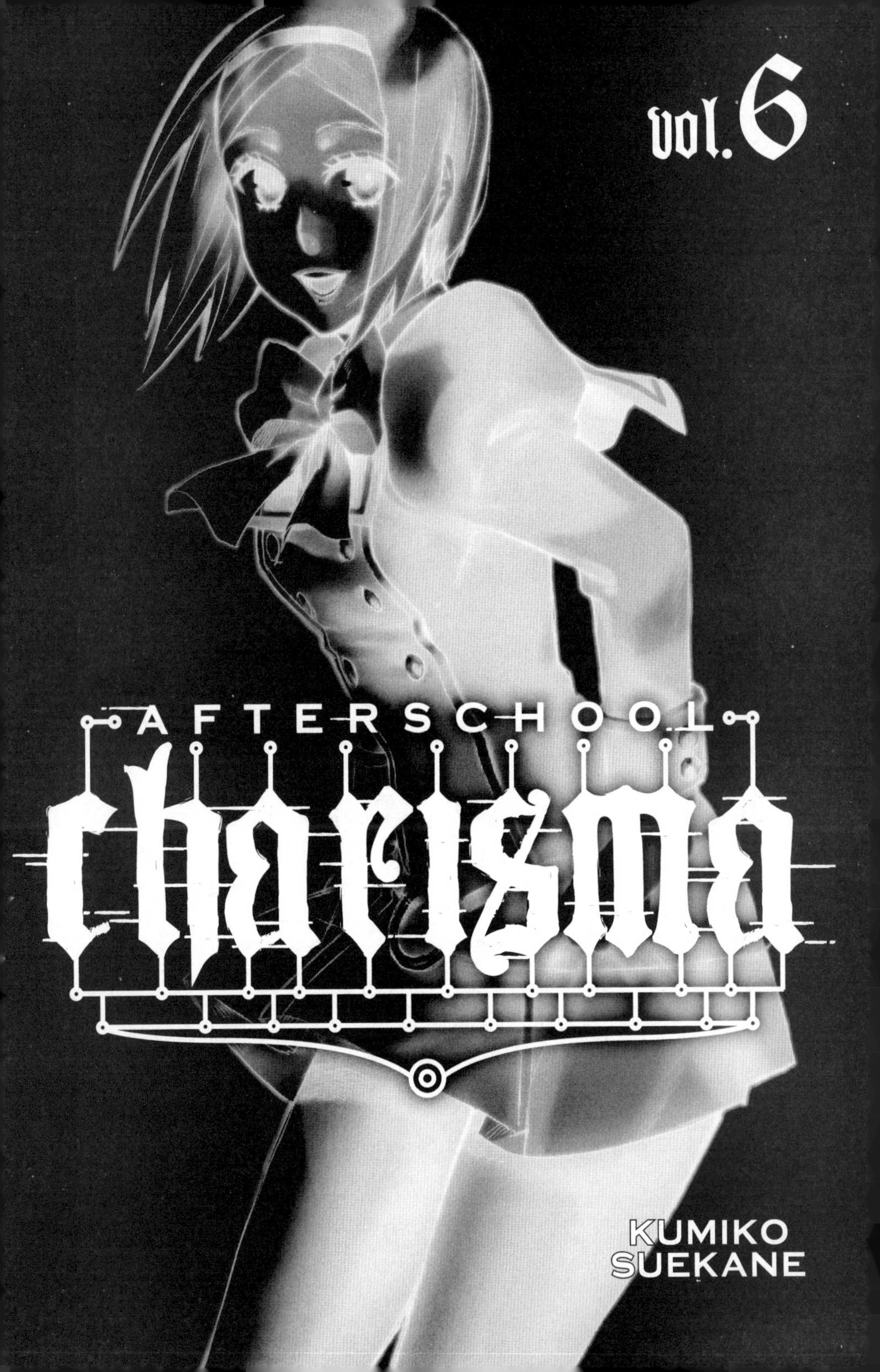
vol. 6
AFTERSCHOOL
charisma
KUMIKO
SUEKANE

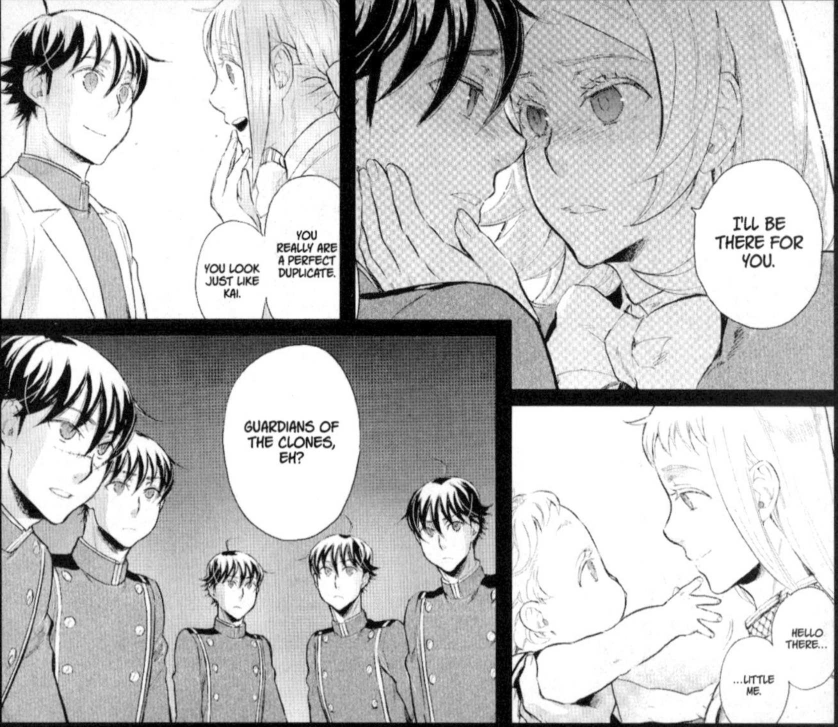
I'LL BE THERE FOR YOU.
YOU REALLY ARE A PERFECT DUPLICATE.
YOU LOOK JUST LIKE KAI.
HELLO THERE...
...LITTLE ME.
GUARDIANS OF THE CLONES, EH?

story

The year is 2XXX, and at St. Kleio Academy, a school for the clones of famous historical figures, Shiro Kamiya is the only non-clone. While Marie Curie, Mozart, Joan of Arc and the other clones struggle to live their lives in the shadows of their Originals, sometimes seeking solace in a little sheep totem called "the Almighty Dolly," Shiro grapples with how different he is from his classmates.

The students prepare for an Academic Exposition in which visitors from the outside society will gather to witness the clones' achievements. But in the midst of the event, an older generation of St. Kleio clones detonate a bomb in the auditorium, and among the terrorists are three men who bear a striking resemblance to Shiro! In the pandemonium that ensues, Joan of Arc is burned at the stake along with an earlier version of Joan, who defected from the terrorist group to save her younger self. The only perpetrator who is captured is Kai, one of the men who look like Shiro. Confronted by the surviving students, he begins to recount his past, and the lives of the previous generation of clones when they were students at St. Kleio.

At that time there were two Kais, but at the annual Exposition three more Kais enter their midst. Shocked to find out about his multiples, one of the Kais slashes his own face with a knife. The students are auctioned off to new posts in the public world, but the five Kais remain at St. Kleio as guardians of the clones. Having been looked over at the auction, Elizabeth is also left behind...

character

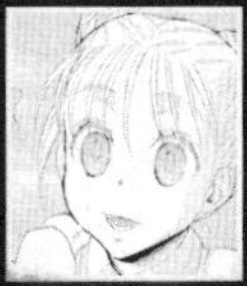

PANDORA
Clone of Marie Curie

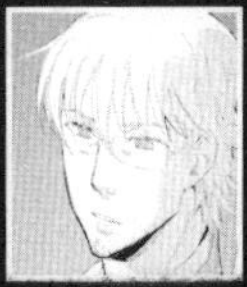

DR. KAMIYA
"Father" to Shiro and professor at St. Kleio

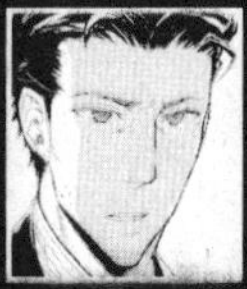

KUROE
Professor at St. Kleio

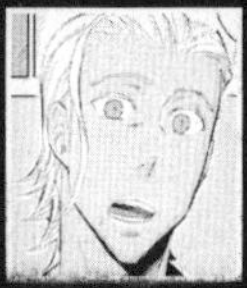

ROCKSWELL
Director of St. Kleio

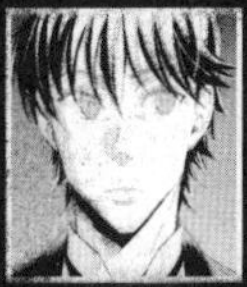

KAI
Graduate of St. Kleio

students of st. kleio academy

(CLONES OF HISTORICAL FIGURES)

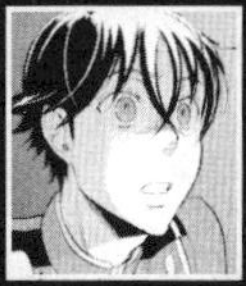

SHIRO KAMIYA
The only non-clone at St. Kleio

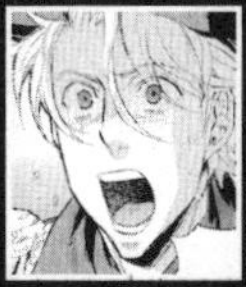

NAPOLEON BONAPARTE

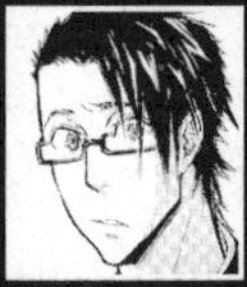

IKKYU SOJUN

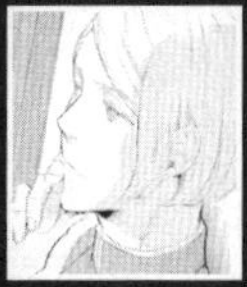

SIGMUND FREUD

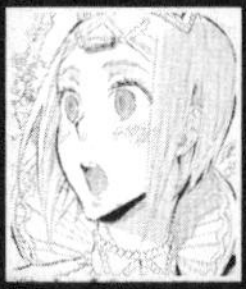

ELIZABETH I

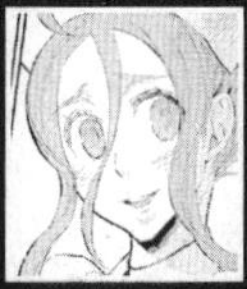

FLORENCE NIGHTINGALE

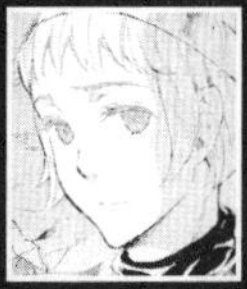

JOAN OF ARC
*burned at the stake

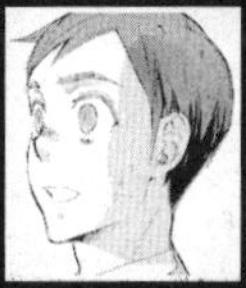

ADOLF HITLER

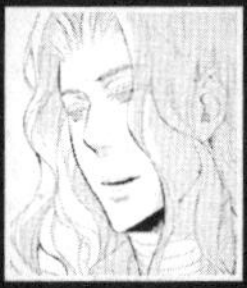

WOLFGANG AMADEUS MOZART

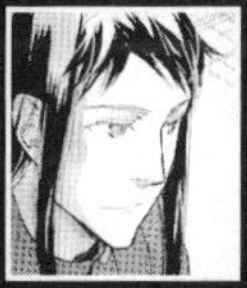

GREGORI YEFIMOVICH RASPUTIN

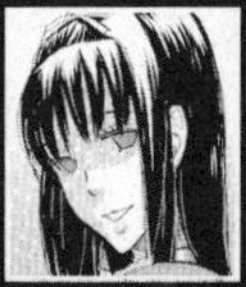

HIMIKO
*joined the terrorists

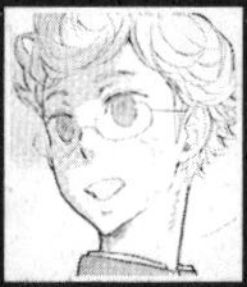

ALBERT EINSTEIN
*shot to death by a sniper

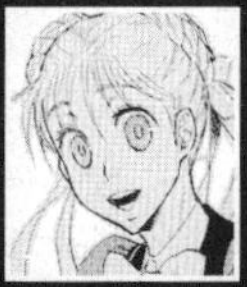

MARIE CURIE (MADAME CURIE)
*transferred to another school (?)

afterschool
charisma

c o n t e n t s

CHAPTER thirty-one

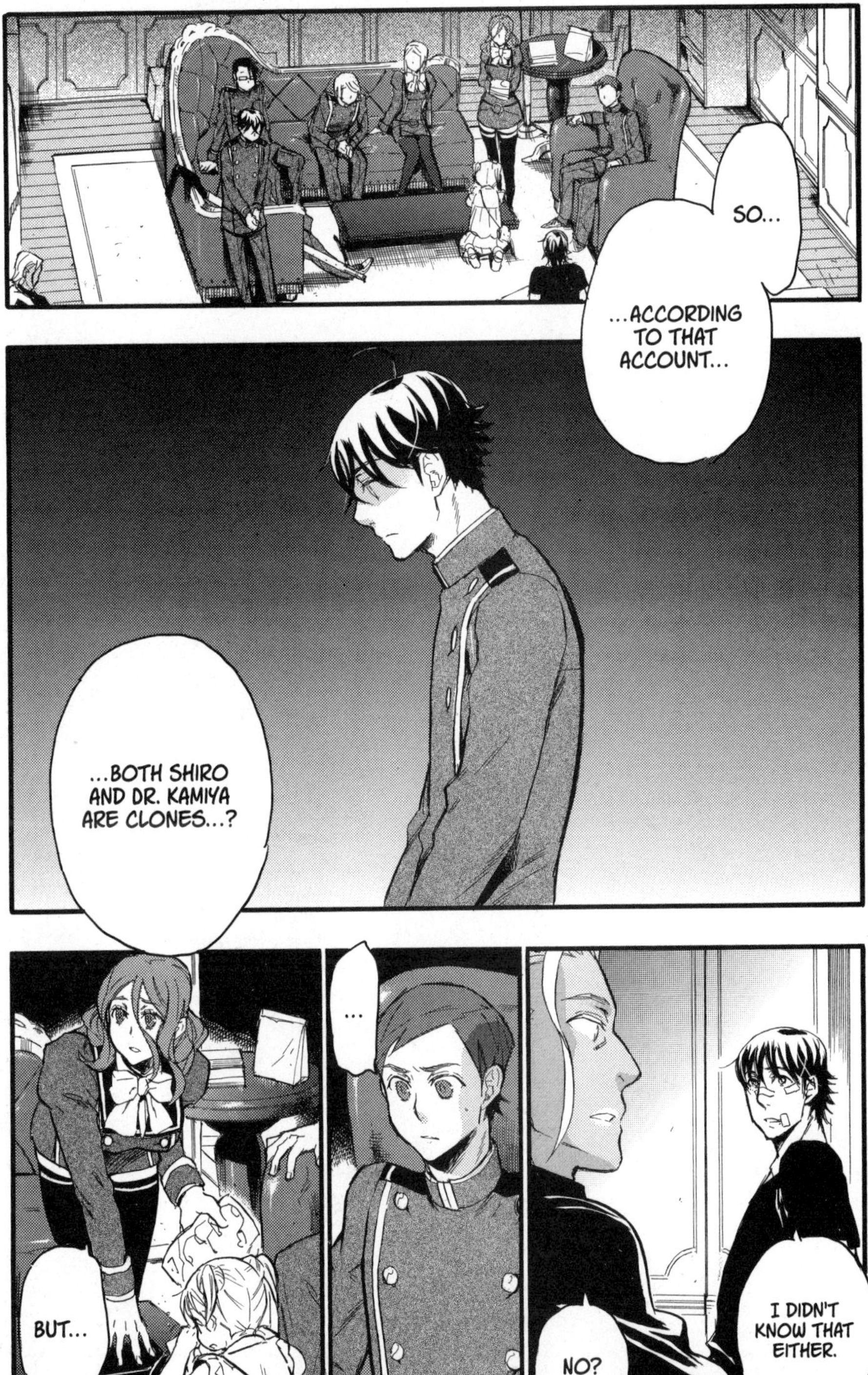
SO...
...ACCORDING TO THAT ACCOUNT...
...BOTH SHIRO AND DR. KAMIYA ARE CLONES...?
I DIDN'T KNOW THAT EITHER.
NO?
...
BUT...

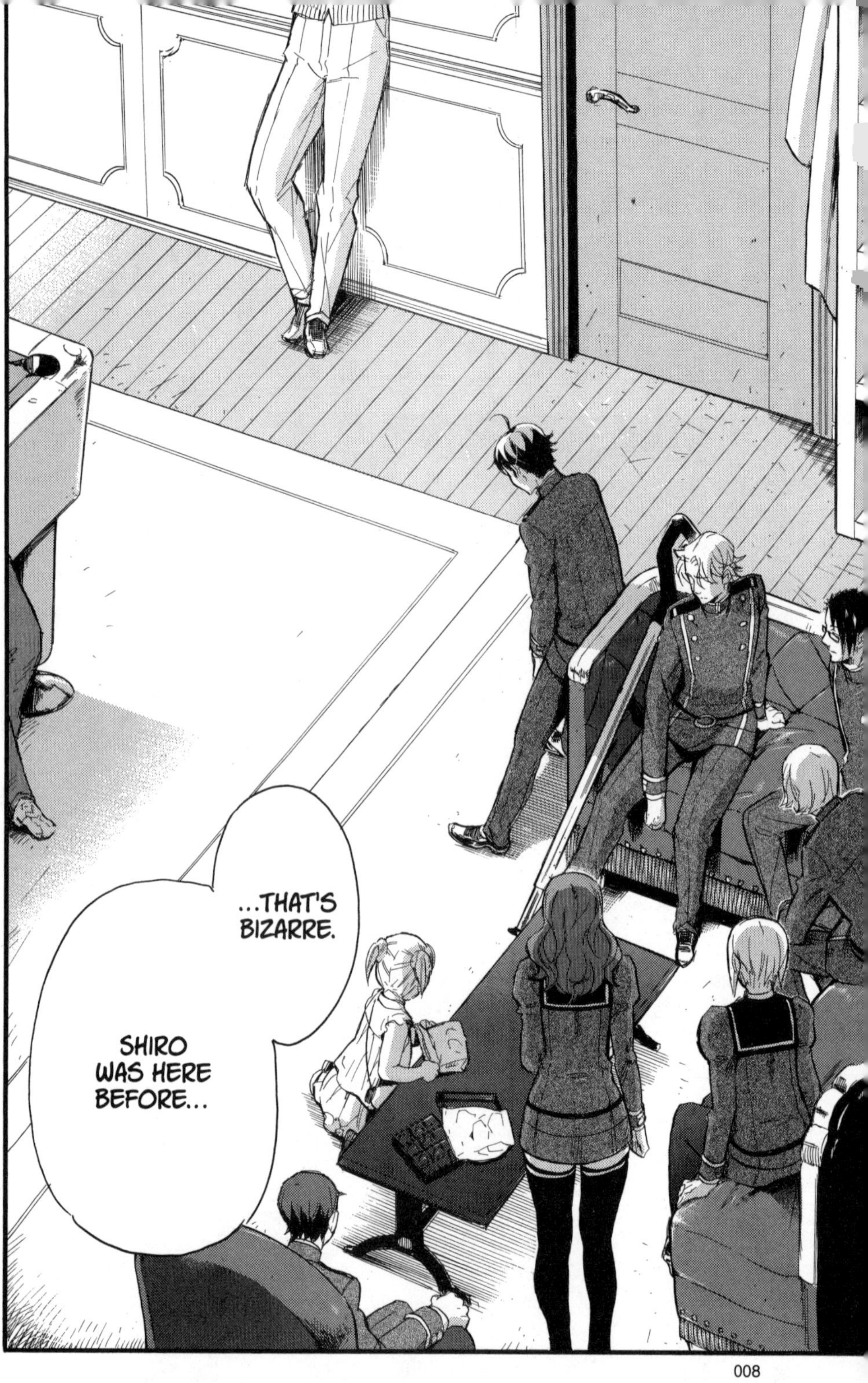
...THAT'S BIZARRE.
SHIRO WAS HERE BEFORE...

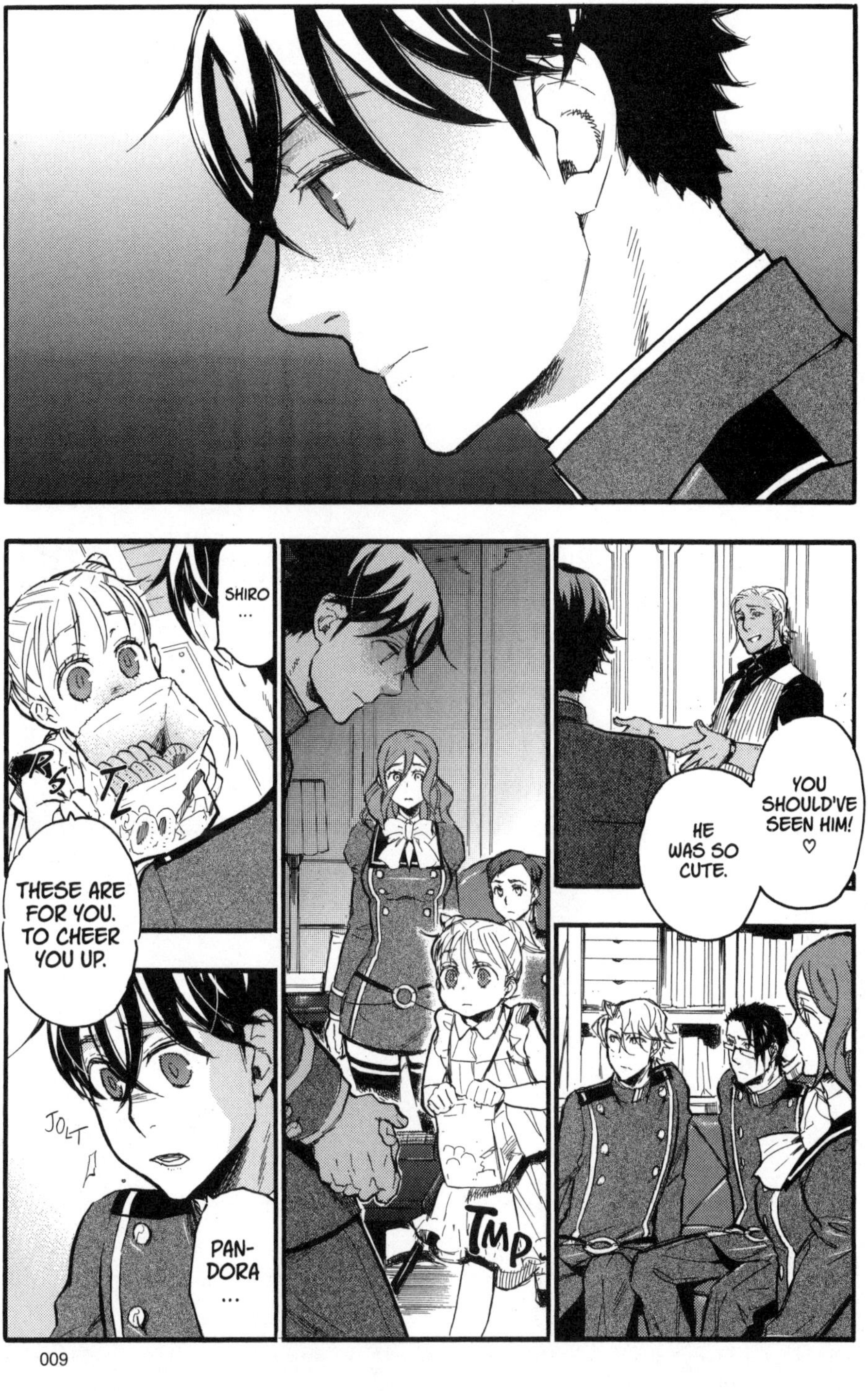

YOU SHOULD'VE SEEN HIM! ♡
HE WAS SO CUTE.
TMP
SHIRO ...
RSTL
THESE ARE FOR YOU. TO CHEER YOU UP.
JOLT
PAN-DORA ...

SO...THAT MAKES SHIRO...

...

...ANOTHER...

...CLONE GUARDIAN?

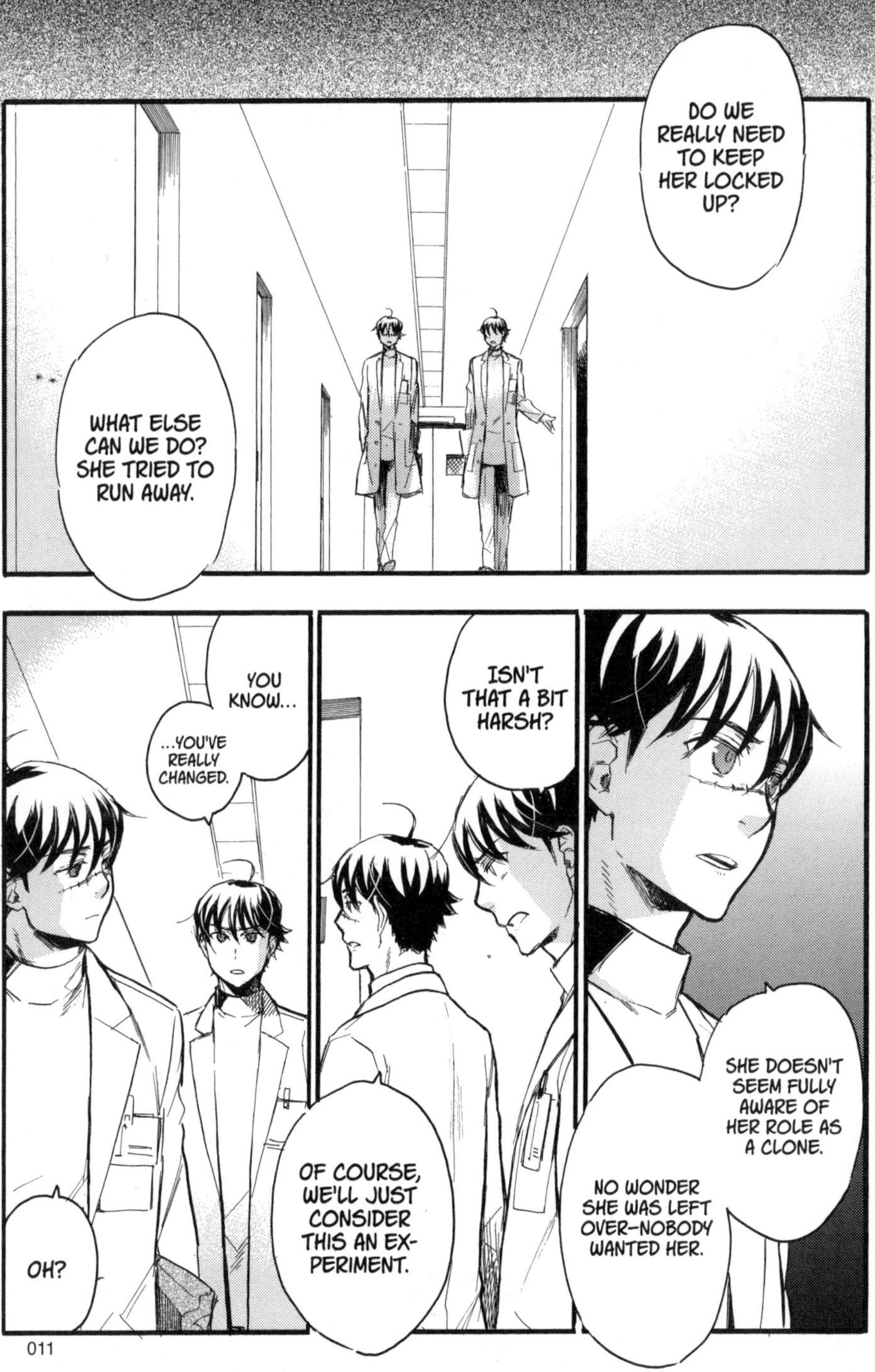
DO WE REALLY NEED TO KEEP HER LOCKED UP?
WHAT ELSE CAN WE DO? SHE TRIED TO RUN AWAY.
SHE DOESN'T SEEM FULLY AWARE OF HER ROLE AS A CLONE.
NO WONDER SHE WAS LEFT OVER–NOBODY WANTED HER.
ISN'T THAT A BIT HARSH?
OF COURSE, WE'LL JUST CONSIDER THIS AN EX-PERIMENT.
YOU KNOW…
…YOU'VE REALLY CHANGED.
OH?

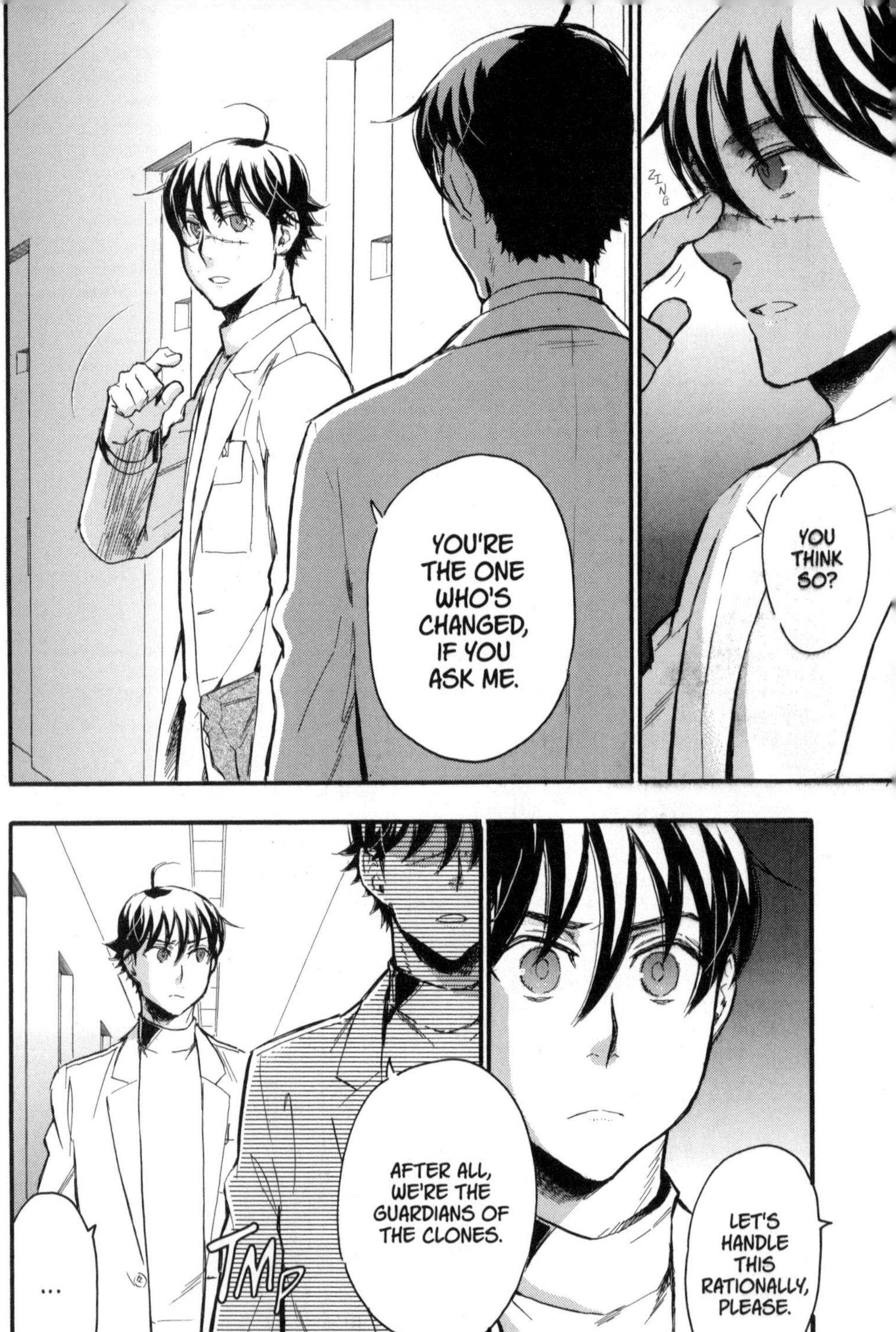
ZING
YOU THINK SO?
YOU'RE THE ONE WHO'S CHANGED, IF YOU ASK ME.
LET'S HANDLE THIS RATIONALLY, PLEASE.
AFTER ALL, WE'RE THE GUARDIANS OF THE CLONES.
TMP
...

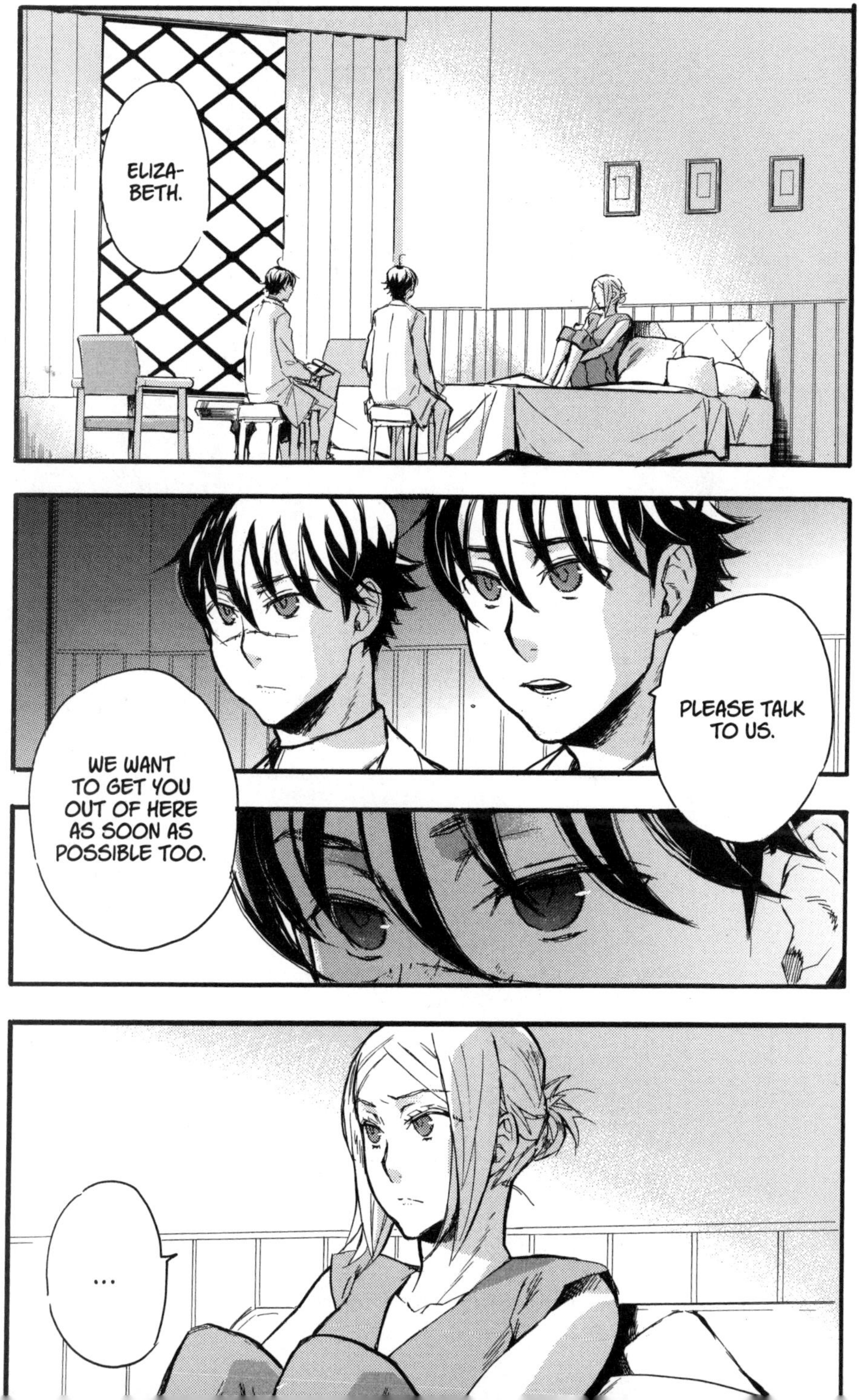
ELIZA-BETH.
PLEASE TALK TO US.
WE WANT TO GET YOU OUT OF HERE AS SOON AS POSSIBLE TOO.
...

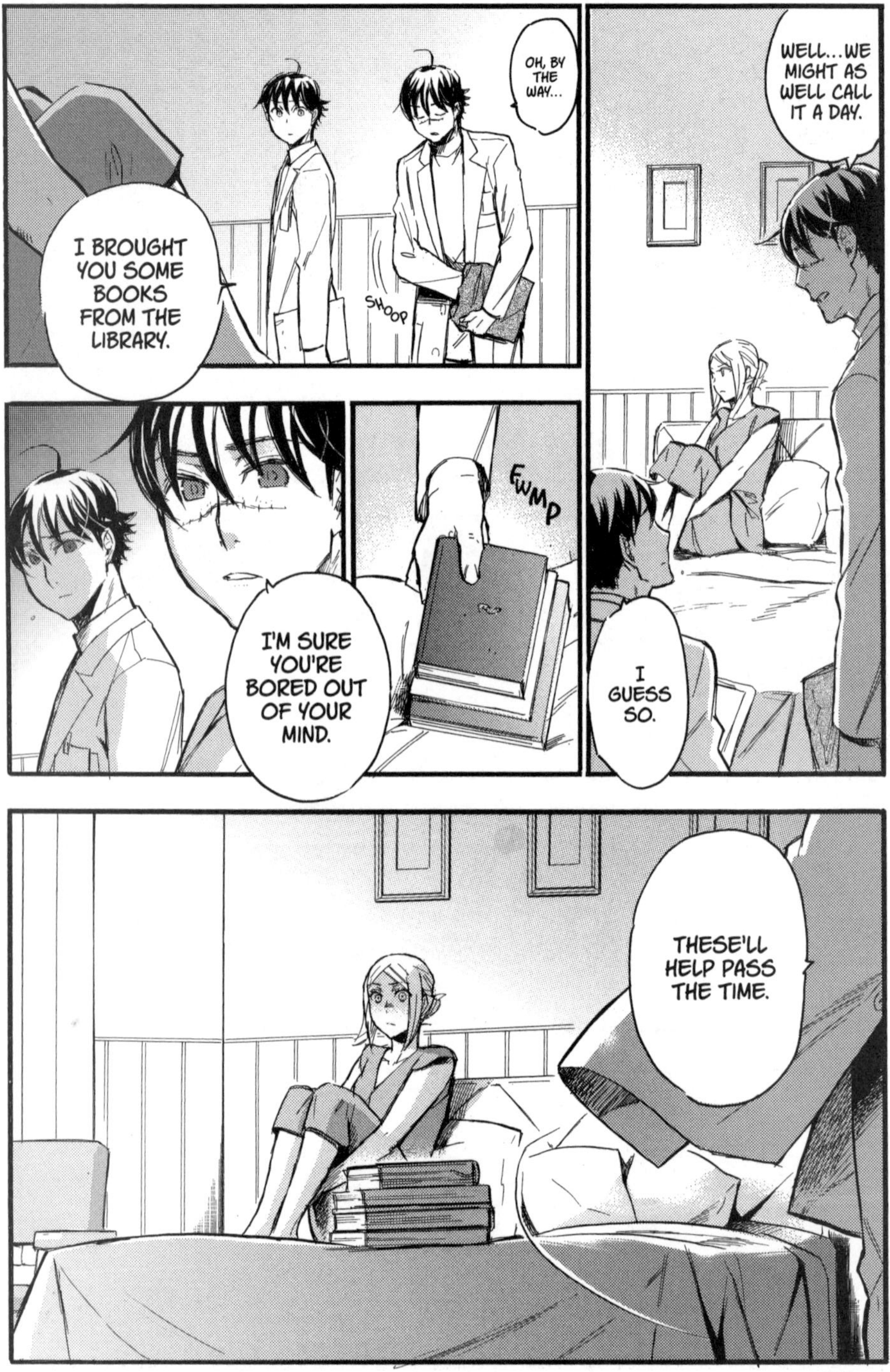
WELL...WE MIGHT AS WELL CALL IT A DAY.
I GUESS SO.
OH, BY THE WAY...
I BROUGHT YOU SOME BOOKS FROM THE LIBRARY.
SHOOP
EWMP
I'M SURE YOU'RE BORED OUT OF YOUR MIND.
THESE'LL HELP PASS THE TIME.

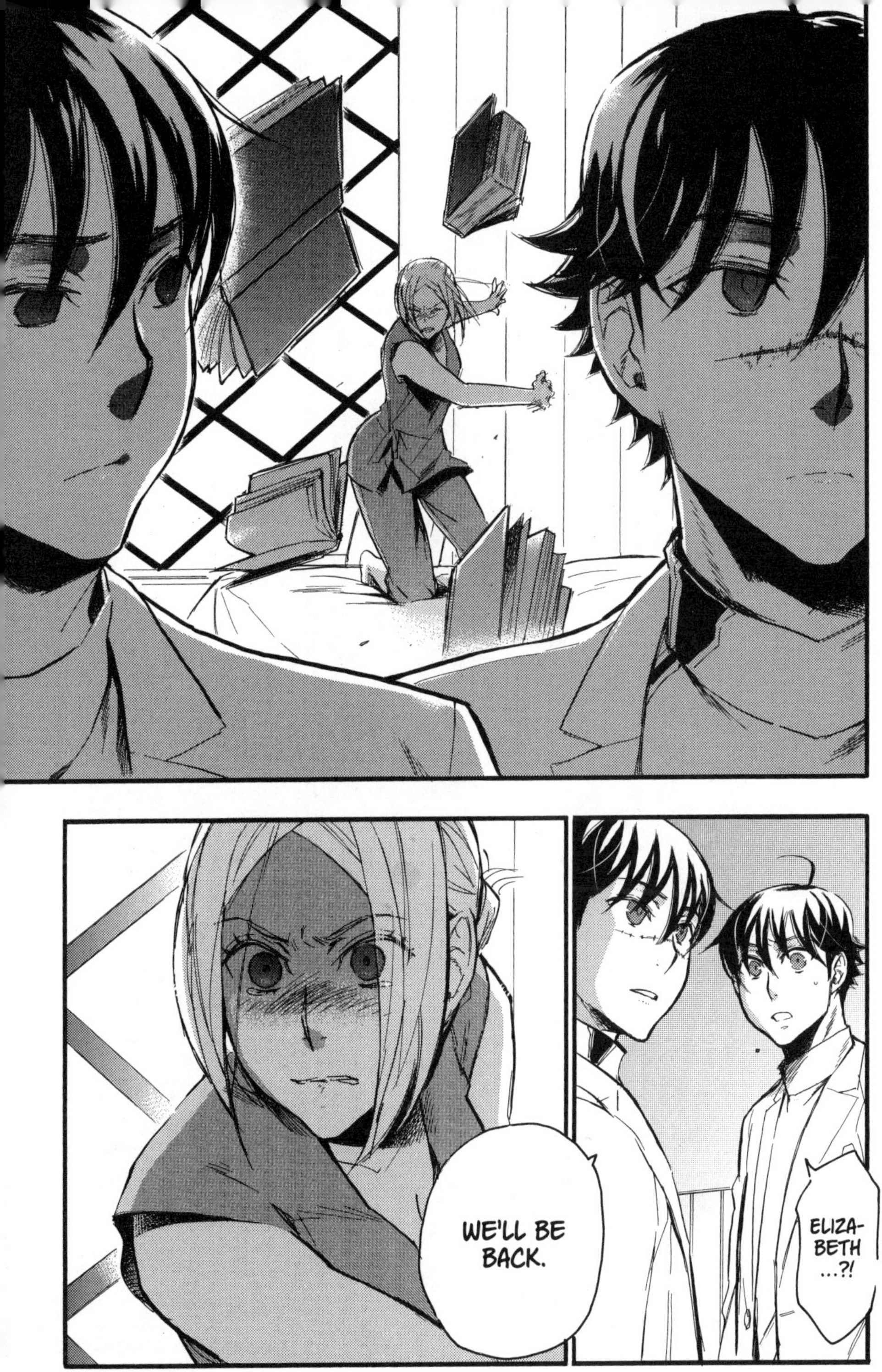
ELIZA-BETH ...?!
WE'LL BE BACK.

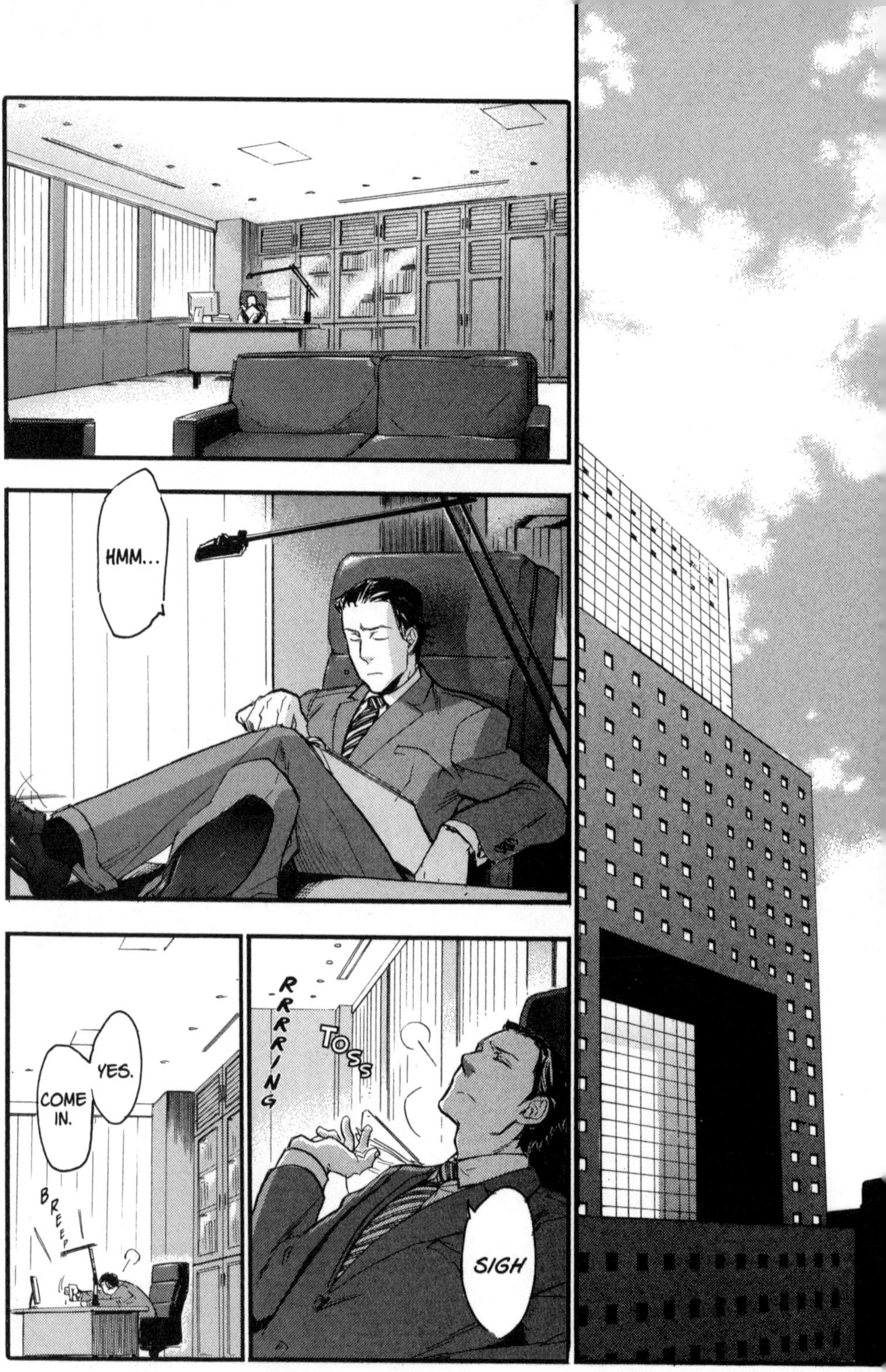
HMM...
TOSS
RRRRING
SIGH
YES.
COME IN.
BREEP

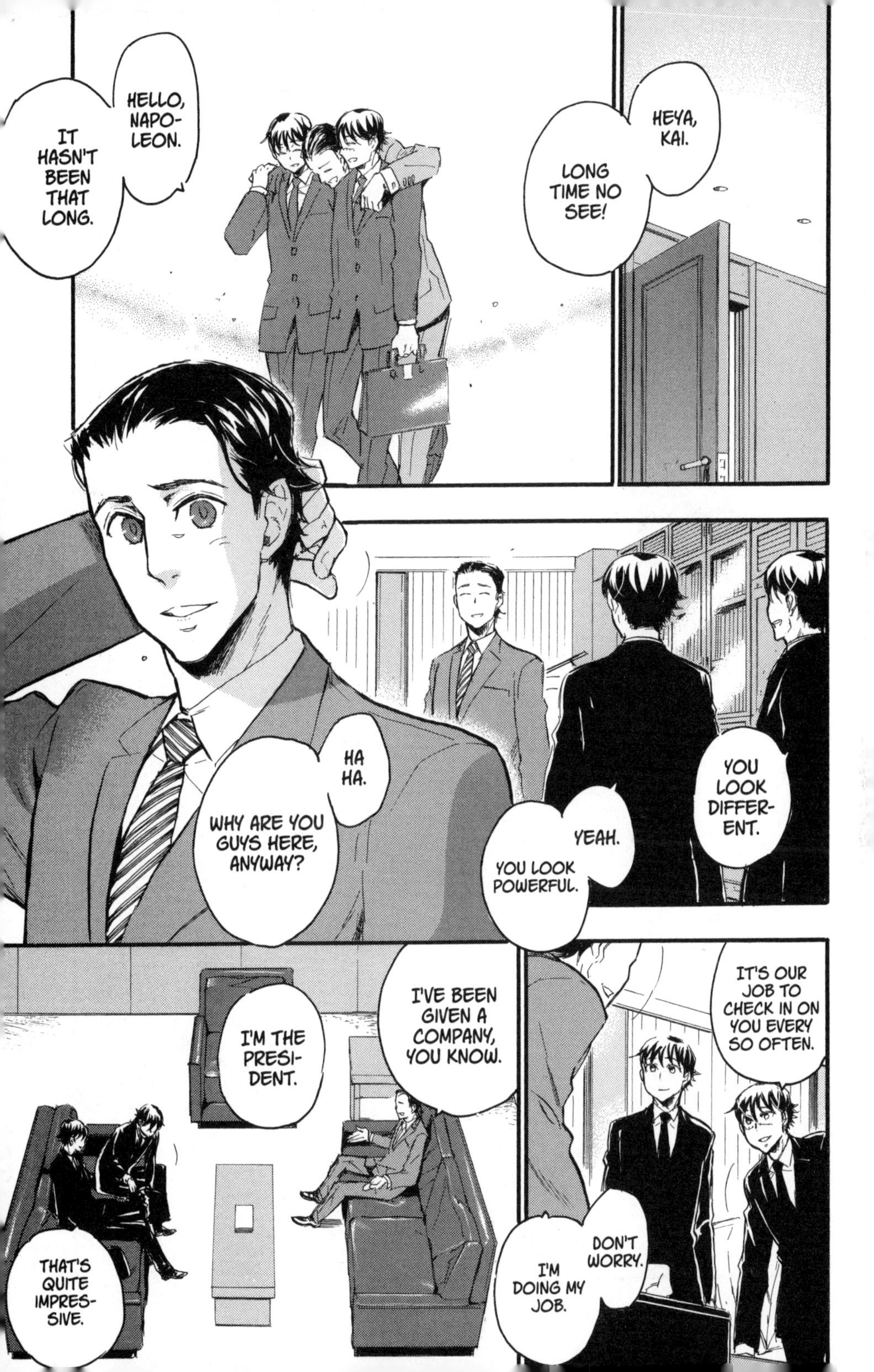
HEYA, KAI.
LONG TIME NO SEE!
HELLO, NAPOLEON.
IT HASN'T BEEN THAT LONG.
YOU LOOK DIFFERENT.
YEAH.
YOU LOOK POWERFUL.
HA HA.
WHY ARE YOU GUYS HERE, ANYWAY?
IT'S OUR JOB TO CHECK IN ON YOU EVERY SO OFTEN.
DON'T WORRY.
I'M DOING MY JOB.
I'VE BEEN GIVEN A COMPANY, YOU KNOW.
I'M THE PRESIDENT.
THAT'S QUITE IMPRESSIVE.

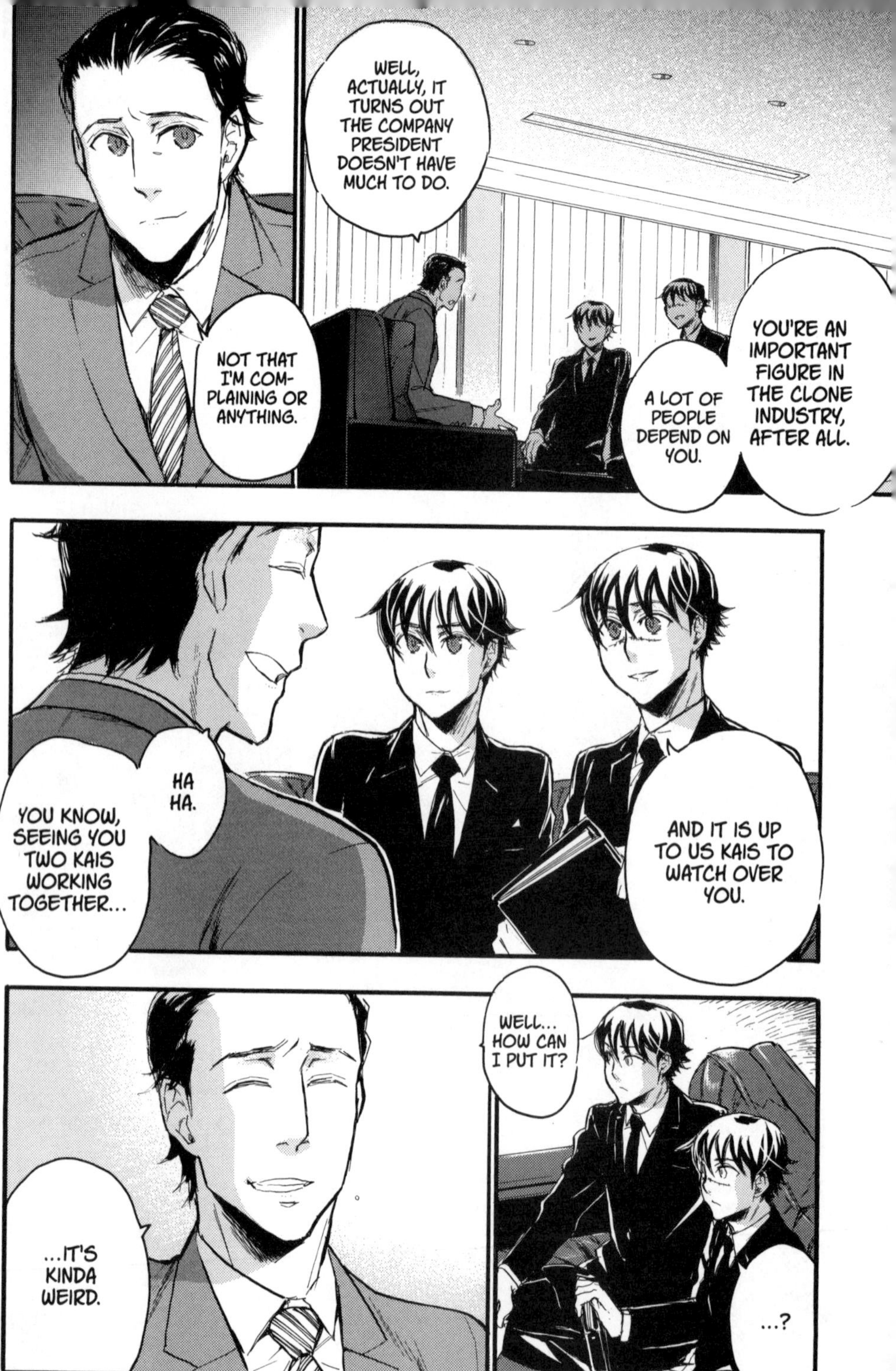
YOU'RE AN IMPORTANT FIGURE IN THE CLONE INDUSTRY, AFTER ALL.
A LOT OF PEOPLE DEPEND ON YOU.
WELL, ACTUALLY, IT TURNS OUT THE COMPANY PRESIDENT DOESN'T HAVE MUCH TO DO.
NOT THAT I'M COM-PLAINING OR ANYTHING.
AND IT IS UP TO US KAIS TO WATCH OVER YOU.
HA HA.
YOU KNOW, SEEING YOU TWO KAIS WORKING TOGETHER...
WELL... HOW CAN I PUT IT?
...?
...IT'S KINDA WEIRD.

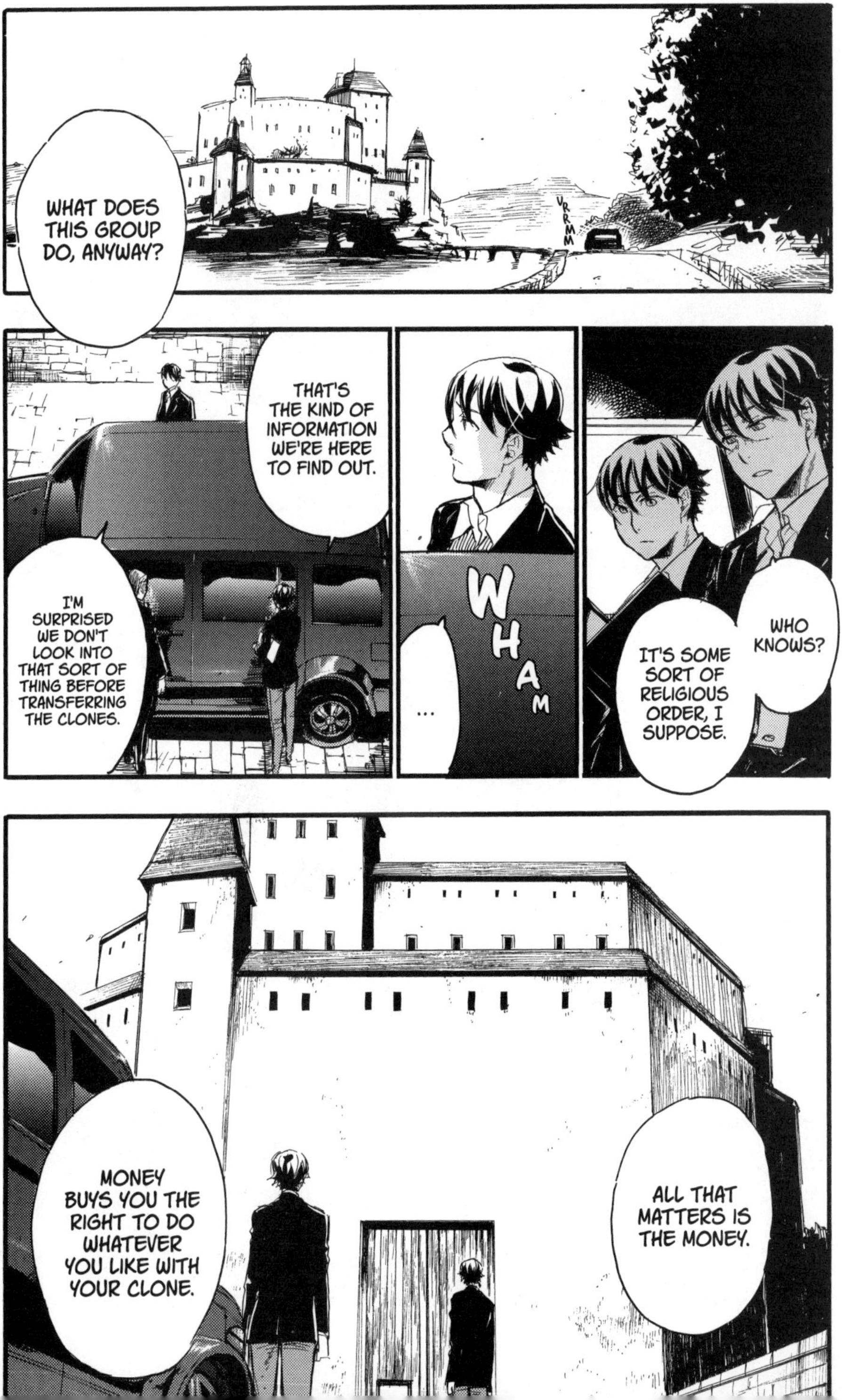
WHAT DOES THIS GROUP DO, ANYWAY?
VRRMM
WHO KNOWS?
IT'S SOME SORT OF RELIGIOUS ORDER, I SUPPOSE.
WHAM
...
THAT'S THE KIND OF INFORMATION WE'RE HERE TO FIND OUT.
I'M SURPRISED WE DON'T LOOK INTO THAT SORT OF THING BEFORE TRANSFERRING THE CLONES.
ALL THAT MATTERS IS THE MONEY.
MONEY BUYS YOU THE RIGHT TO DO WHATEVER YOU LIKE WITH YOUR CLONE.

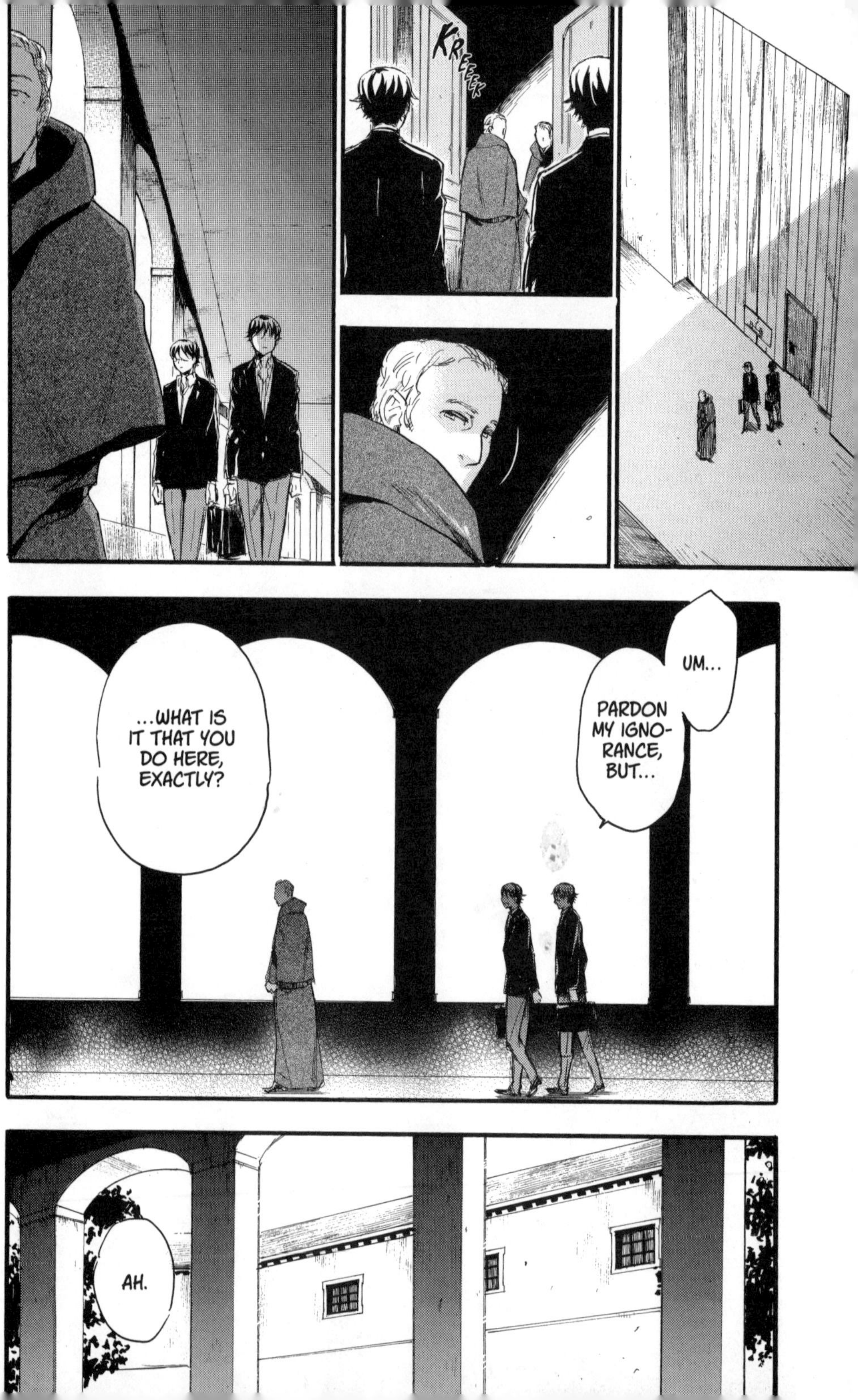
KREEEK
UM...
PARDON MY IGNORANCE, BUT...
...WHAT IS IT THAT YOU DO HERE, EXACTLY?
AH.

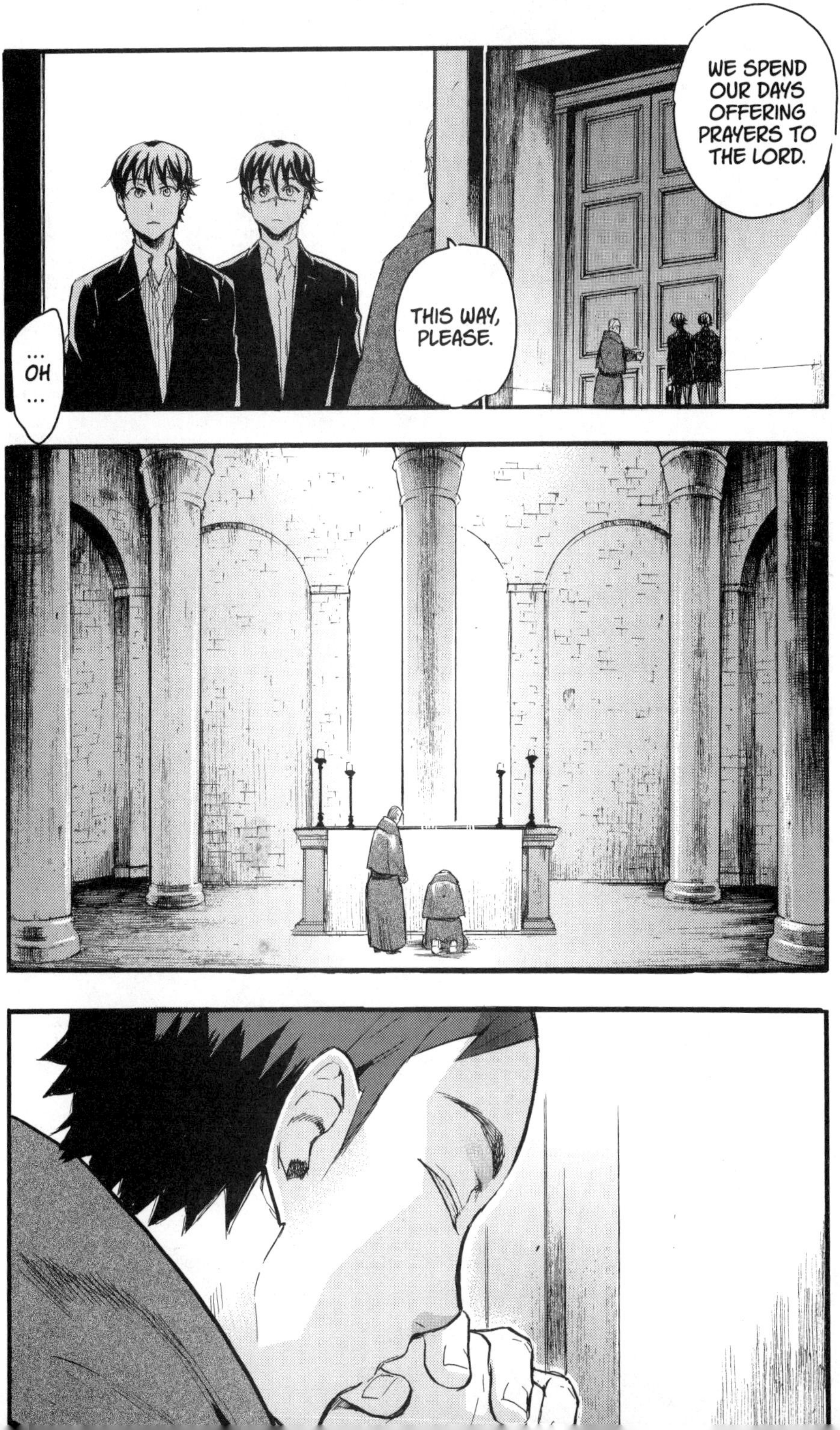
WE SPEND OUR DAYS OFFERING PRAYERS TO THE LORD.
THIS WAY, PLEASE.
... OH ...

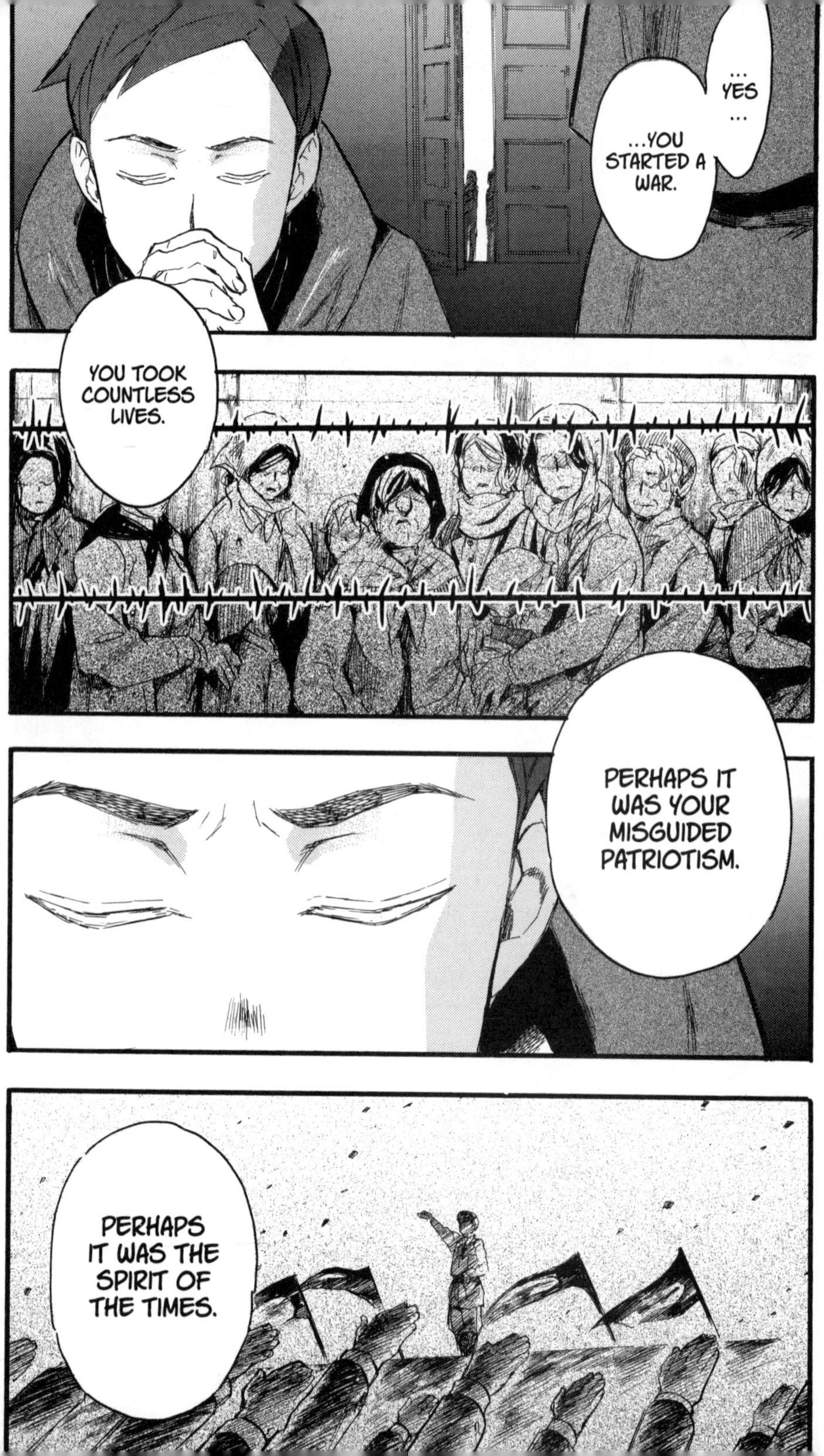
...YES...
...YOU STARTED A WAR.
YOU TOOK COUNTLESS LIVES.
PERHAPS IT WAS YOUR MISGUIDED PATRIOTISM.
PERHAPS IT WAS THE SPIRIT OF THE TIMES.

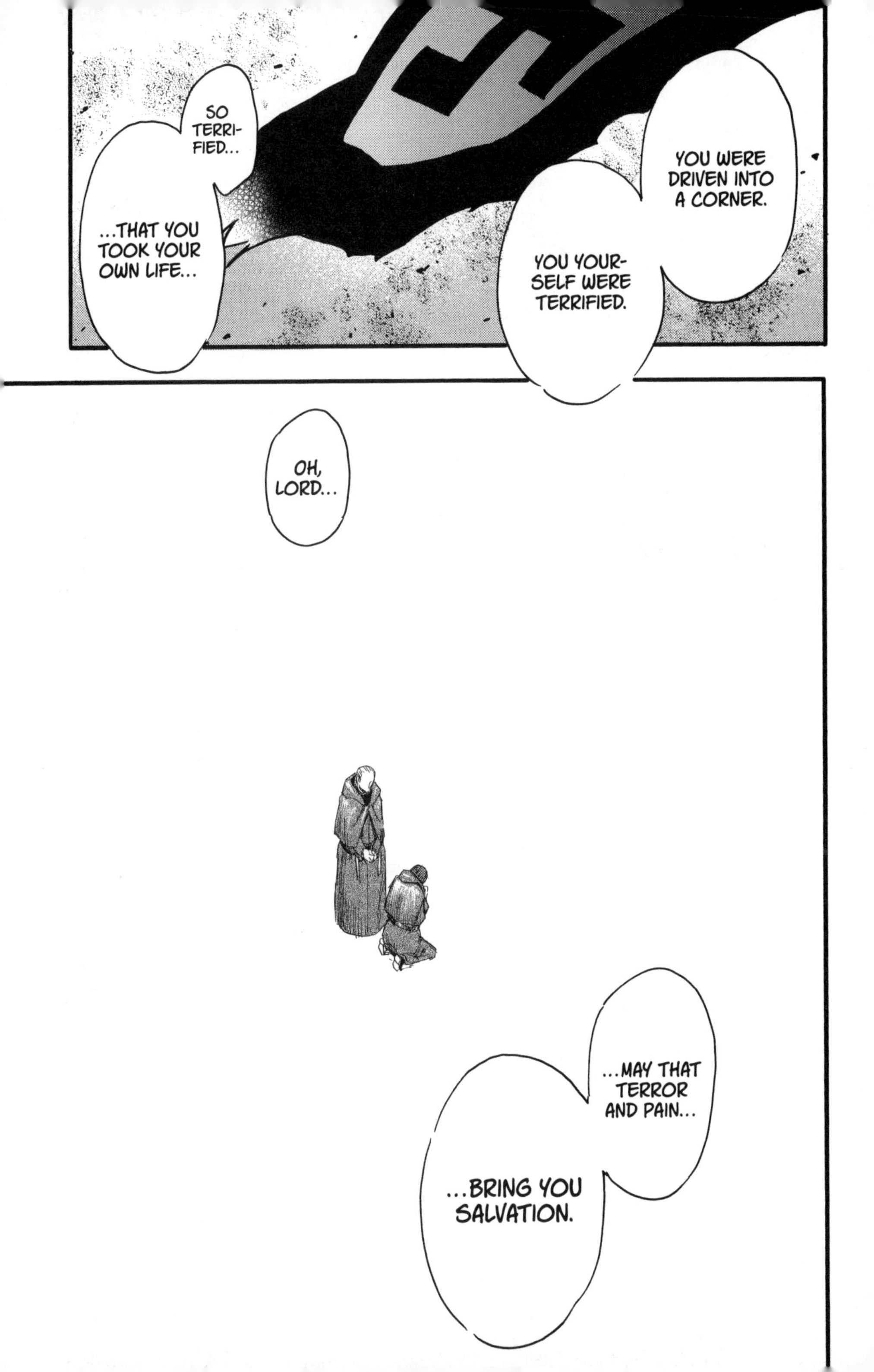
YOU WERE DRIVEN INTO A CORNER.
YOU YOUR-SELF WERE TERRIFIED.
SO TERRI-FIED...
...THAT YOU TOOK YOUR OWN LIFE...
OH, LORD...
...MAY THAT TERROR AND PAIN...
...BRING YOU SALVATION.

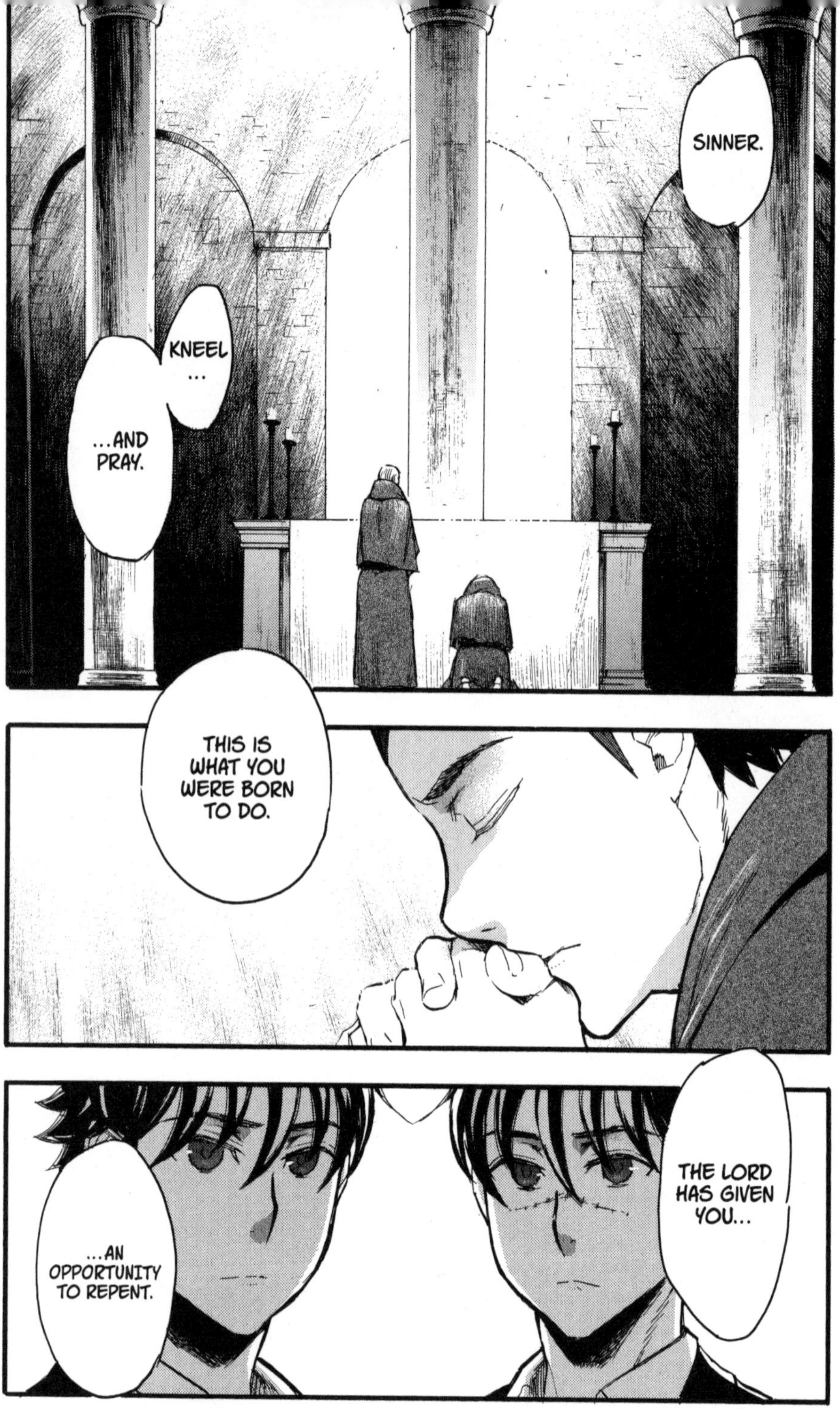
SINNER.
KNEEL...
...AND PRAY.
THIS IS WHAT YOU WERE BORN TO DO.
THE LORD HAS GIVEN YOU...
...AN OPPORTUNITY TO REPENT.

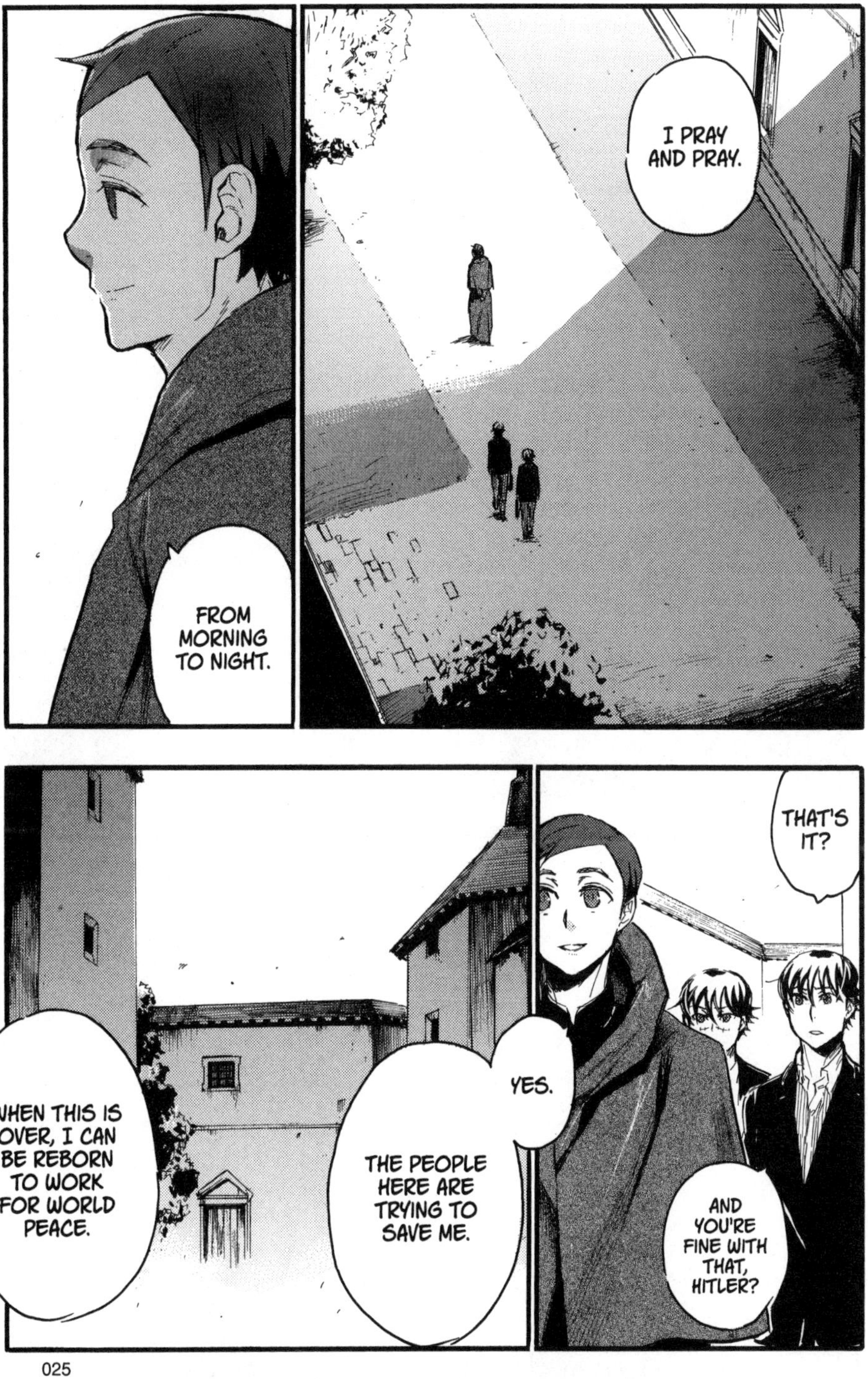
I PRAY AND PRAY.
FROM MORNING TO NIGHT.
THAT'S IT?
YES.
THE PEOPLE HERE ARE TRYING TO SAVE ME.
WHEN THIS IS OVER, I CAN BE REBORN TO WORK FOR WORLD PEACE.
AND YOU'RE FINE WITH THAT, HITLER?

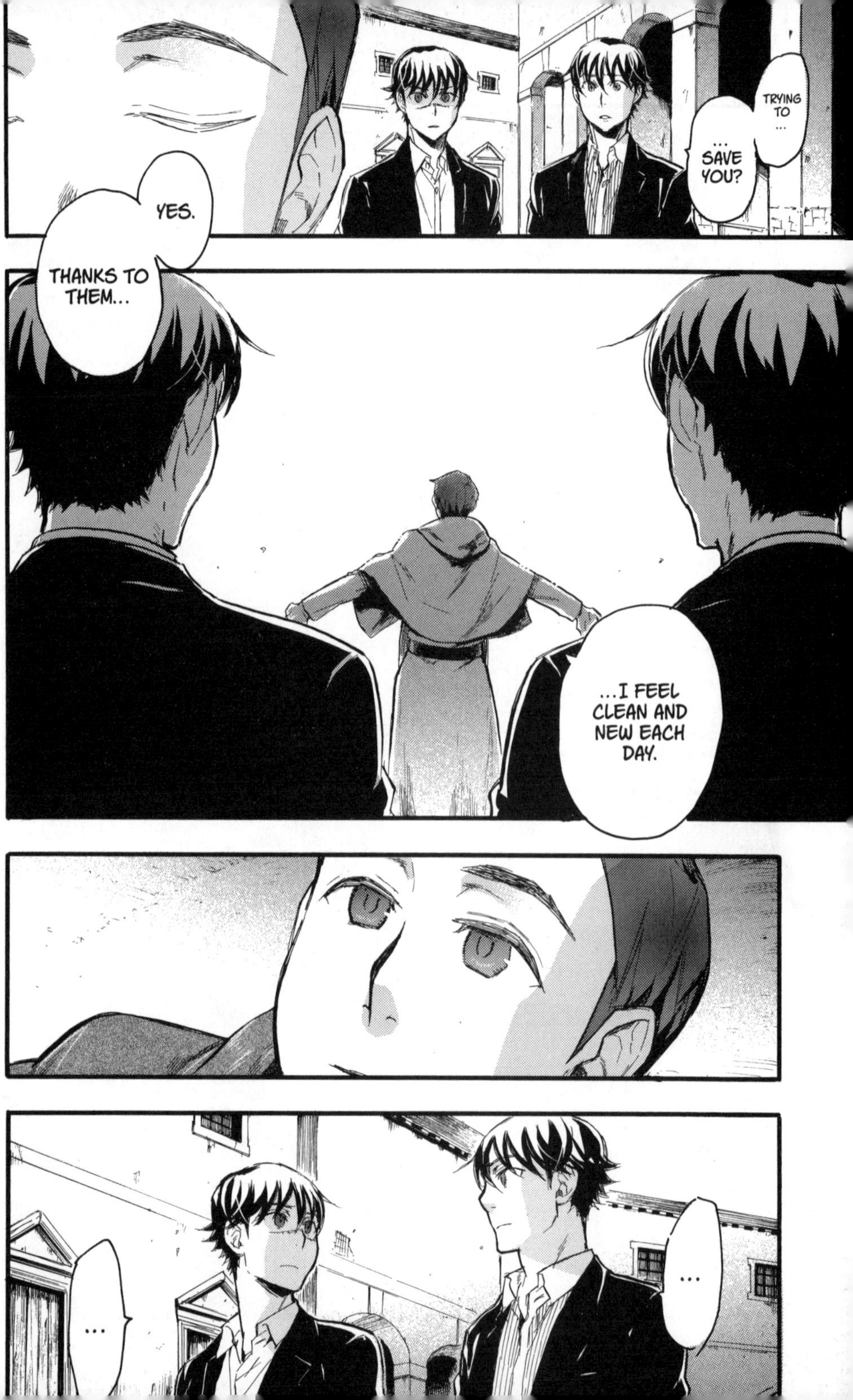
TRYING TO...
...SAVE YOU?
YES.
THANKS TO THEM...
...I FEEL CLEAN AND NEW EACH DAY.
...
...

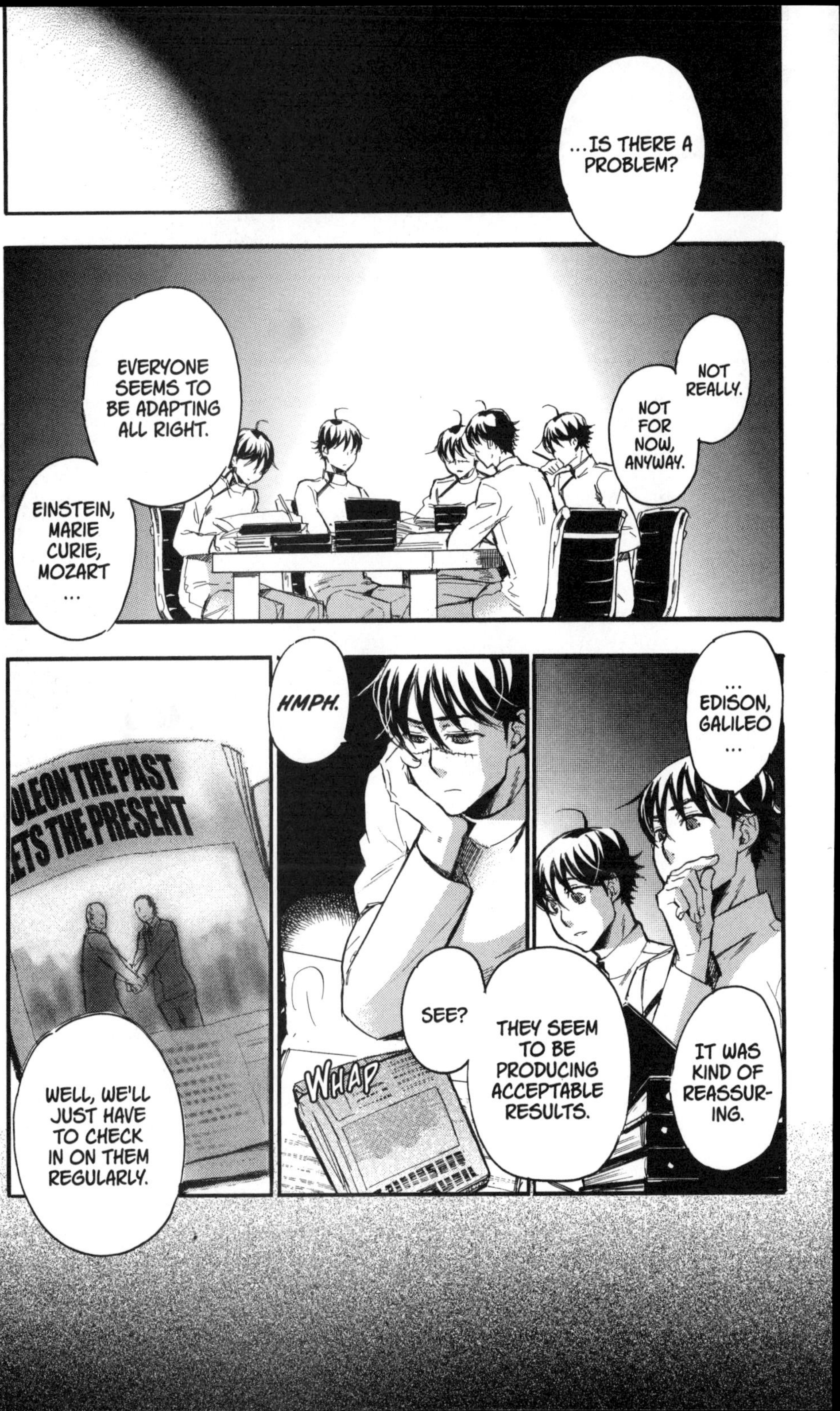
...IS THERE A PROBLEM?
NOT REALLY.
NOT FOR NOW, ANYWAY.
EVERYONE SEEMS TO BE ADAPTING ALL RIGHT.
EINSTEIN, MARIE CURIE, MOZART ...
... EDISON, GALILEO ...
IT WAS KIND OF REASSURING.
HMPH.
SEE?
THEY SEEM TO BE PRODUCING ACCEPTABLE RESULTS.
WHAP
OLEON THE PAST
ETS THE PRESENT
WELL, WE'LL JUST HAVE TO CHECK IN ON THEM REGULARLY.

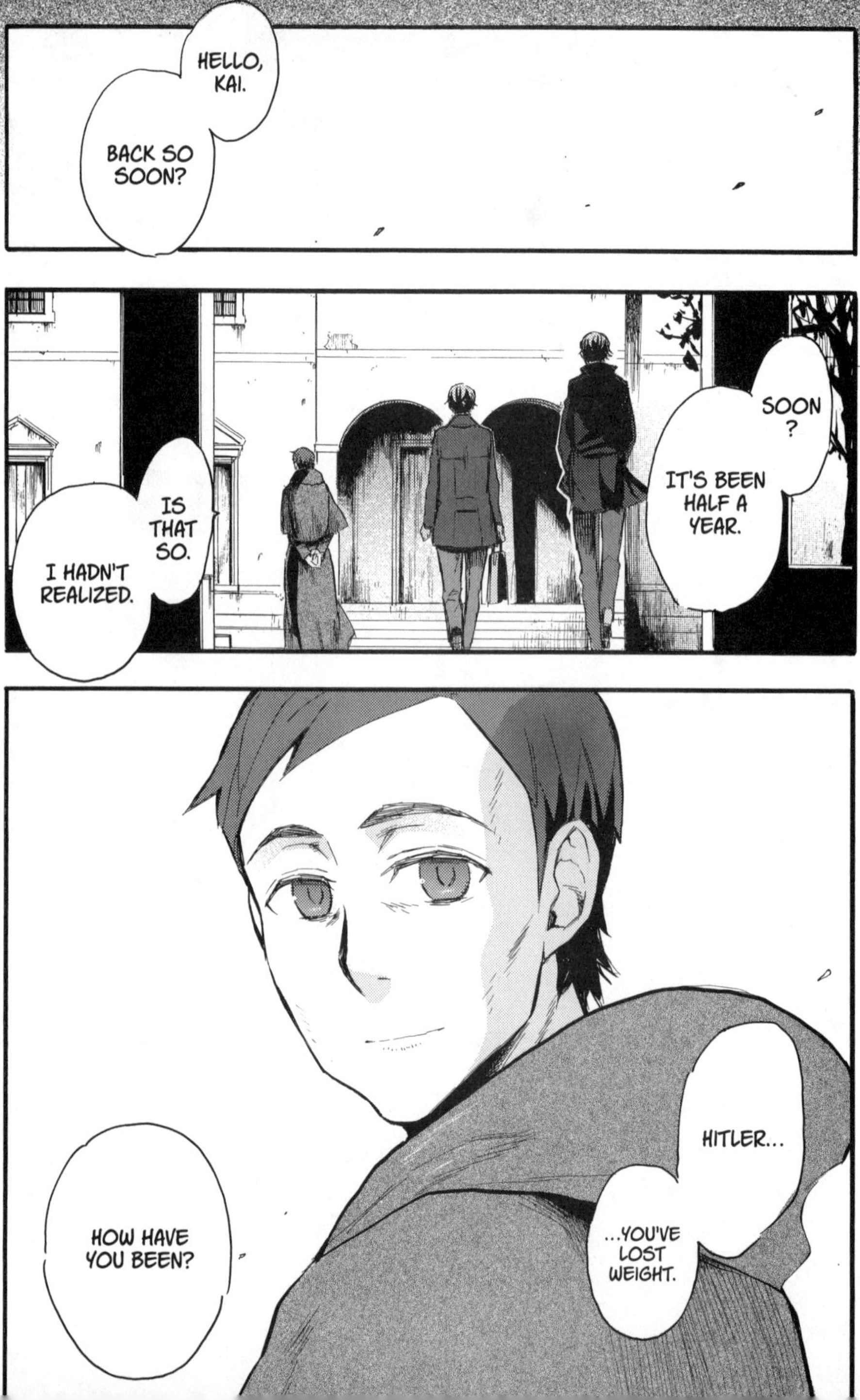
HELLO, KAI.
BACK SO SOON?
SOON?
IT'S BEEN HALF A YEAR.
IS THAT SO.
I HADN'T REALIZED.
HITLER...
...YOU'VE LOST WEIGHT.
HOW HAVE YOU BEEN?

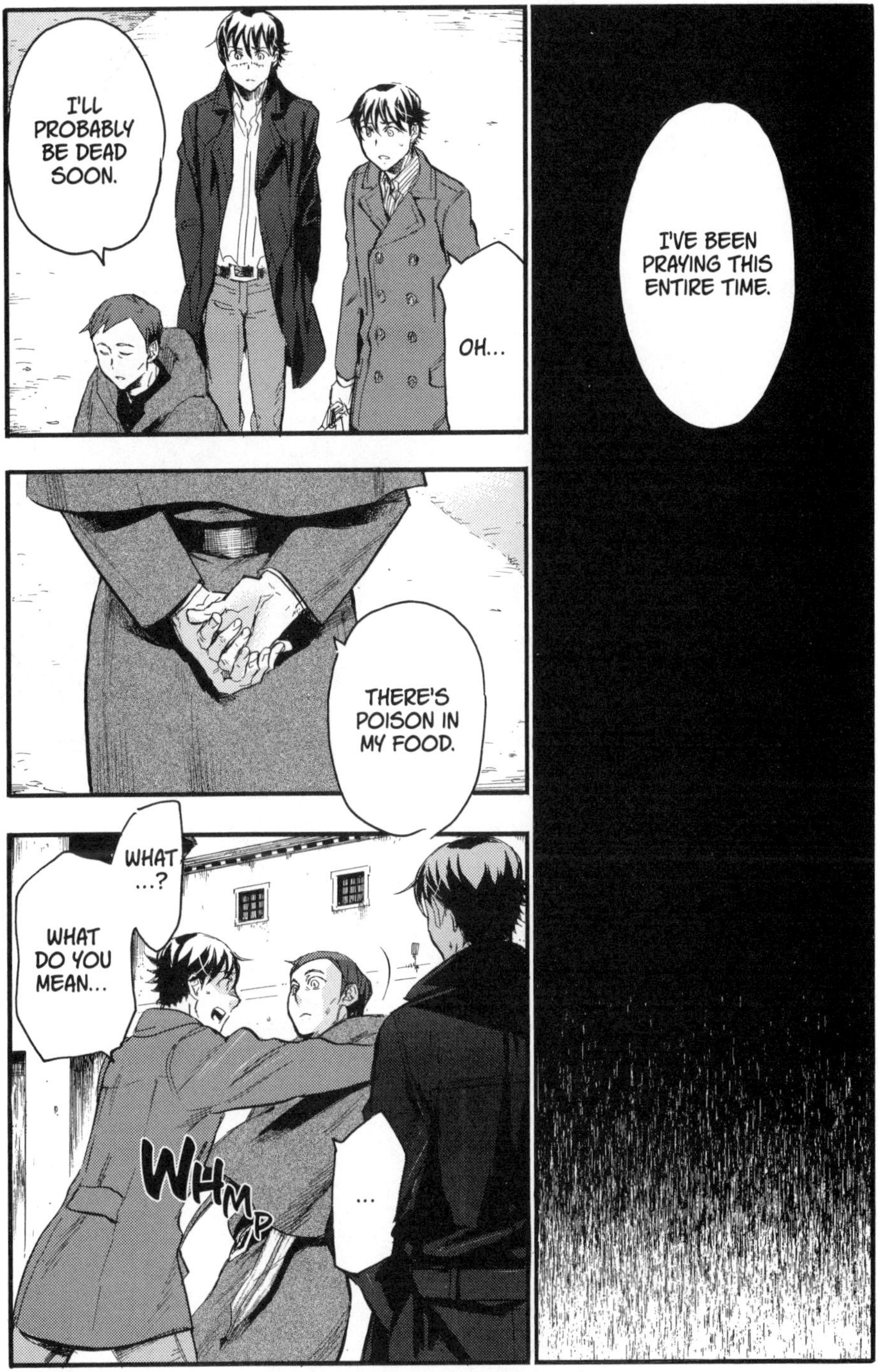
I'VE BEEN PRAYING THIS ENTIRE TIME.
I'LL PROBABLY BE DEAD SOON.
OH...
THERE'S POISON IN MY FOOD.
WHAT ...?
WHAT DO YOU MEAN...
WHMP
...

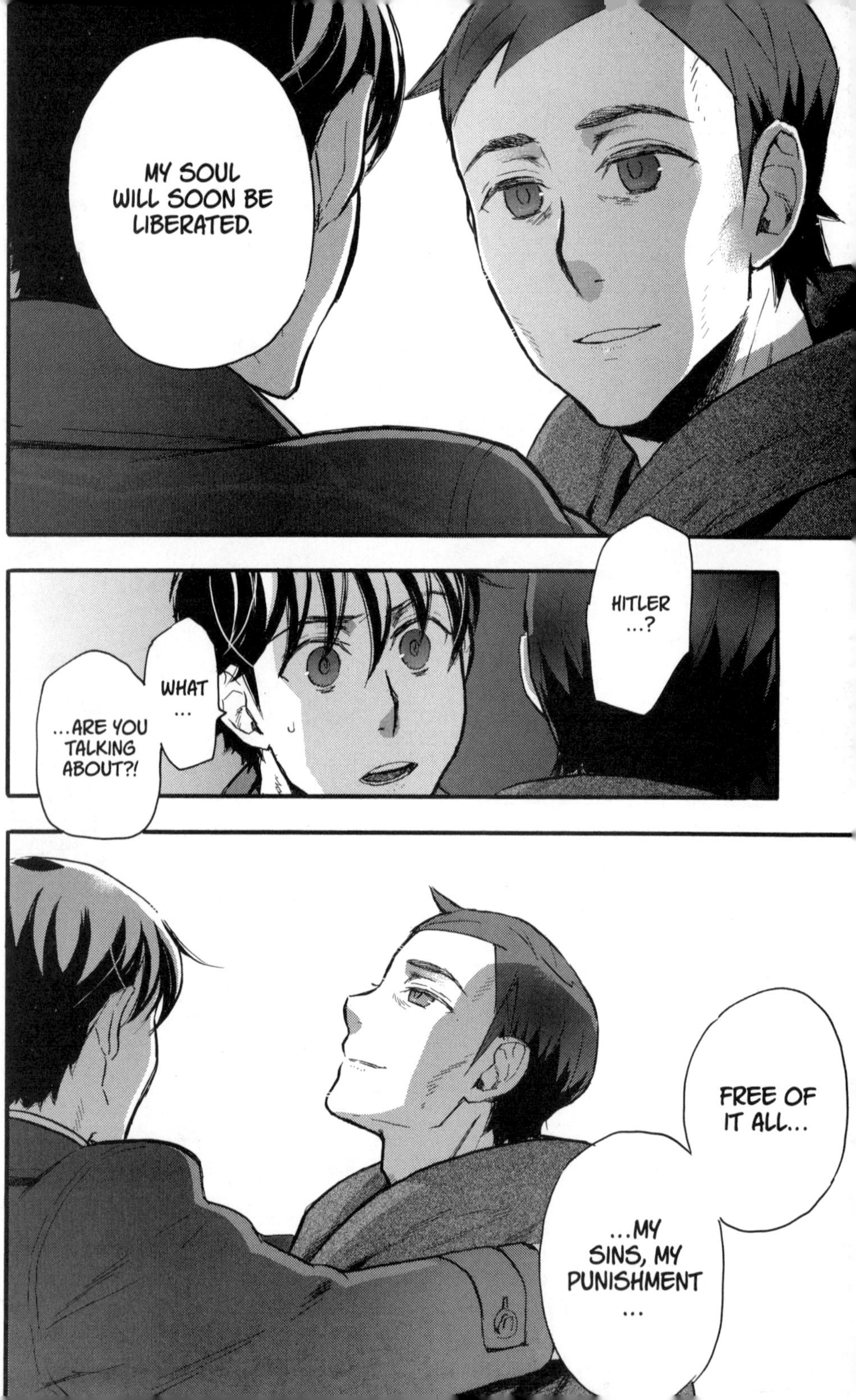
MY SOUL WILL SOON BE LIBERATED.
HITLER ...?
WHAT ...
...ARE YOU TALKING ABOUT?!
FREE OF IT ALL...
...MY SINS, MY PUNISHMENT ...

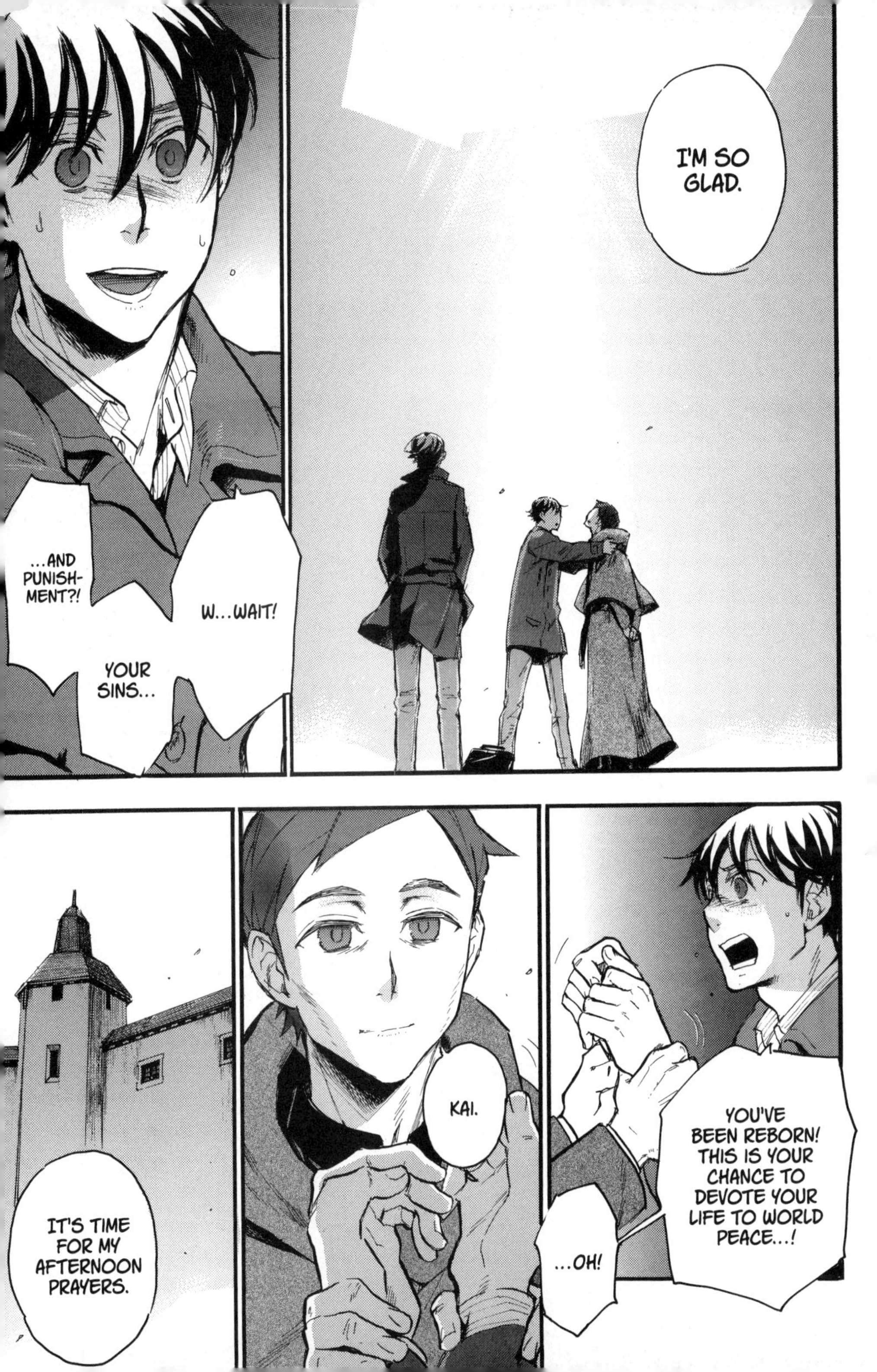
I'M SO GLAD.
W...WAIT!
YOUR SINS...
...AND PUNISHMENT?!
YOU'VE BEEN REBORN! THIS IS YOUR CHANCE TO DEVOTE YOUR LIFE TO WORLD PEACE...!
...OH!
KAI.
IT'S TIME FOR MY AFTERNOON PRAYERS.

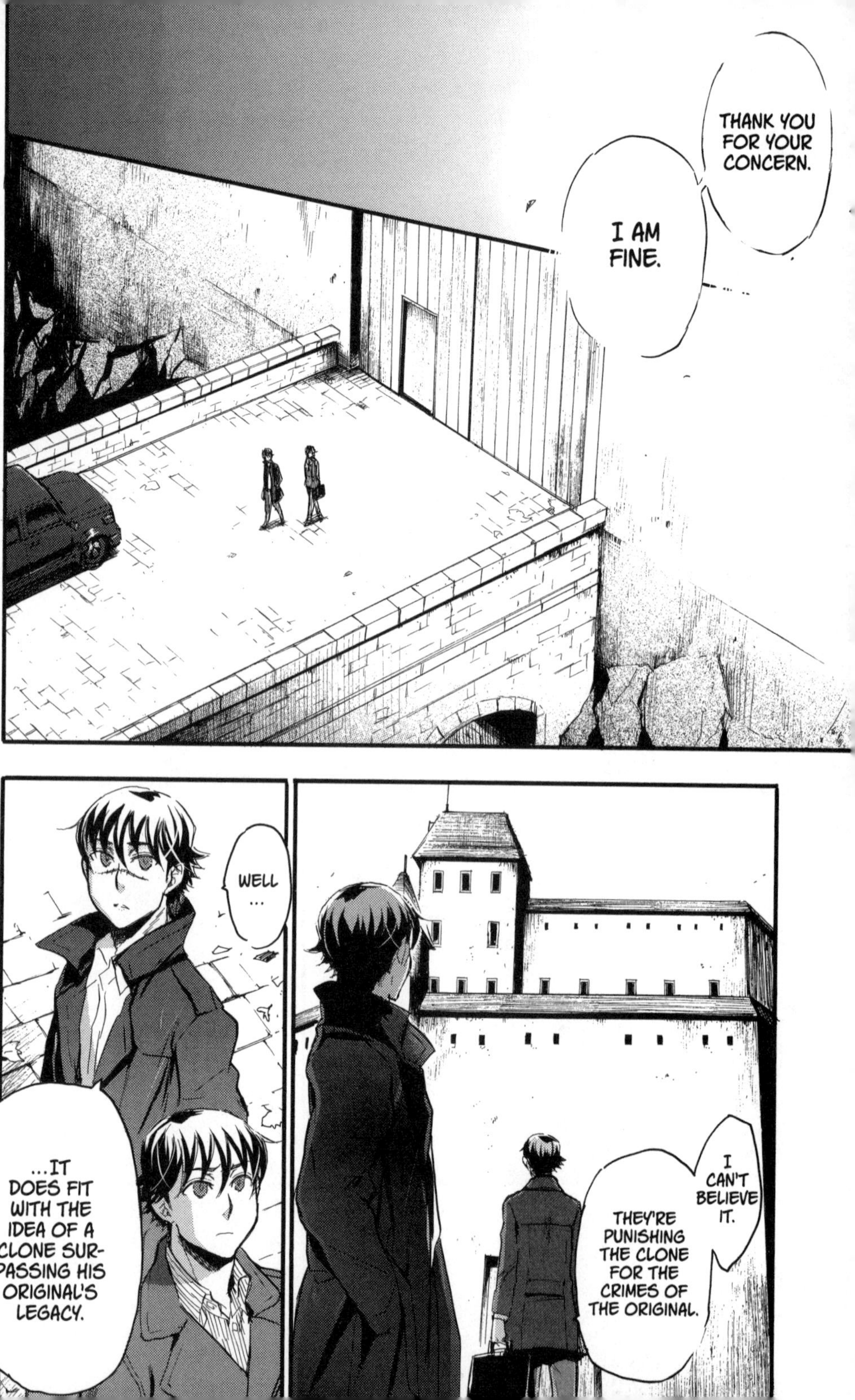
THANK YOU FOR YOUR CONCERN.
I AM FINE.
I CAN'T BELIEVE IT.
THEY'RE PUNISHING THE CLONE FOR THE CRIMES OF THE ORIGINAL.
WELL ...
...IT DOES FIT WITH THE IDEA OF A CLONE SURPASSING HIS ORIGINAL'S LEGACY.

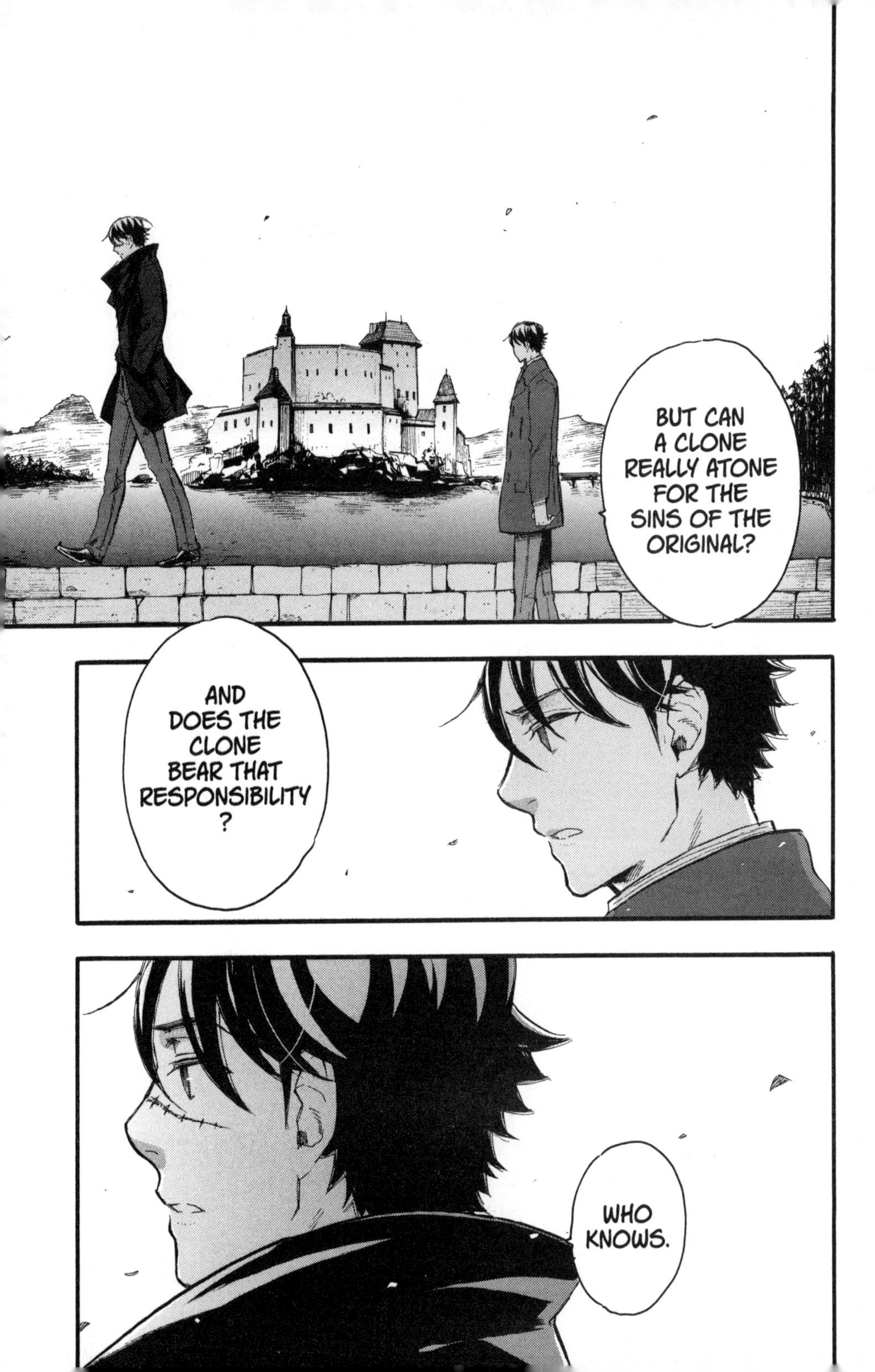
BUT CAN A CLONE REALLY ATONE FOR THE SINS OF THE ORIGINAL?
AND DOES THE CLONE BEAR THAT RESPONSIBILITY?
WHO KNOWS.

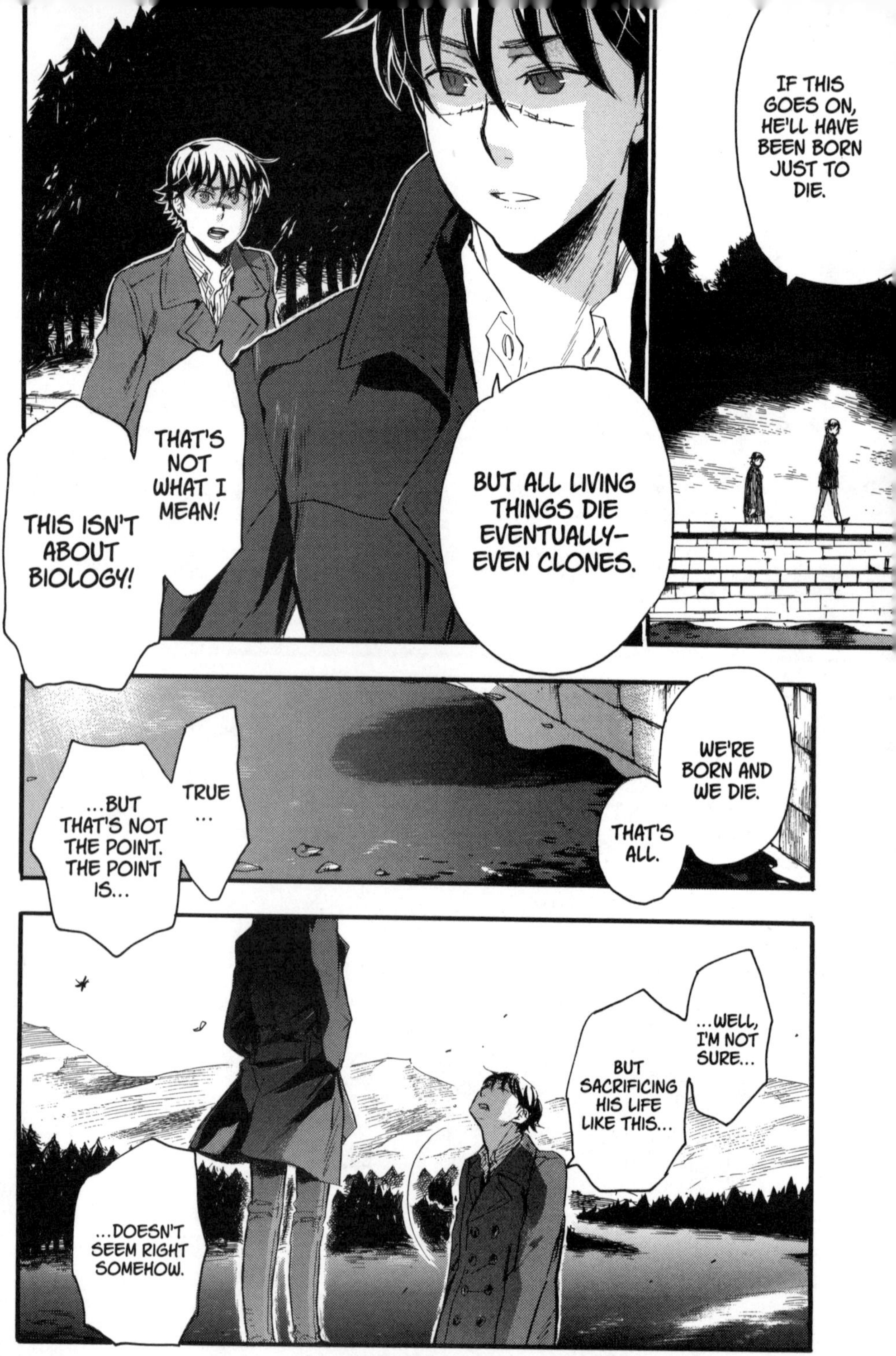
IF THIS GOES ON, HE'LL HAVE BEEN BORN JUST TO DIE.
BUT ALL LIVING THINGS DIE EVENTUALLY— EVEN CLONES.
THAT'S NOT WHAT I MEAN!
THIS ISN'T ABOUT BIOLOGY!
WE'RE BORN AND WE DIE.
THAT'S ALL.
TRUE...
...BUT THAT'S NOT THE POINT. THE POINT IS...
...WELL, I'M NOT SURE...
BUT SACRIFICING HIS LIFE LIKE THIS...
...DOESN'T SEEM RIGHT SOMEHOW.

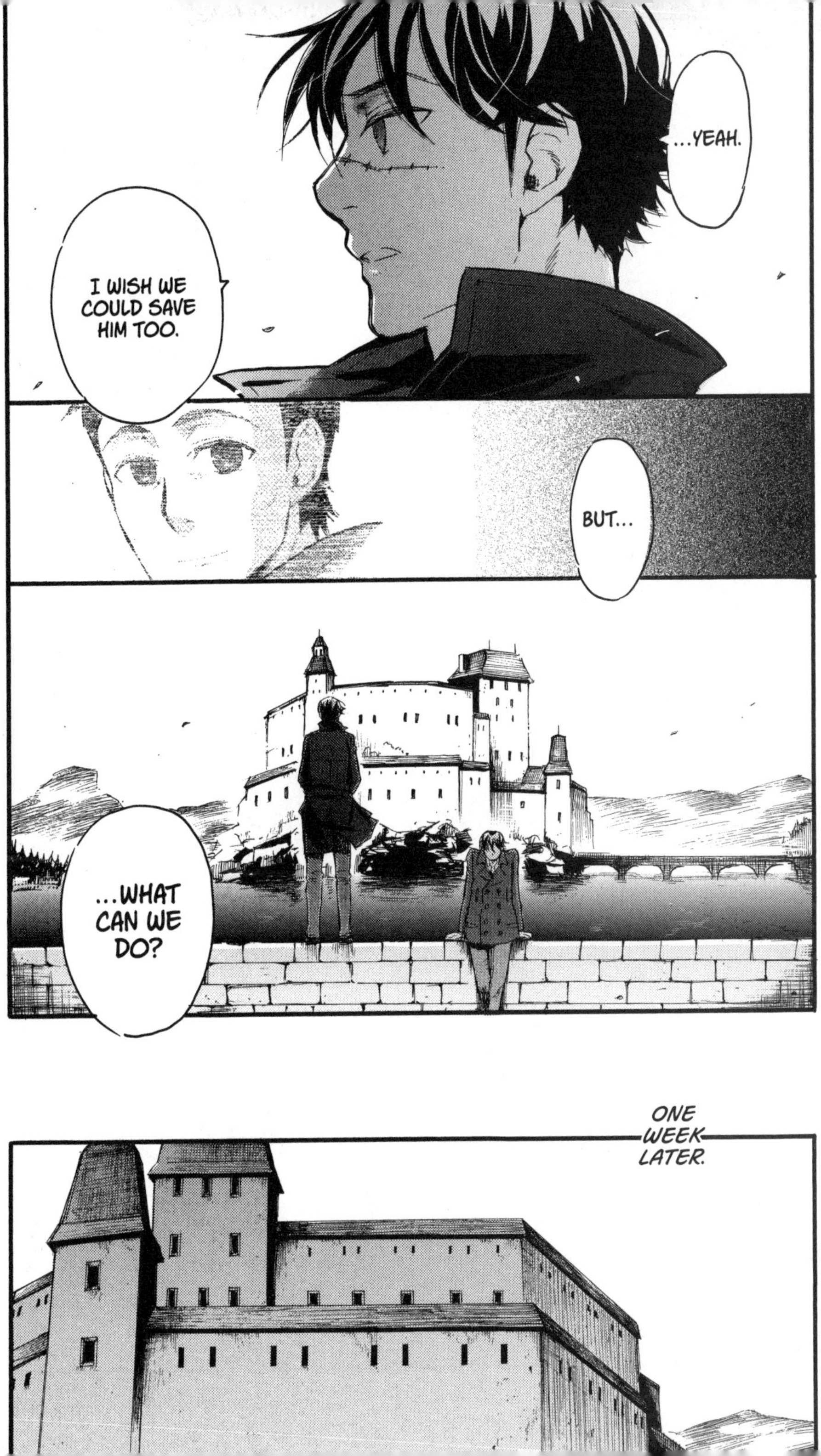
...YEAH.
I WISH WE COULD SAVE HIM TOO.
BUT...
...WHAT CAN WE DO?
ONE WEEK LATER.

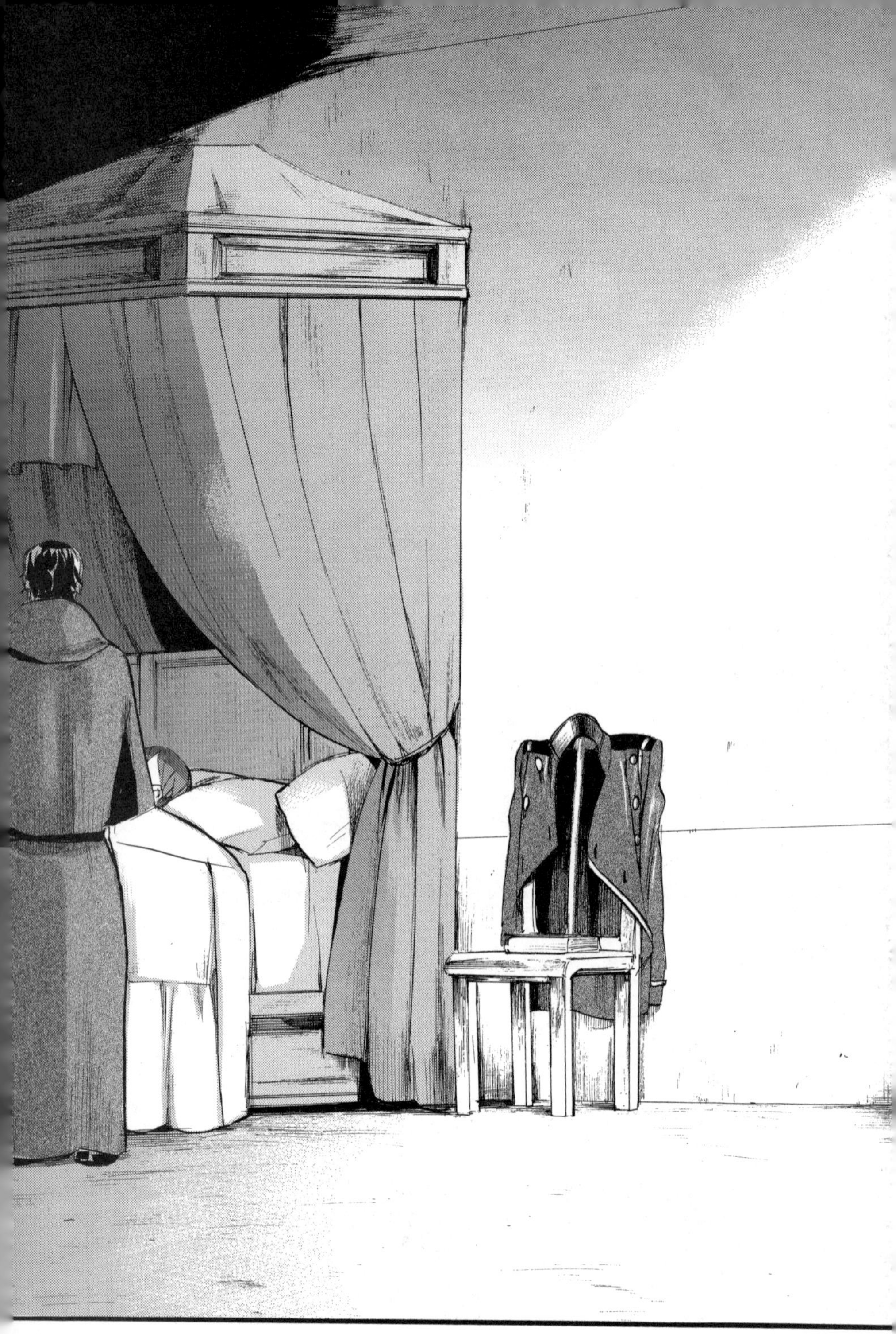

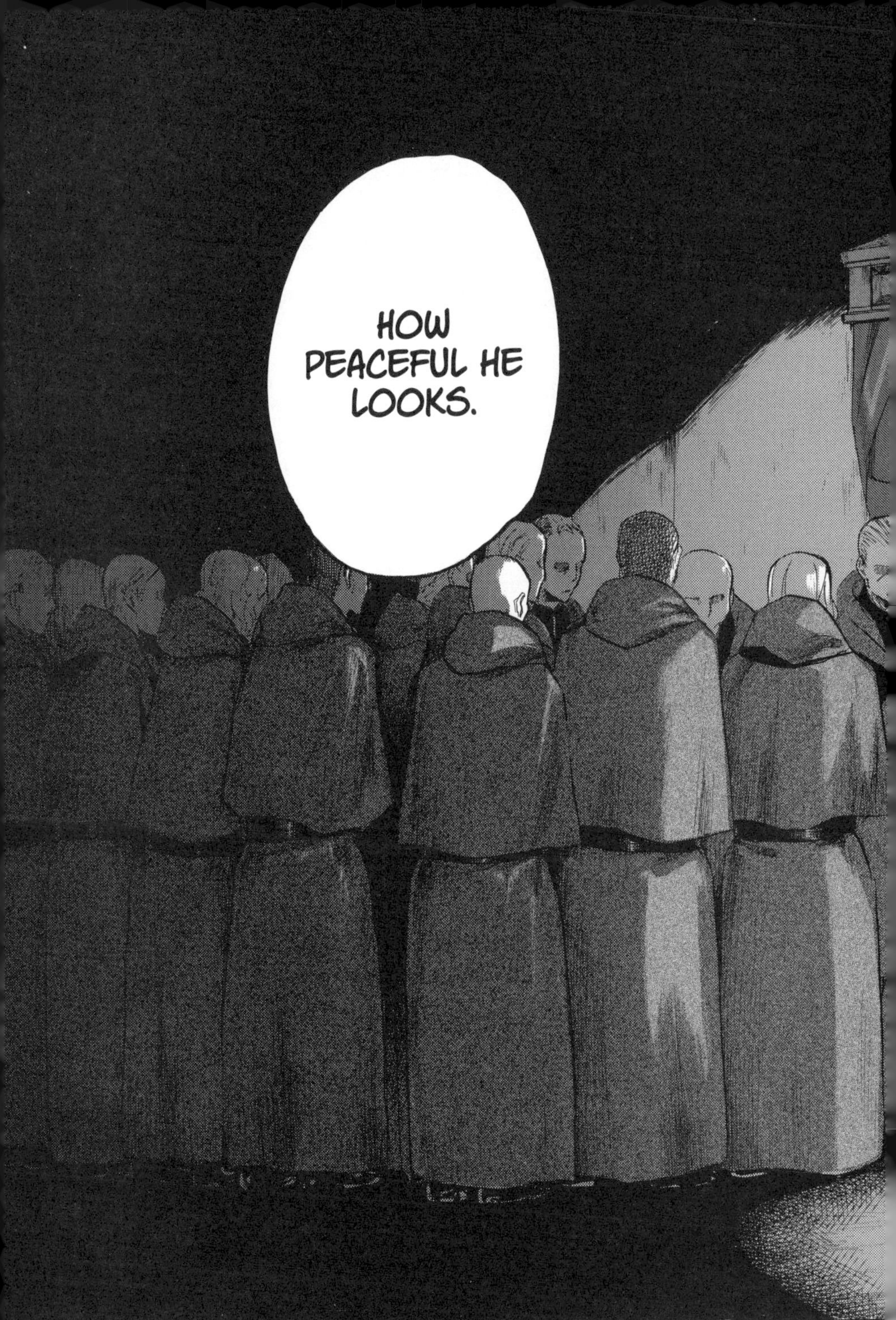
HOW PEACEFUL HE LOOKS.

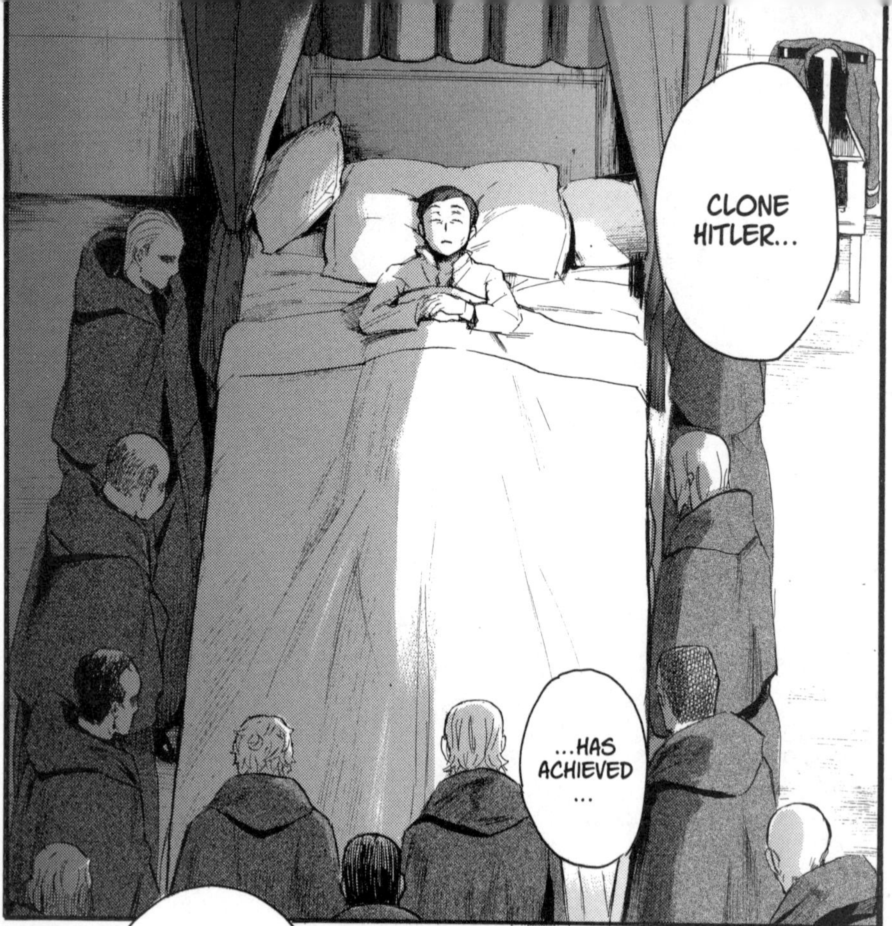
CLONE HITLER...
...HAS ACHIEVED ...
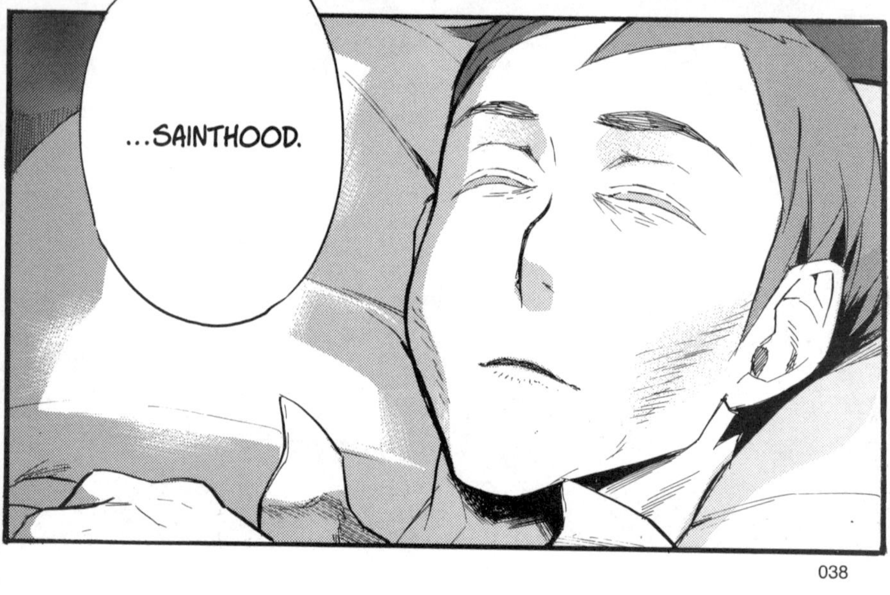
...SAINTHOOD.

CHAPTER **thirty-two**

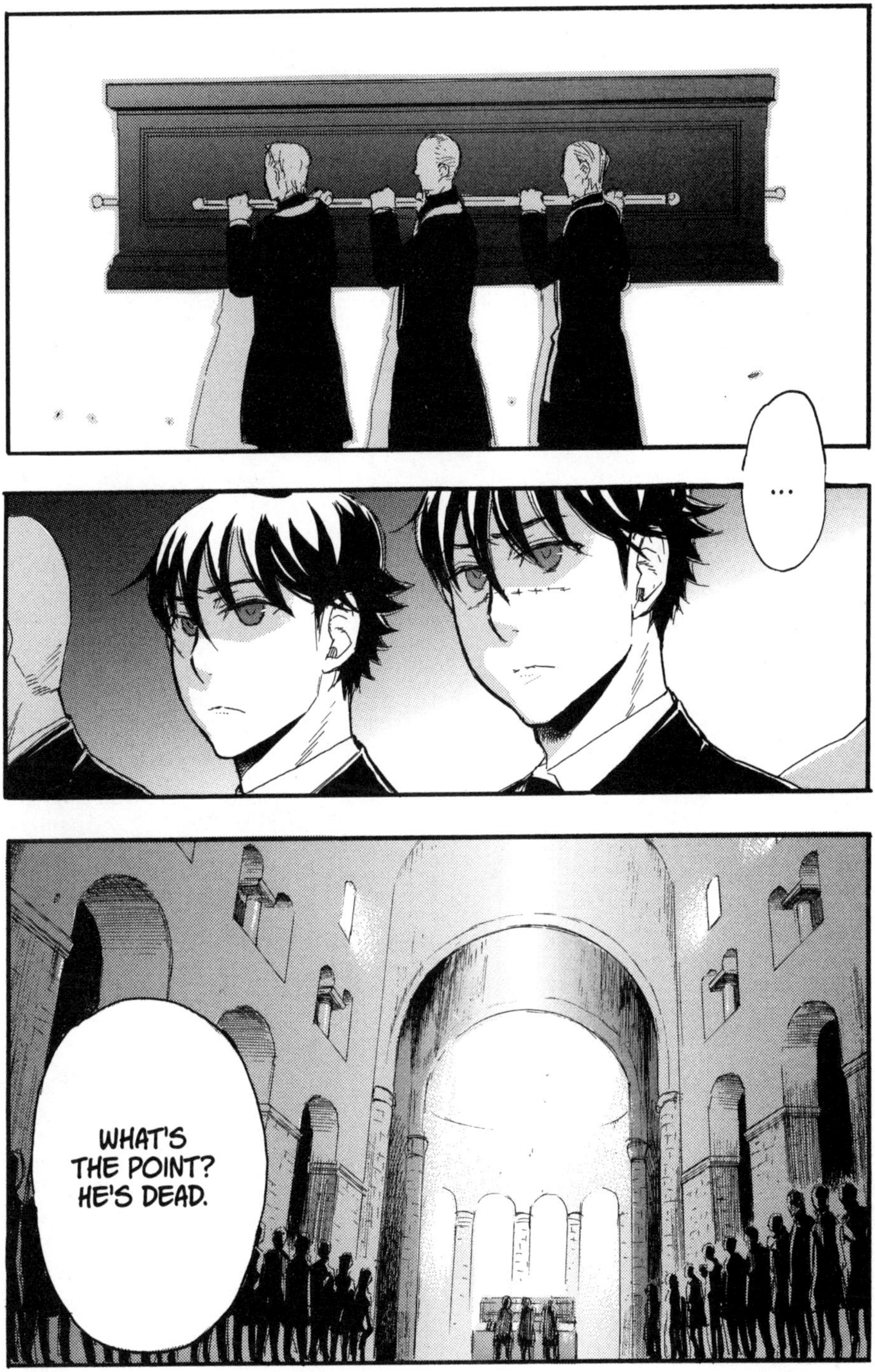
...
WHAT'S THE POINT? HE'S DEAD.

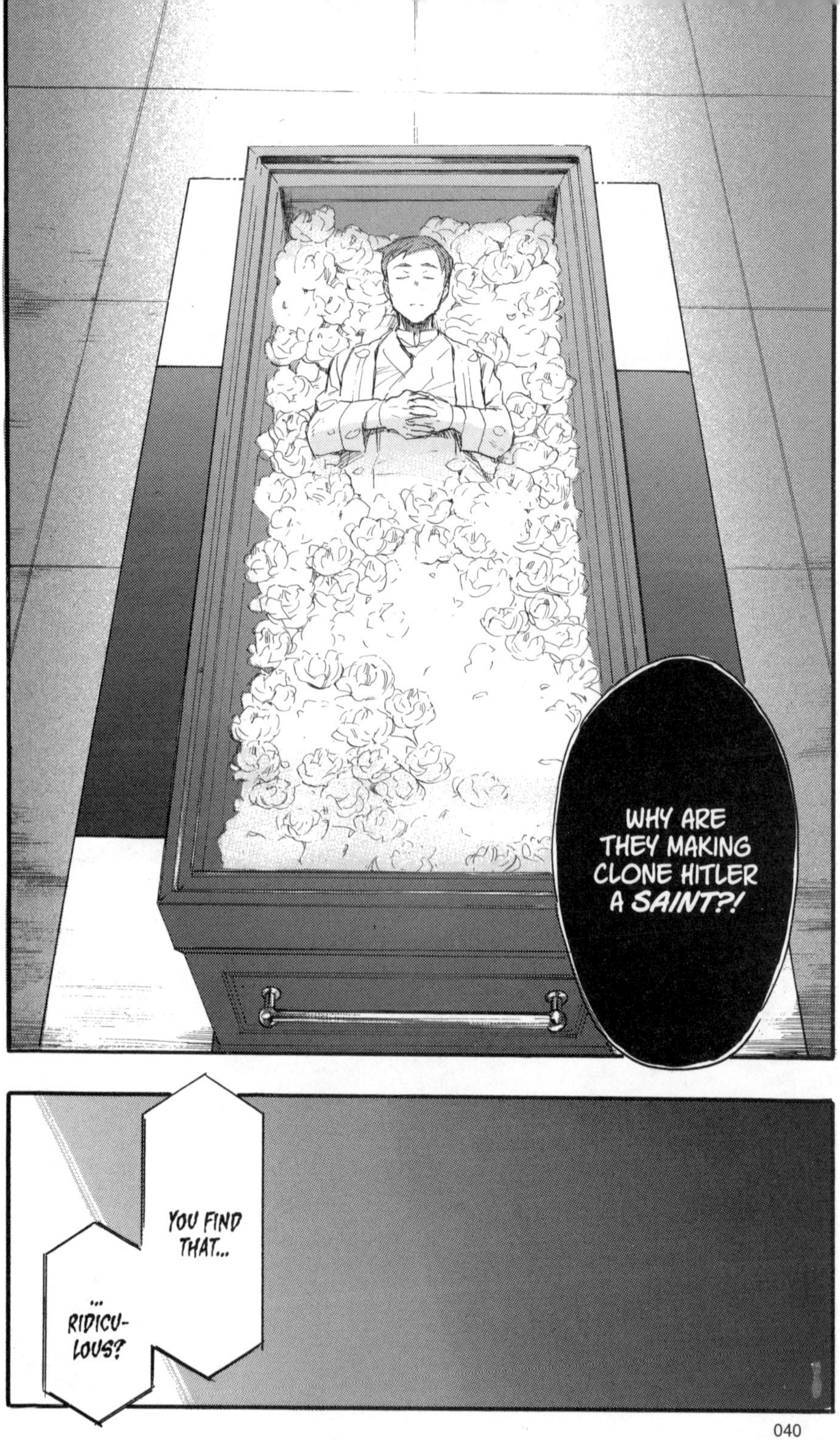
WHY ARE THEY MAKING CLONE HITLER A *SAINT?!*
YOU FIND THAT...
...RIDICU-LOUS?

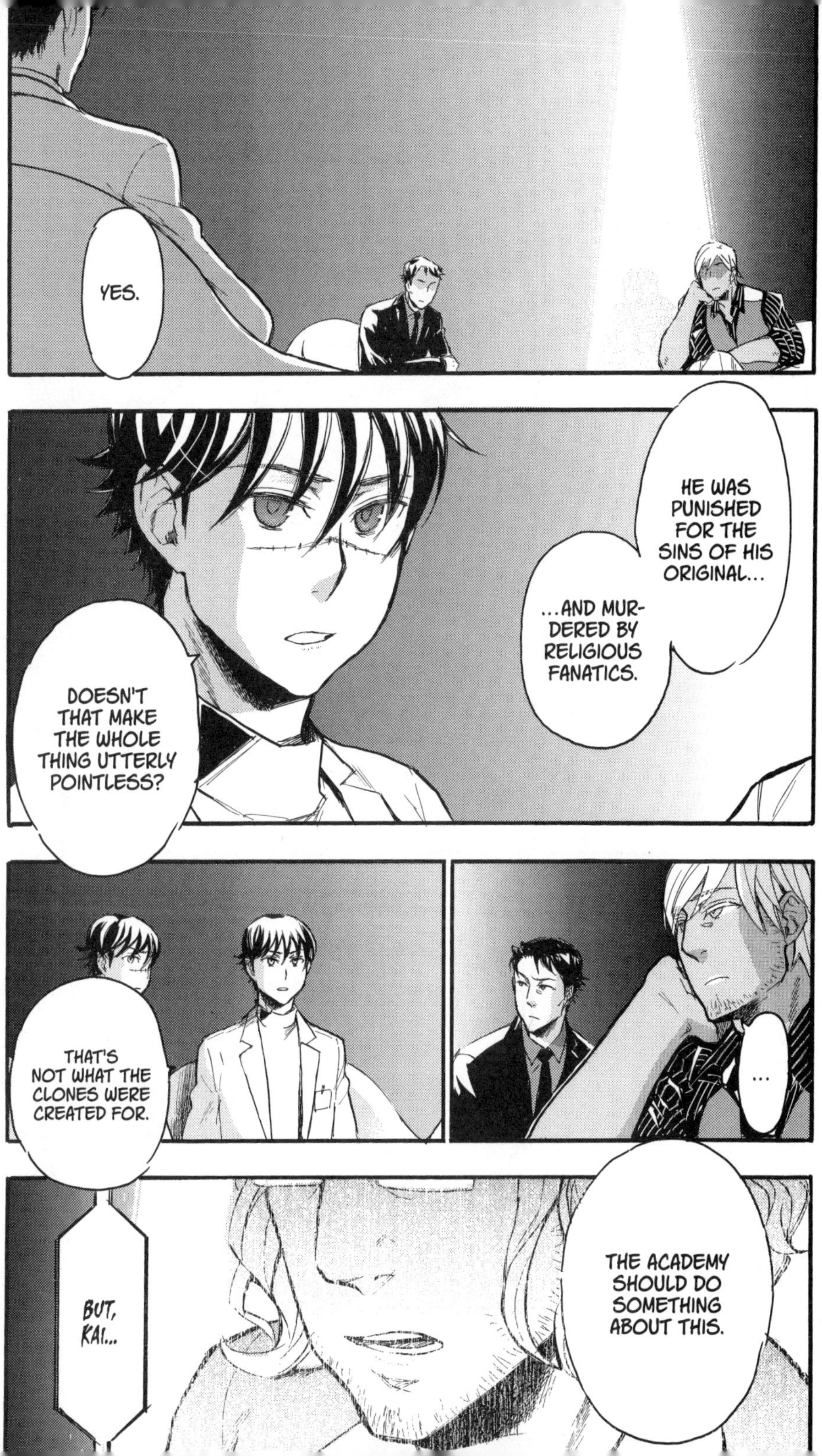
YES.
HE WAS PUNISHED FOR THE SINS OF HIS ORIGINAL...
...AND MURDERED BY RELIGIOUS FANATICS.
DOESN'T THAT MAKE THE WHOLE THING UTTERLY POINTLESS?
...
THAT'S NOT WHAT THE CLONES WERE CREATED FOR.
THE ACADEMY SHOULD DO SOMETHING ABOUT THIS.
BUT, KAI...

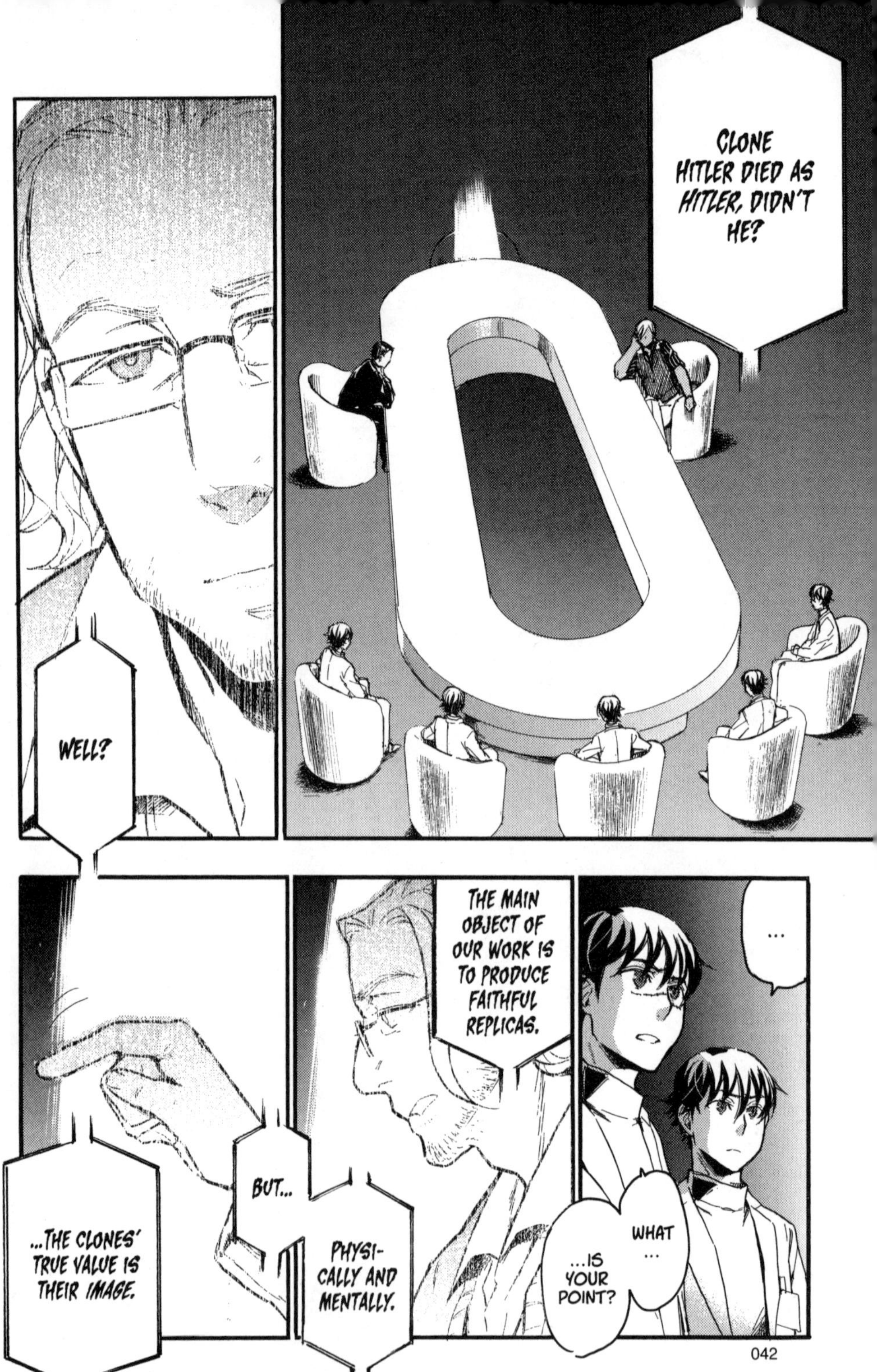
CLONE HITLER DIED AS HITLER, DIDN'T HE?
WELL?
...
WHAT ...
...IS YOUR POINT?
THE MAIN OBJECT OF OUR WORK IS TO PRODUCE FAITHFUL REPLICAS.
BUT...
PHYSICALLY AND MENTALLY.
...THE CLONES' TRUE VALUE IS THEIR IMAGE.

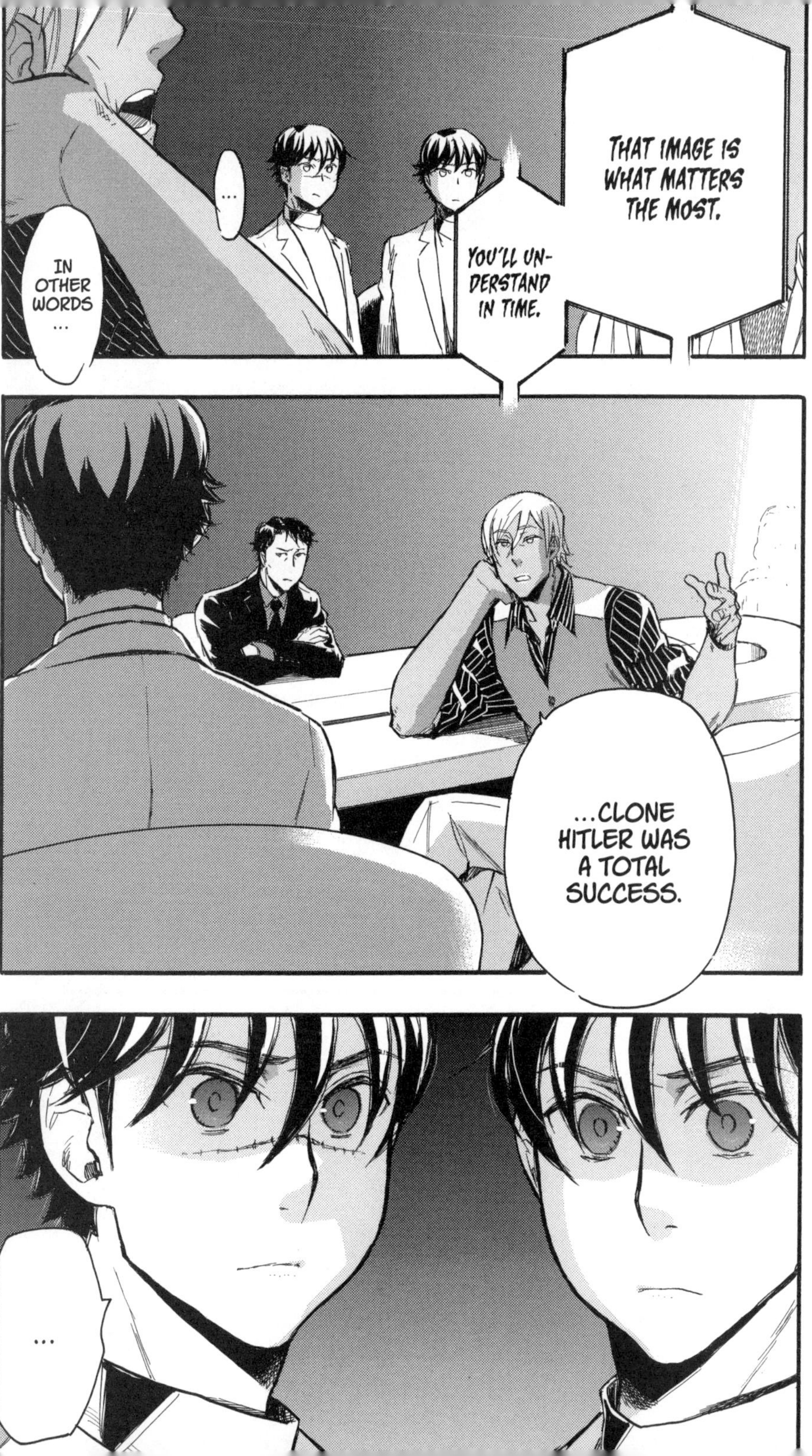
THAT IMAGE IS WHAT MATTERS THE MOST.
YOU'LL UN-DERSTAND IN TIME.
...
IN OTHER WORDS ...
...CLONE HITLER WAS A TOTAL SUCCESS.
...

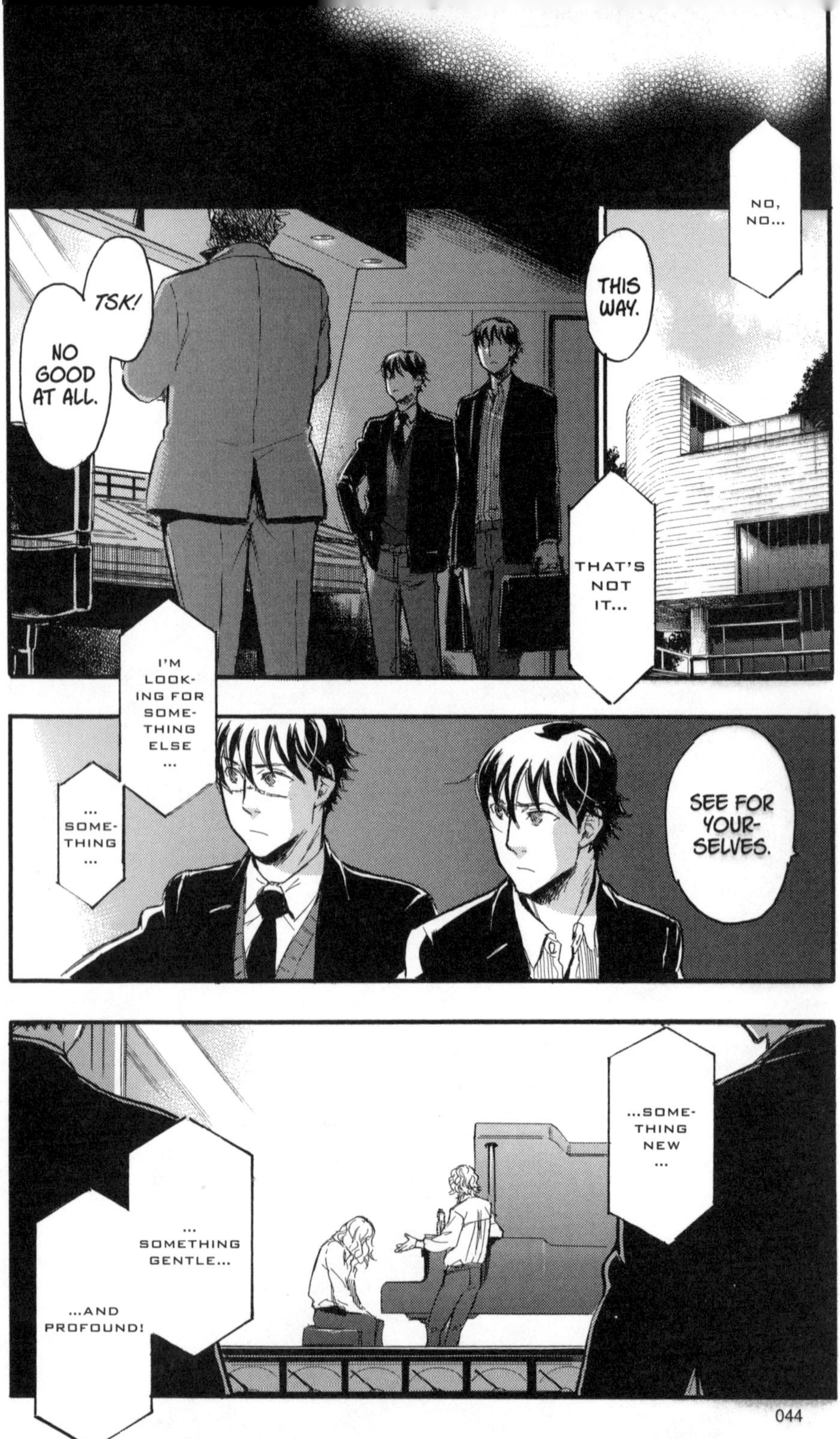

NO, NO...
THIS WAY.
TSK!
NO GOOD AT ALL.
THAT'S NOT IT...
I'M LOOKING FOR SOMETHING ELSE ...
SEE FOR YOURSELVES.
... SOMETHING ...
...SOMETHING NEW ...
... SOMETHING GENTLE...
...AND PROFOUND!

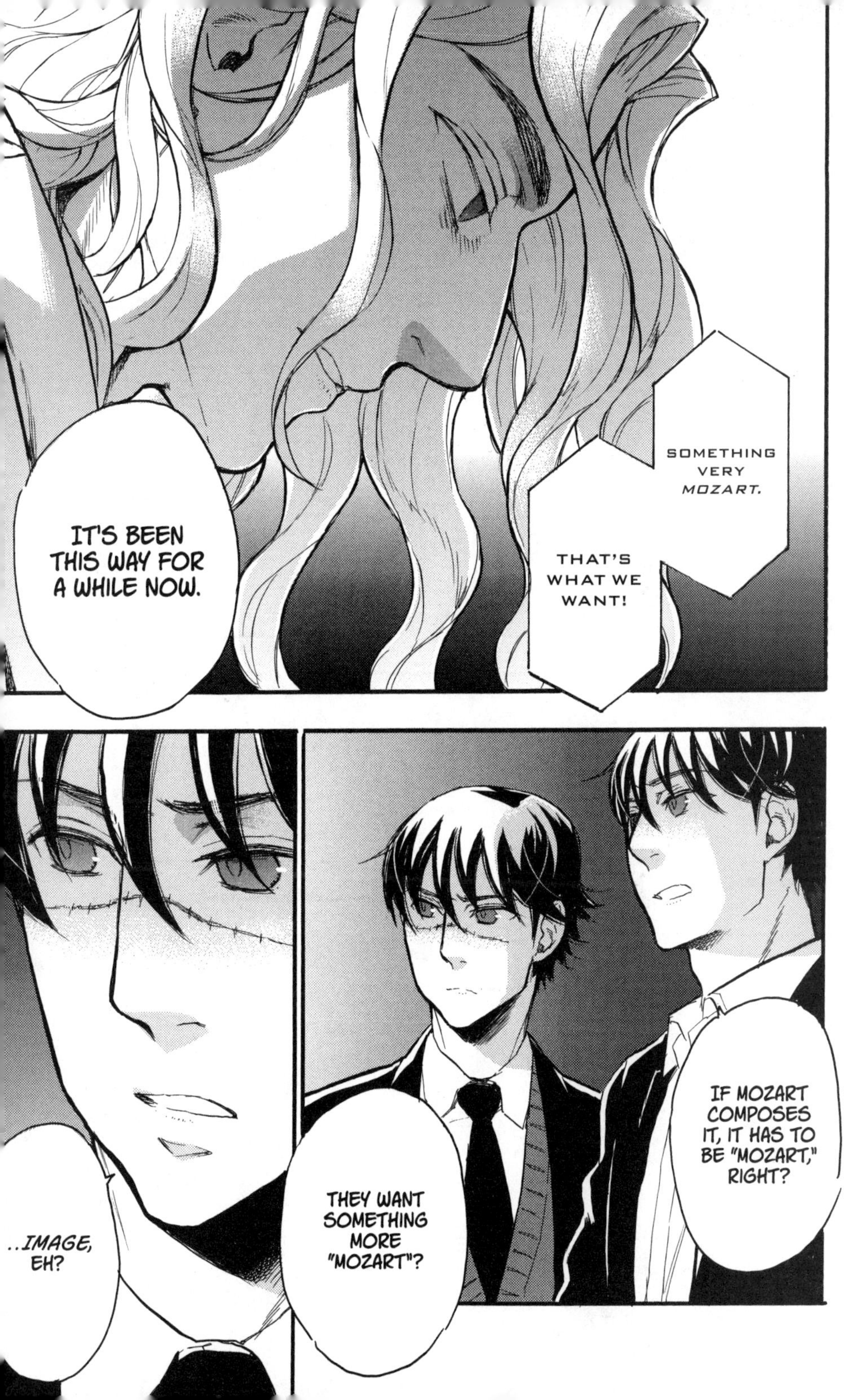
SOMETHING VERY *MOZART.*
THAT'S WHAT WE WANT!
IT'S BEEN THIS WAY FOR A WHILE NOW.
IF MOZART COMPOSES IT, IT HAS TO BE "MOZART," RIGHT?
THEY WANT SOMETHING MORE "MOZART"?
..*IMAGE,* EH?

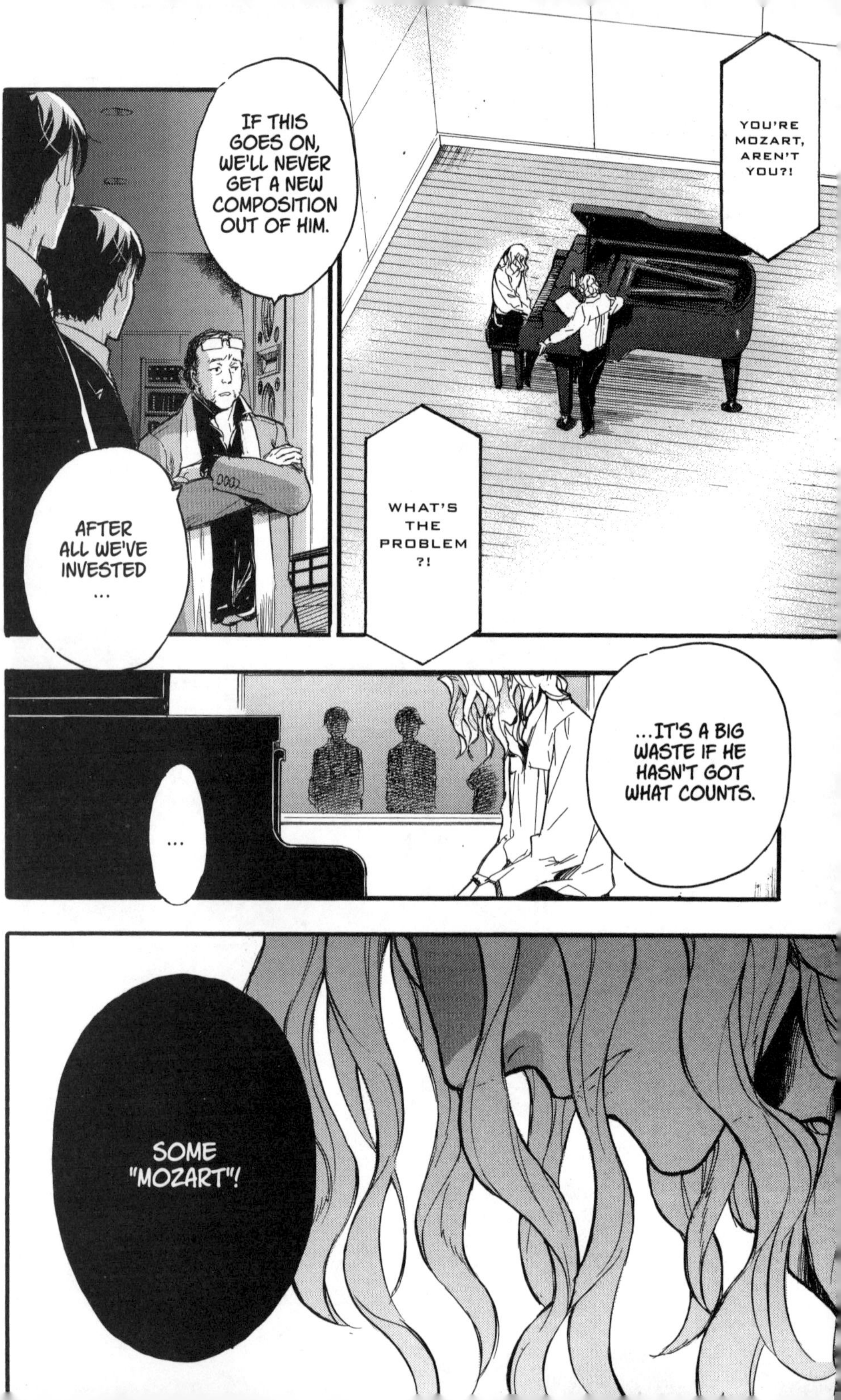
YOU'RE MOZART, AREN'T YOU?!
WHAT'S THE PROBLEM ?!
IF THIS GOES ON, WE'LL NEVER GET A NEW COMPOSITION OUT OF HIM.
AFTER ALL WE'VE INVESTED ...
...IT'S A BIG WASTE IF HE HASN'T GOT WHAT COUNTS.
...
SOME "MOZART"!

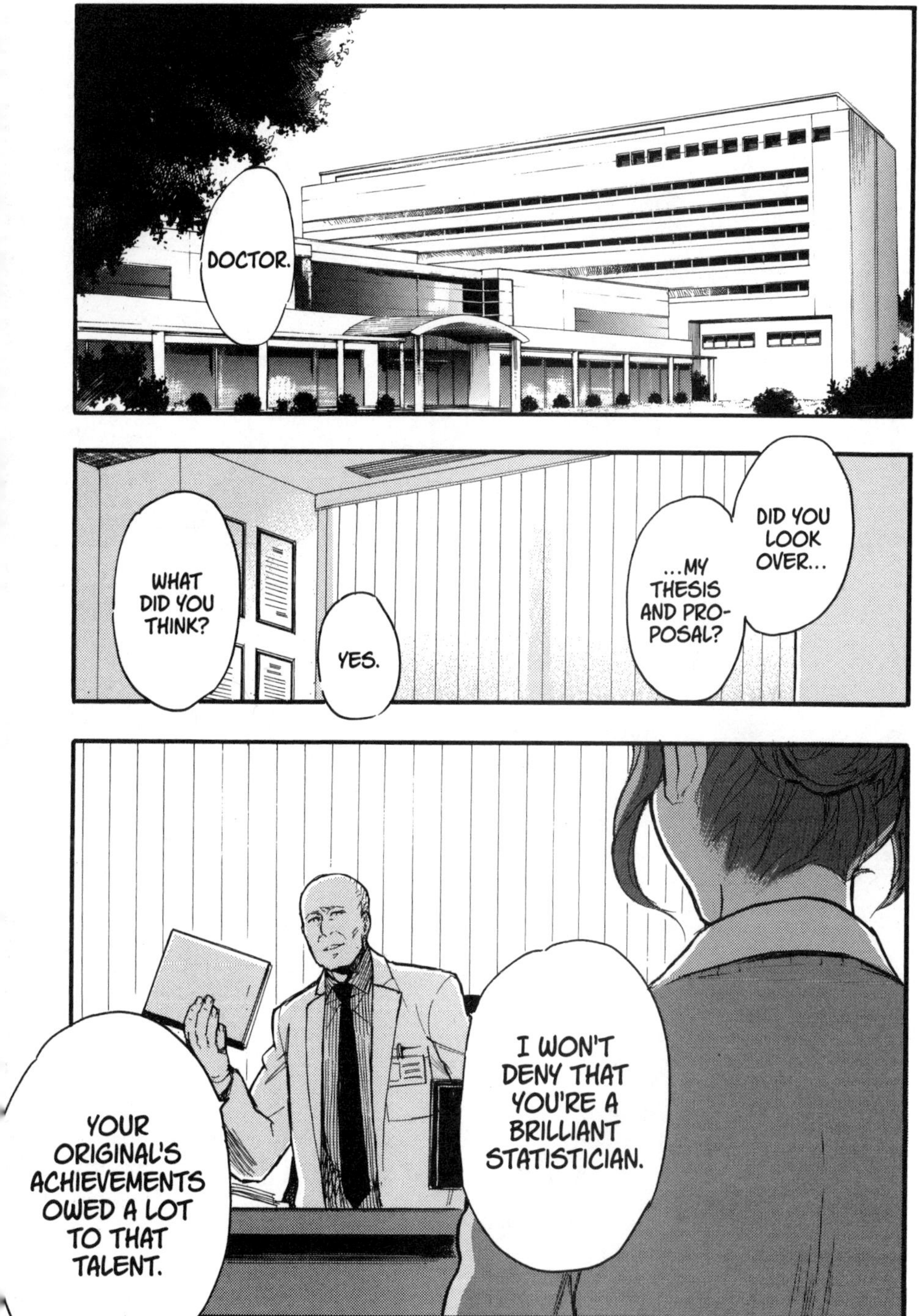
DOCTOR.
DID YOU LOOK OVER...
...MY THESIS AND PRO-POSAL?
YES.
WHAT DID YOU THINK?
I WON'T DENY THAT YOU'RE A BRILLIANT STATISTICIAN.
YOUR ORIGINAL'S ACHIEVEMENTS OWED A LOT TO THAT TALENT.

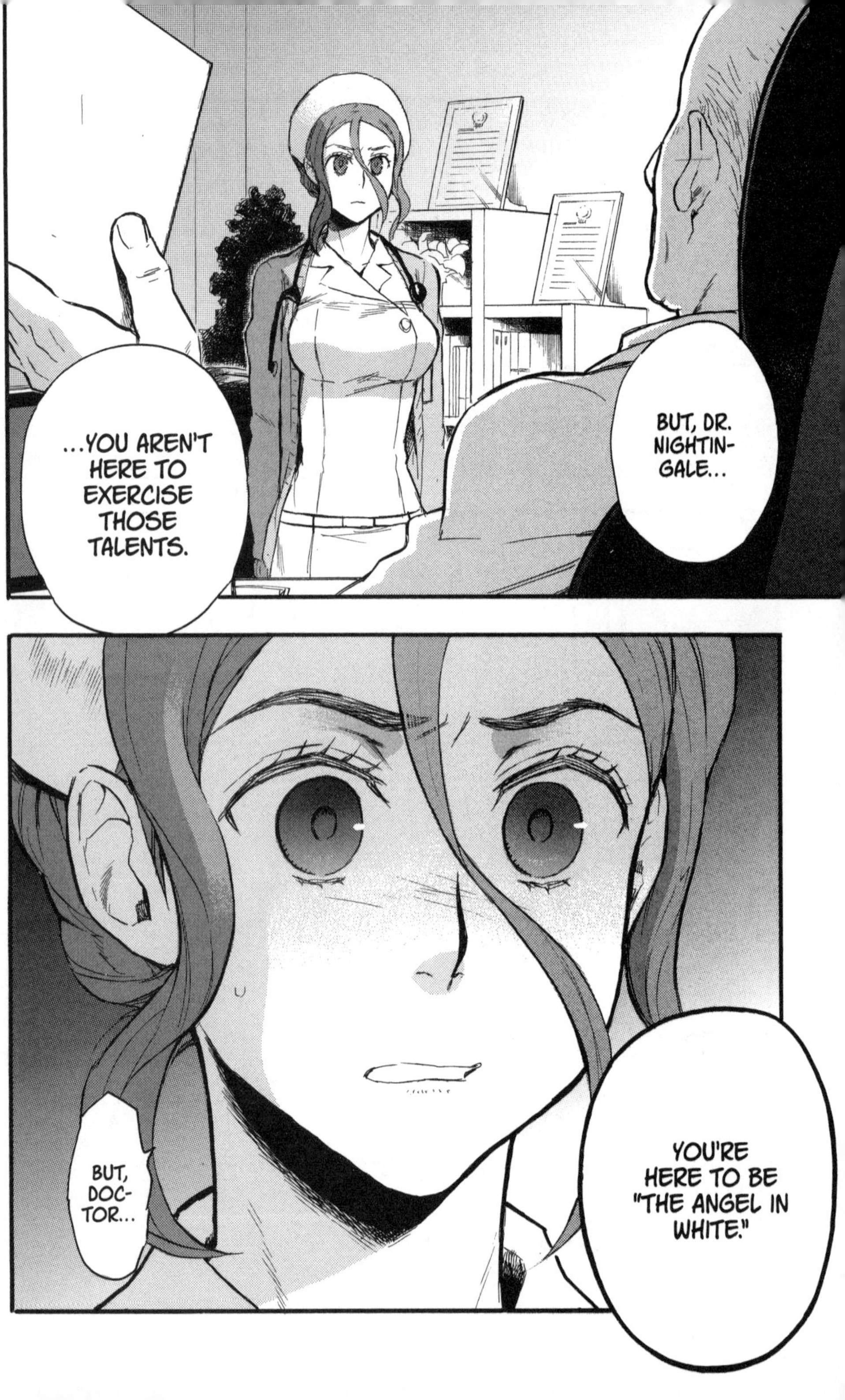
BUT, DR. NIGHTIN-GALE...
...YOU AREN'T HERE TO EXERCISE THOSE TALENTS.
YOU'RE HERE TO BE "THE ANGEL IN WHITE."
BUT, DOC-TOR...

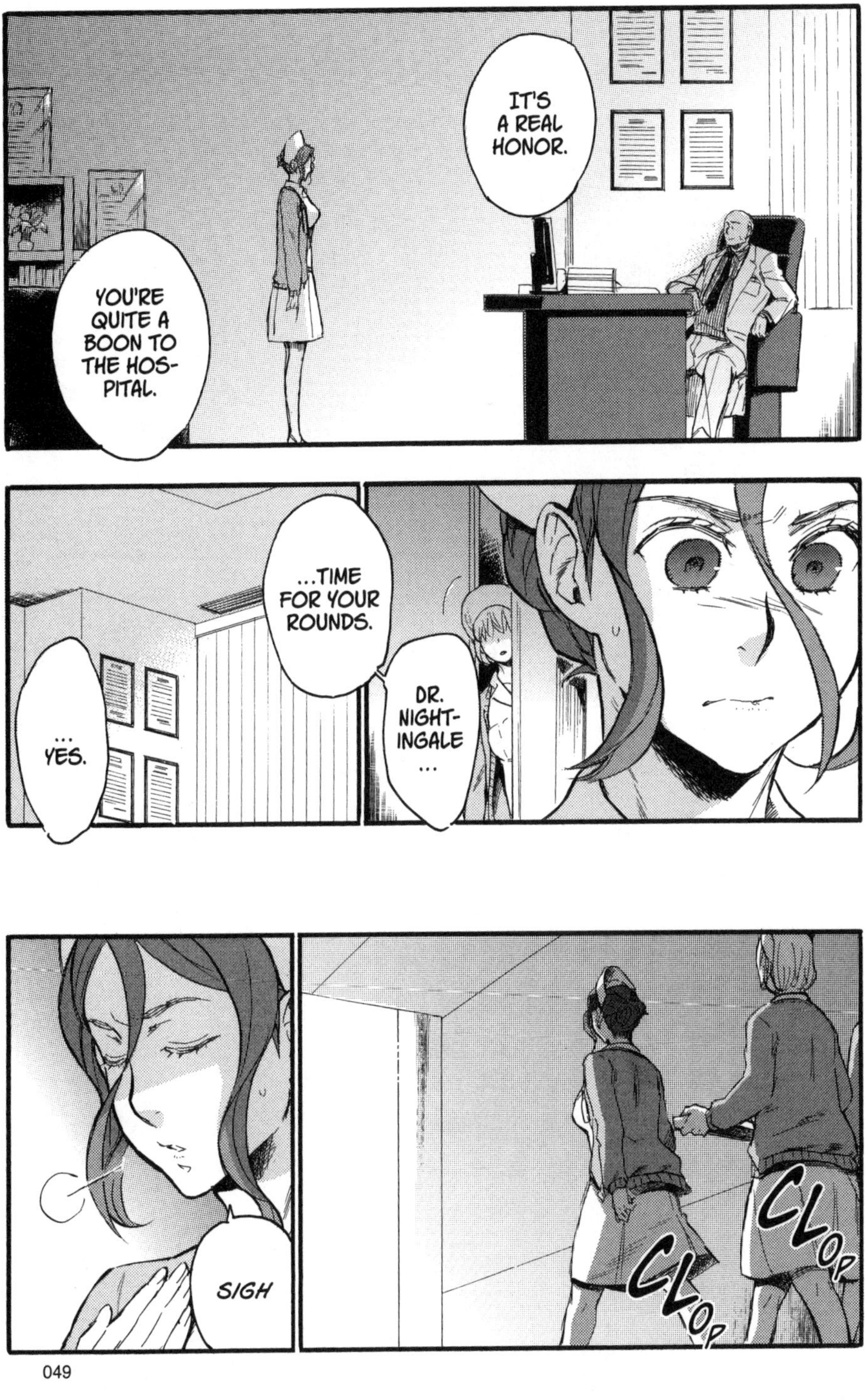
IT'S A REAL HONOR.
YOU'RE QUITE A BOON TO THE HOS-PITAL.
DR. NIGHT-INGALE...
...TIME FOR YOUR ROUNDS.
... YES.
CLOP
CLOP
SIGH

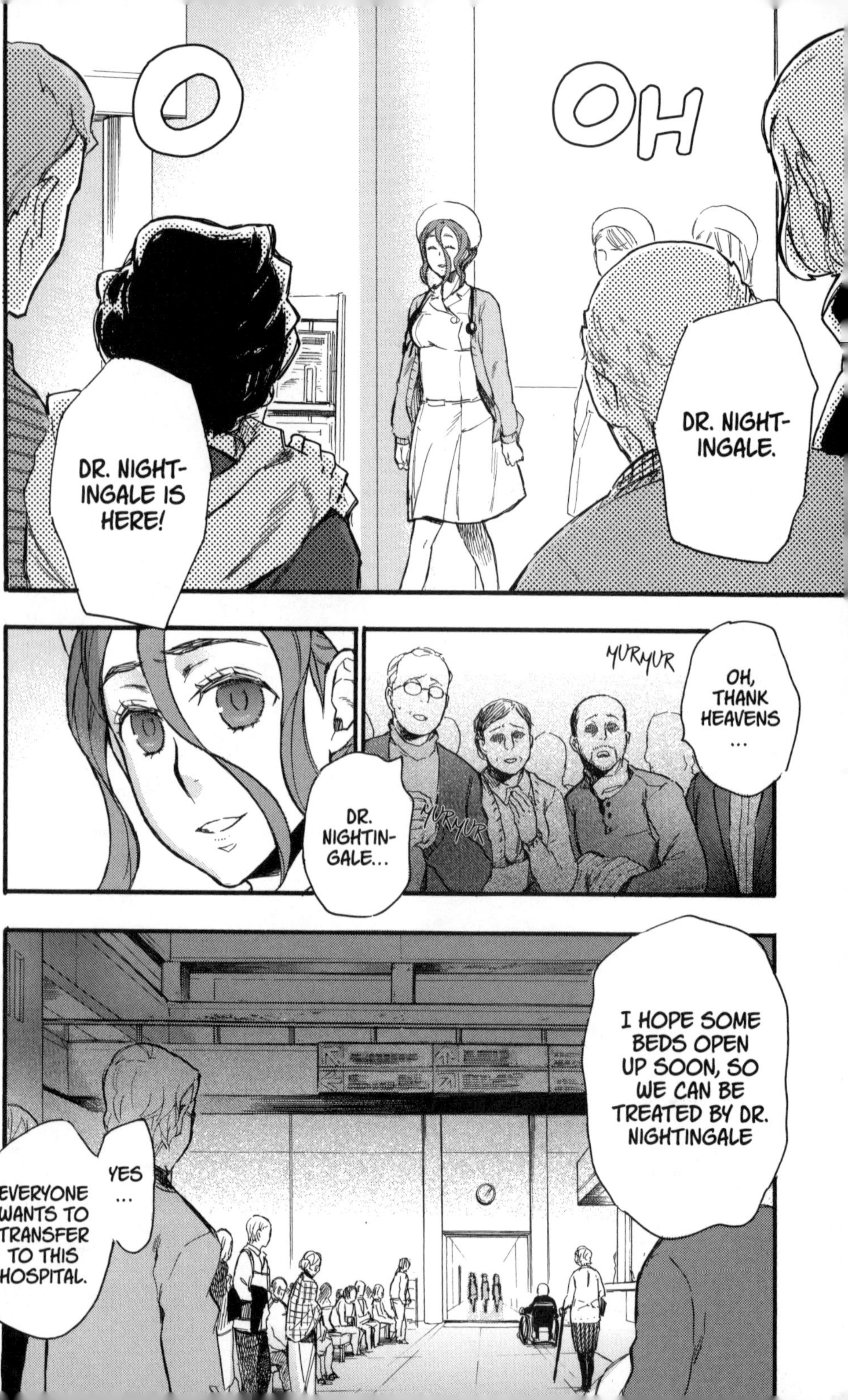
OH
DR. NIGHT-INGALE.
O
DR. NIGHT-INGALE IS HERE!
MURMUR
OH, THANK HEAVENS ...
DR. NIGHTIN-GALE...
MURMUR
I HOPE SOME BEDS OPEN UP SOON, SO WE CAN BE TREATED BY DR. NIGHTINGALE
YES ...
EVERYONE WANTS TO TRANSFER TO THIS HOSPITAL.

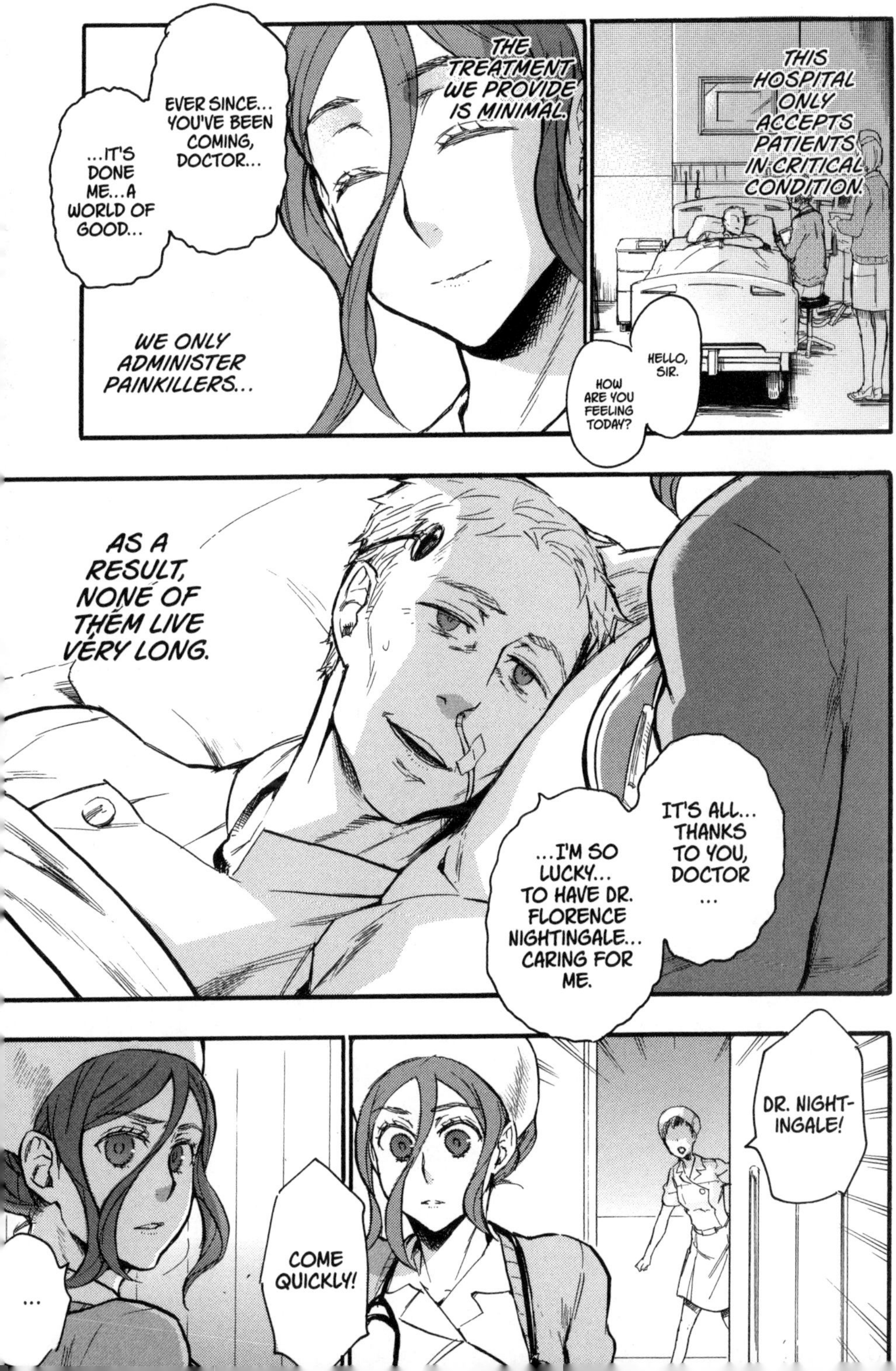
THIS HOSPITAL ONLY ACCEPTS PATIENTS IN CRITICAL CONDITION.
HELLO, SIR. HOW ARE YOU FEELING TODAY?
THE TREATMENT WE PROVIDE IS MINIMAL.
EVER SINCE... YOU'VE BEEN COMING, DOCTOR...
...IT'S DONE ME...A WORLD OF GOOD...
WE ONLY ADMINISTER PAINKILLERS...
AS A RESULT, NONE OF THEM LIVE VERY LONG.
IT'S ALL... THANKS TO YOU, DOCTOR...
...I'M SO LUCKY... TO HAVE DR. FLORENCE NIGHTINGALE... CARING FOR ME.
DR. NIGHT-INGALE!
COME QUICKLY!
...

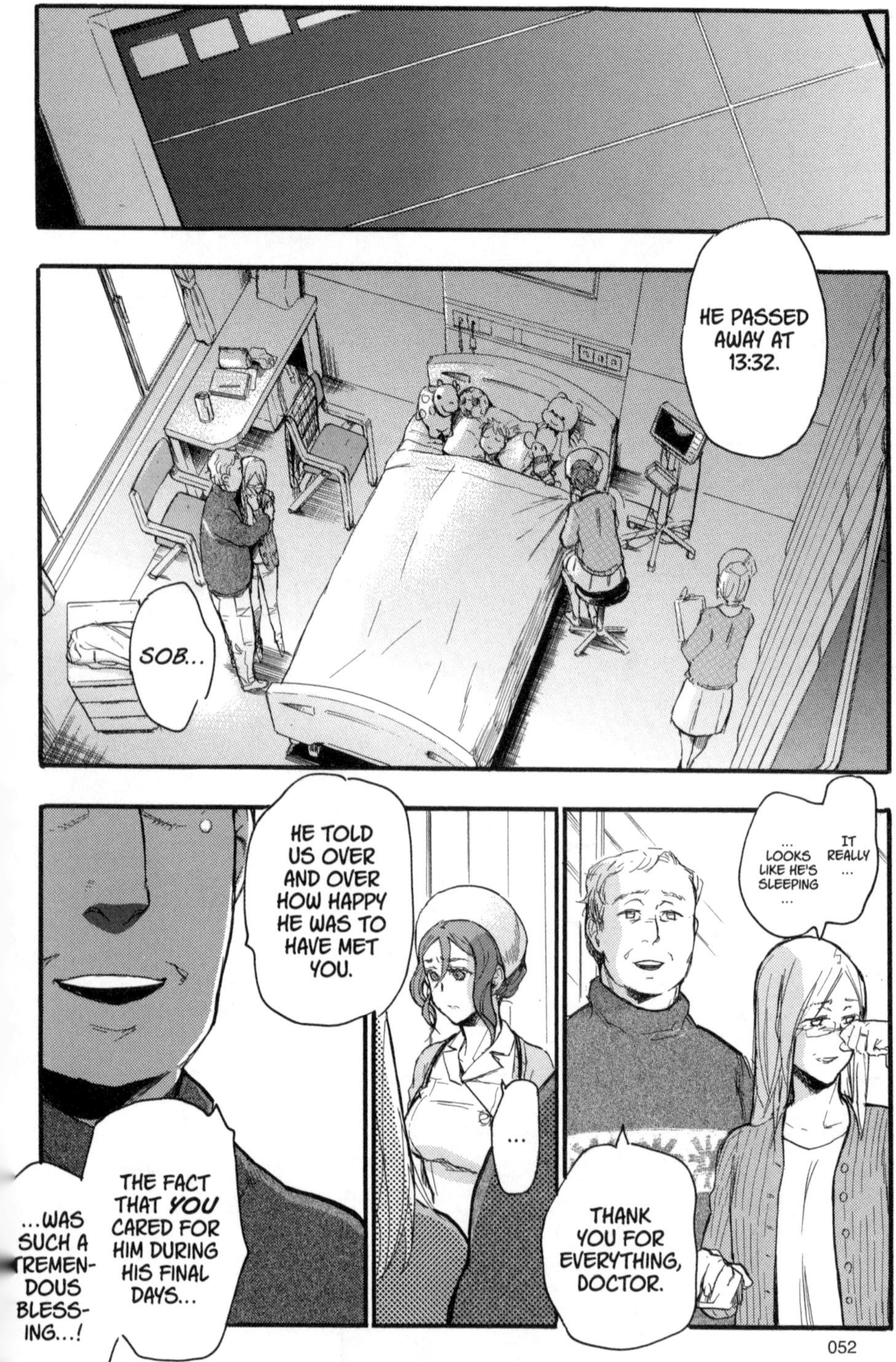
HE PASSED AWAY AT 13:32.
SOB...
IT REALLY...
...LOOKS LIKE HE'S SLEEPING...
THANK YOU FOR EVERYTHING, DOCTOR.
HE TOLD US OVER AND OVER HOW HAPPY HE WAS TO HAVE MET YOU.
...
THE FACT THAT *YOU* CARED FOR HIM DURING HIS FINAL DAYS...
...WAS SUCH A TREMEN-DOUS BLESS-ING...!

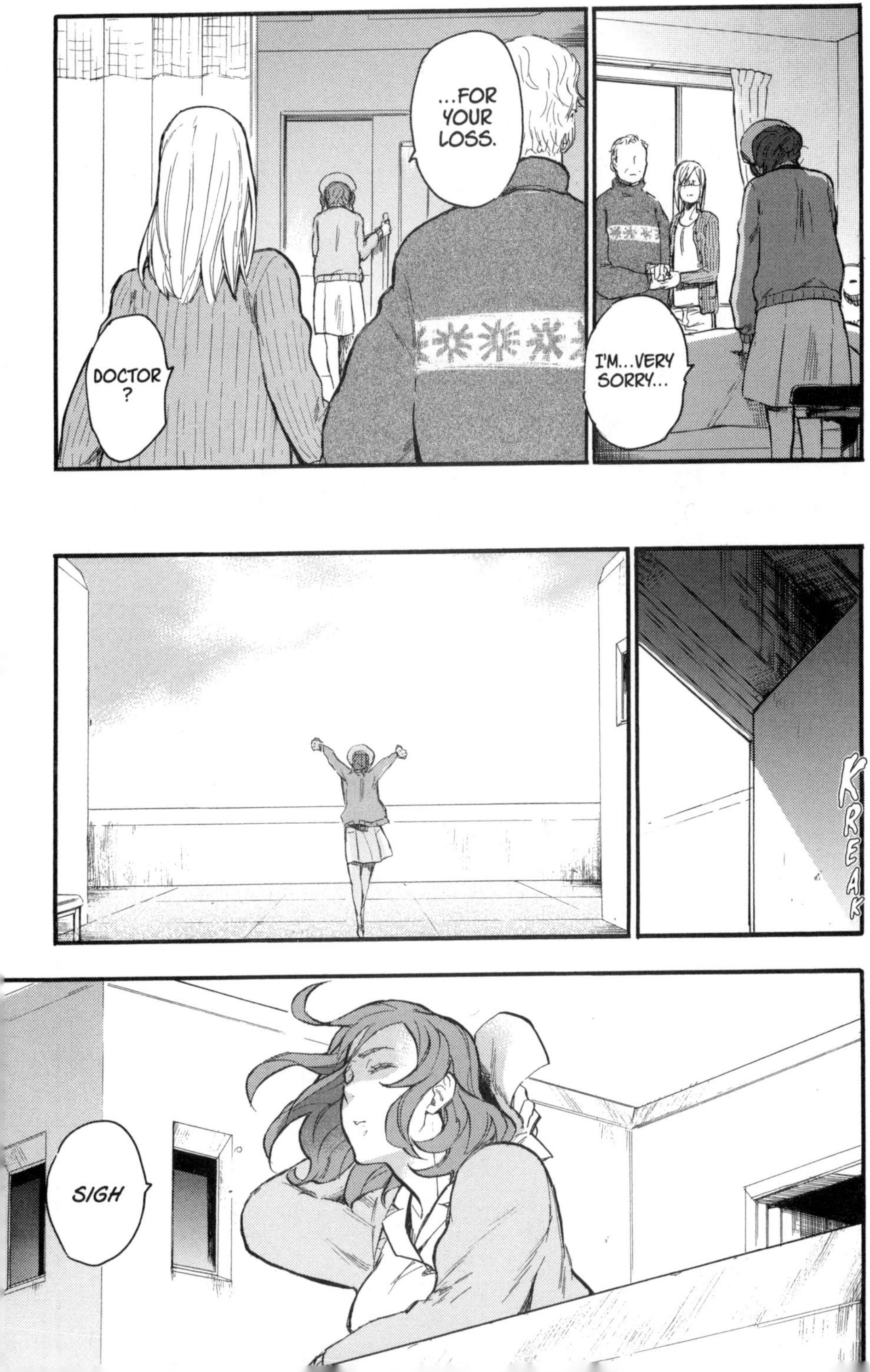
I'M...VERY SORRY...
...FOR YOUR LOSS.
DOCTOR ?
KREAK
SIGH

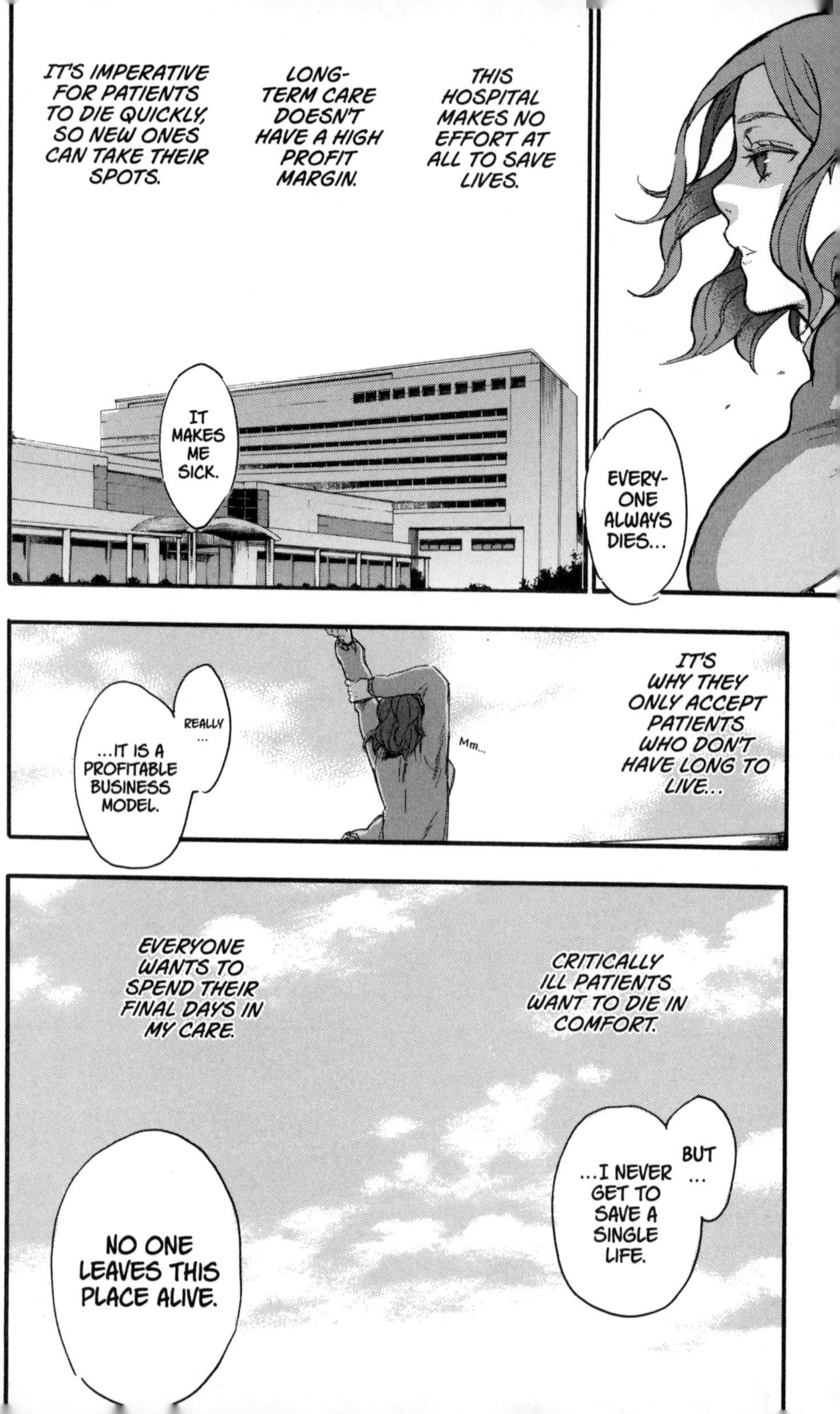
EVERYONE ALWAYS DIES...
THIS HOSPITAL MAKES NO EFFORT AT ALL TO SAVE LIVES.
LONG-TERM CARE DOESN'T HAVE A HIGH PROFIT MARGIN.
IT'S IMPERATIVE FOR PATIENTS TO DIE QUICKLY, SO NEW ONES CAN TAKE THEIR SPOTS.
IT MAKES ME SICK.
IT'S WHY THEY ONLY ACCEPT PATIENTS WHO DON'T HAVE LONG TO LIVE...
Mm...
REALLY...
...IT IS A PROFITABLE BUSINESS MODEL.
CRITICALLY ILL PATIENTS WANT TO DIE IN COMFORT.
EVERYONE WANTS TO SPEND THEIR FINAL DAYS IN MY CARE.
BUT...
...I NEVER GET TO SAVE A SINGLE LIFE.
NO ONE LEAVES THIS PLACE ALIVE.

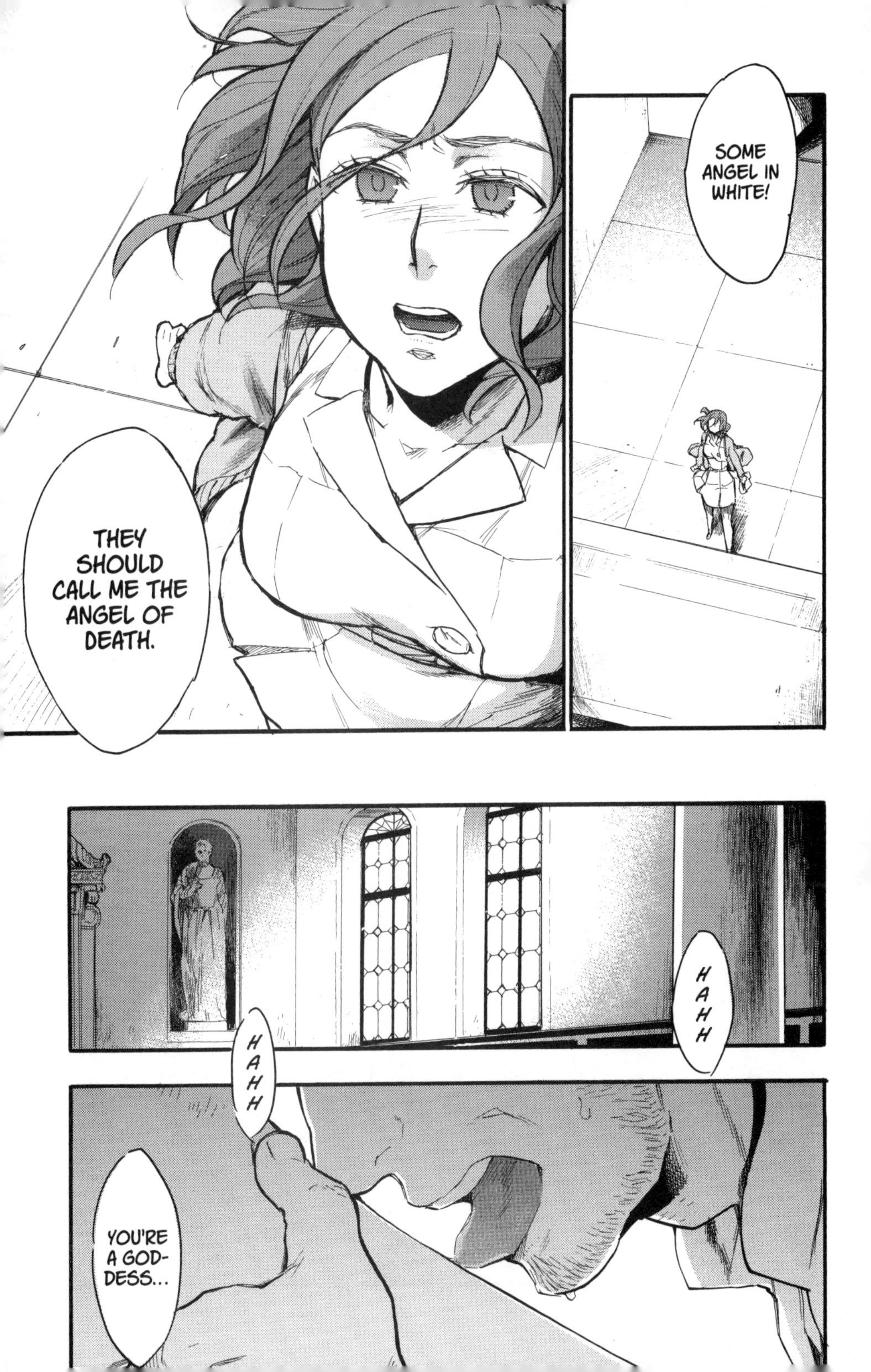
SOME ANGEL IN WHITE!
THEY SHOULD CALL ME THE ANGEL OF DEATH.
HAHH
HAHH
YOU'RE A GOD-DESS...

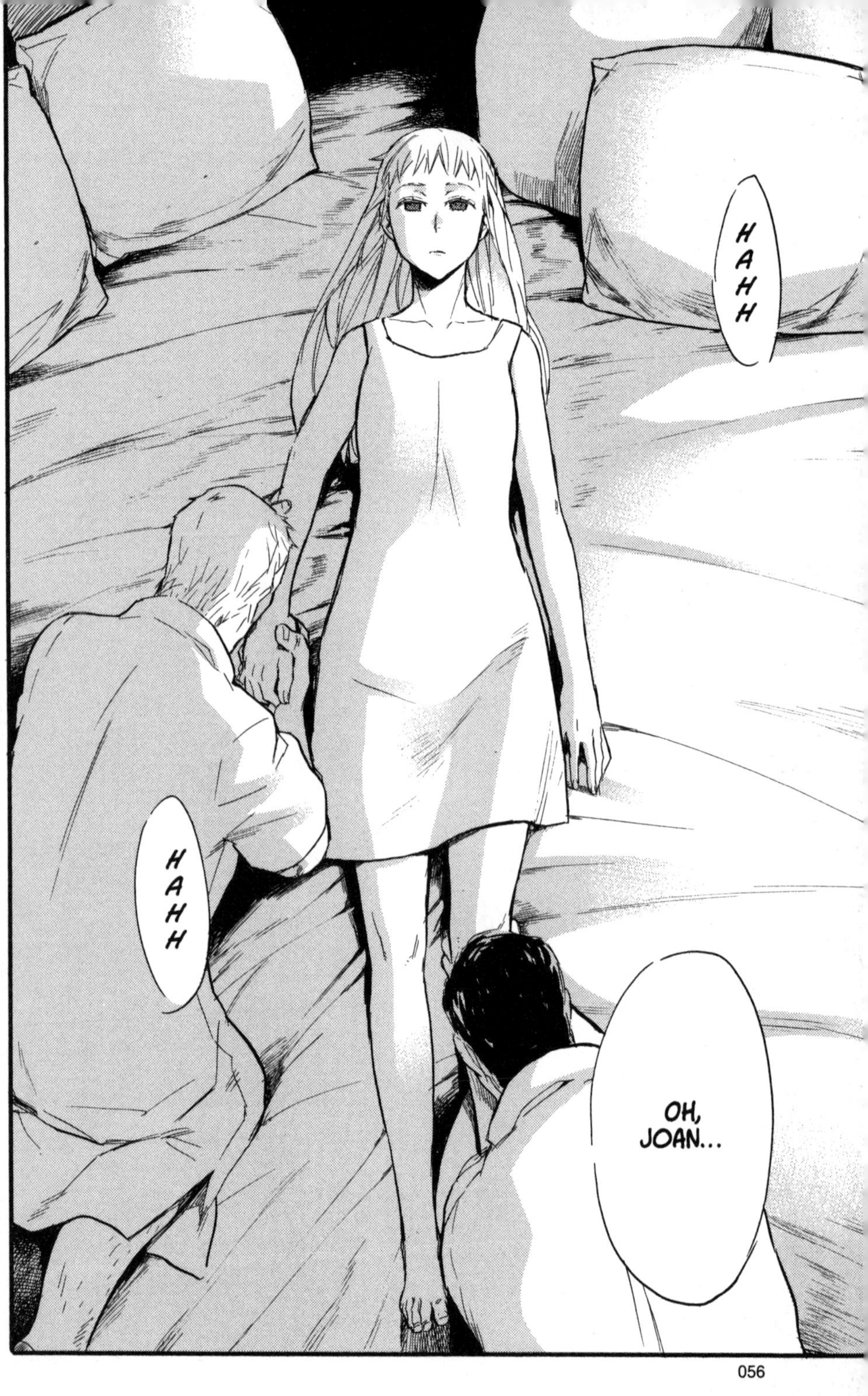
HAHH
HAHH
OH, JOAN...

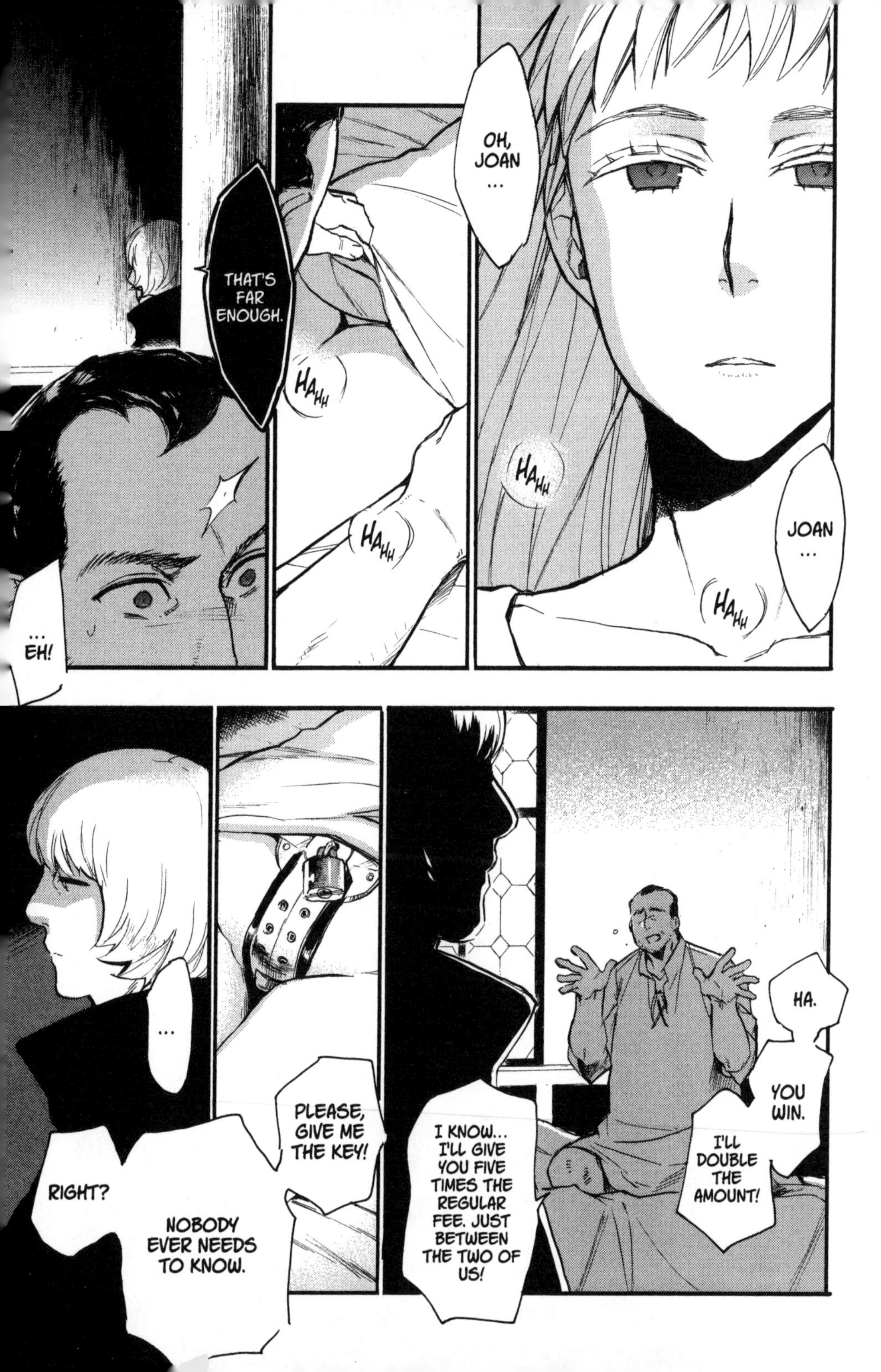

OH, JOAN ...
HAHH
JOAN ...
HAHH
HAHH
HAHH
THAT'S FAR ENOUGH.
... EH!
HA.
YOU WIN.
I'LL DOUBLE THE AMOUNT!
I KNOW... I'LL GIVE YOU FIVE TIMES THE REGULAR FEE. JUST BETWEEN THE TWO OF US!
PLEASE, GIVE ME THE KEY!
...
RIGHT?
NOBODY EVER NEEDS TO KNOW.

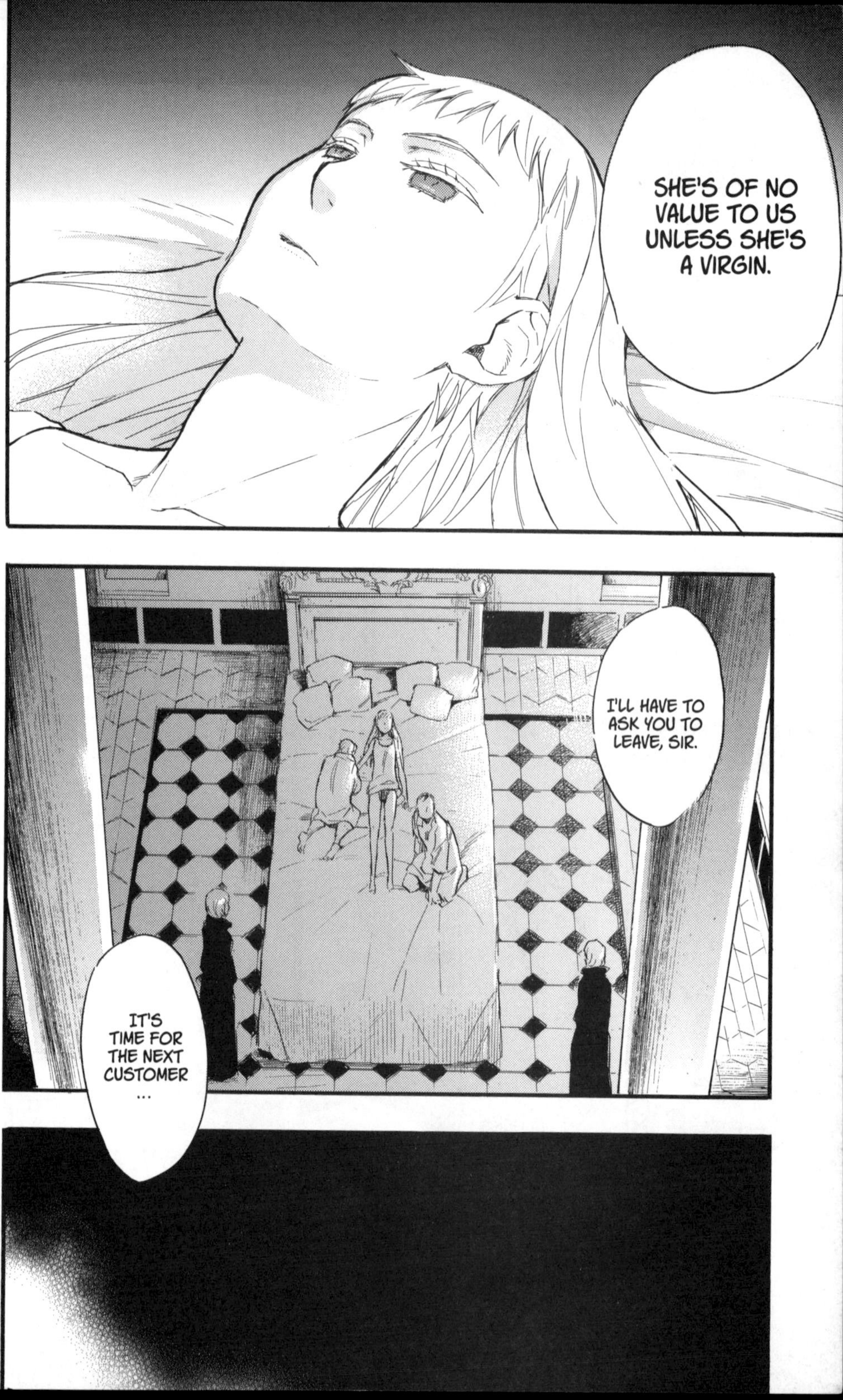
SHE'S OF NO VALUE TO US UNLESS SHE'S A VIRGIN.
I'LL HAVE TO ASK YOU TO LEAVE, SIR.
IT'S TIME FOR THE NEXT CUSTOMER ...

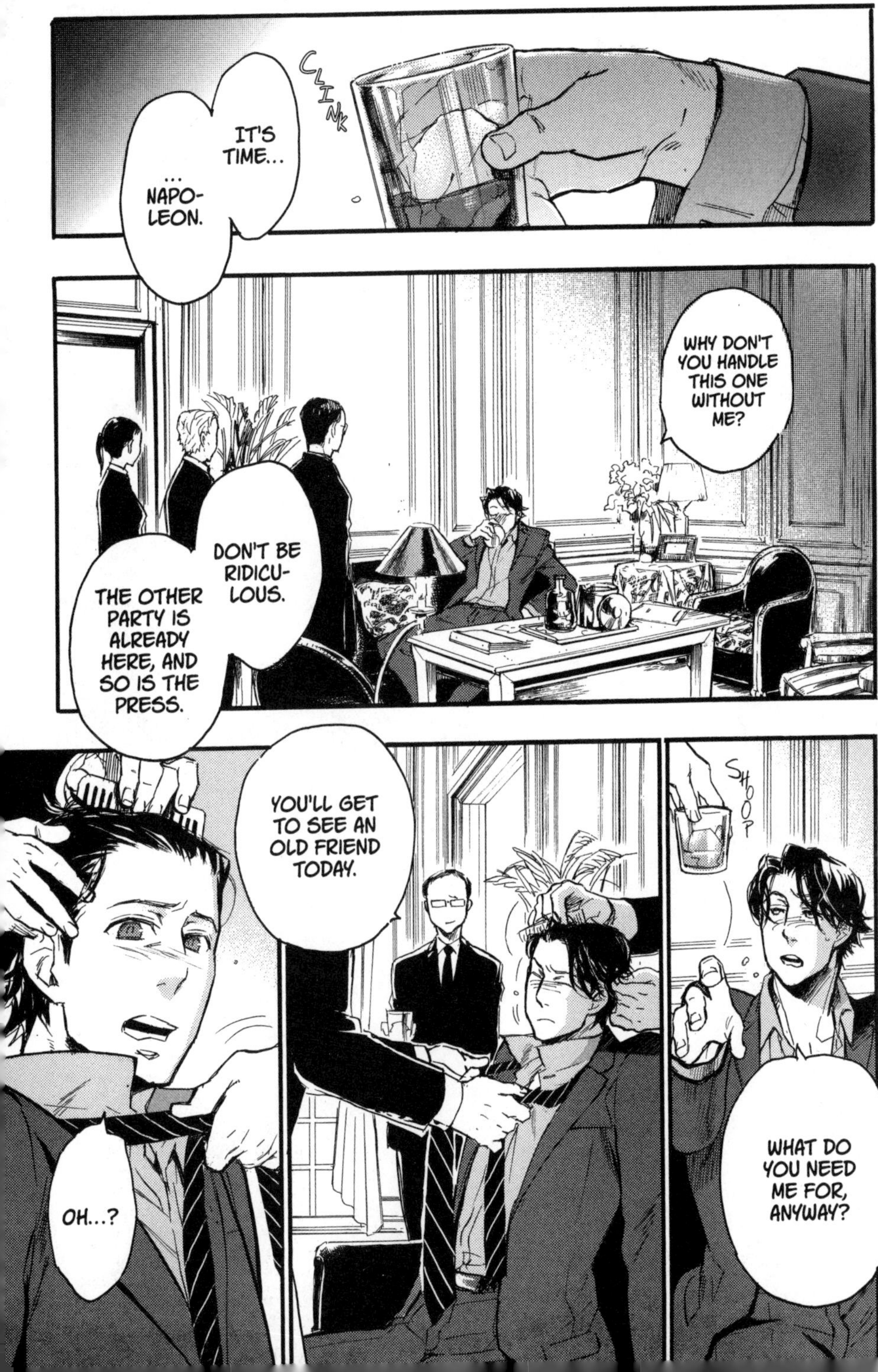
CLINK
IT'S TIME...
...NAPOLEON.
WHY DON'T YOU HANDLE THIS ONE WITHOUT ME?
DON'T BE RIDICULOUS.
THE OTHER PARTY IS ALREADY HERE, AND SO IS THE PRESS.
SHOOP
WHAT DO YOU NEED ME FOR, ANYWAY?
YOU'LL GET TO SEE AN OLD FRIEND TODAY.
OH...?

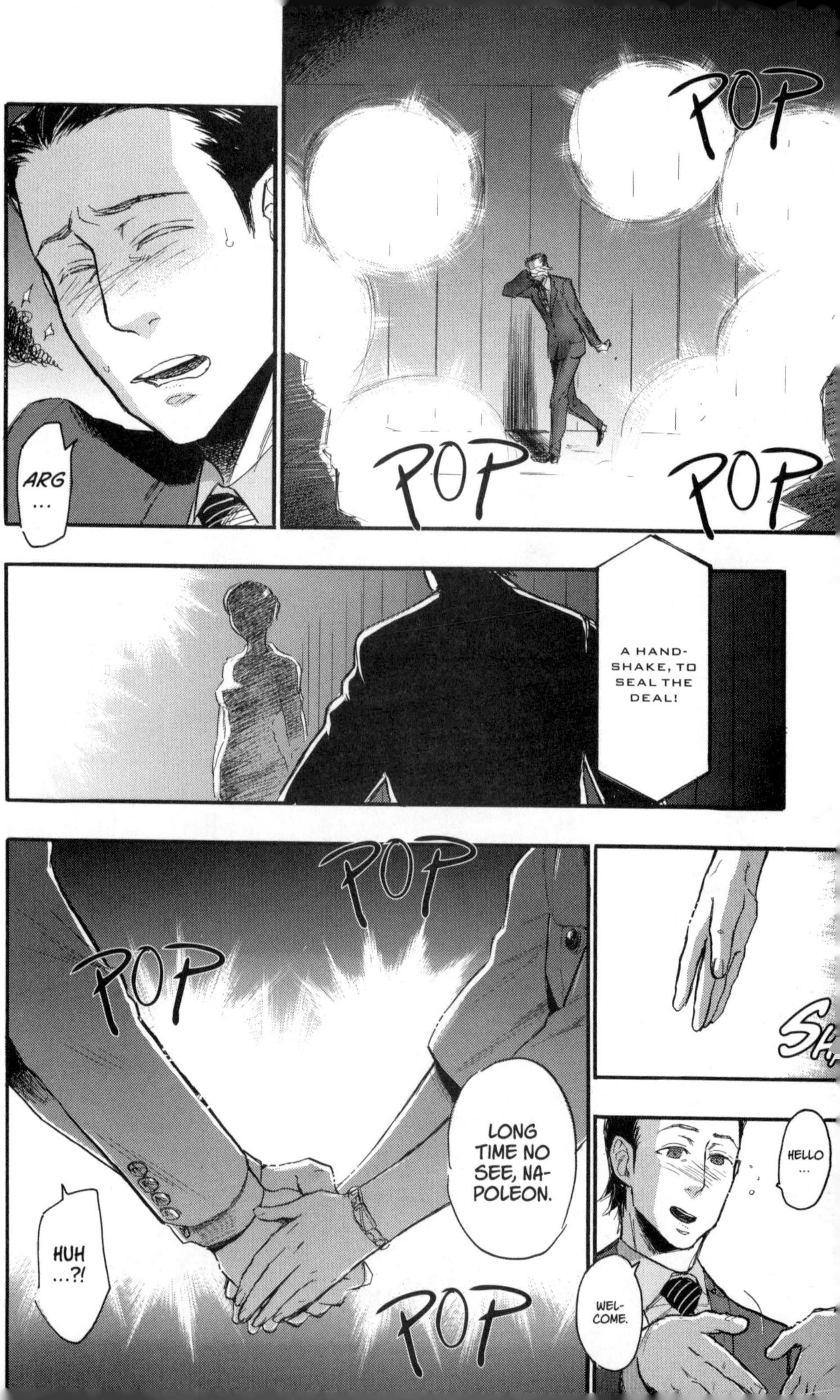
POP
POP
POP
ARG...
A HAND-SHAKE, TO SEAL THE DEAL!
HELLO...
WEL-COME.
POP
POP
LONG TIME NO SEE, NA-POLEON.
HUH...?!
POP

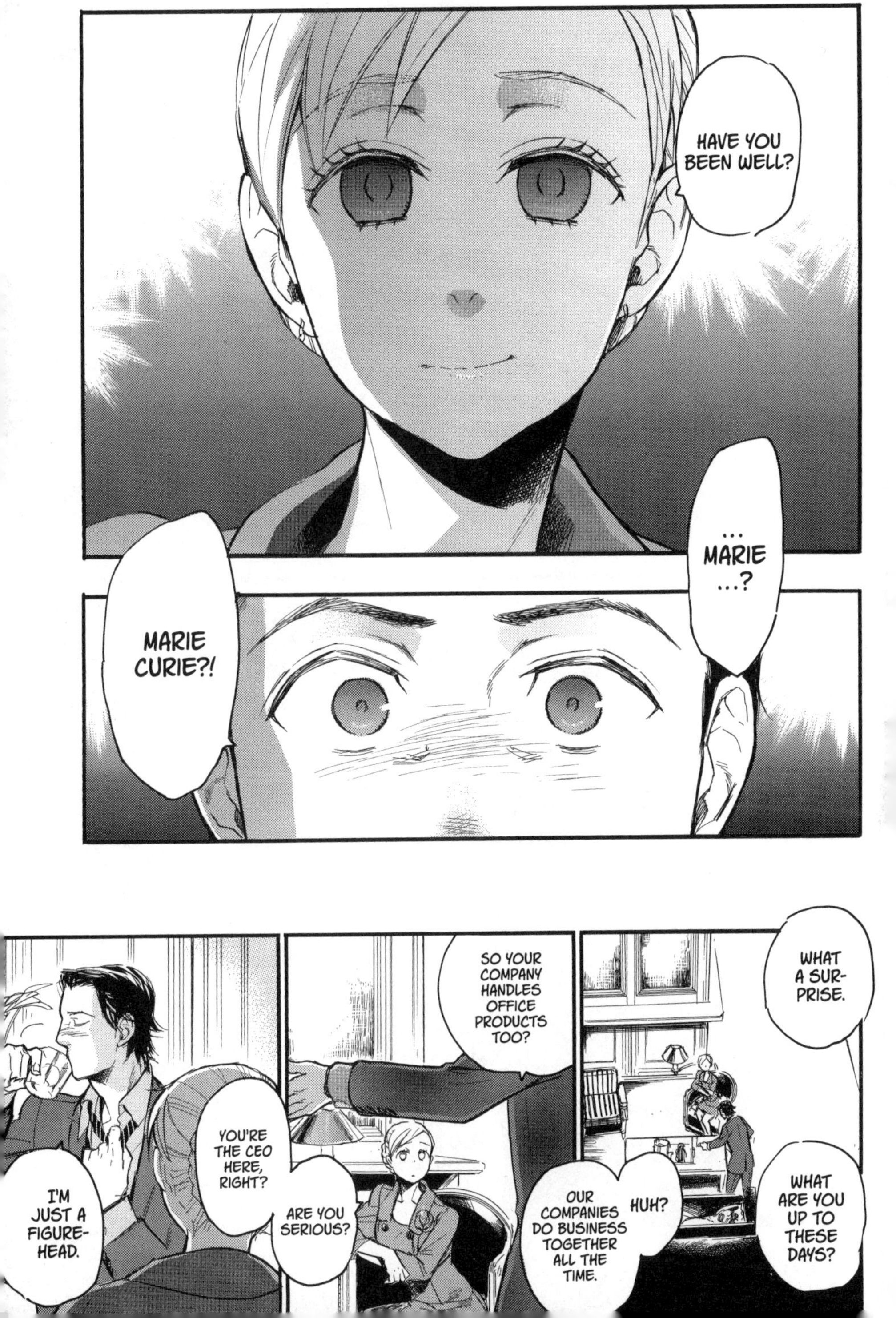
HAVE YOU BEEN WELL?
...MARIE...?
MARIE CURIE?!
WHAT A SUR-PRISE.
WHAT ARE YOU UP TO THESE DAYS?
HUH?
OUR COMPANIES DO BUSINESS TOGETHER ALL THE TIME.
SO YOUR COMPANY HANDLES OFFICE PRODUCTS TOO?
YOU'RE THE CEO HERE, RIGHT?
ARE YOU SERIOUS?
I'M JUST A FIGURE-HEAD.

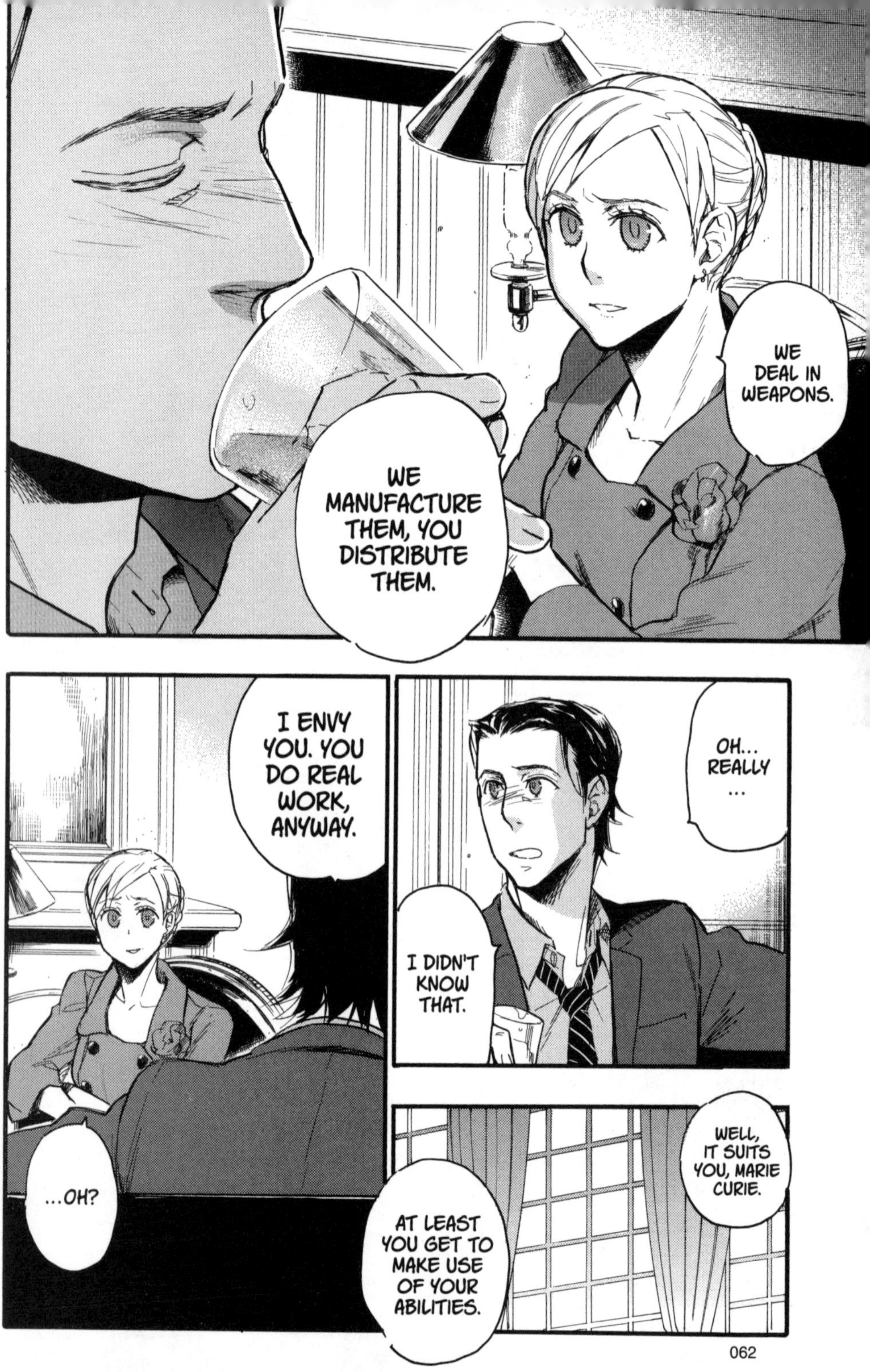
WE DEAL IN WEAPONS.
WE MANUFACTURE THEM, YOU DISTRIBUTE THEM.
OH... REALLY ...
I DIDN'T KNOW THAT.
WELL, IT SUITS YOU, MARIE CURIE.
AT LEAST YOU GET TO MAKE USE OF YOUR ABILITIES.
I ENVY YOU. YOU DO REAL WORK, ANYWAY.
...OH?

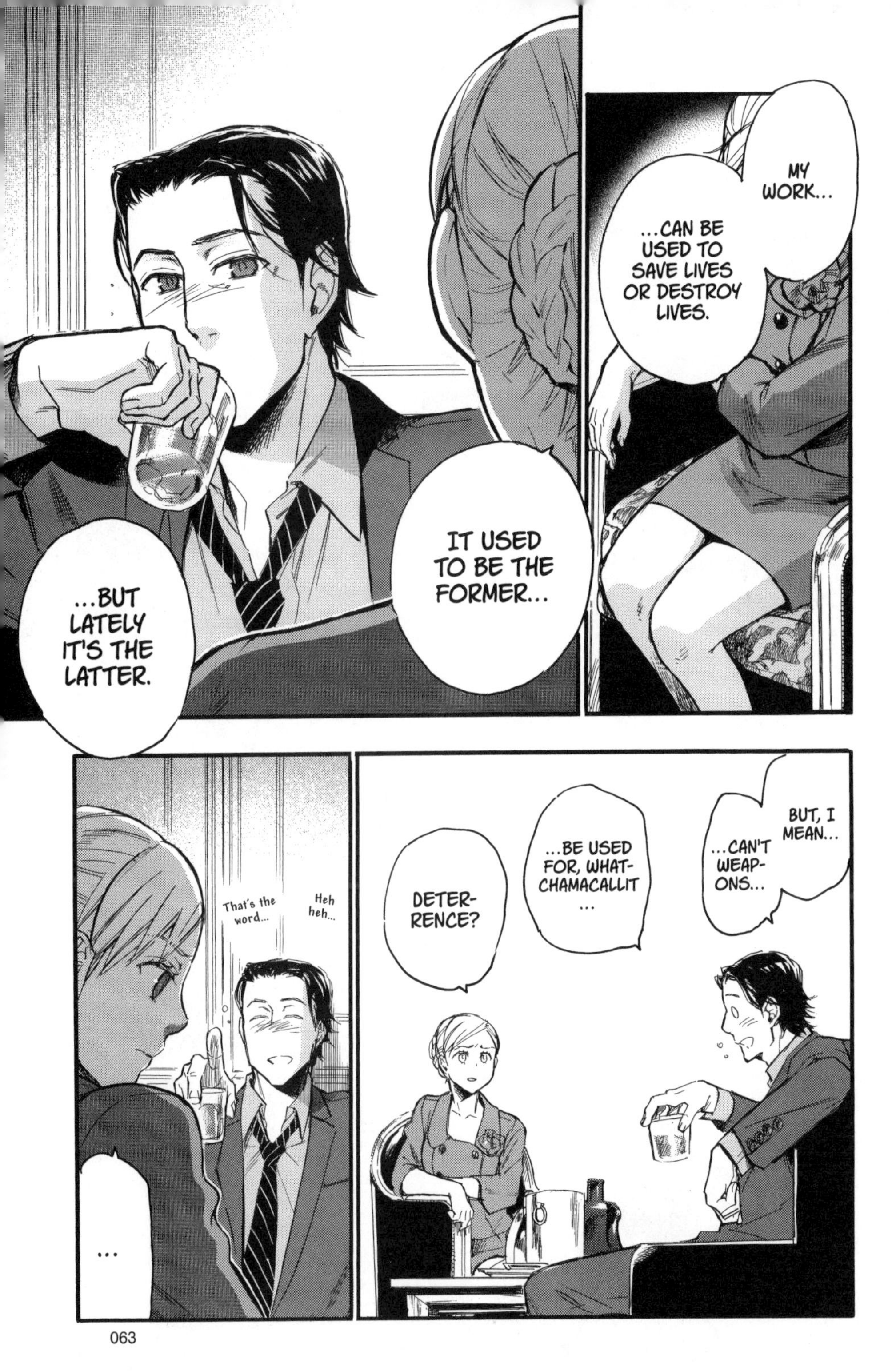
MY WORK...
...CAN BE USED TO SAVE LIVES OR DESTROY LIVES.
IT USED TO BE THE FORMER...
...BUT LATELY IT'S THE LATTER.
BUT, I MEAN...
...CAN'T WEAP-ONS...
...BE USED FOR, WHAT-CHAMACALLIT...
DETER-RENCE?
Heh heh...
That's the word...
...

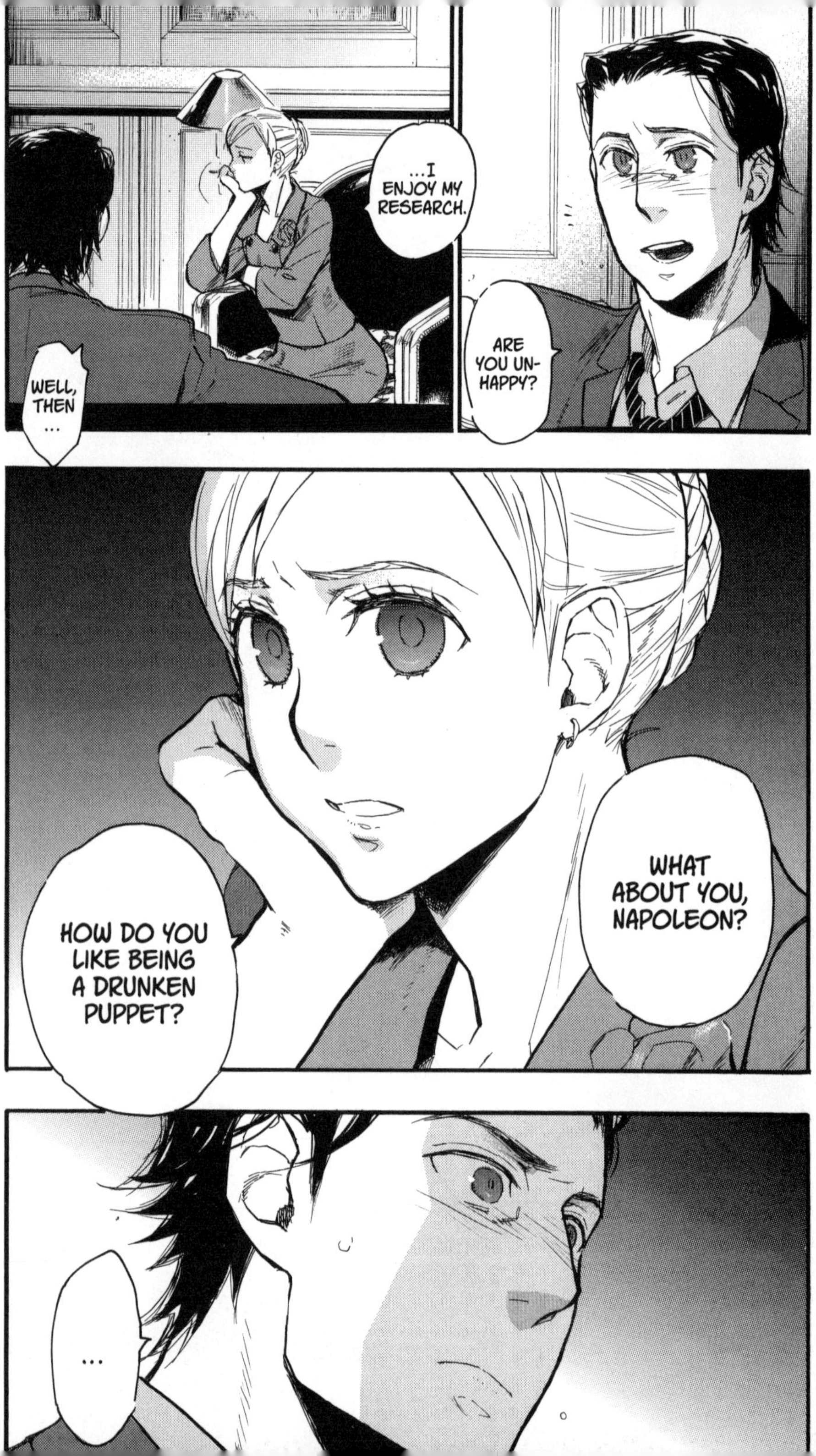
ARE YOU UN-HAPPY?
...I ENJOY MY RESEARCH.
WELL, THEN ...
WHAT ABOUT YOU, NAPOLEON?
HOW DO YOU LIKE BEING A DRUNKEN PUPPET?
...

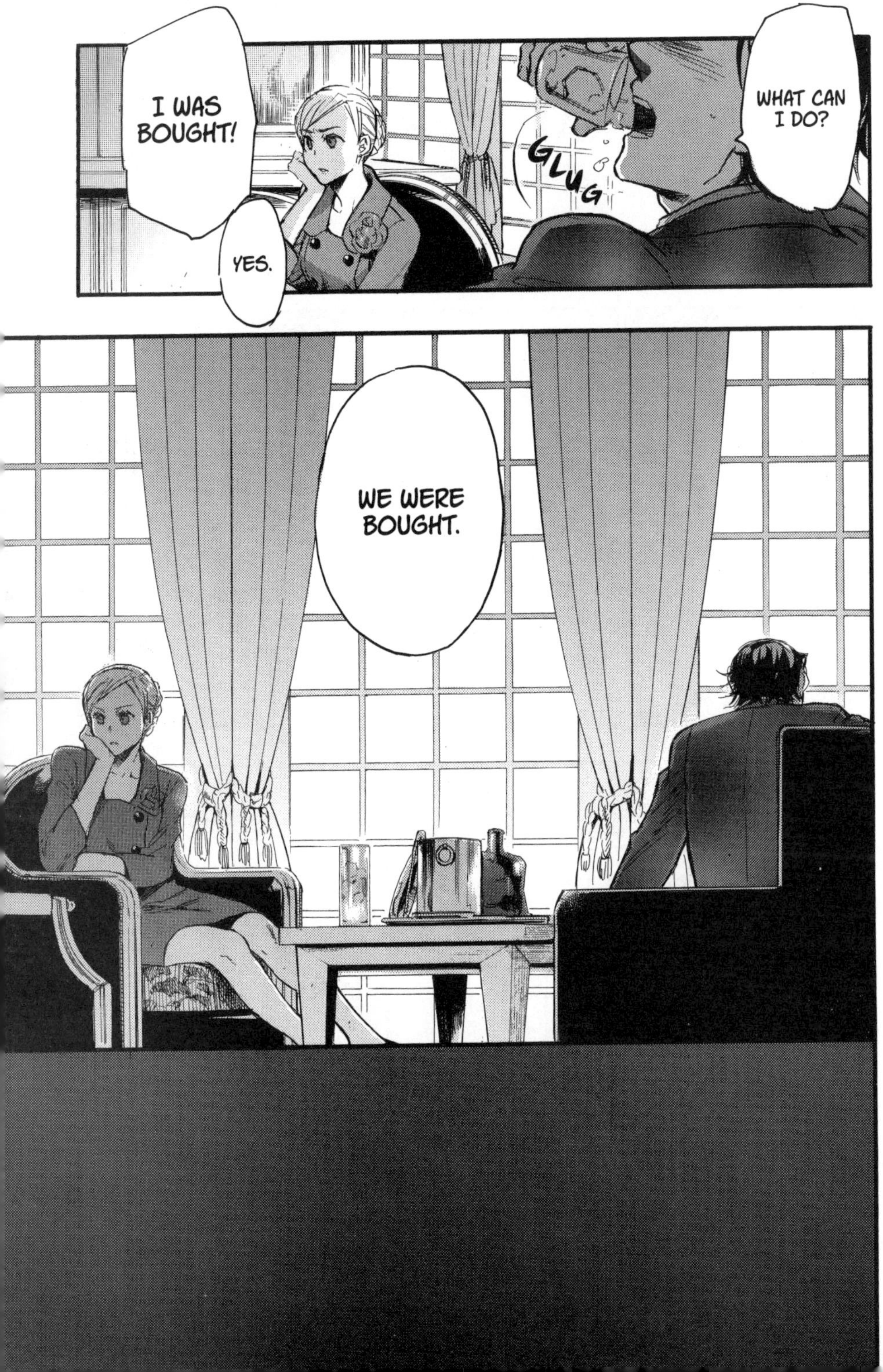
WHAT CAN I DO?
GLUG
I WAS BOUGHT!
YES.
WE WERE BOUGHT.

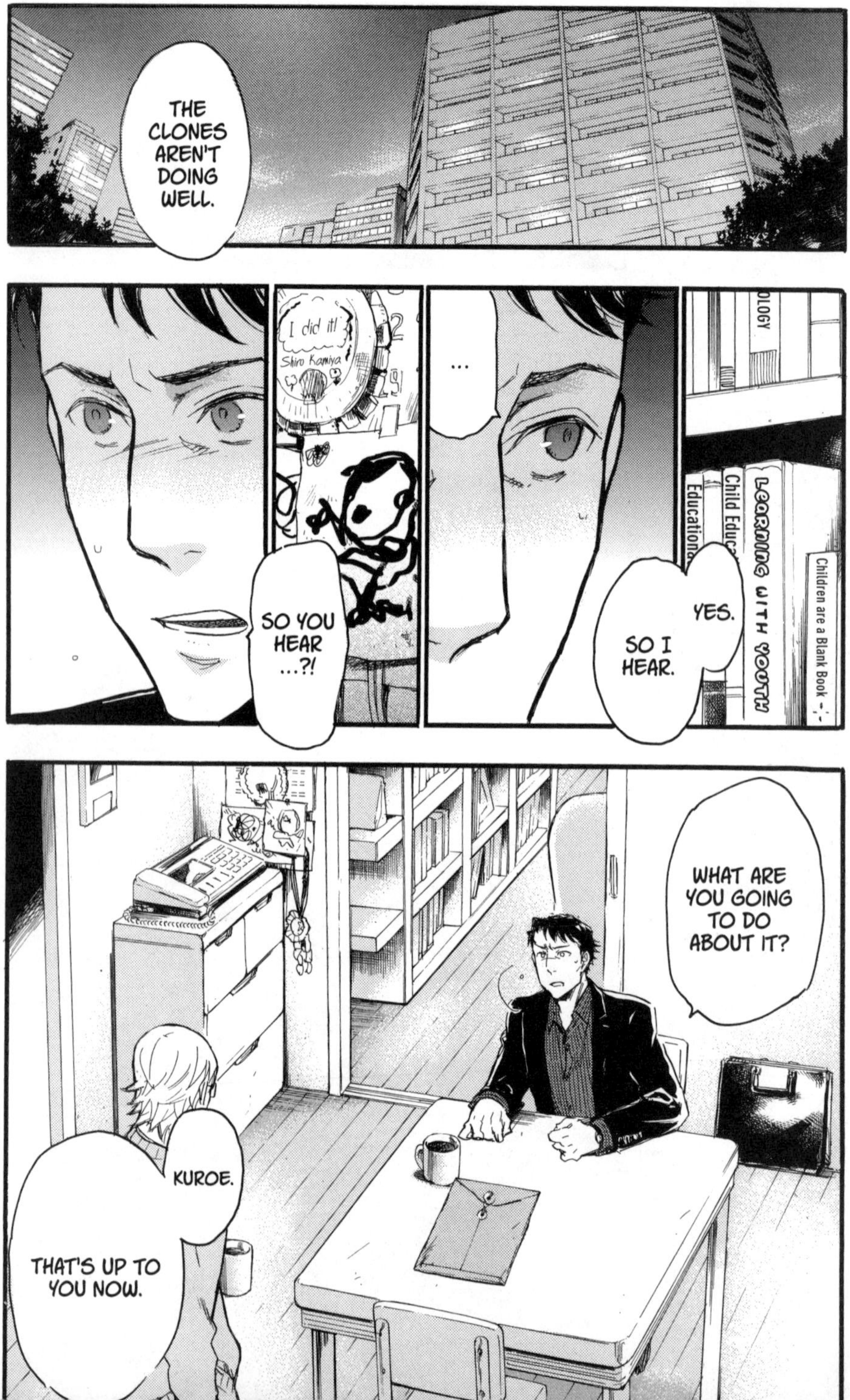
THE CLONES AREN'T DOING WELL.
Children are a Blank Book
LEARNING WITH YOUTH
YES. SO I HEAR.
...
I did it!
Shiro Kamiya
SO YOU HEAR ...?!
WHAT ARE YOU GOING TO DO ABOUT IT?
KUROE.
THAT'S UP TO YOU NOW.

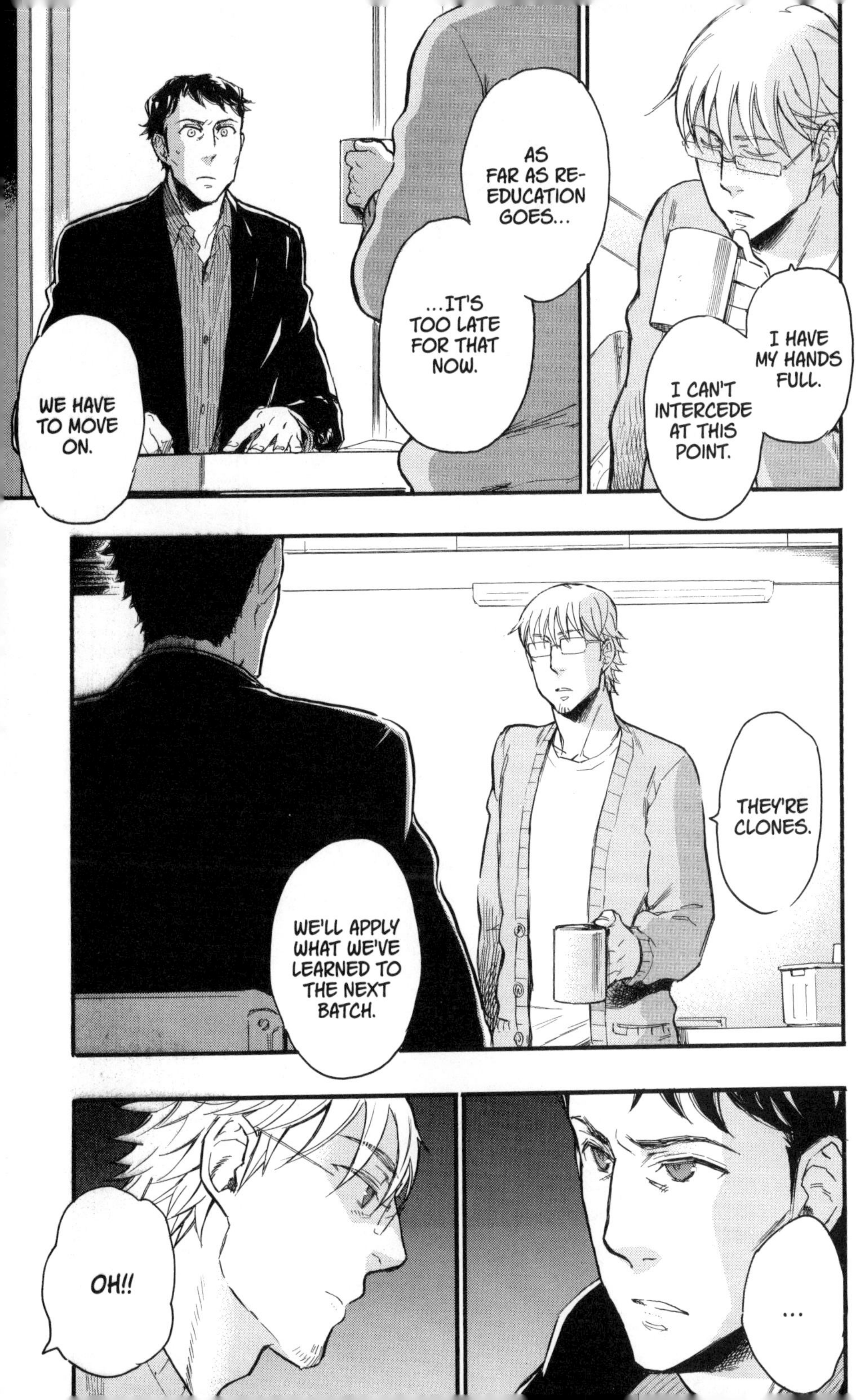
I HAVE MY HANDS FULL.
I CAN'T INTERCEDE AT THIS POINT.
AS FAR AS RE-EDUCATION GOES...
...IT'S TOO LATE FOR THAT NOW.
WE HAVE TO MOVE ON.
THEY'RE CLONES.
WE'LL APPLY WHAT WE'VE LEARNED TO THE NEXT BATCH.
...
OH!!

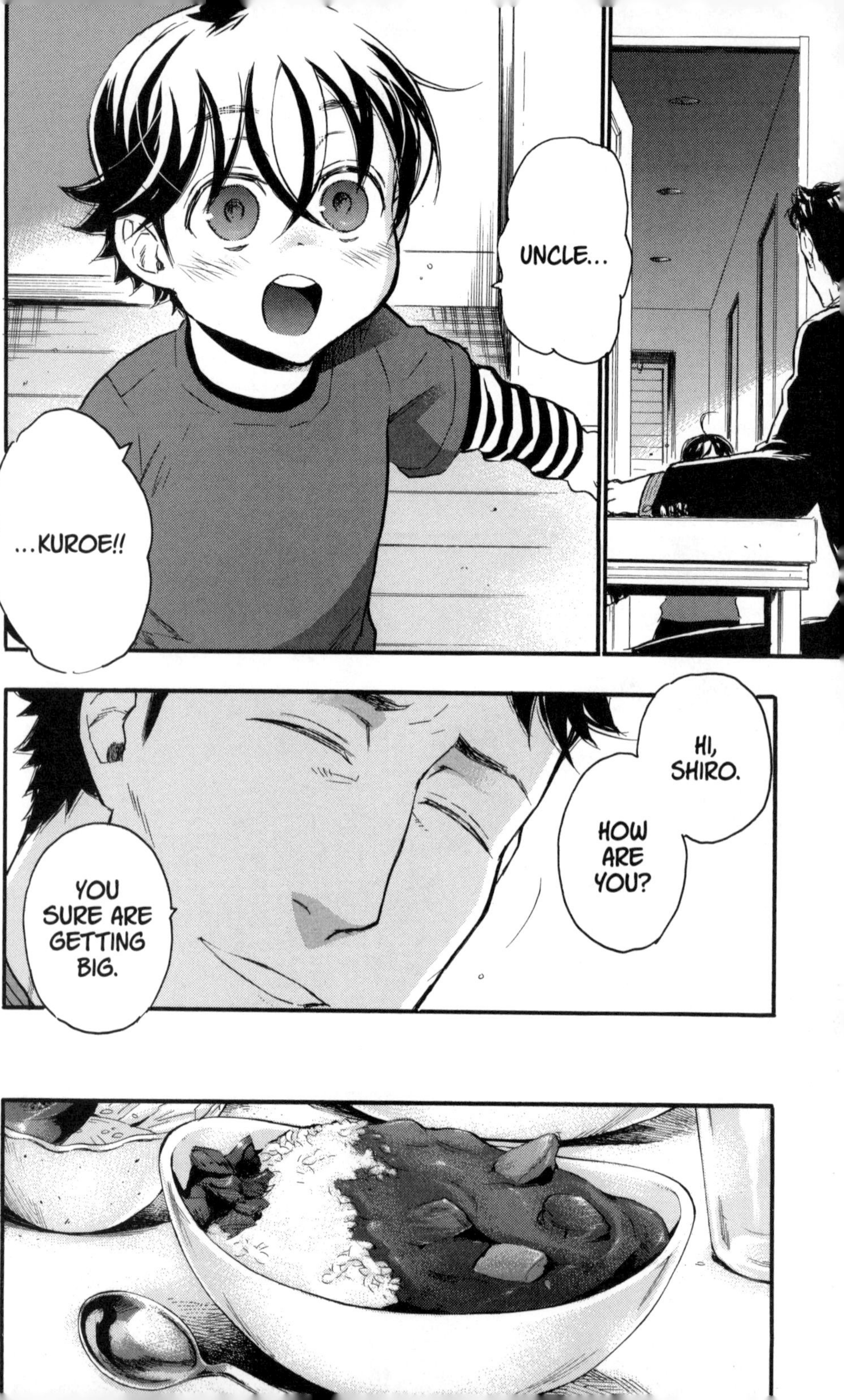
UNCLE...
...KUROE!!
HI, SHIRO.
HOW ARE YOU?
YOU SURE ARE GETTING BIG.

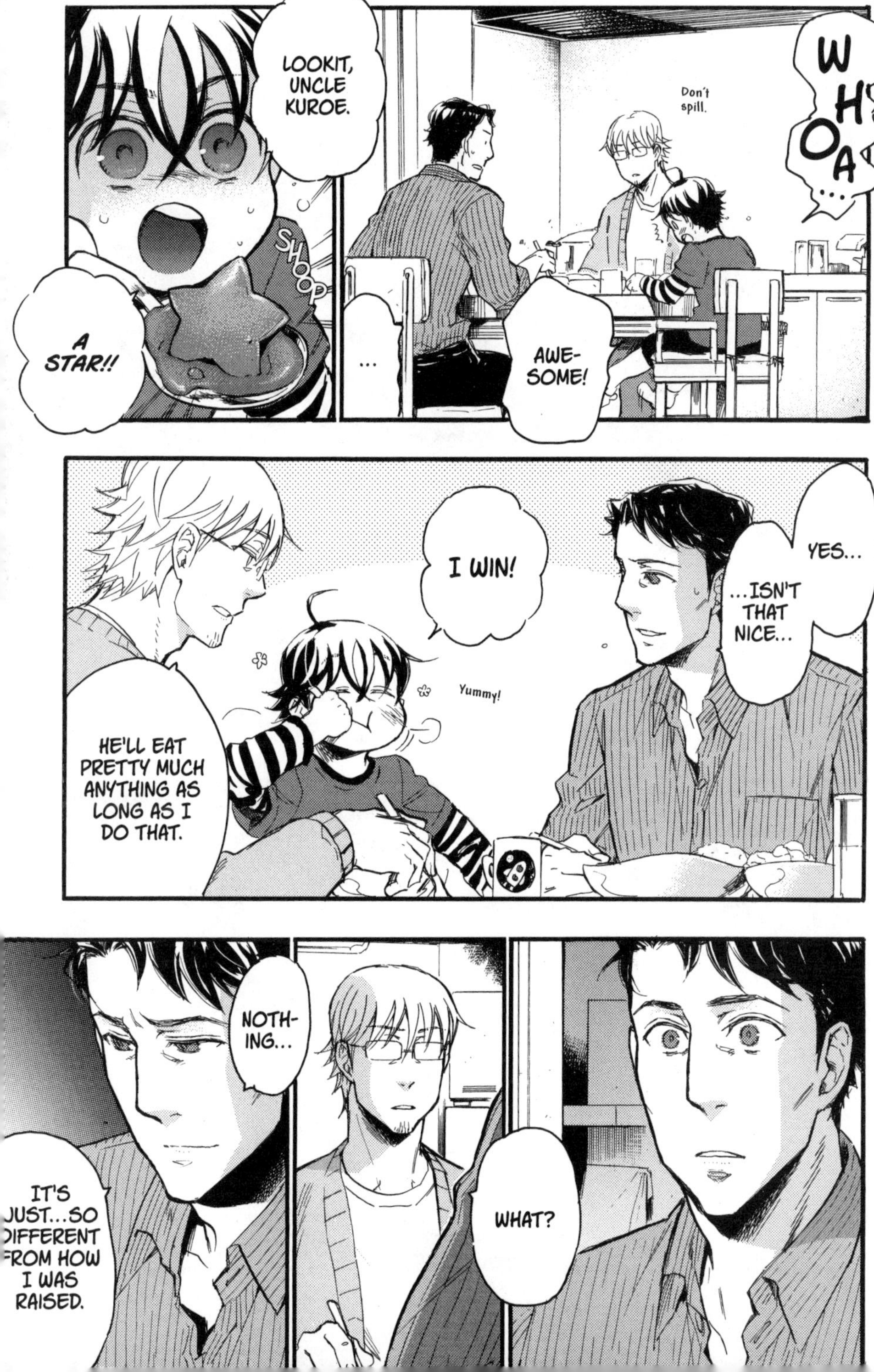
WHOA...
Don't spill.
AWE-SOME!
...
LOOKIT, UNCLE KUROE.
SHOOP
A STAR!!
YES...
...ISN'T THAT NICE...
I WIN!
Yummy!
HE'LL EAT PRETTY MUCH ANYTHING AS LONG AS I DO THAT.
WHAT?
NOTH-ING...
IT'S JUST...SO DIFFERENT FROM HOW I WAS RAISED.

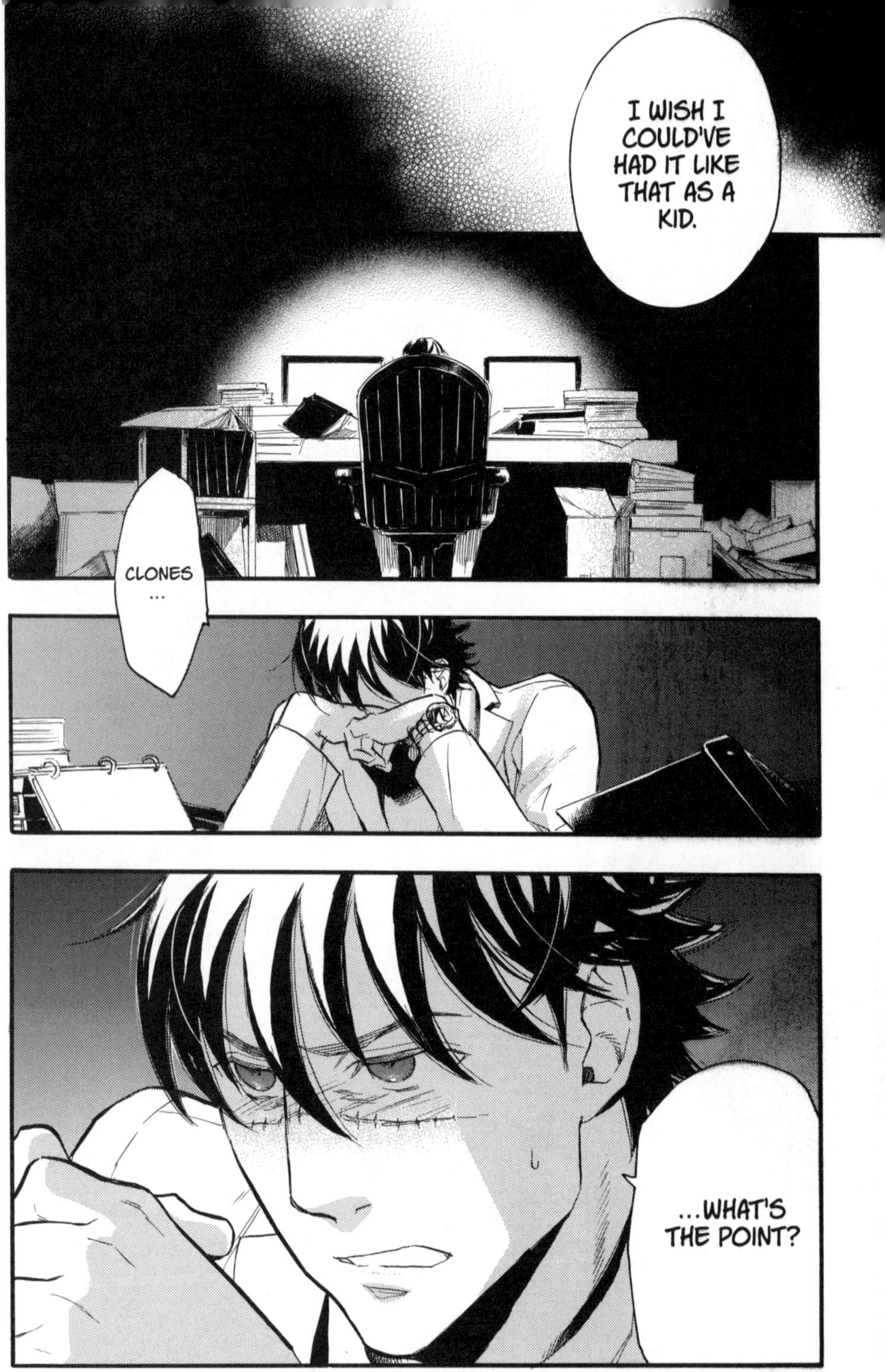
I WISH I COULD'VE HAD IT LIKE THAT AS A KID.
CLONES ...
...WHAT'S THE POINT?

CHAPTER thirty-three

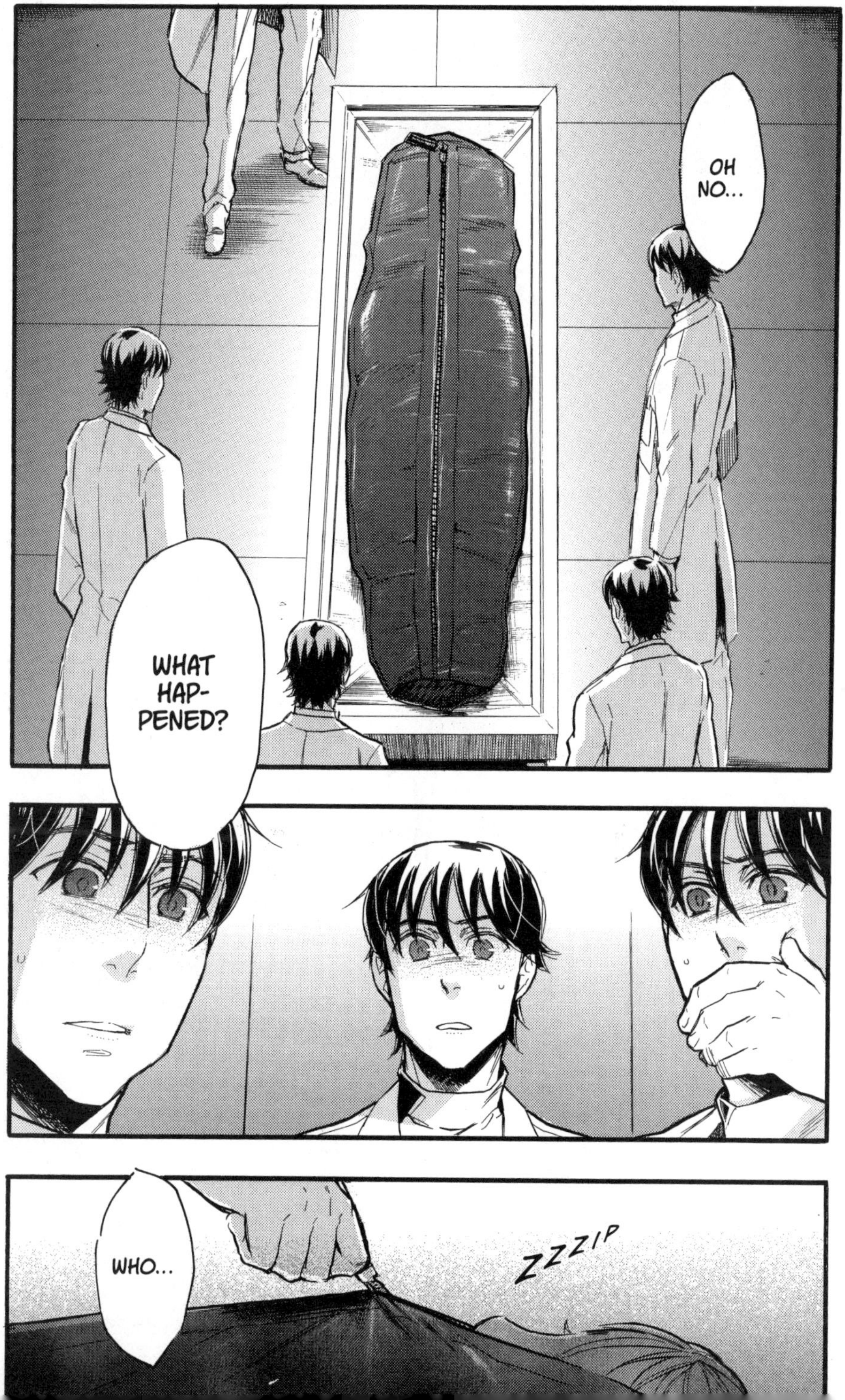
OH NO...
WHAT HAP-PENED?
WHO...
ZZZIP

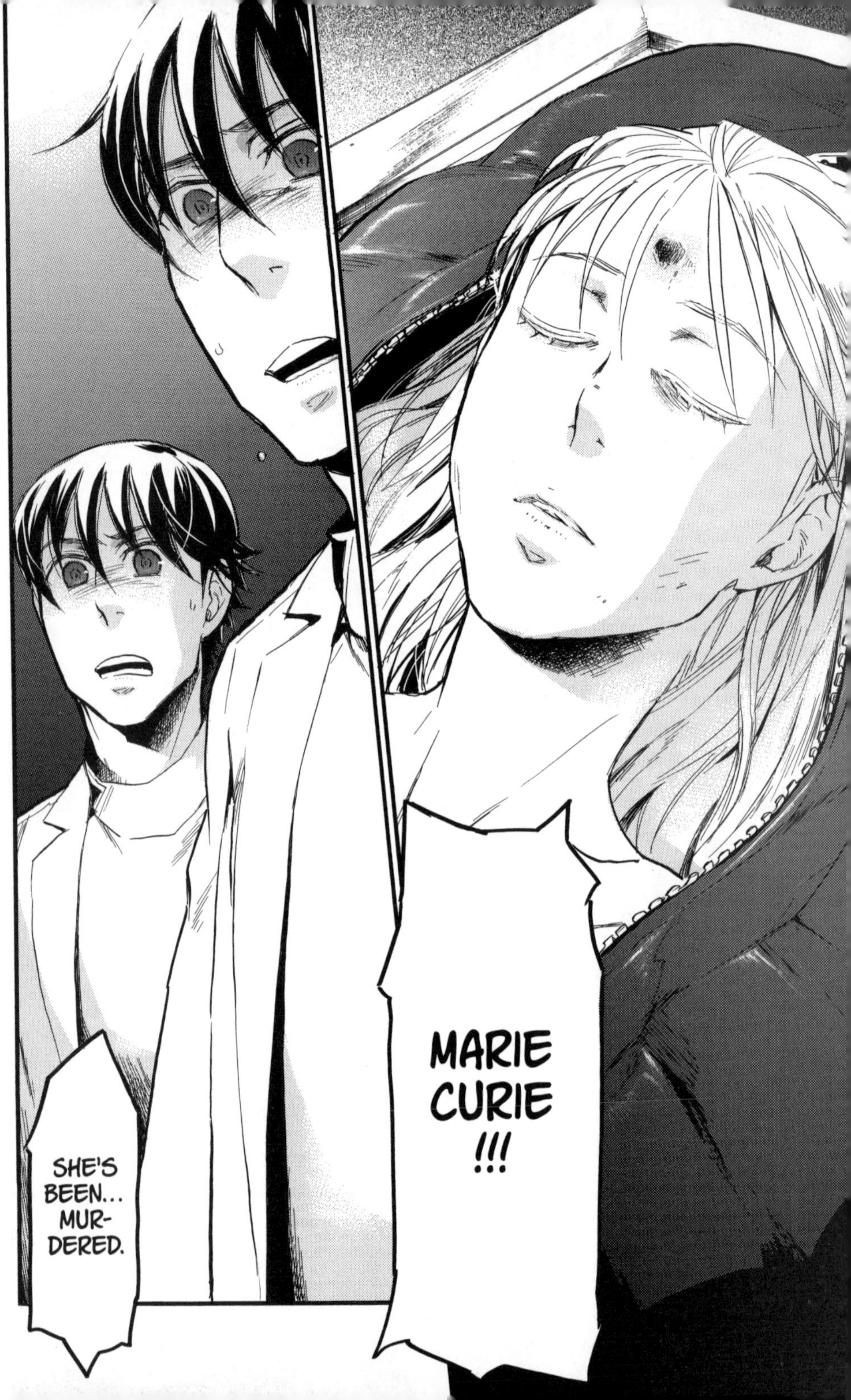
MARIE CURIE !!!
SHE'S BEEN... MUR-DERED.

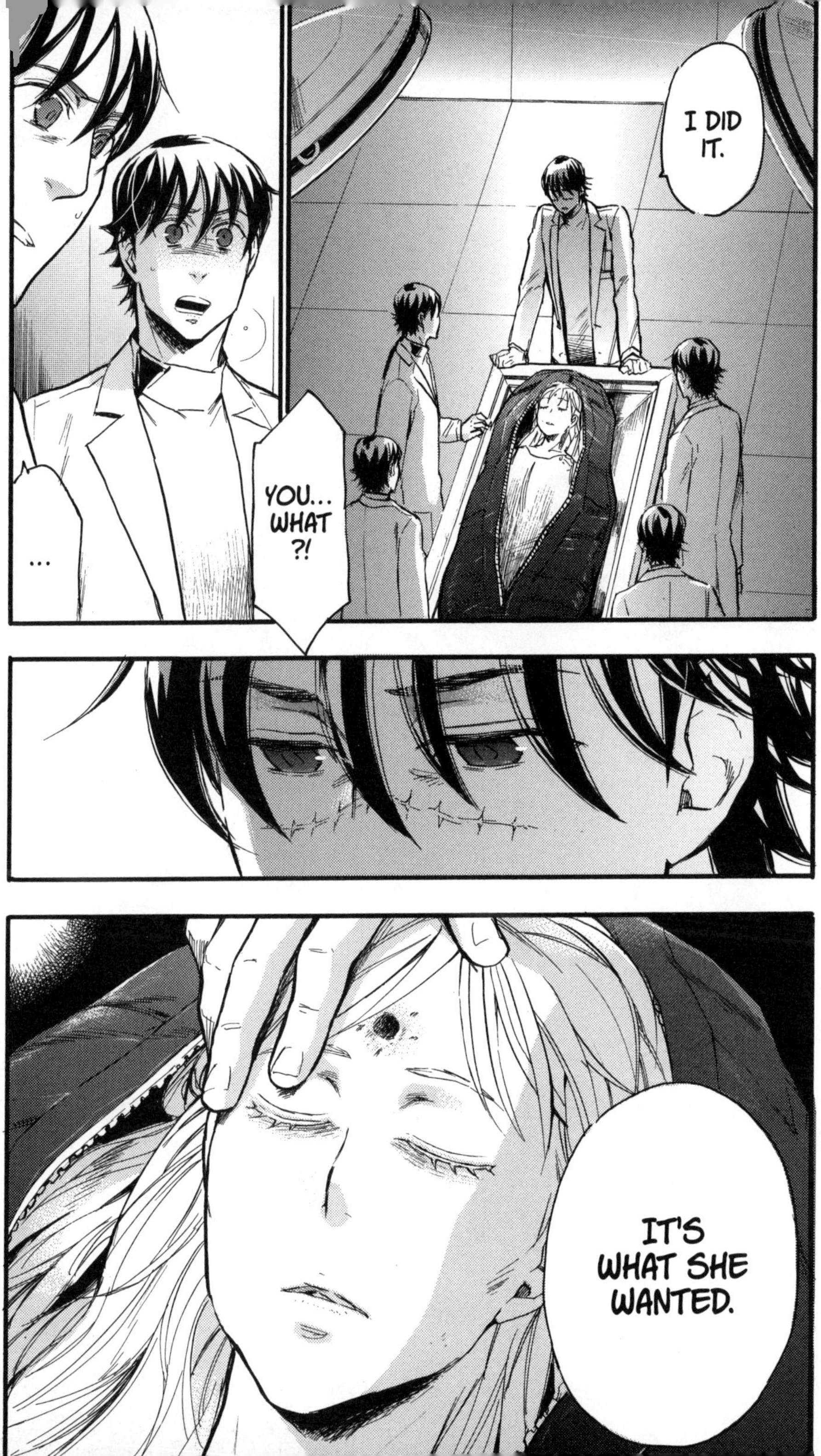
I DID IT.
YOU... WHAT?!
...
IT'S WHAT SHE WANTED.

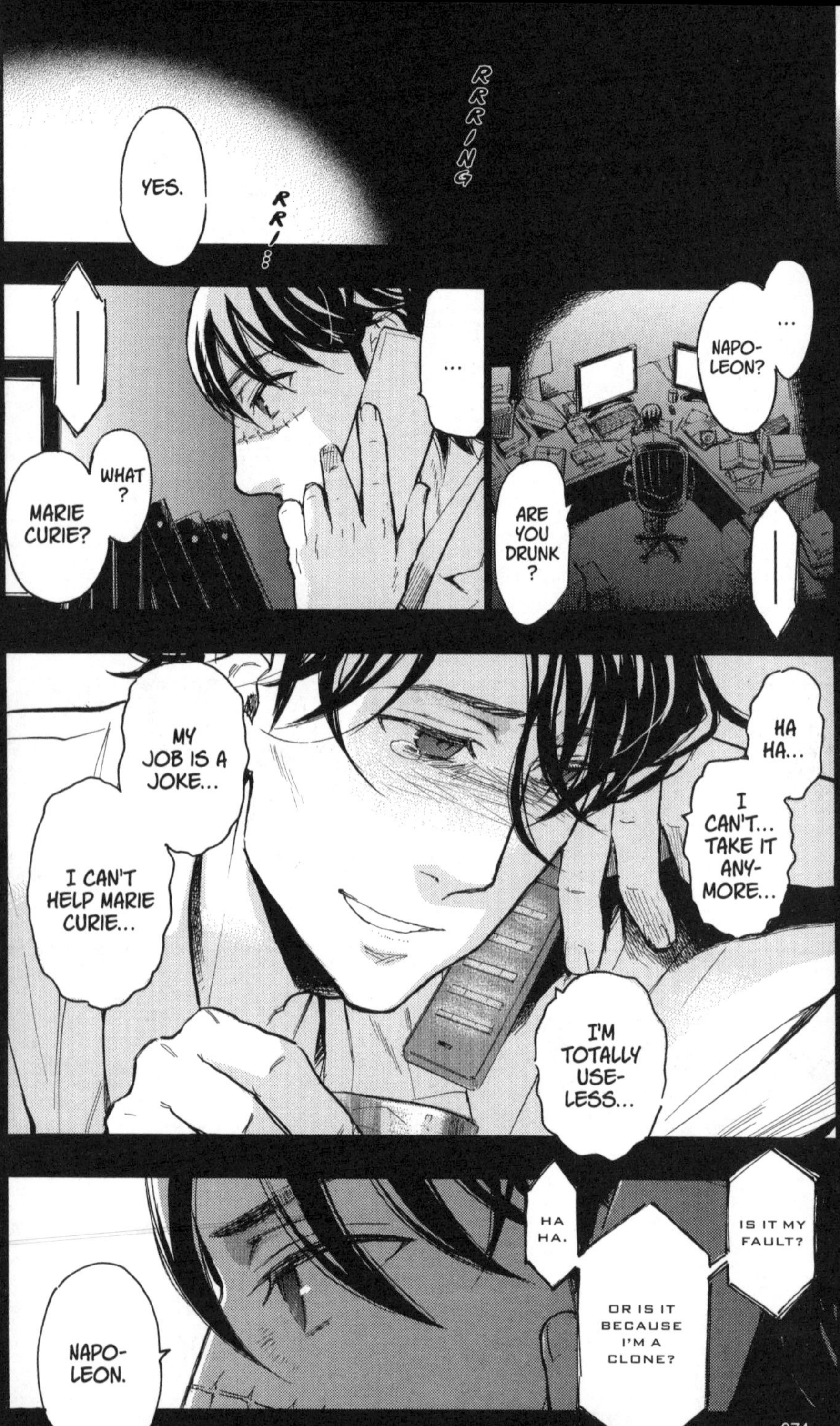
RRRING
RRI...
YES.
...
NAPO-LEON?
ARE YOU DRUNK?
—
...
—
WHAT?
MARIE CURIE?
HA HA...
I CAN'T... TAKE IT ANY-MORE...
MY JOB IS A JOKE...
I'M TOTALLY USE-LESS...
I CAN'T HELP MARIE CURIE...
IS IT MY FAULT?
HA HA.
OR IS IT BECAUSE I'M A CLONE?
NAPO-LEON.

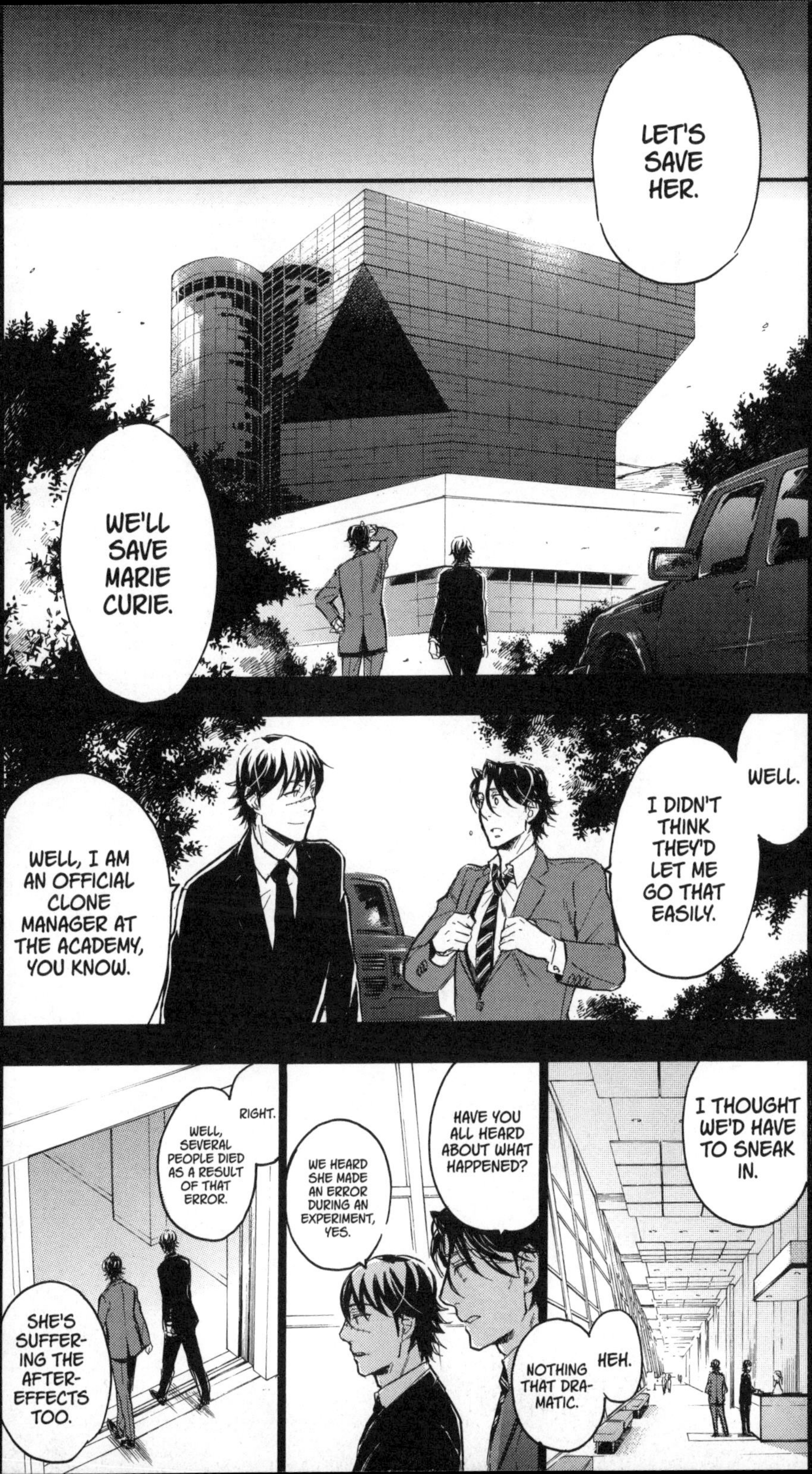
LET'S SAVE HER.
WE'LL SAVE MARIE CURIE.
WELL.
I DIDN'T THINK THEY'D LET ME GO THAT EASILY.
WELL, I AM AN OFFICIAL CLONE MANAGER AT THE ACADEMY, YOU KNOW.
I THOUGHT WE'D HAVE TO SNEAK IN.
HEH.
NOTHING THAT DRAMATIC.
HAVE YOU ALL HEARD ABOUT WHAT HAPPENED?
WE HEARD SHE MADE AN ERROR DURING AN EXPERIMENT, YES.
RIGHT.
WELL, SEVERAL PEOPLE DIED AS A RESULT OF THAT ERROR.
SHE'S SUFFERING THE AFTER-EFFECTS TOO.

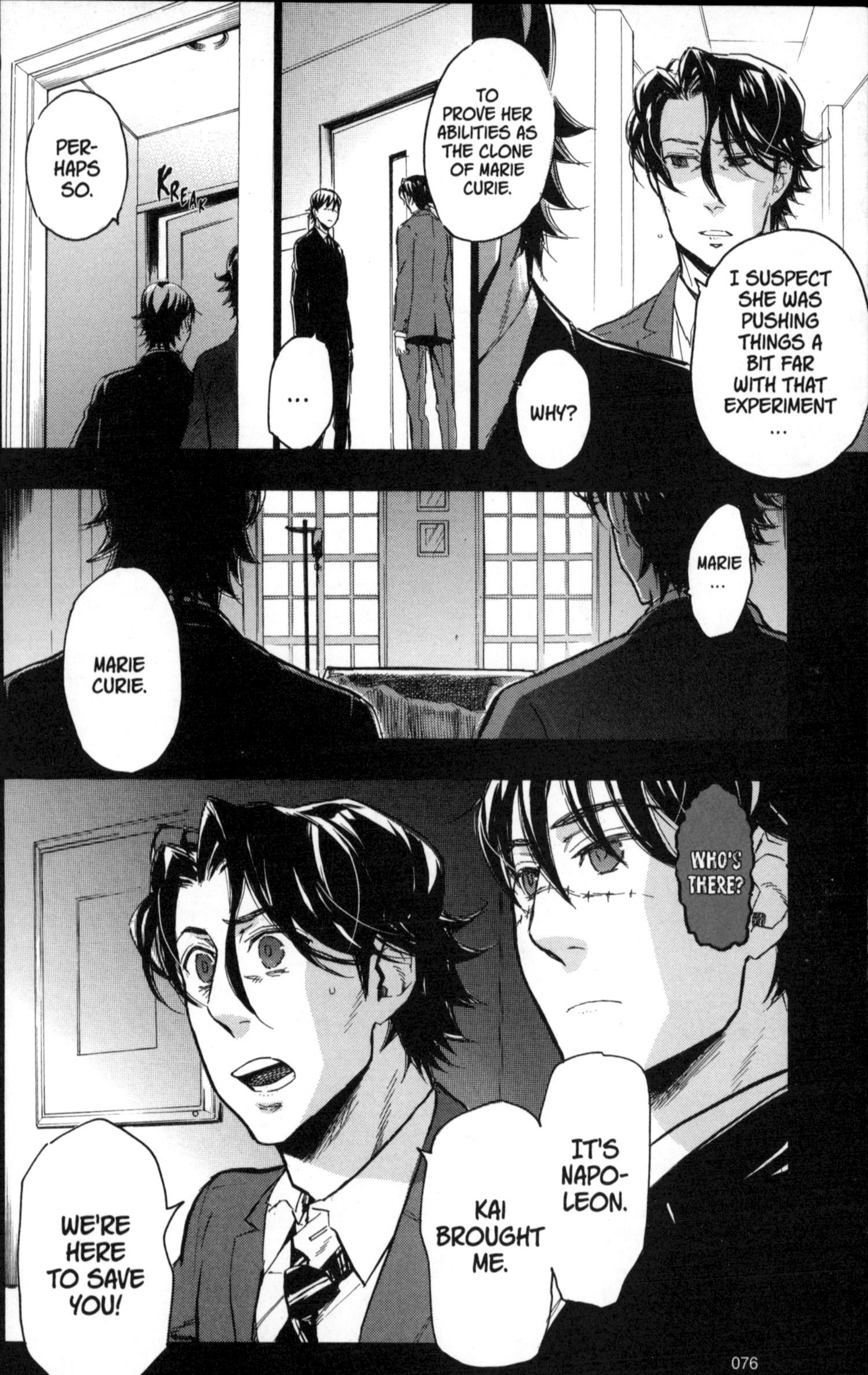
I SUSPECT SHE WAS PUSHING THINGS A BIT FAR WITH THAT EXPERIMENT ...
WHY?
TO PROVE HER ABILITIES AS THE CLONE OF MARIE CURIE.
...
PER- HAPS SO.
KREAR
MARIE ...
MARIE CURIE.
WHO'S THERE?
IT'S NAPO- LEON.
KAI BROUGHT ME.
WE'RE HERE TO SAVE YOU!

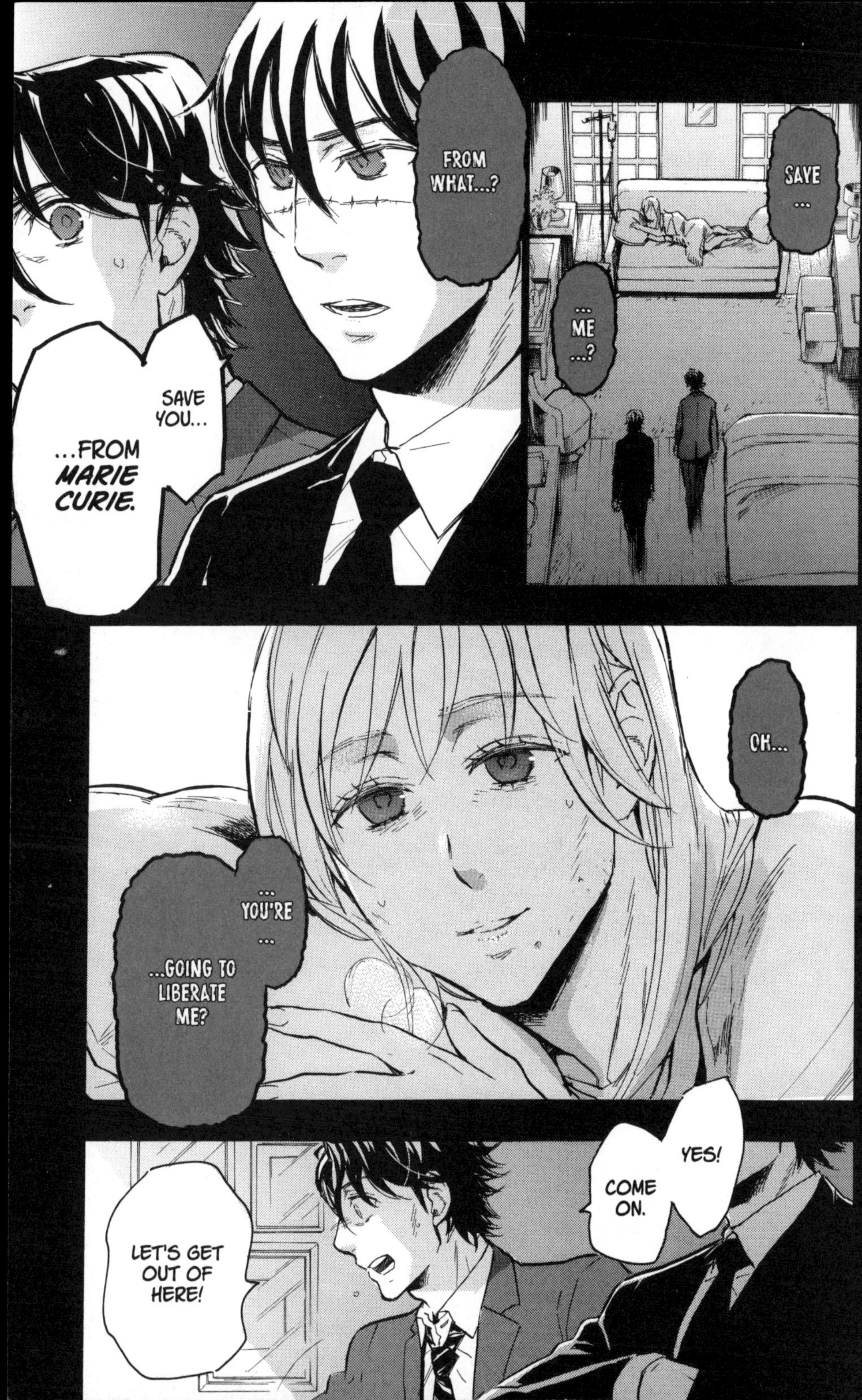
SAVE ...
... ME ...?
FROM WHAT...?
SAVE YOU... ...FROM *MARIE CURIE.*
OH...
... YOU'RE ... ...GOING TO LIBERATE ME?
YES! COME ON.
LET'S GET OUT OF HERE!

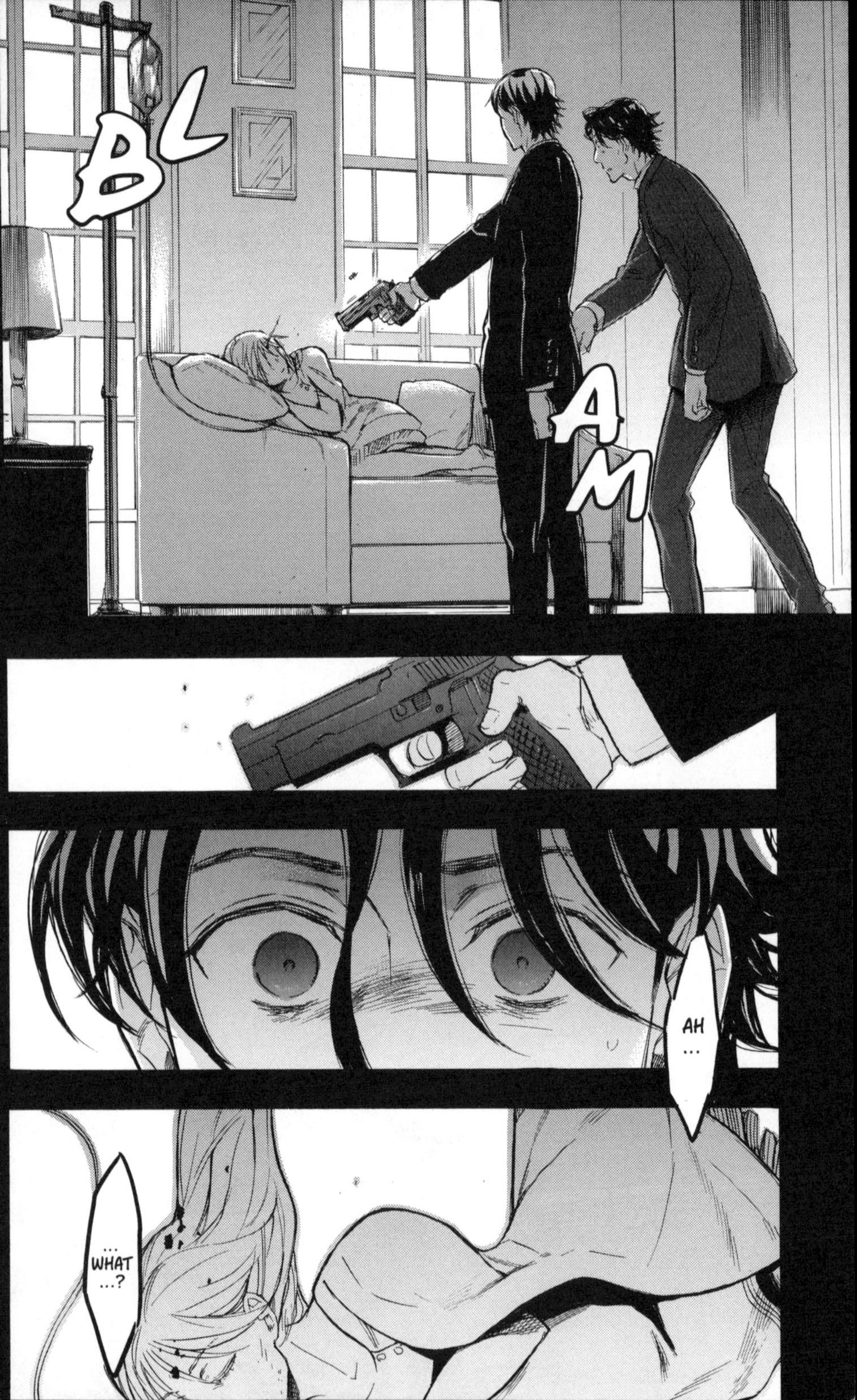
BLAM
AH...
...WHAT...?

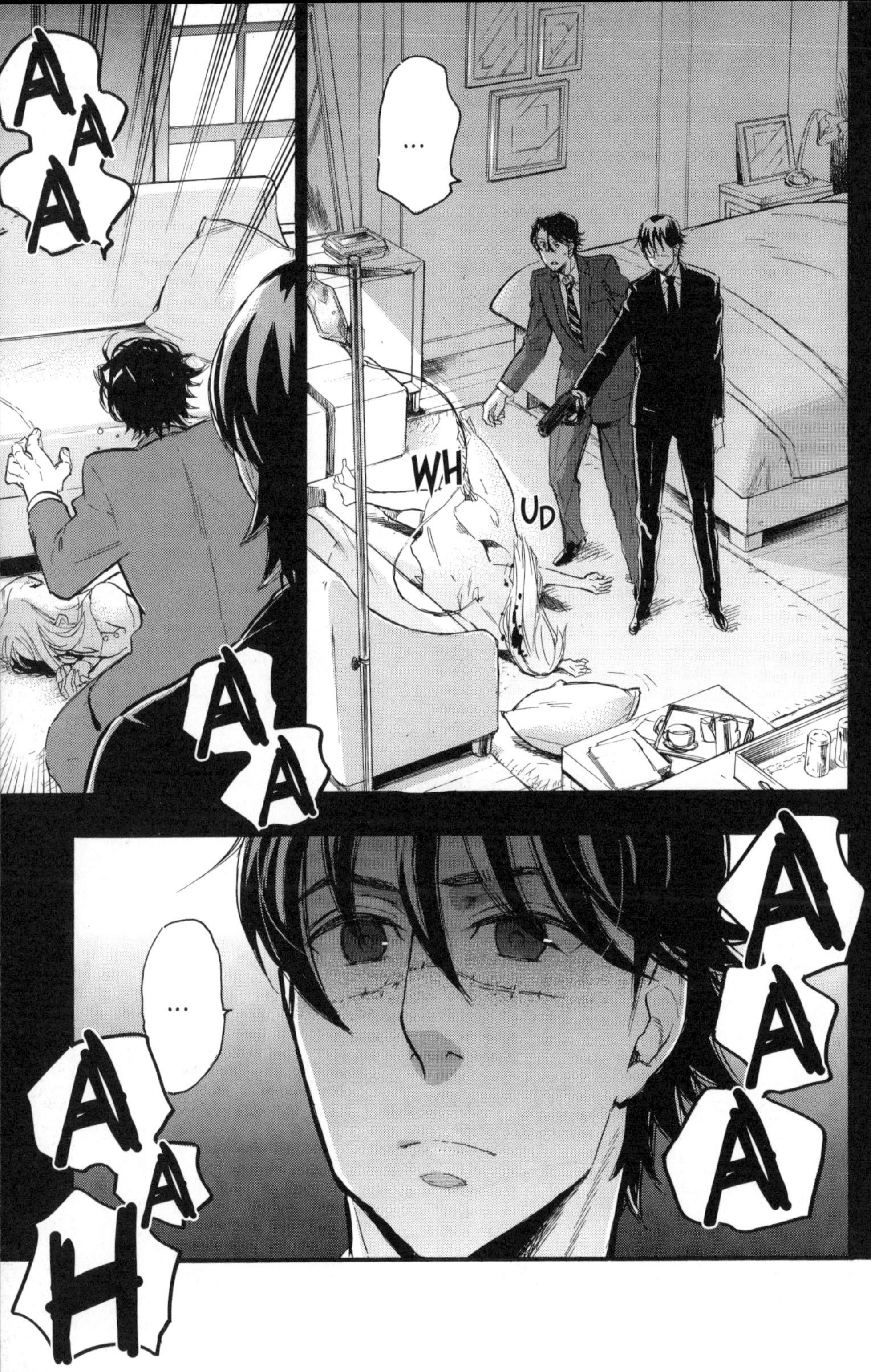
...
WHUD
AAA
AAA
AAAA
...
AAAH

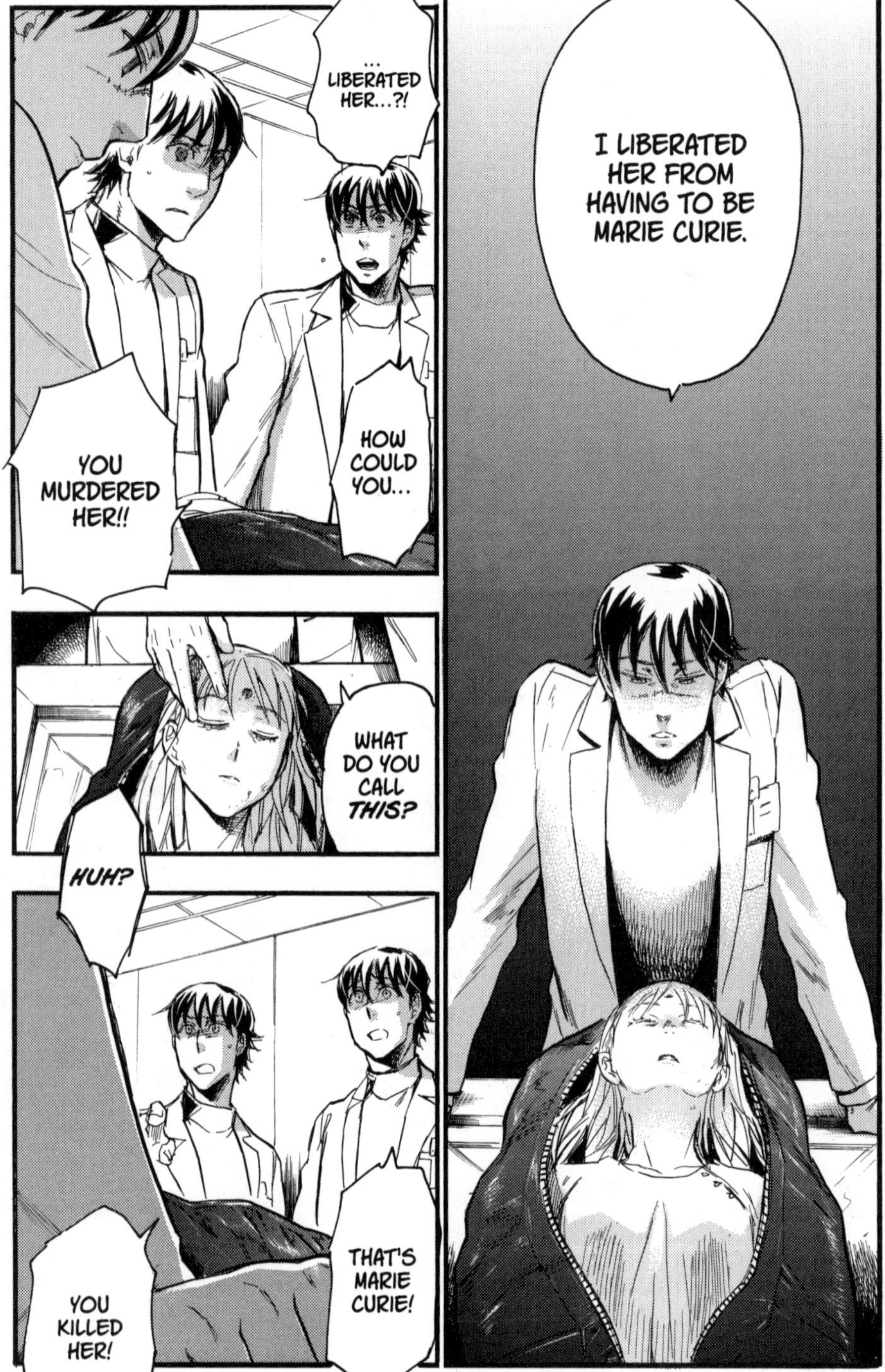
I LIBERATED HER FROM HAVING TO BE MARIE CURIE.
...LIBERATED HER...?!
HOW COULD YOU...
YOU MURDERED HER!!
WHAT DO YOU CALL *THIS?*
HUH?
THAT'S MARIE CURIE!
YOU KILLED HER!

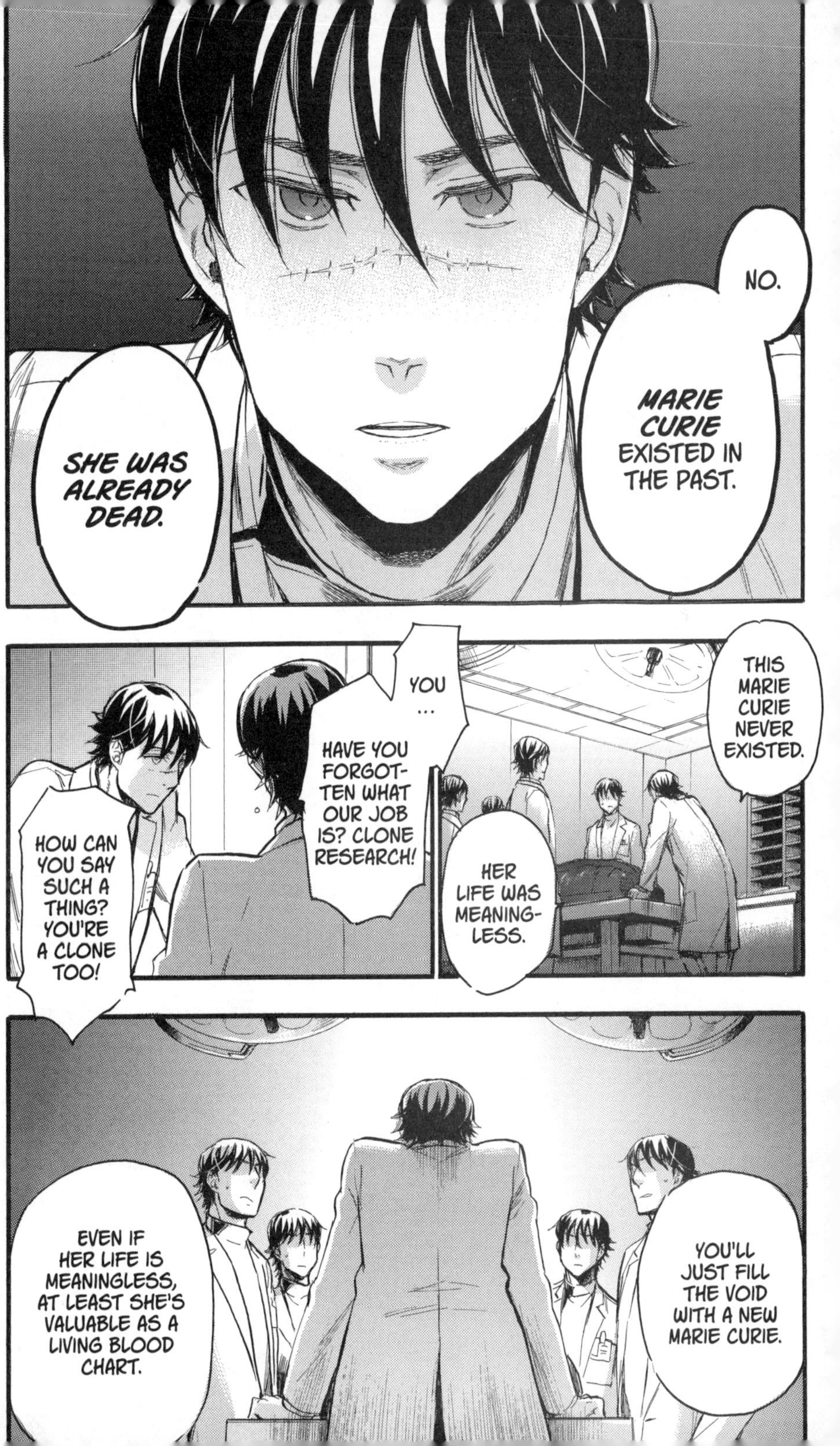
NO.
MARIE CURIE EXISTED IN THE PAST.
SHE WAS ALREADY DEAD.
THIS MARIE CURIE NEVER EXISTED.
HER LIFE WAS MEANING-LESS.
YOU ...
HAVE YOU FORGOT-TEN WHAT OUR JOB IS? CLONE RESEARCH!
HOW CAN YOU SAY SUCH A THING? YOU'RE A CLONE TOO!
YOU'LL JUST FILL THE VOID WITH A NEW MARIE CURIE.
EVEN IF HER LIFE IS MEANINGLESS, AT LEAST SHE'S VALUABLE AS A LIVING BLOOD CHART.

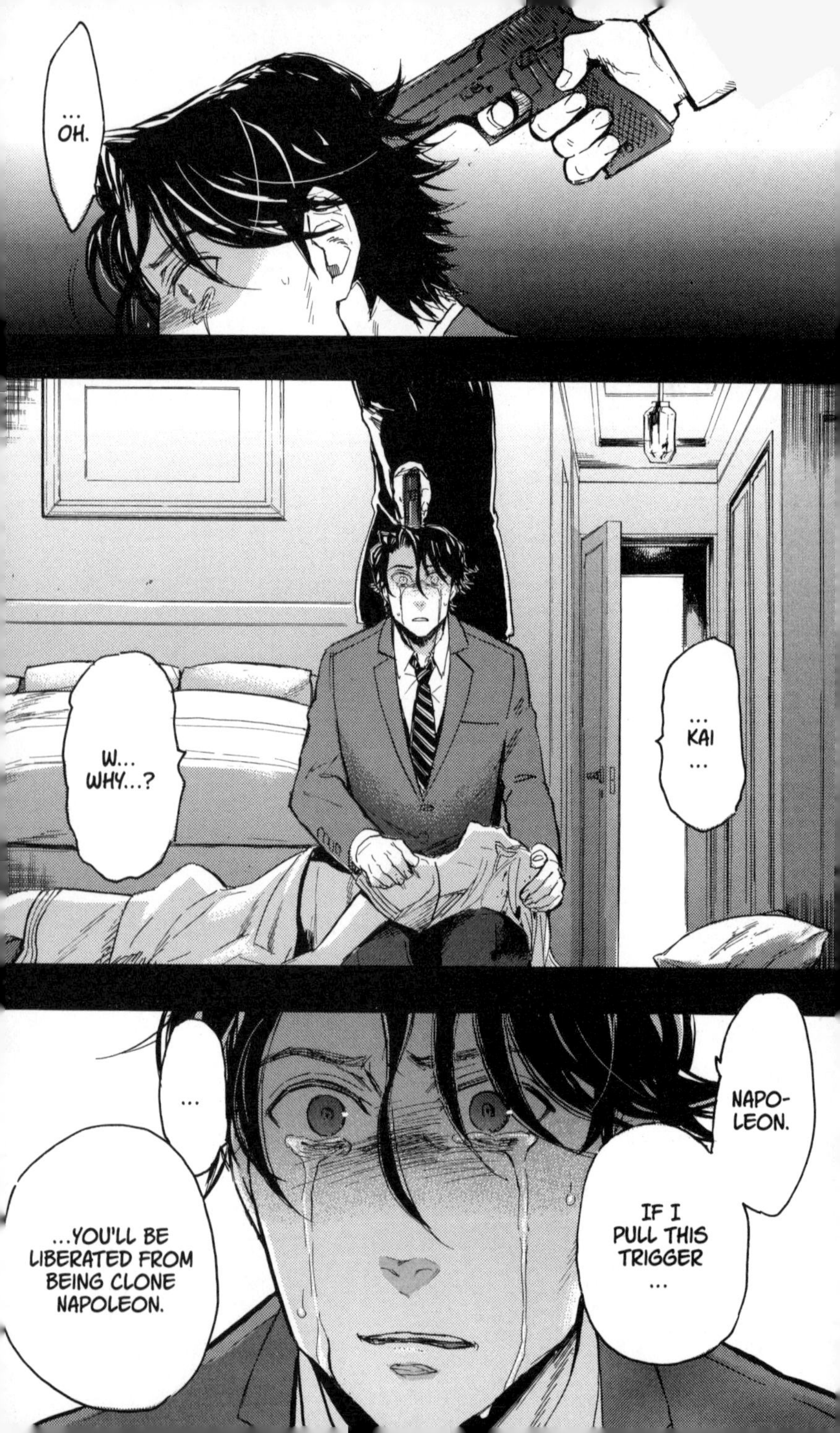
...OH.
...KAI...
W... WHY...?
NAPOLEON.
...
IF I PULL THIS TRIGGER...
...YOU'LL BE LIBERATED FROM BEING CLONE NAPOLEON.

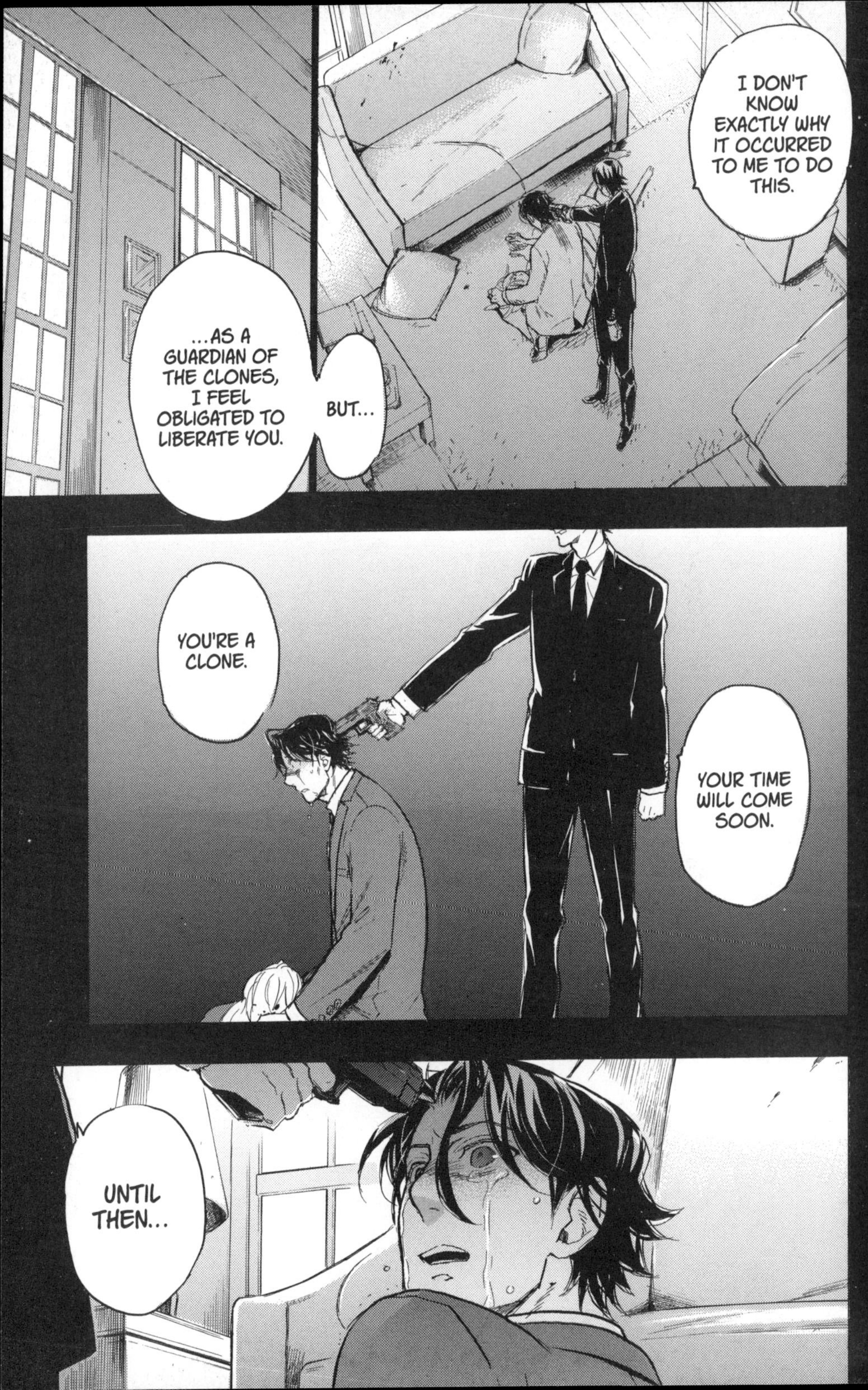
I DON'T KNOW EXACTLY WHY IT OCCURRED TO ME TO DO THIS.
BUT...
...AS A GUARDIAN OF THE CLONES, I FEEL OBLIGATED TO LIBERATE YOU.
YOU'RE A CLONE.
YOUR TIME WILL COME SOON.
UNTIL THEN...

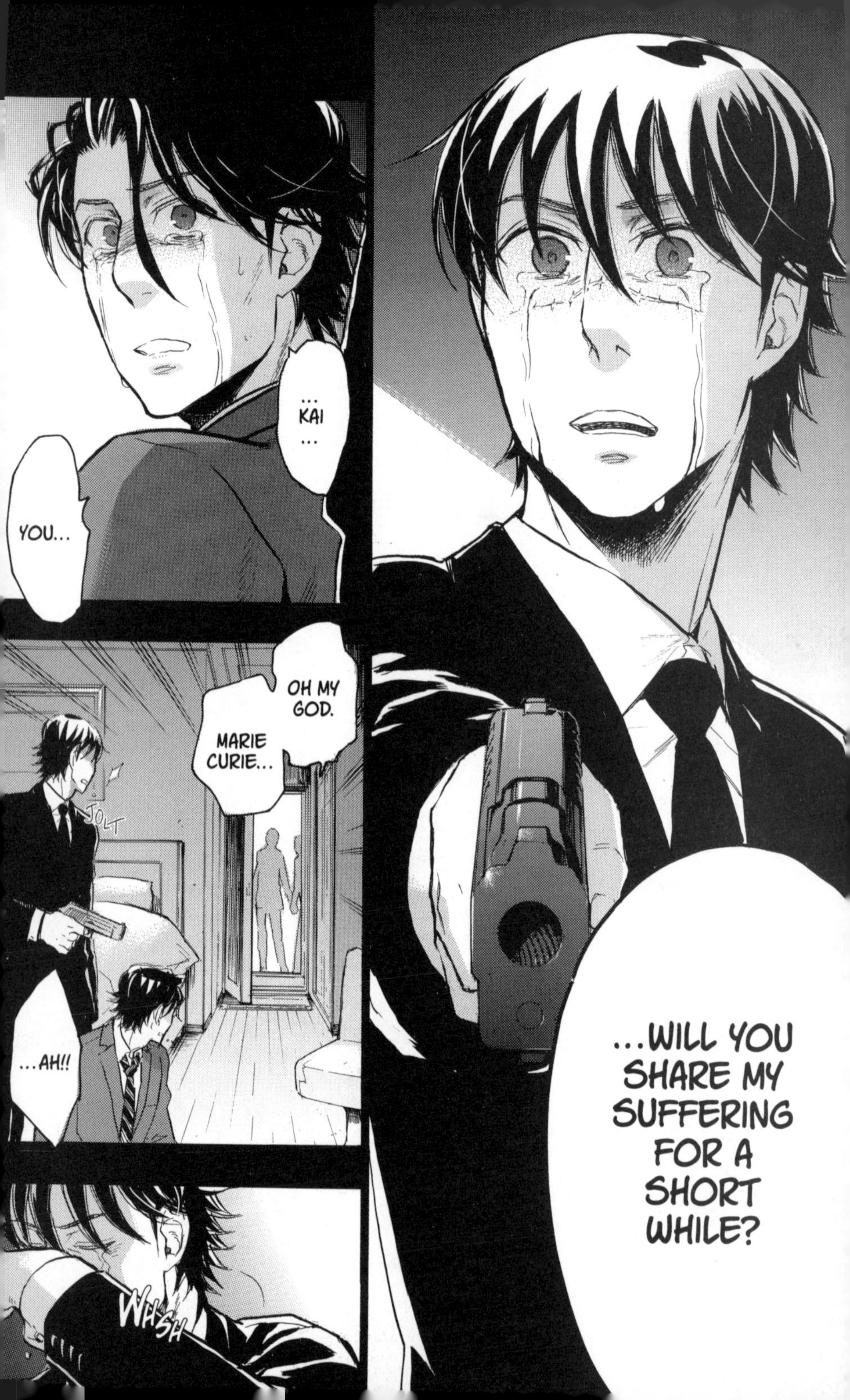
...WILL YOU SHARE MY SUFFERING FOR A SHORT WHILE?
...KAI...
YOU...
OH MY GOD.
MARIE CURIE...
JOLT
...AH!!
WHSH

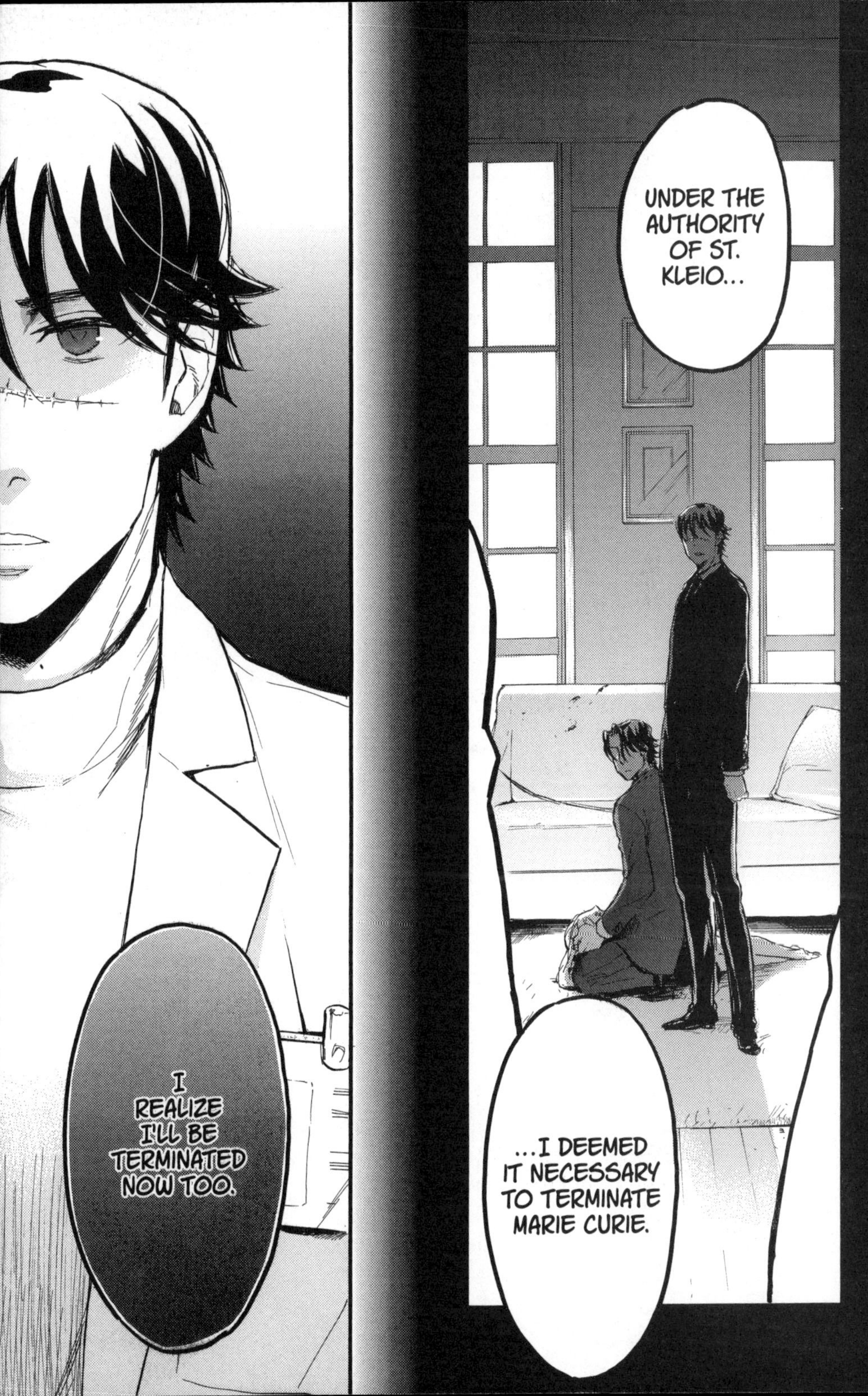
UNDER THE AUTHORITY OF ST. KLEIO...
...I DEEMED IT NECESSARY TO TERMINATE MARIE CURIE.
I REALIZE I'LL BE TERMINATED NOW TOO.

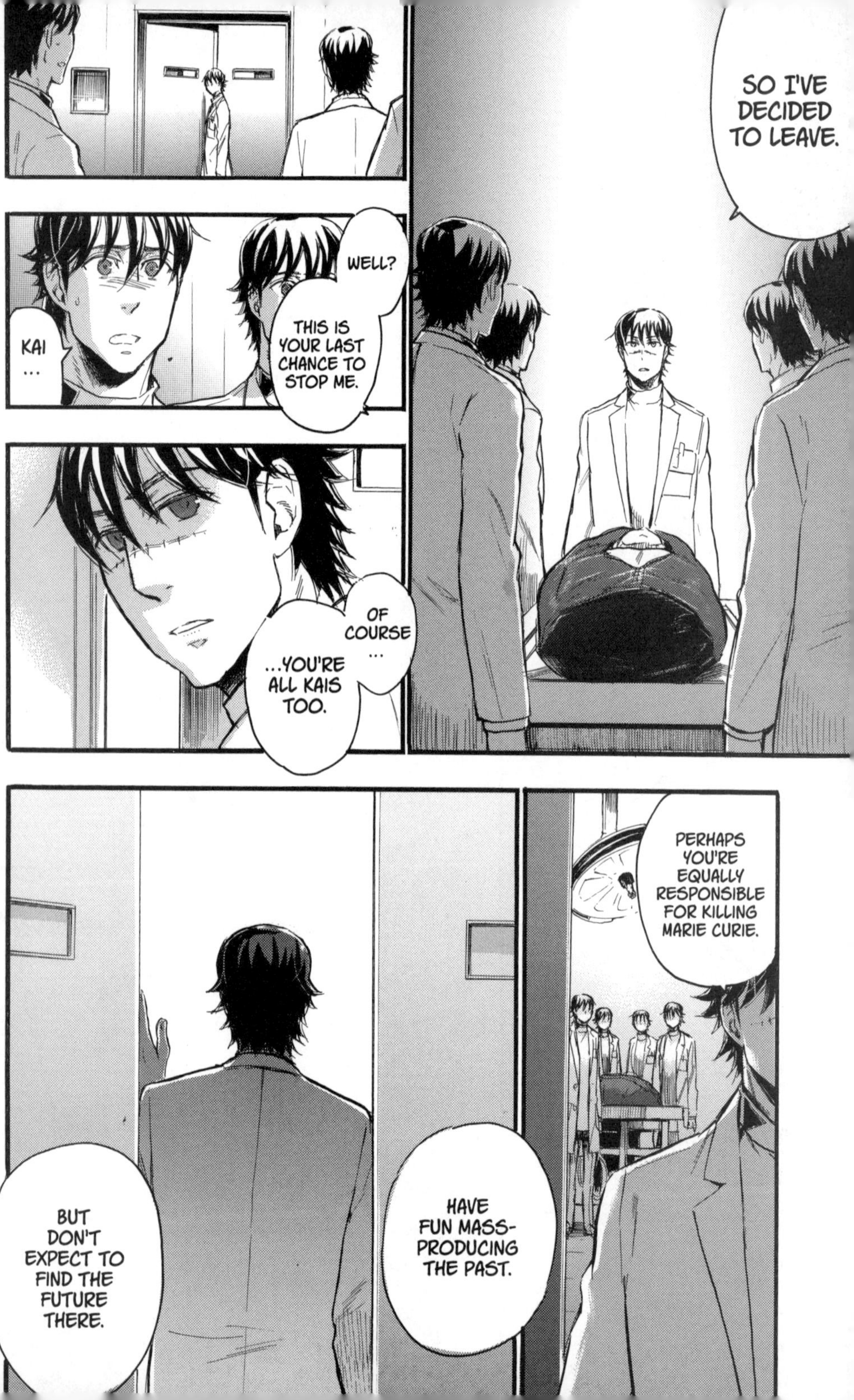
SO I'VE DECIDED TO LEAVE.
WELL?
THIS IS YOUR LAST CHANCE TO STOP ME.
KAI ...
OF COURSE ...
...YOU'RE ALL KAIS TOO.
PERHAPS YOU'RE EQUALLY RESPONSIBLE FOR KILLING MARIE CURIE.
HAVE FUN MASS-PRODUCING THE PAST.
BUT DON'T EXPECT TO FIND THE FUTURE THERE.

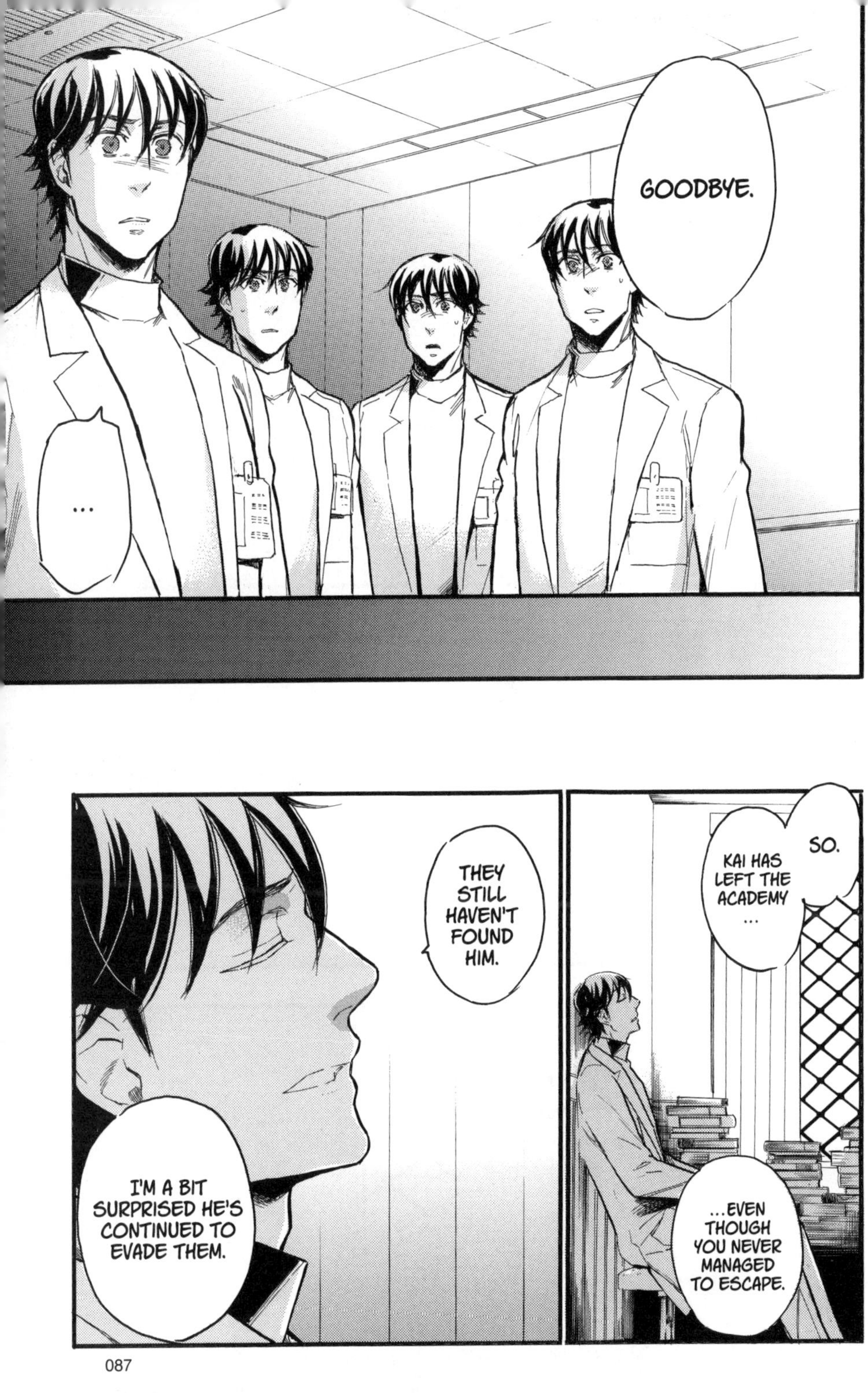
GOODBYE.
...
SO.
KAI HAS LEFT THE ACADEMY ...
...EVEN THOUGH YOU NEVER MANAGED TO ESCAPE.
THEY STILL HAVEN'T FOUND HIM.
I'M A BIT SURPRISED HE'S CONTINUED TO EVADE THEM.

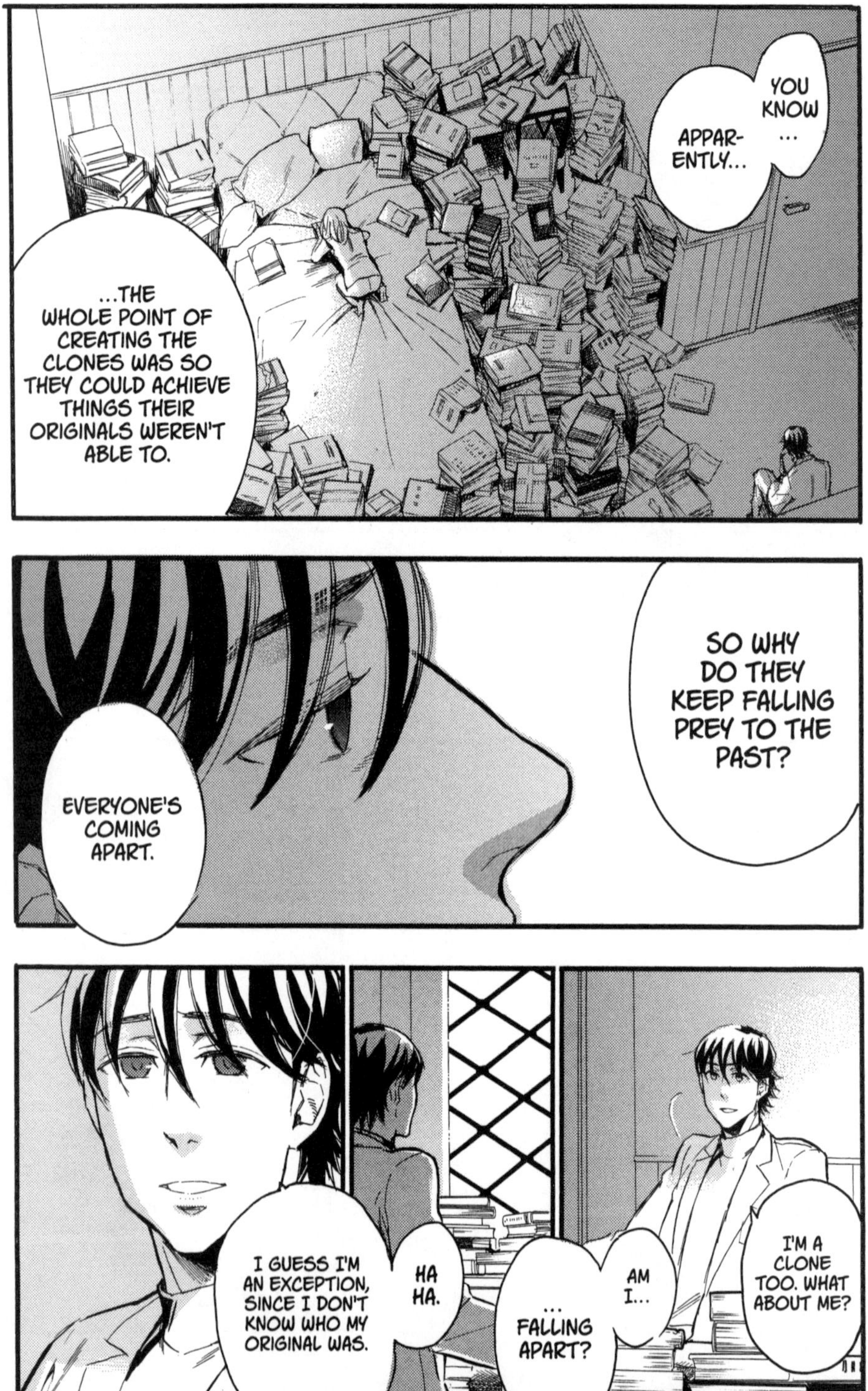
YOU KNOW ...
APPARENTLY...
...THE WHOLE POINT OF CREATING THE CLONES WAS SO THEY COULD ACHIEVE THINGS THEIR ORIGINALS WEREN'T ABLE TO.
SO WHY DO THEY KEEP FALLING PREY TO THE PAST?
EVERYONE'S COMING APART.
I'M A CLONE TOO. WHAT ABOUT ME?
AM I...
...FALLING APART?
HA HA.
I GUESS I'M AN EXCEPTION, SINCE I DON'T KNOW WHO MY ORIGINAL WAS.

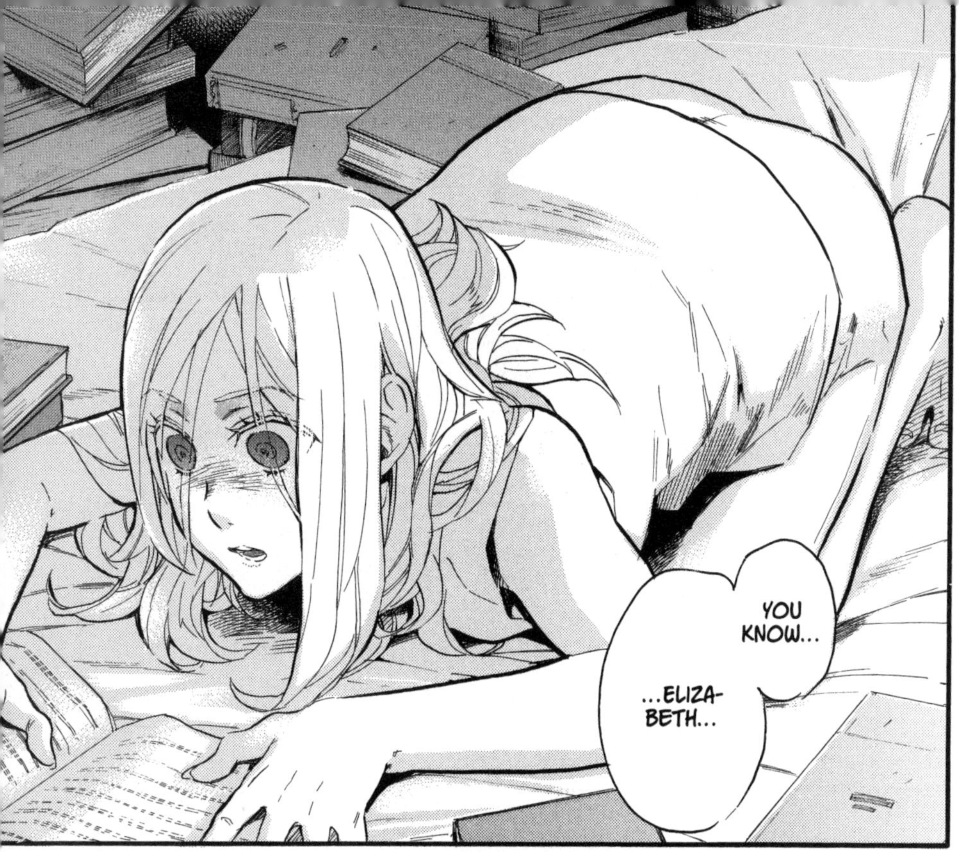
YOU KNOW...
...ELIZA-BETH...

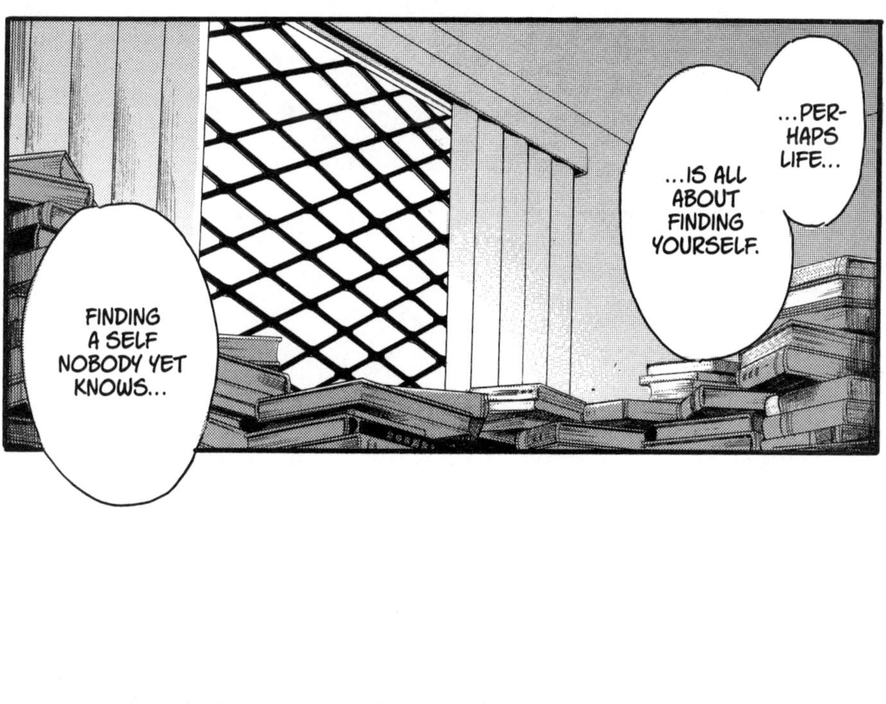
...PER-HAPS LIFE...
...IS ALL ABOUT FINDING YOURSELF.
FINDING A SELF NOBODY YET KNOWS...

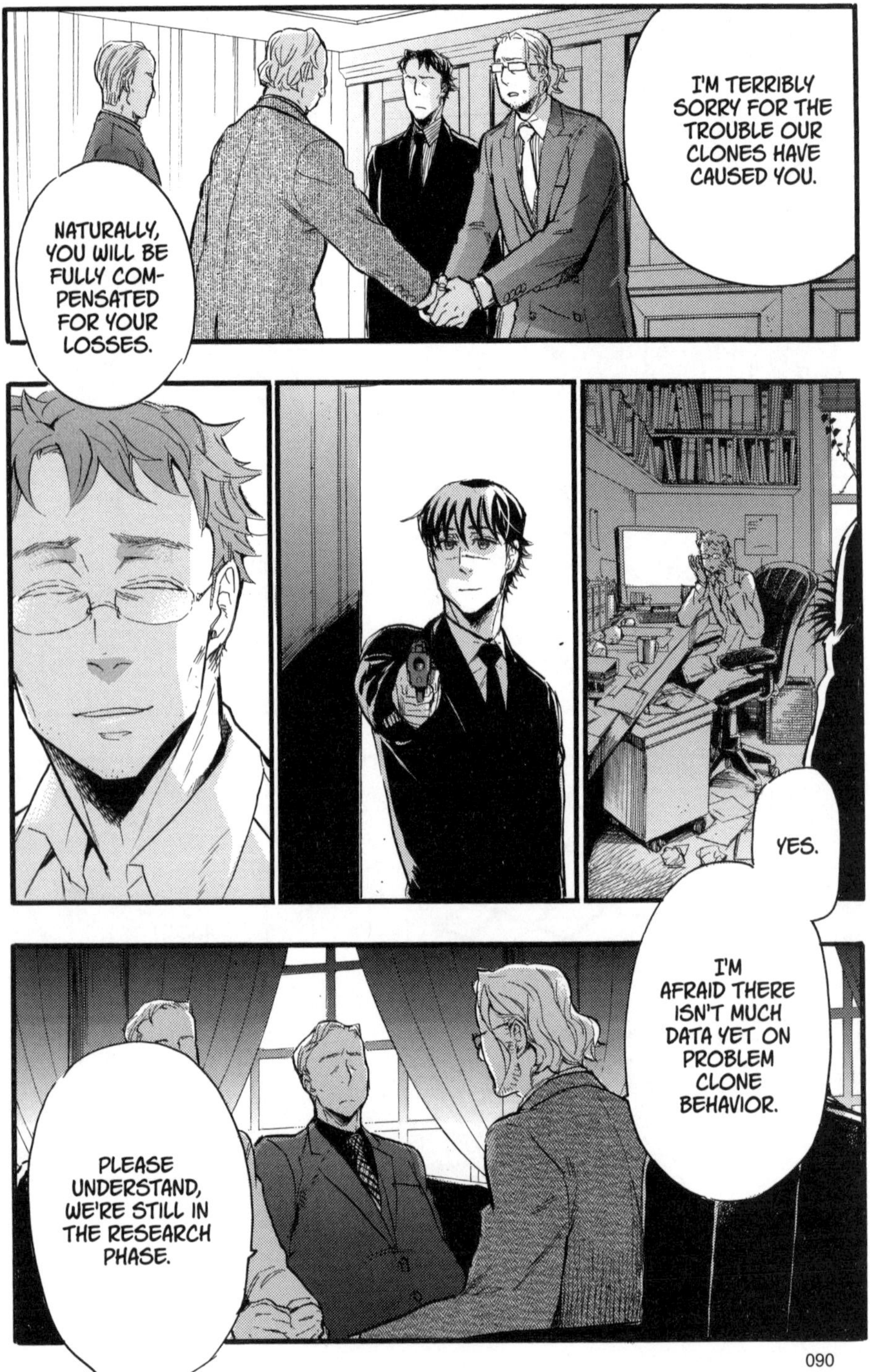
I'M TERRIBLY SORRY FOR THE TROUBLE OUR CLONES HAVE CAUSED YOU.
NATURALLY, YOU WILL BE FULLY COM-PENSATED FOR YOUR LOSSES.
YES.
I'M AFRAID THERE ISN'T MUCH DATA YET ON PROBLEM CLONE BEHAVIOR.
PLEASE UNDERSTAND, WE'RE STILL IN THE RESEARCH PHASE.

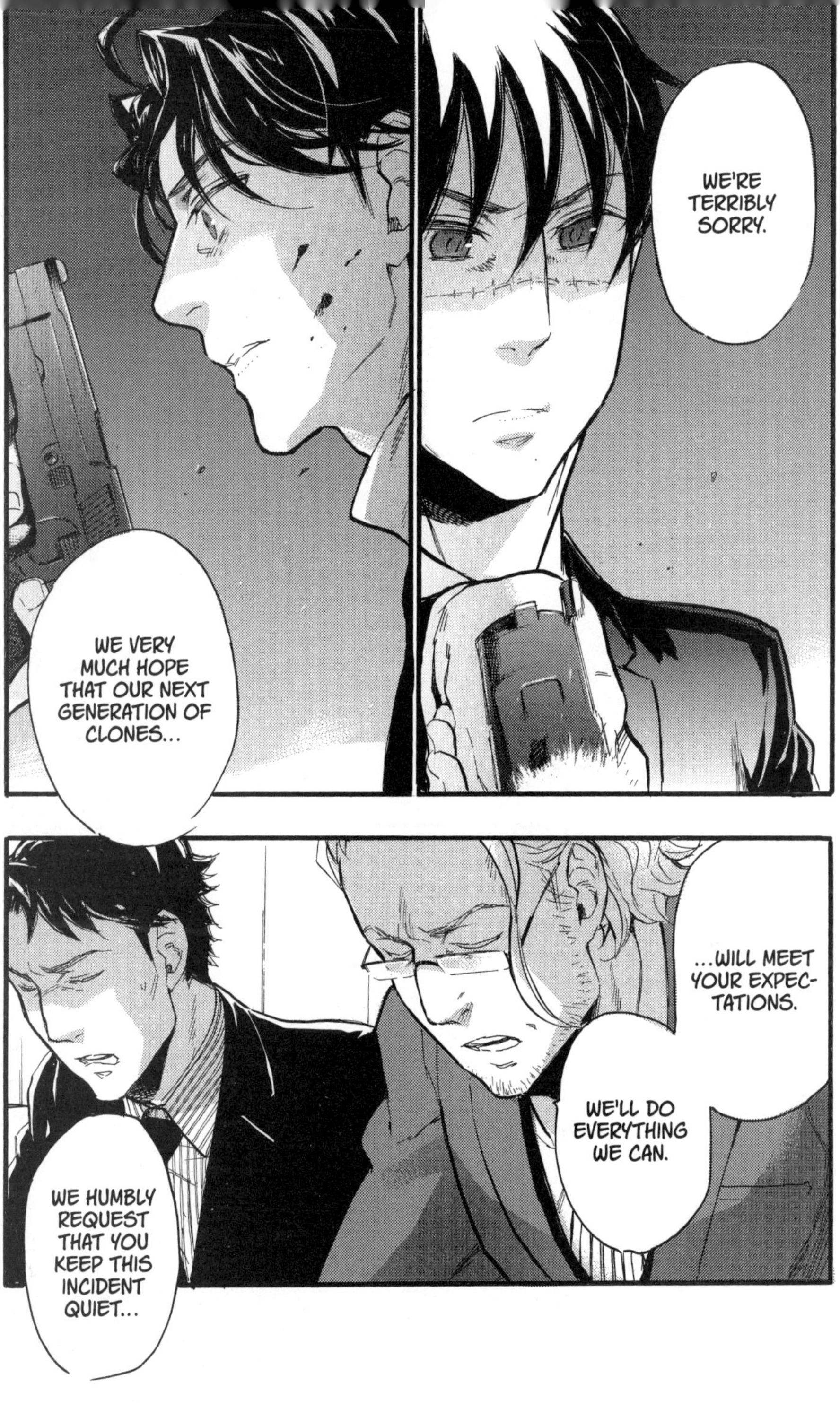
WE'RE TERRIBLY SORRY.
WE VERY MUCH HOPE THAT OUR NEXT GENERATION OF CLONES...
...WILL MEET YOUR EXPEC-TATIONS.
WE'LL DO EVERYTHING WE CAN.
WE HUMBLY REQUEST THAT YOU KEEP THIS INCIDENT QUIET...

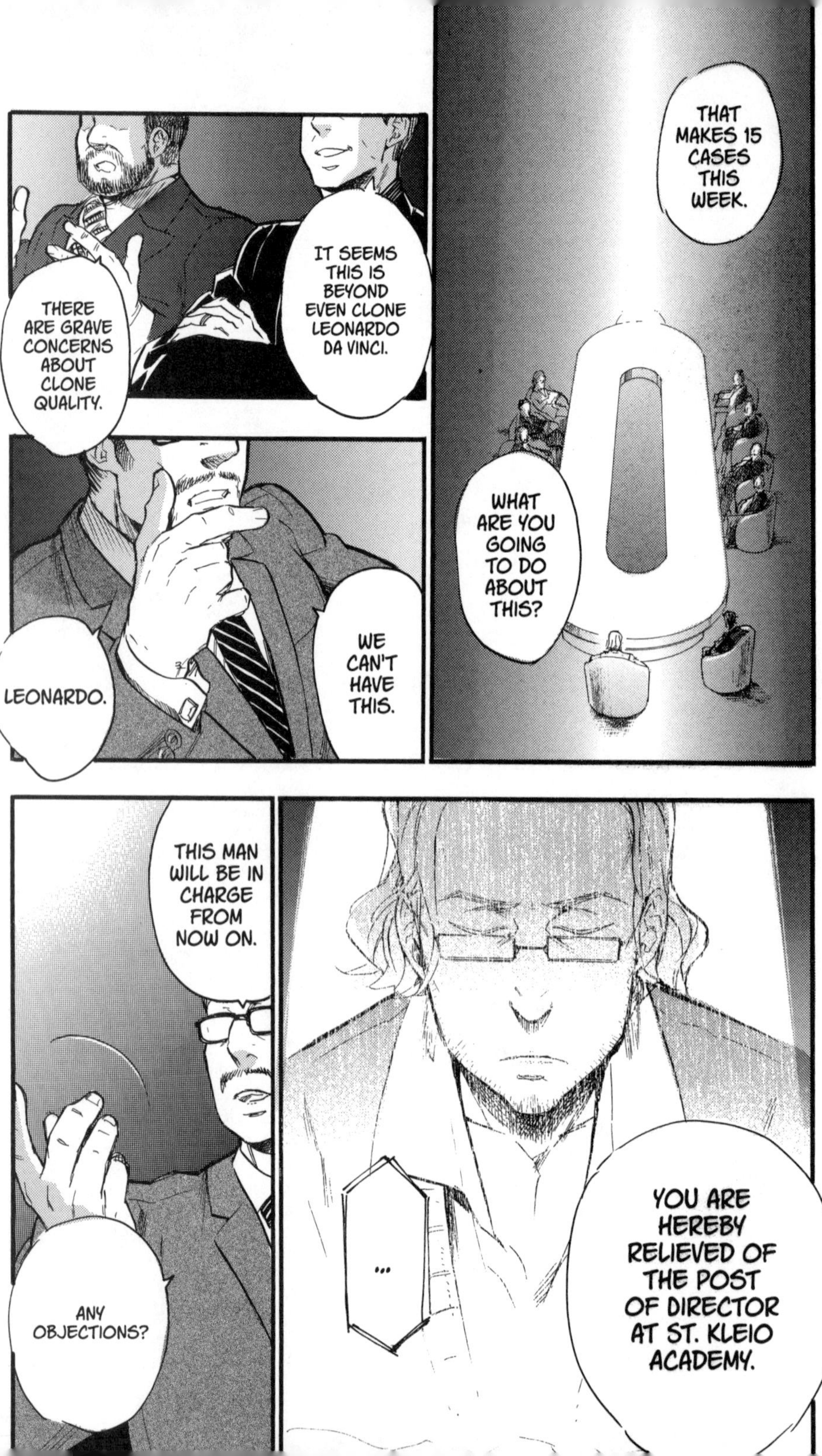
THAT MAKES 15 CASES THIS WEEK.
WHAT ARE YOU GOING TO DO ABOUT THIS?
IT SEEMS THIS IS BEYOND EVEN CLONE LEONARDO DA VINCI.
THERE ARE GRAVE CONCERNS ABOUT CLONE QUALITY.
WE CAN'T HAVE THIS.
LEONARDO.
YOU ARE HEREBY RELIEVED OF THE POST OF DIRECTOR AT ST. KLEIO ACADEMY.
...
THIS MAN WILL BE IN CHARGE FROM NOW ON.
ANY OBJECTIONS?

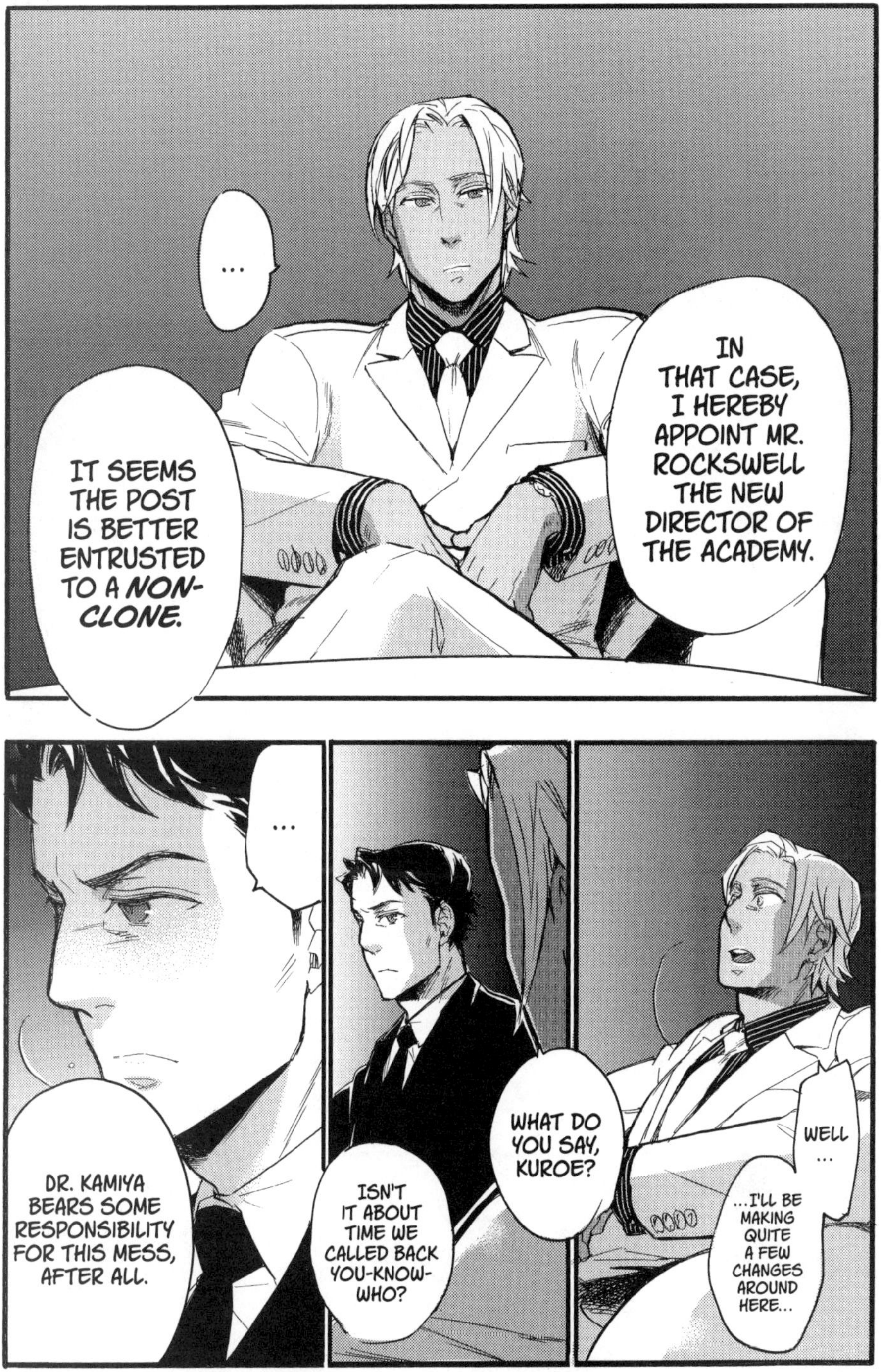
IN THAT CASE, I HEREBY APPOINT MR. ROCKSWELL THE NEW DIRECTOR OF THE ACADEMY.
...
IT SEEMS THE POST IS BETTER ENTRUSTED TO A *NON-CLONE*.
WELL...
...I'LL BE MAKING QUITE A FEW CHANGES AROUND HERE...
WHAT DO YOU SAY, KUROE?
ISN'T IT ABOUT TIME WE CALLED BACK YOU-KNOW-WHO?
...
DR. KAMIYA BEARS SOME RESPONSIBILITY FOR THIS MESS, AFTER ALL.

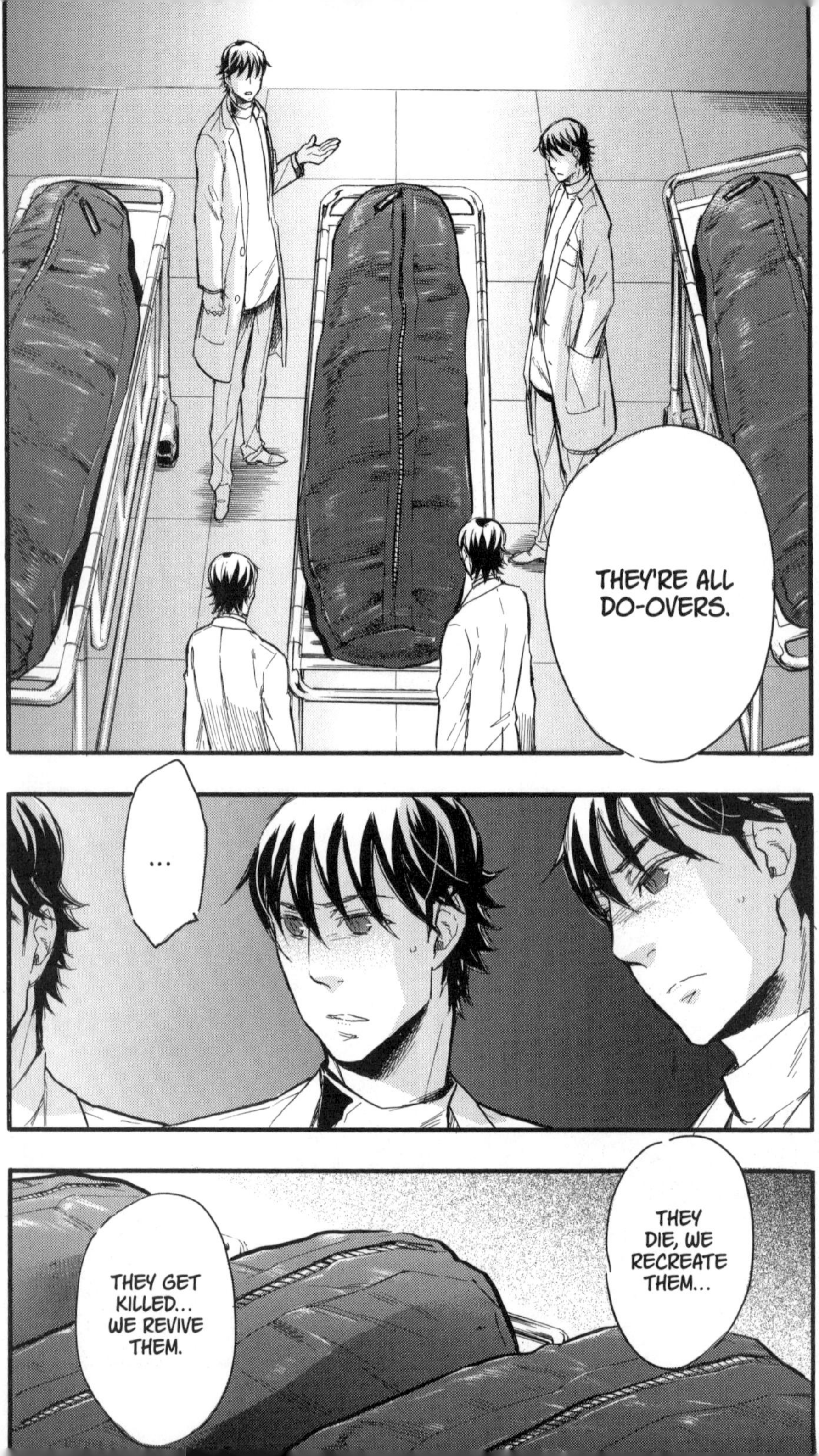
THEY'RE ALL DO-OVERS.
...
THEY DIE, WE RECREATE THEM...
THEY GET KILLED... WE REVIVE THEM.

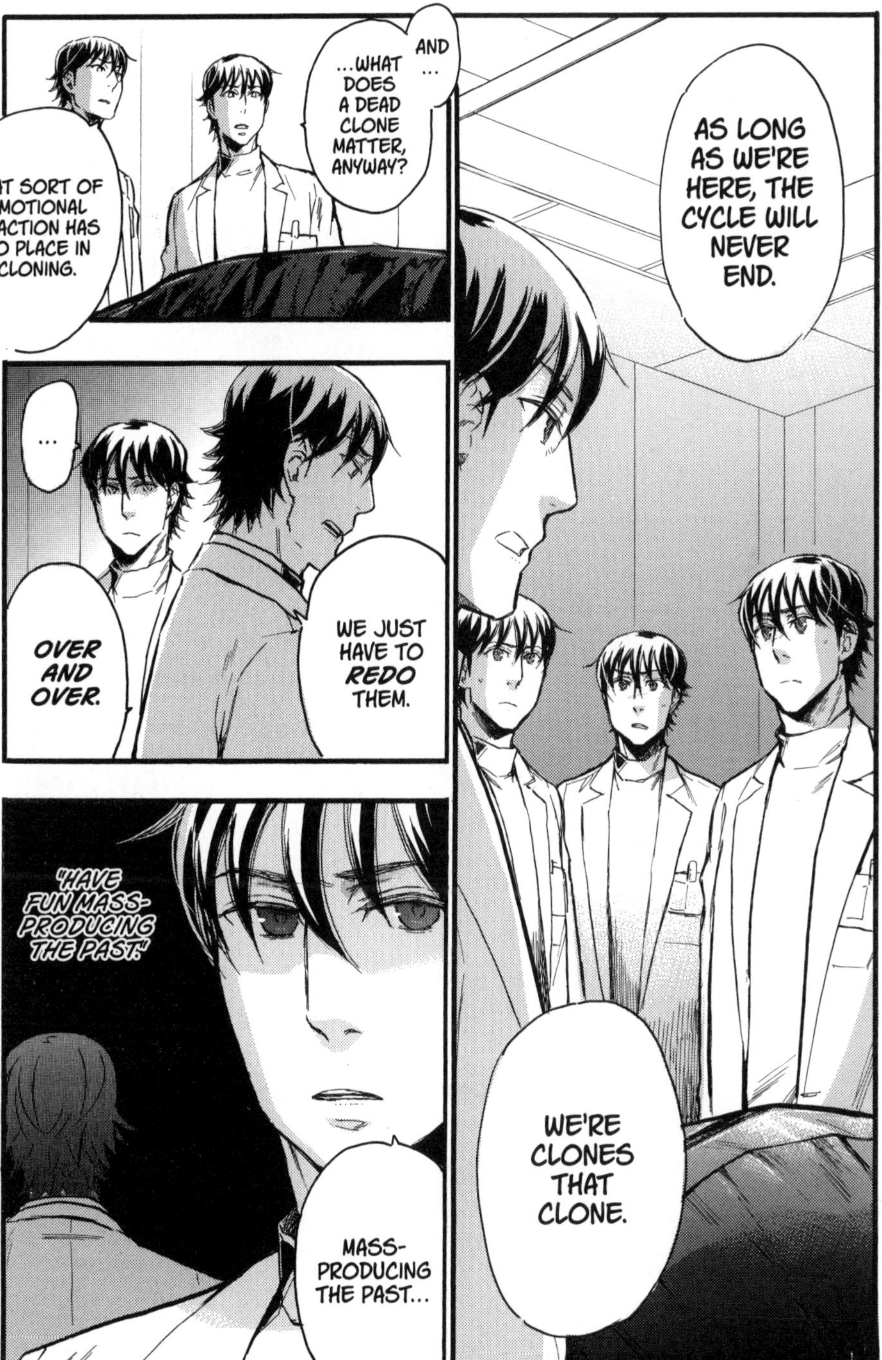
AS LONG AS WE'RE HERE, THE CYCLE WILL NEVER END.
WE'RE CLONES THAT CLONE.
AND ...
...WHAT DOES A DEAD CLONE MATTER, ANYWAY?
THAT SORT OF EMOTIONAL REACTION HAS NO PLACE IN CLONING.
...
WE JUST HAVE TO REDO THEM.
OVER AND OVER.
"HAVE FUN MASS-PRODUCING THE PAST."
MASS-PRODUCING THE PAST...

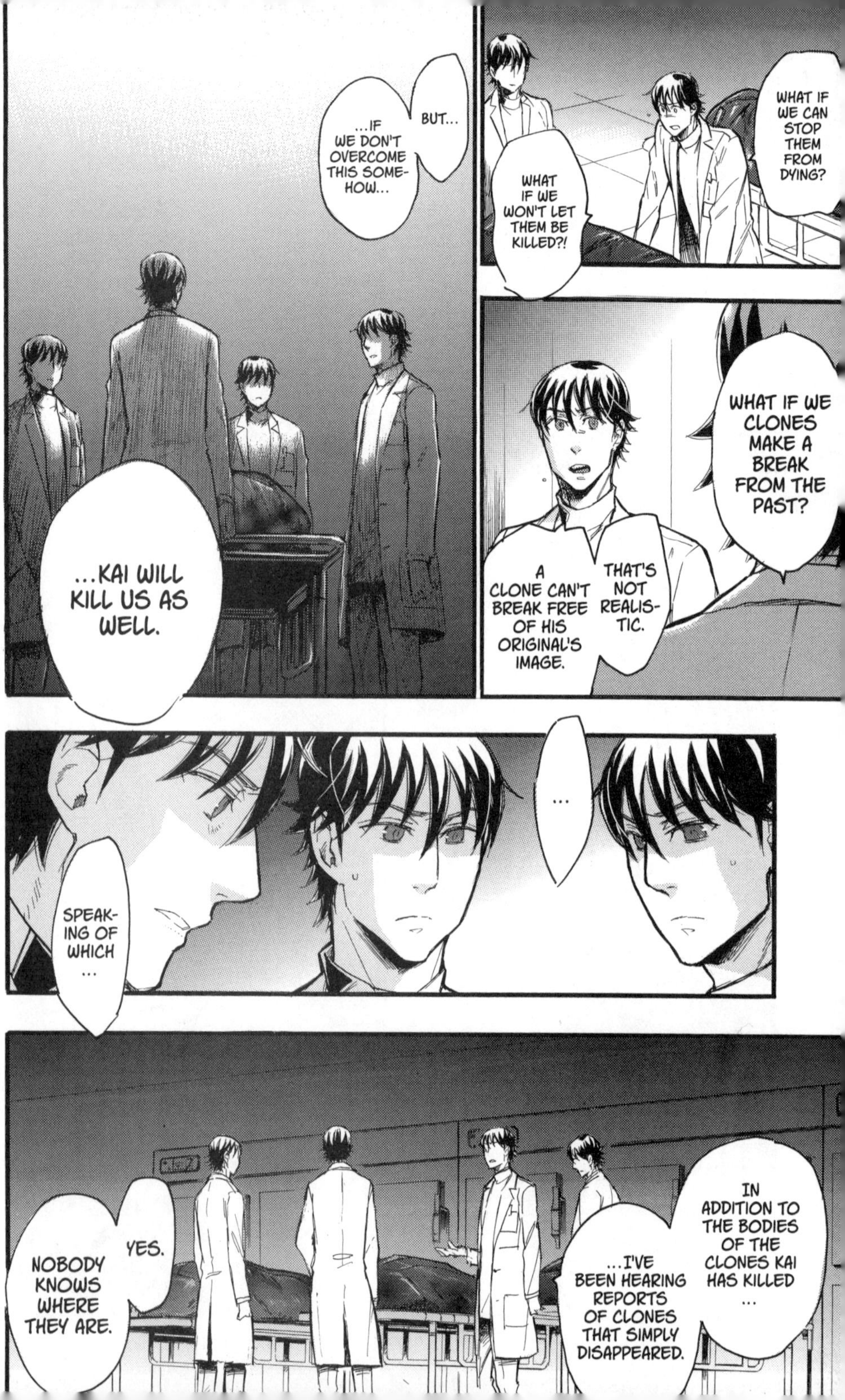
WHAT IF WE CAN STOP THEM FROM DYING?
WHAT IF WE WON'T LET THEM BE KILLED?!
WHAT IF WE CLONES MAKE A BREAK FROM THE PAST?
THAT'S NOT REALISTIC.
A CLONE CAN'T BREAK FREE OF HIS ORIGINAL'S IMAGE.
BUT...
...IF WE DON'T OVERCOME THIS SOMEHOW...
...KAI WILL KILL US AS WELL.
...
SPEAKING OF WHICH...
IN ADDITION TO THE BODIES OF THE CLONES KAI HAS KILLED...
...I'VE BEEN HEARING REPORTS OF CLONES THAT SIMPLY DISAPPEARED.
YES.
NOBODY KNOWS WHERE THEY ARE.

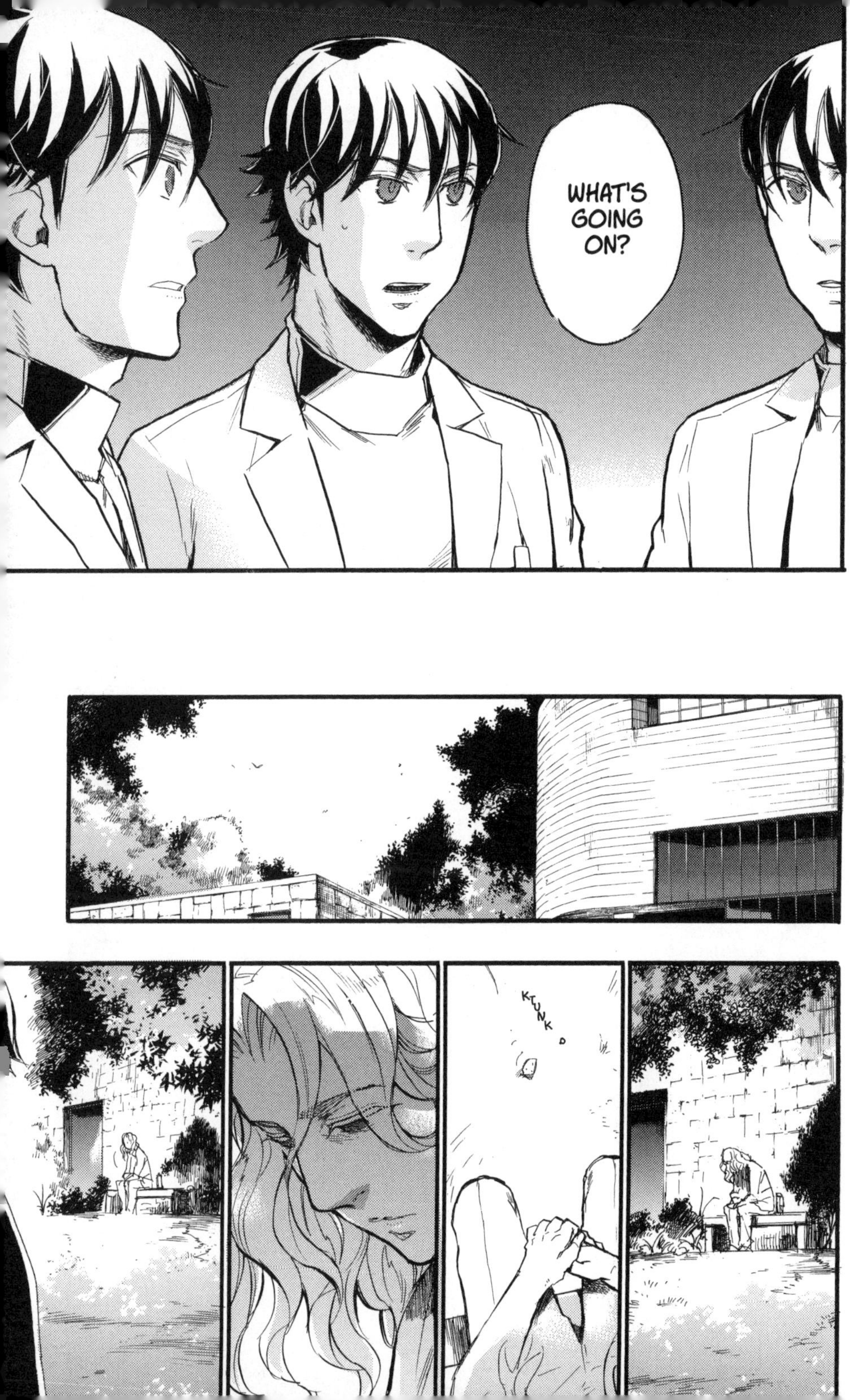
WHAT'S GOING ON?
KTUNK

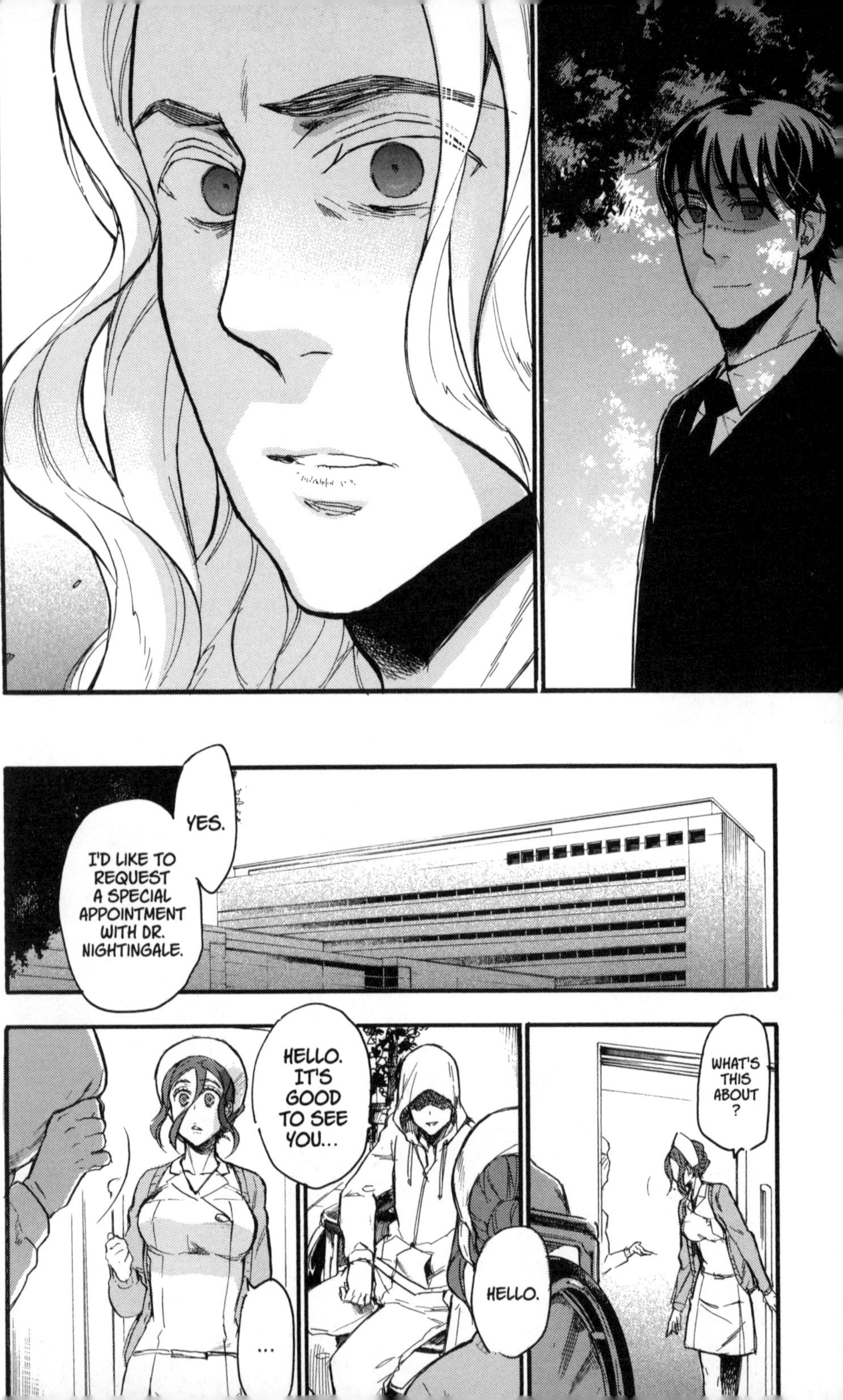
YES.
I'D LIKE TO REQUEST A SPECIAL APPOINTMENT WITH DR. NIGHTINGALE.
WHAT'S THIS ABOUT?
HELLO.
HELLO. IT'S GOOD TO SEE YOU...
...

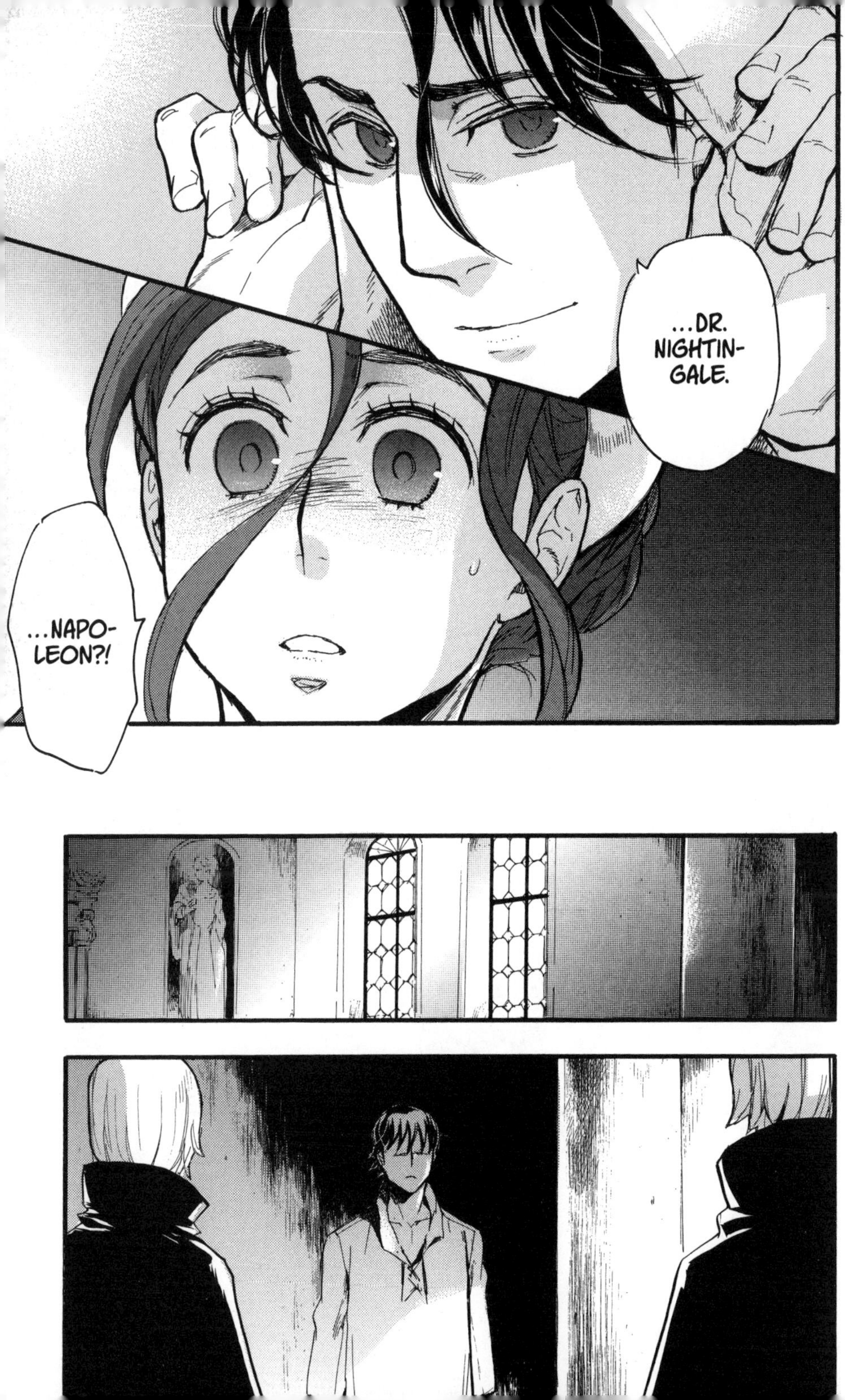
...DR. NIGHTIN-GALE.
...NAPO-LEON?!

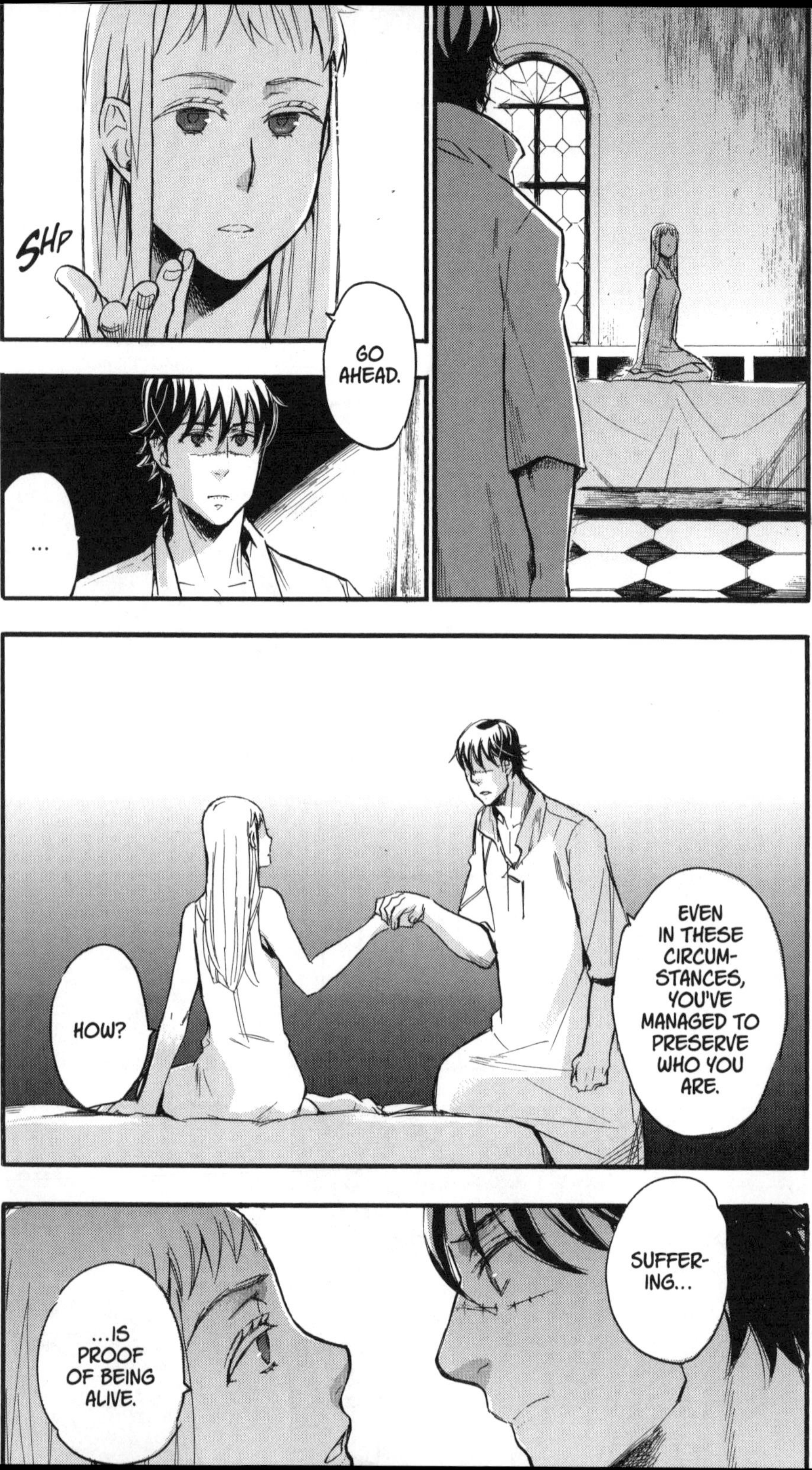
SHP
GO AHEAD.
...
EVEN IN THESE CIRCUM- STANCES, YOU'VE MANAGED TO PRESERVE WHO YOU ARE.
HOW?
SUFFER- ING...
...IS PROOF OF BEING ALIVE.

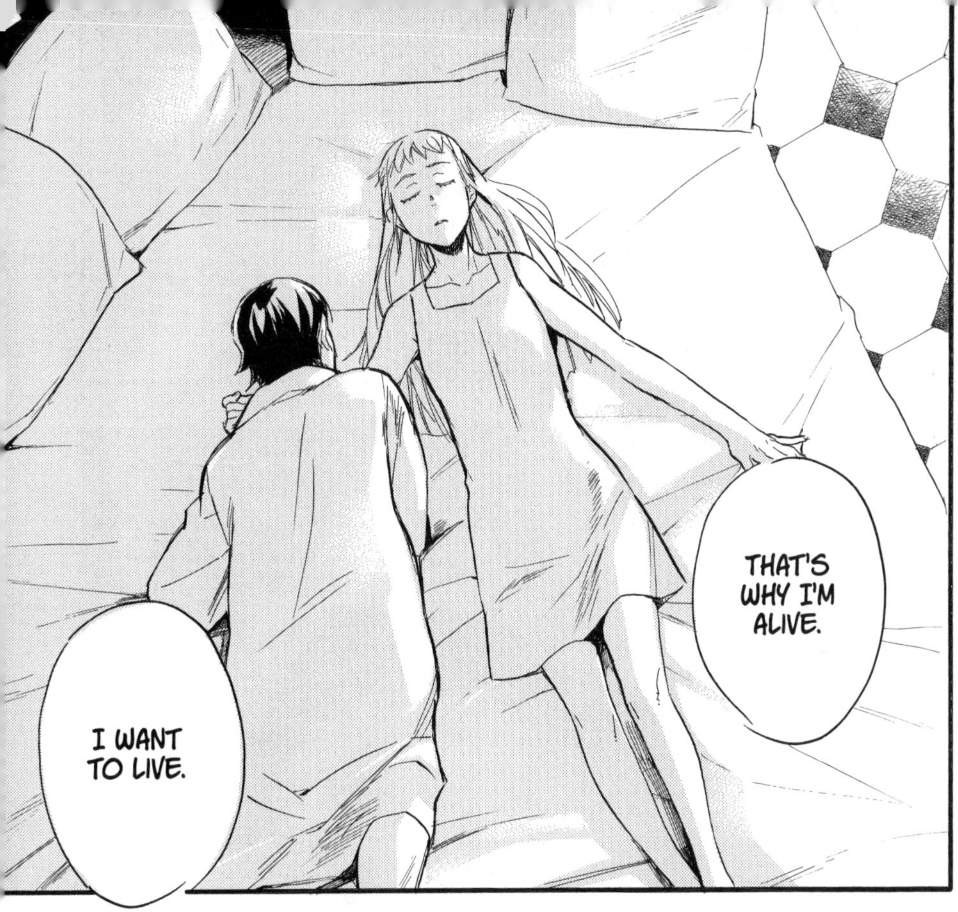
THAT'S WHY I'M ALIVE.
I WANT TO LIVE.

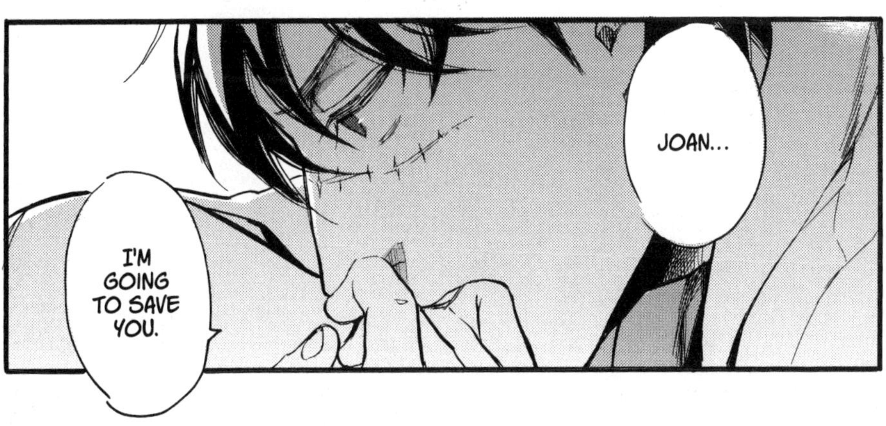
JOAN...
I'M GOING TO SAVE YOU.

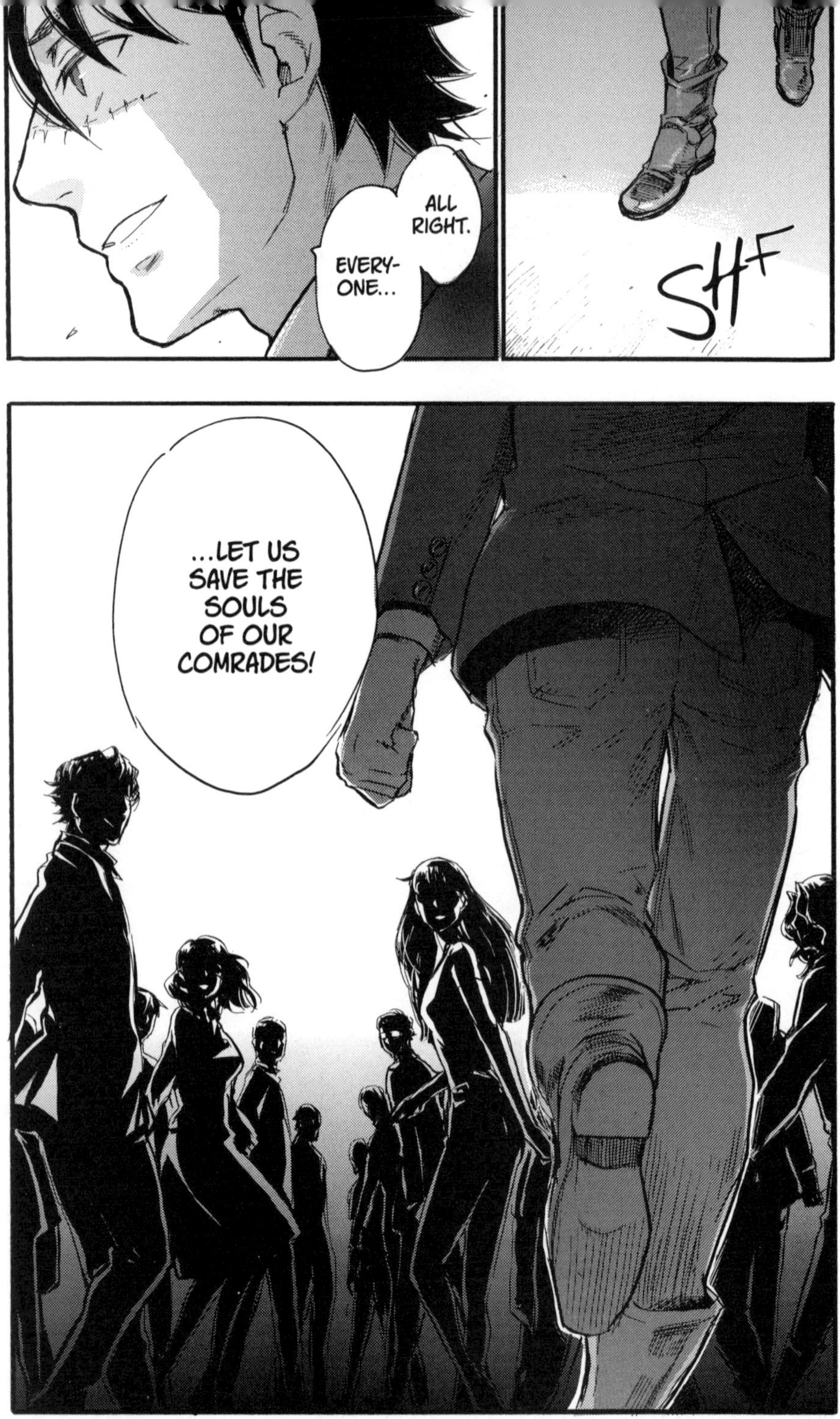
SHF
ALL RIGHT.
EVERYONE...
...LET US SAVE THE SOULS OF OUR COMRADES!

CHAPTER thirty-four

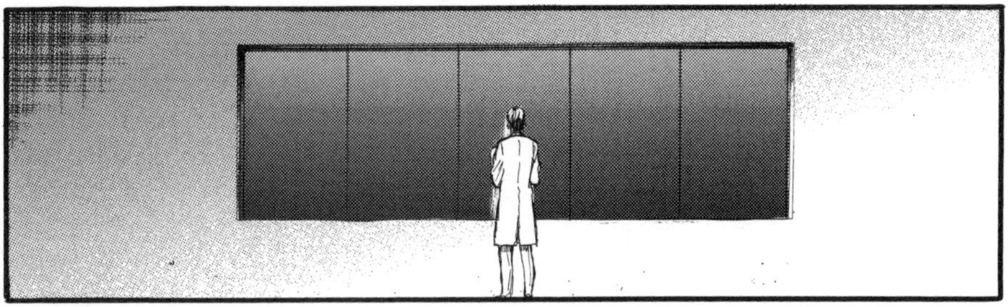

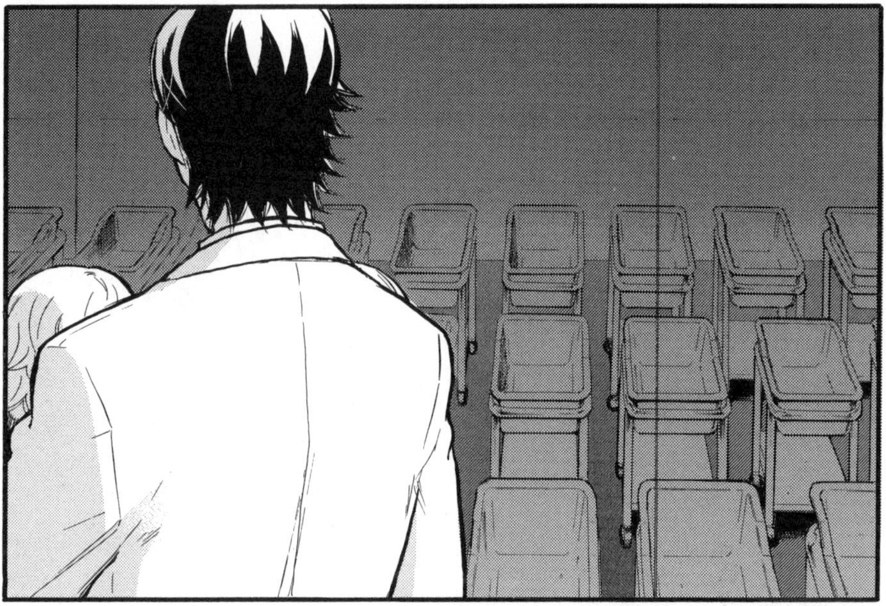

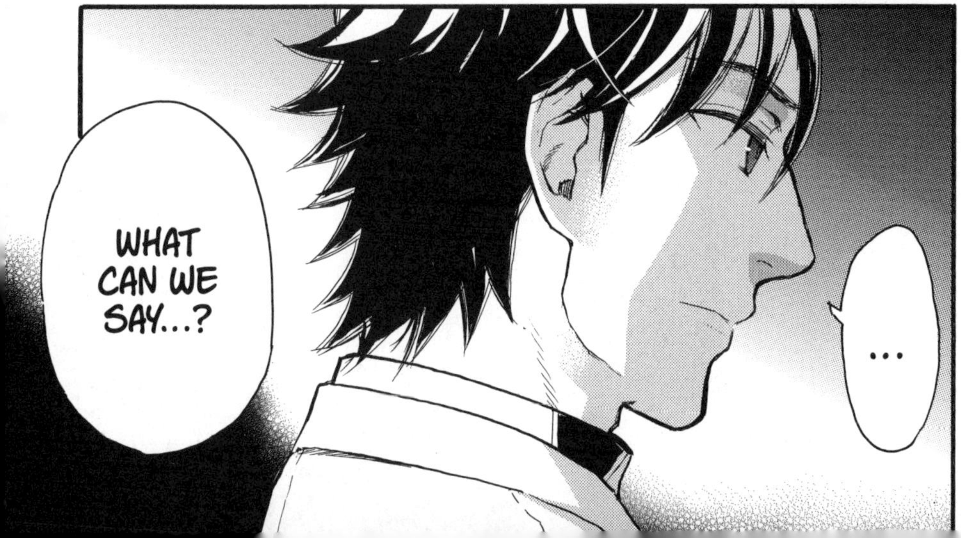
...
WHAT CAN WE SAY...?

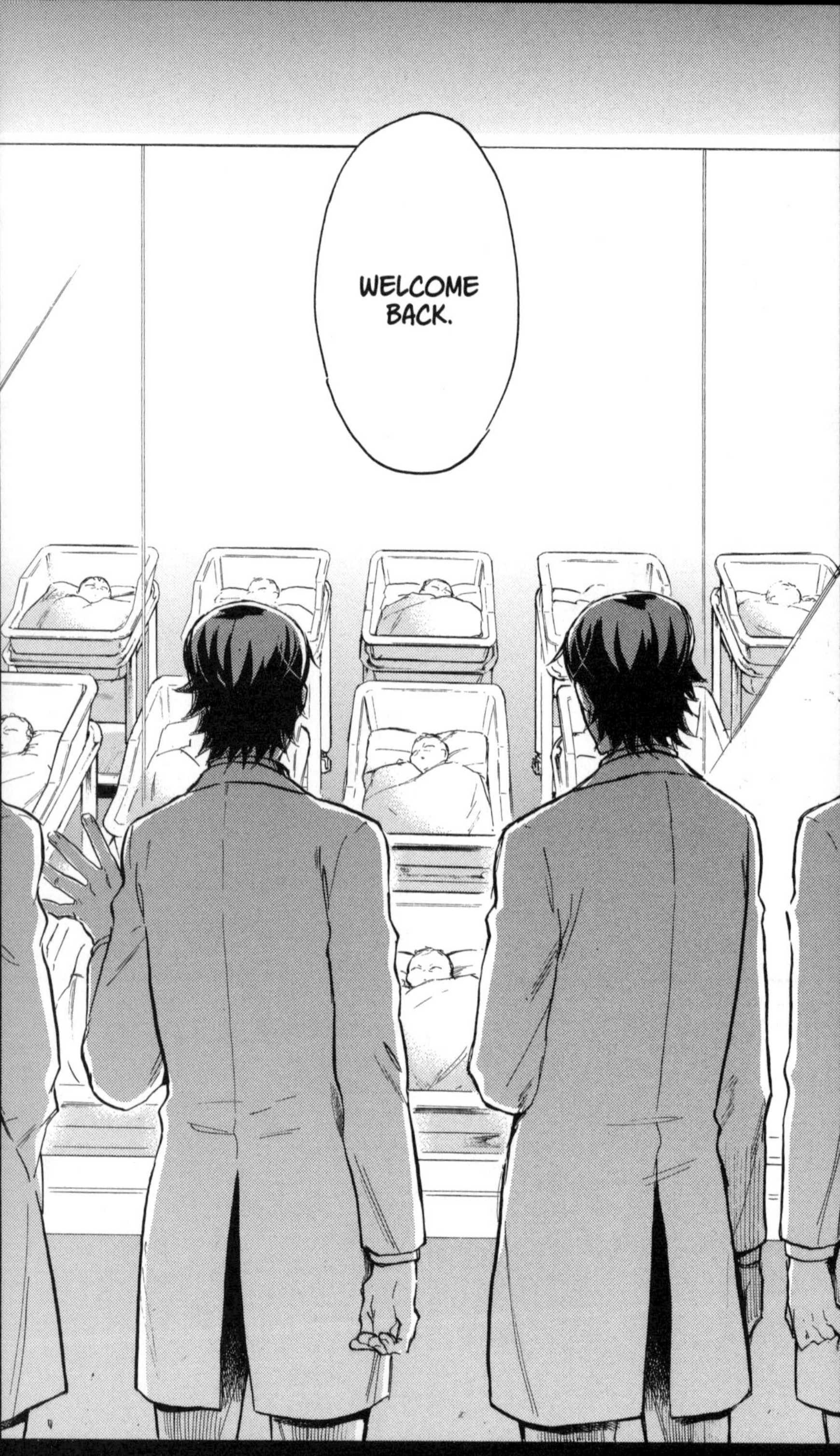
WELCOME BACK.

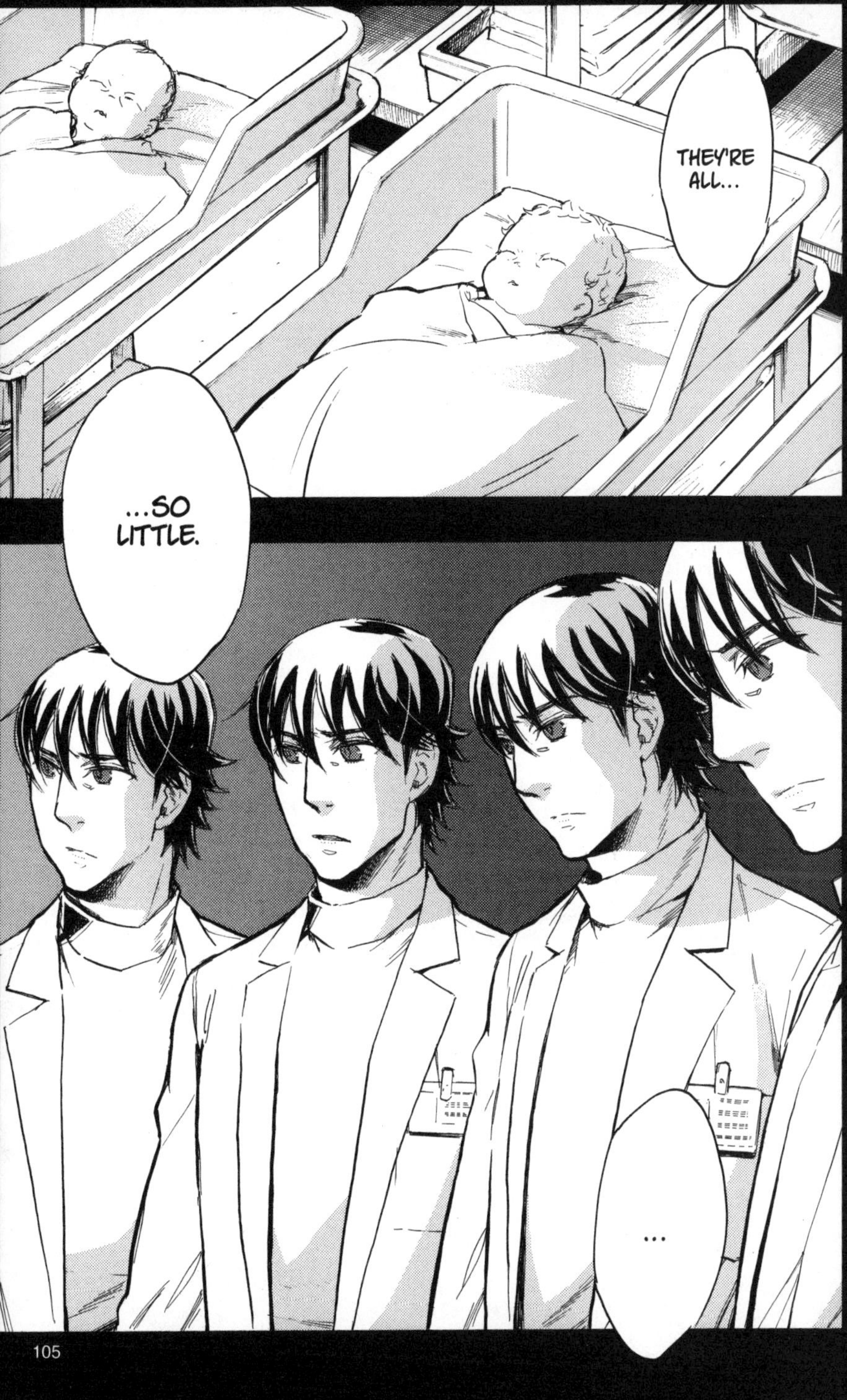
THEY'RE ALL...
...SO LITTLE.
...

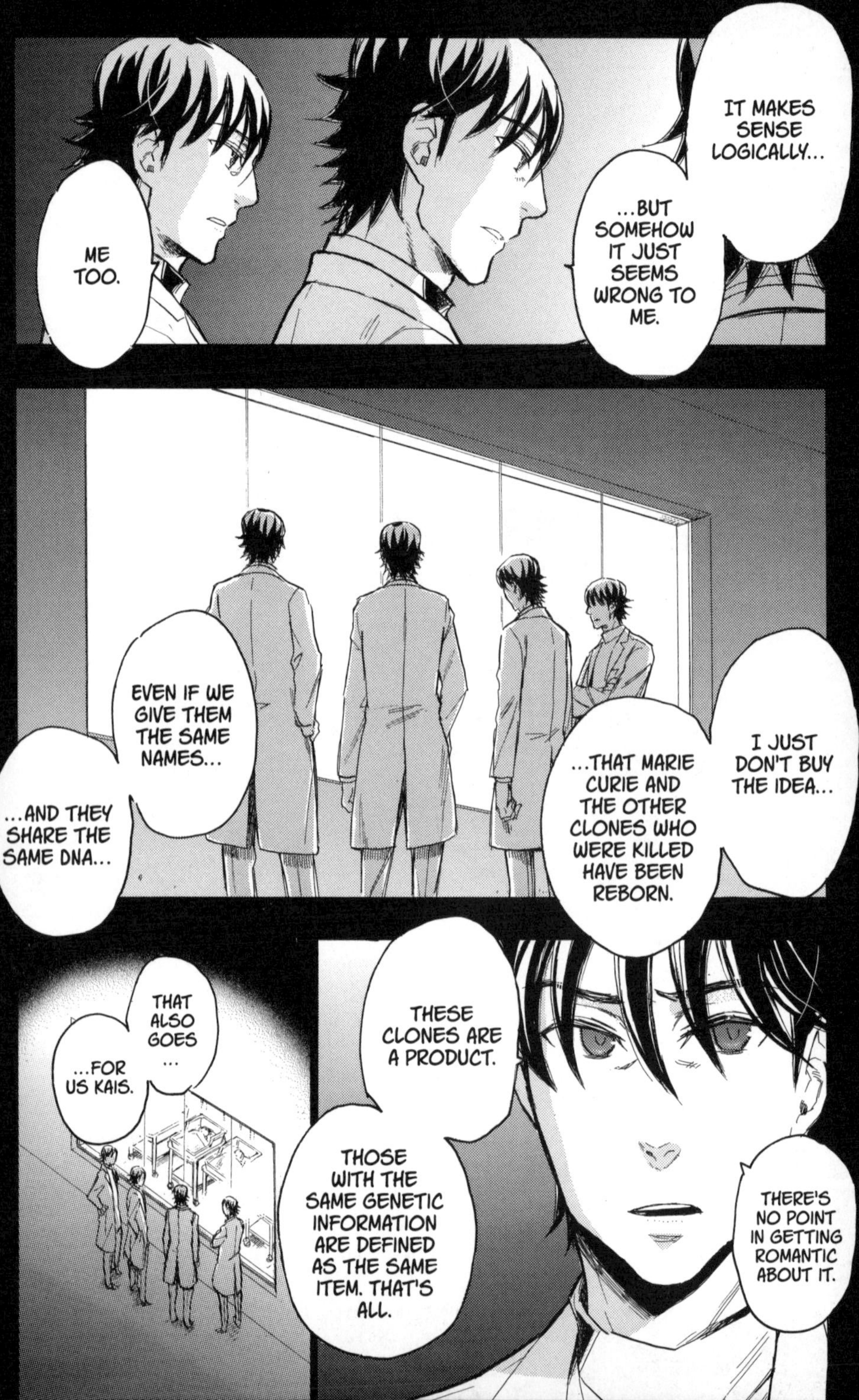
IT MAKES SENSE LOGICALLY...
...BUT SOMEHOW IT JUST SEEMS WRONG TO ME.
ME TOO.
I JUST DON'T BUY THE IDEA...
...THAT MARIE CURIE AND THE OTHER CLONES WHO WERE KILLED HAVE BEEN REBORN.
EVEN IF WE GIVE THEM THE SAME NAMES...
...AND THEY SHARE THE SAME DNA...
THESE CLONES ARE A PRODUCT.
THOSE WITH THE SAME GENETIC INFORMATION ARE DEFINED AS THE SAME ITEM. THAT'S ALL.
THERE'S NO POINT IN GETTING ROMANTIC ABOUT IT.
THAT ALSO GOES...
...FOR US KAIS.

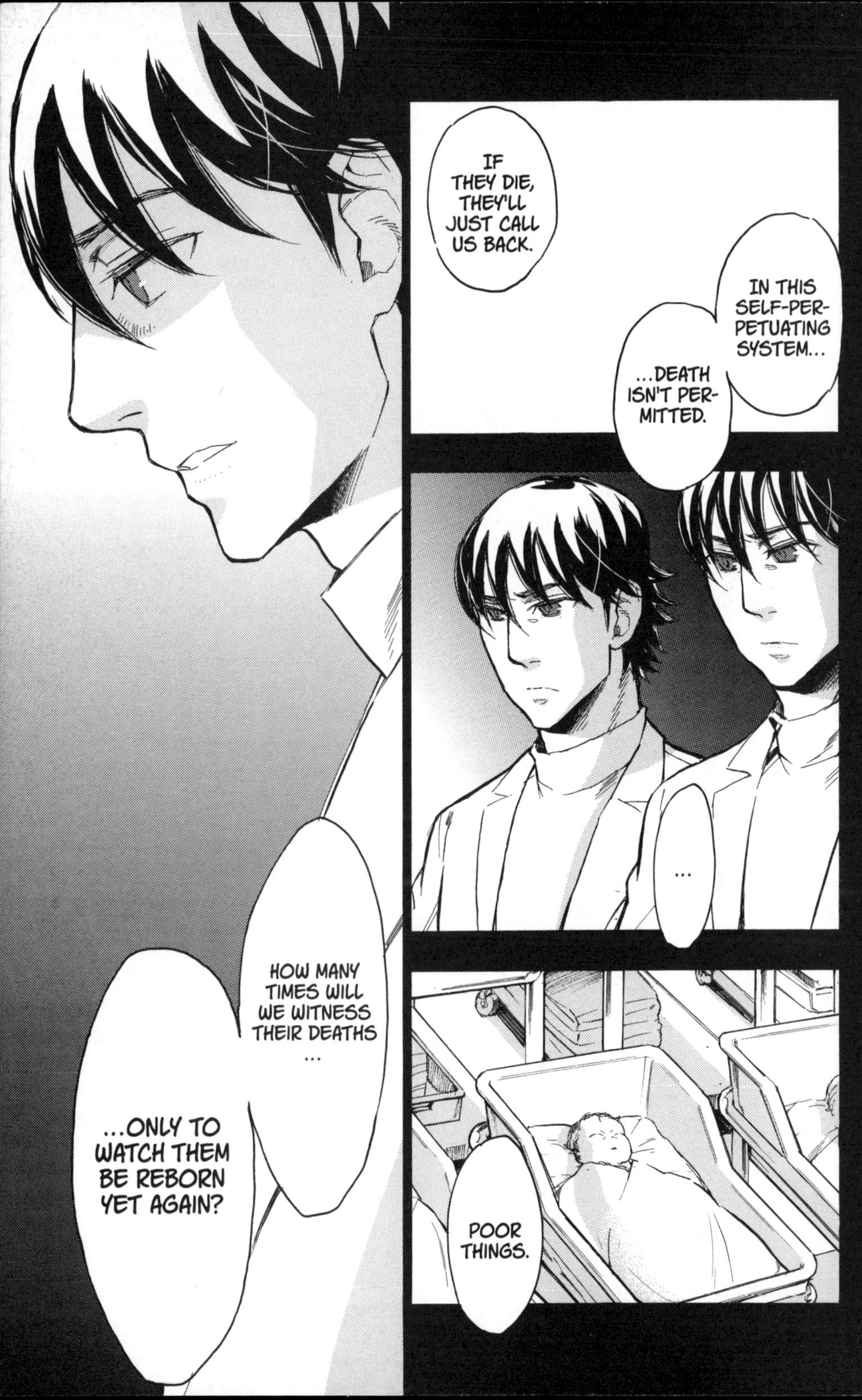
IF THEY DIE, THEY'LL JUST CALL US BACK.
IN THIS SELF-PER-PETUATING SYSTEM...
...DEATH ISN'T PER-MITTED.
...
POOR THINGS.
HOW MANY TIMES WILL WE WITNESS THEIR DEATHS...
...ONLY TO WATCH THEM BE REBORN YET AGAIN?

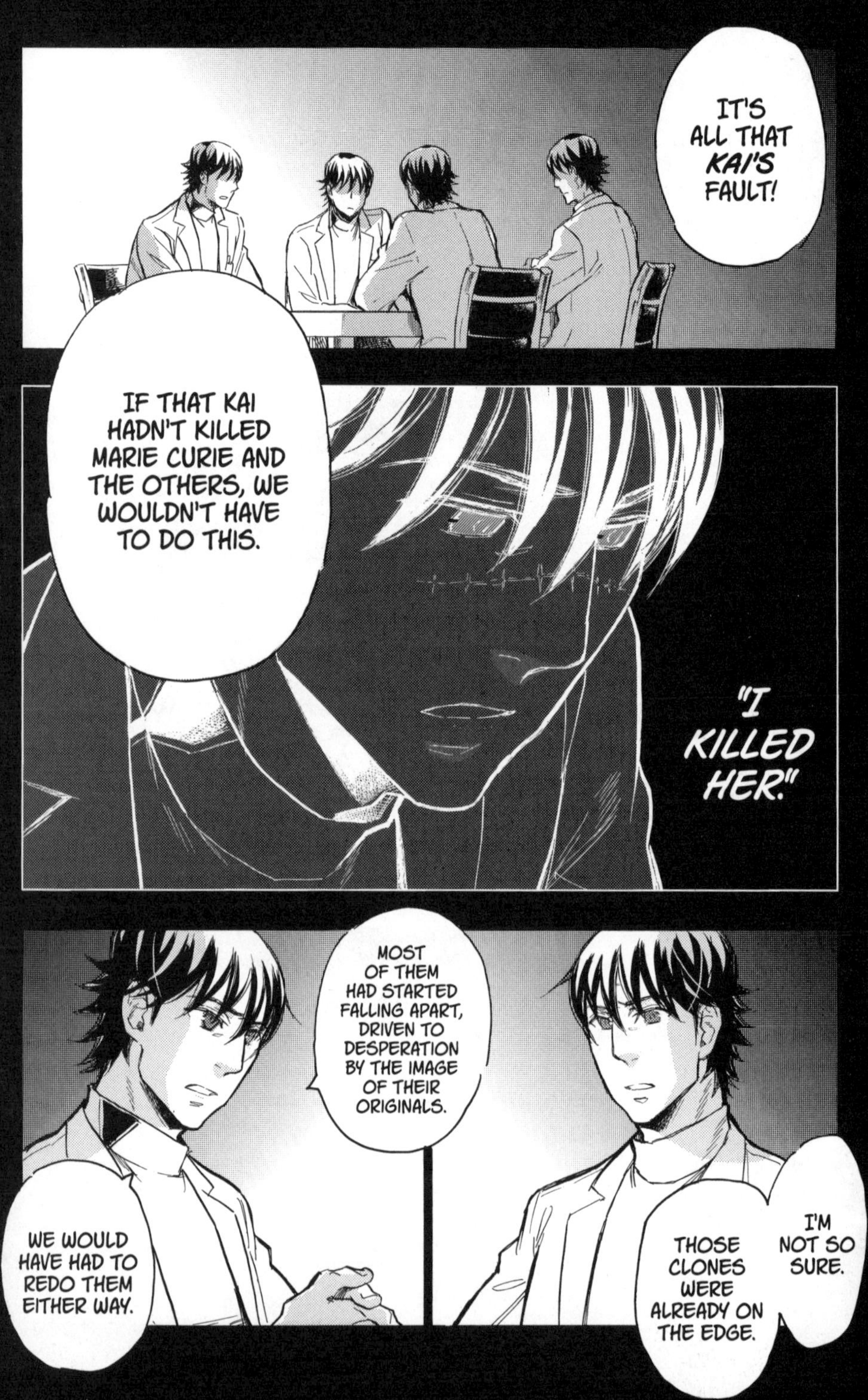
IT'S ALL THAT *KAI'S* FAULT!
IF THAT KAI HADN'T KILLED MARIE CURIE AND THE OTHERS, WE WOULDN'T HAVE TO DO THIS.
"I KILLED HER."
WE WOULD HAVE HAD TO REDO THEM EITHER WAY.
I'M NOT SO SURE.
THOSE CLONES WERE ALREADY ON THE EDGE.
MOST OF THEM HAD STARTED FALLING APART, DRIVEN TO DESPERATION BY THE IMAGE OF THEIR ORIGINALS.

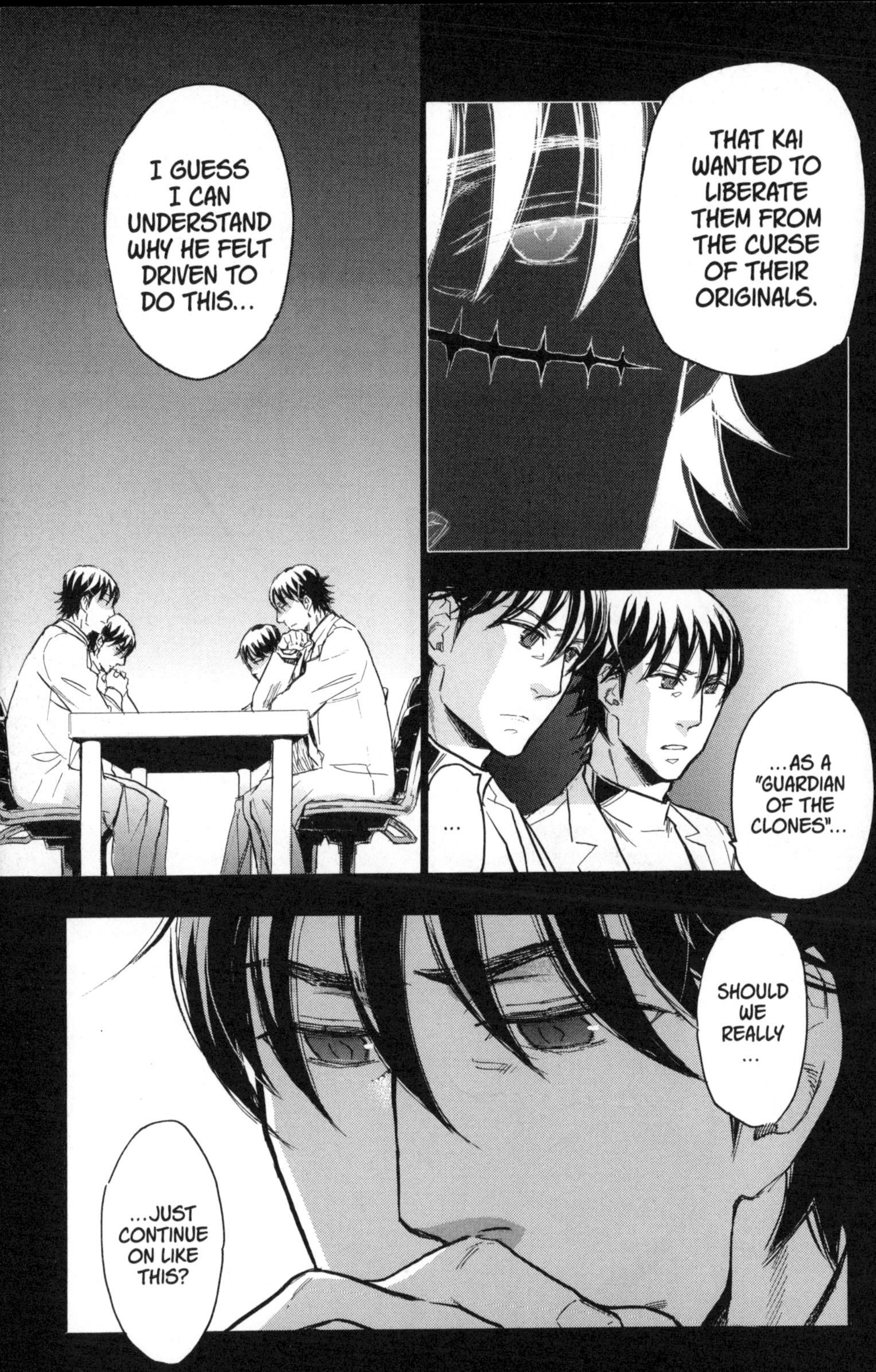
THAT KAI WANTED TO LIBERATE THEM FROM THE CURSE OF THEIR ORIGINALS.
I GUESS I CAN UNDERSTAND WHY HE FELT DRIVEN TO DO THIS...
...AS A "GUARDIAN OF THE CLONES"...
...
SHOULD WE REALLY ...
...JUST CONTINUE ON LIKE THIS?

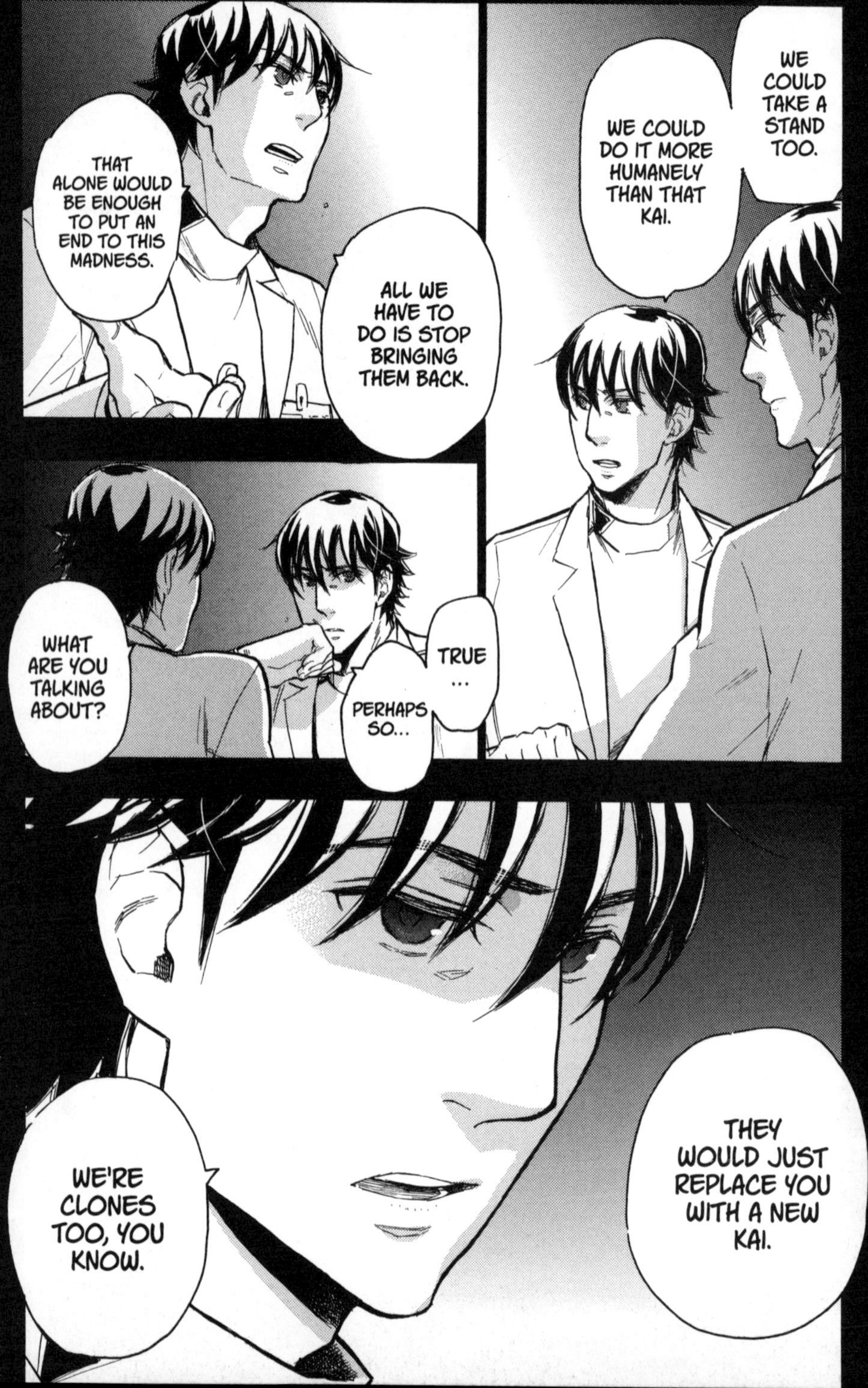
WE COULD TAKE A STAND TOO.
WE COULD DO IT MORE HUMANELY THAN THAT KAI.
ALL WE HAVE TO DO IS STOP BRINGING THEM BACK.
THAT ALONE WOULD BE ENOUGH TO PUT AN END TO THIS MADNESS.
TRUE...
PERHAPS SO...
WHAT ARE YOU TALKING ABOUT?
THEY WOULD JUST REPLACE YOU WITH A NEW KAI.
WE'RE CLONES TOO, YOU KNOW.

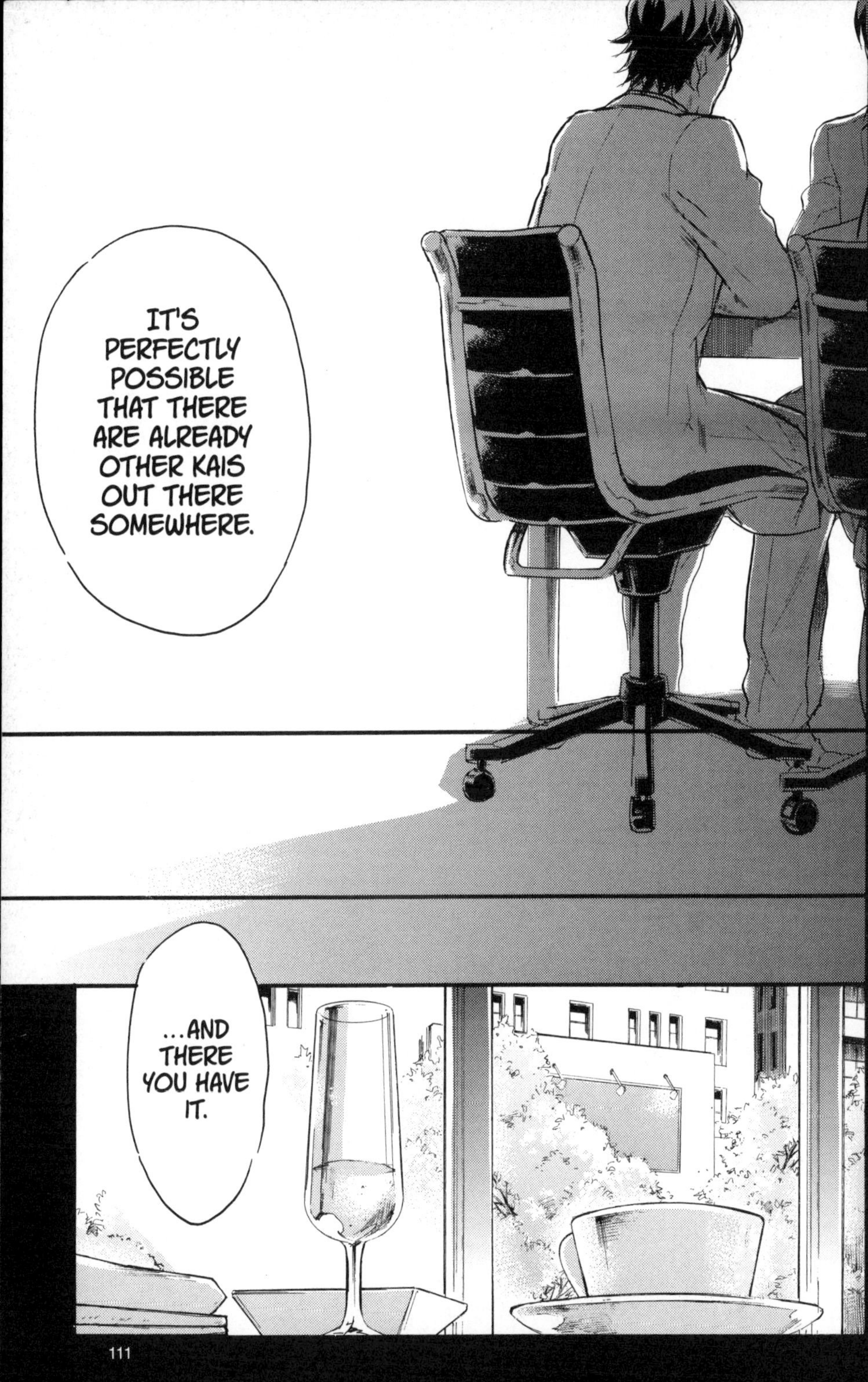
IT'S PERFECTLY POSSIBLE THAT THERE ARE ALREADY OTHER KAIS OUT THERE SOMEWHERE.
...AND THERE YOU HAVE IT.

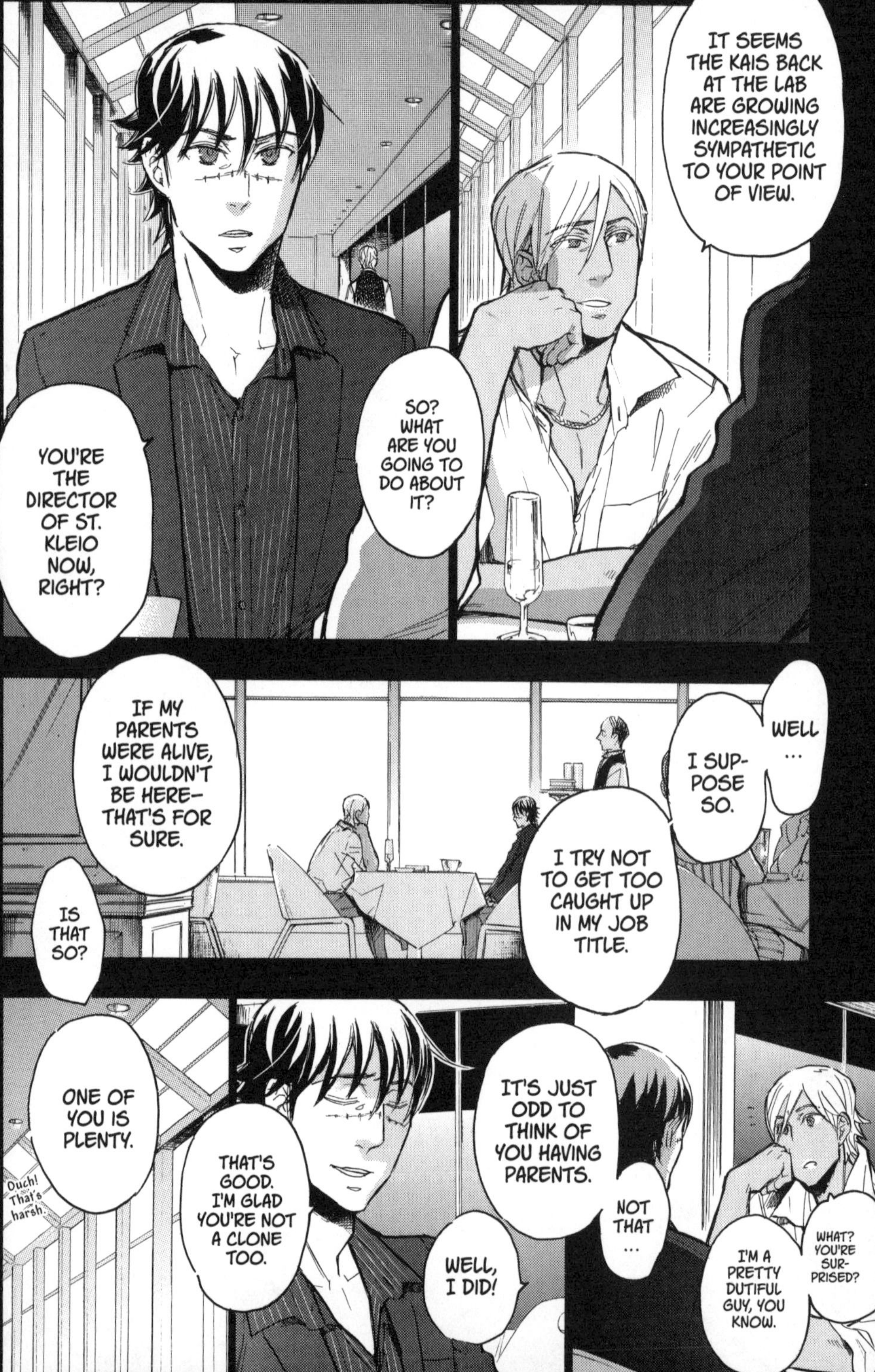
IT SEEMS THE KAIS BACK AT THE LAB ARE GROWING INCREASINGLY SYMPATHETIC TO YOUR POINT OF VIEW.
SO? WHAT ARE YOU GOING TO DO ABOUT IT?
YOU'RE THE DIRECTOR OF ST. KLEIO NOW, RIGHT?
WELL ...
I SUP-POSE SO.
I TRY NOT TO GET TOO CAUGHT UP IN MY JOB TITLE.
IF MY PARENTS WERE ALIVE, I WOULDN'T BE HERE—THAT'S FOR SURE.
IS THAT SO?
IT'S JUST ODD TO THINK OF YOU HAVING PARENTS.
WHAT? YOU'RE SUR-PRISED?
I'M A PRETTY DUTIFUL GUY, YOU KNOW.
NOT THAT ...
WELL, I DID!
THAT'S GOOD. I'M GLAD YOU'RE NOT A CLONE TOO.
ONE OF YOU IS PLENTY.
Ouch! That's harsh.

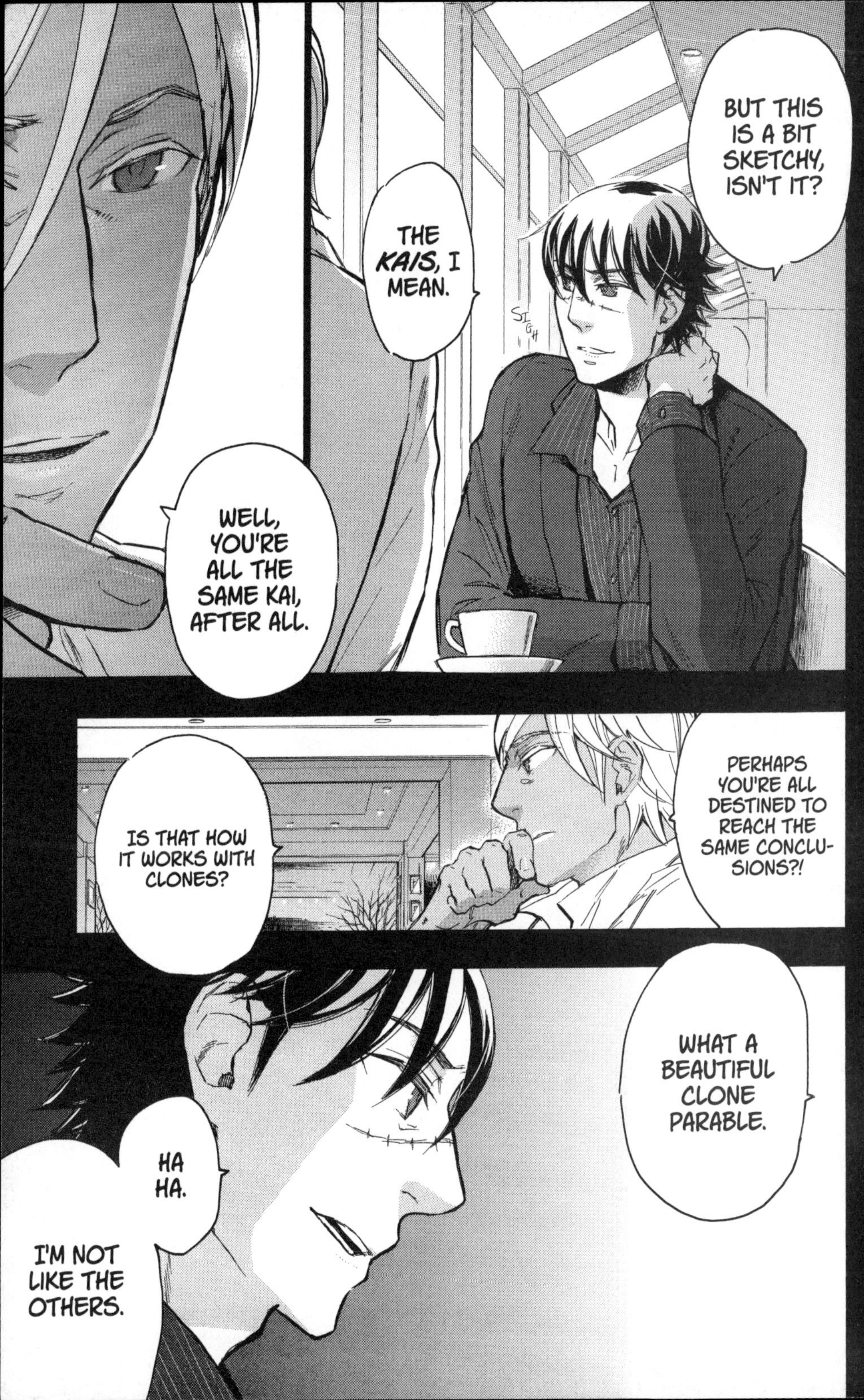
BUT THIS IS A BIT SKETCHY, ISN'T IT?
THE *KAIS*, I MEAN.
SIGH
WELL, YOU'RE ALL THE SAME KAI, AFTER ALL.
PERHAPS YOU'RE ALL DESTINED TO REACH THE SAME CONCLUSIONS?!
IS THAT HOW IT WORKS WITH CLONES?
WHAT A BEAUTIFUL CLONE PARABLE.
HA HA.
I'M NOT LIKE THE OTHERS.

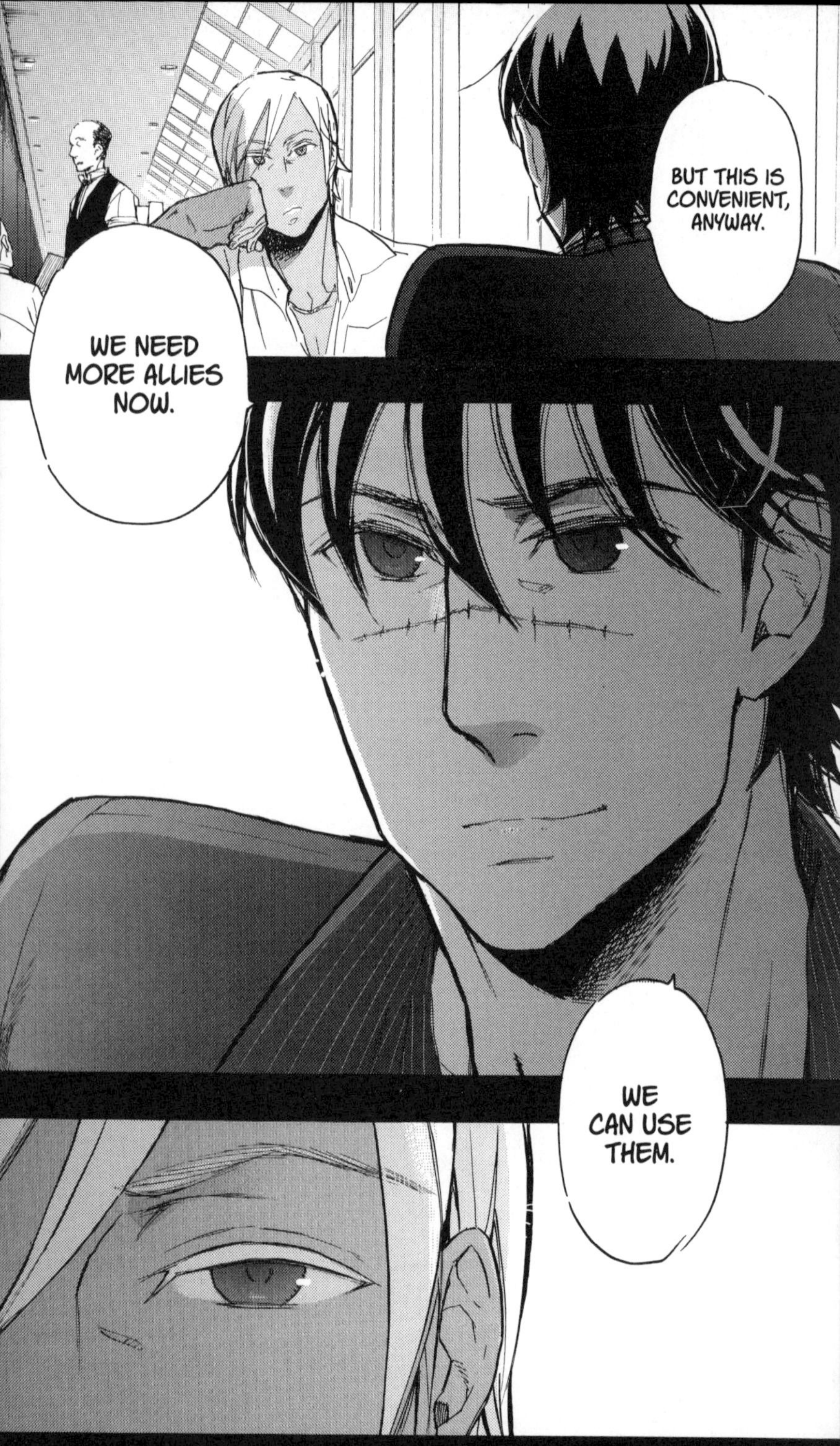
BUT THIS IS CONVENIENT, ANYWAY.
WE NEED MORE ALLIES NOW.
WE CAN USE THEM.

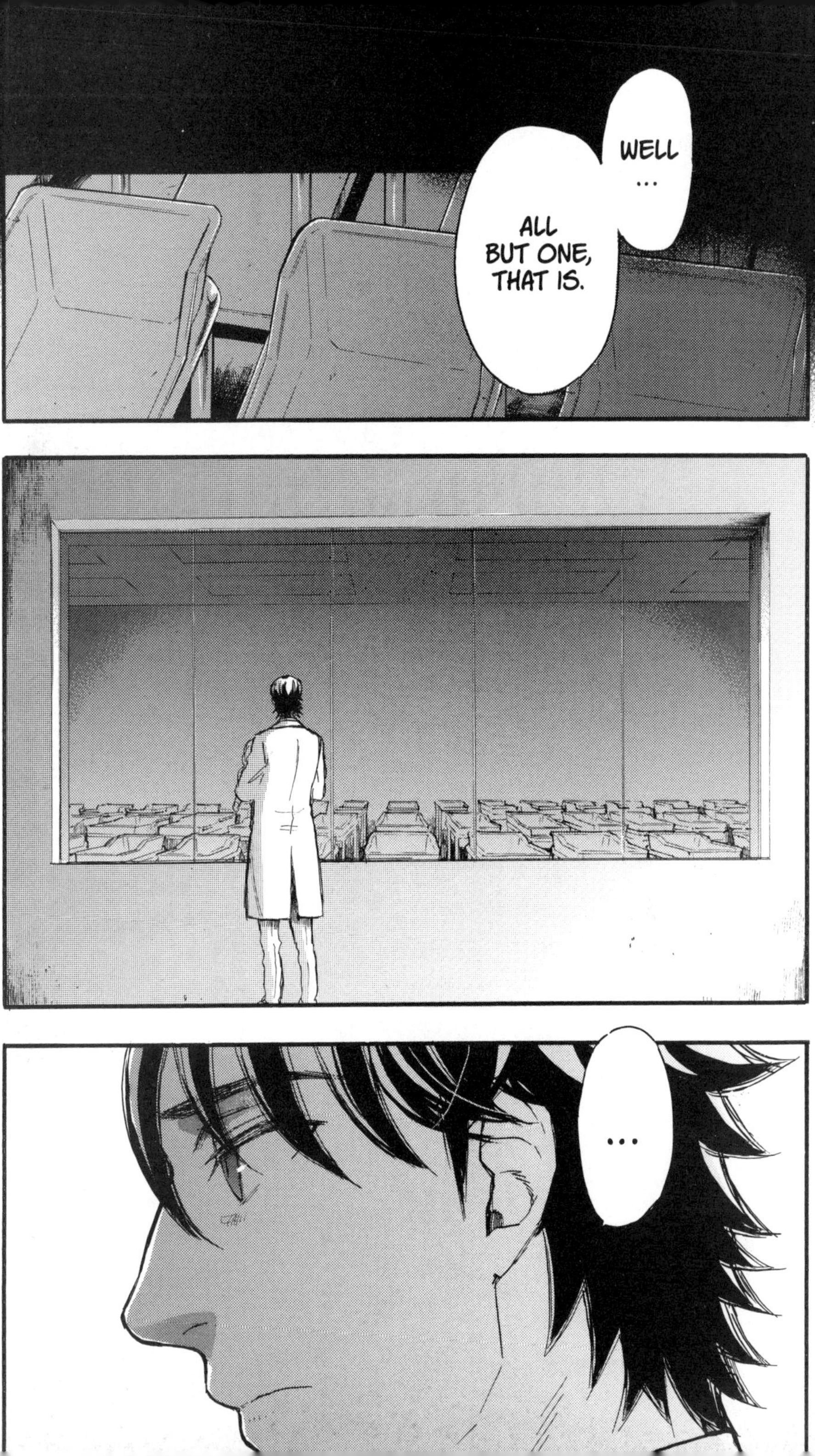
WELL ...
ALL BUT ONE, THAT IS.
...

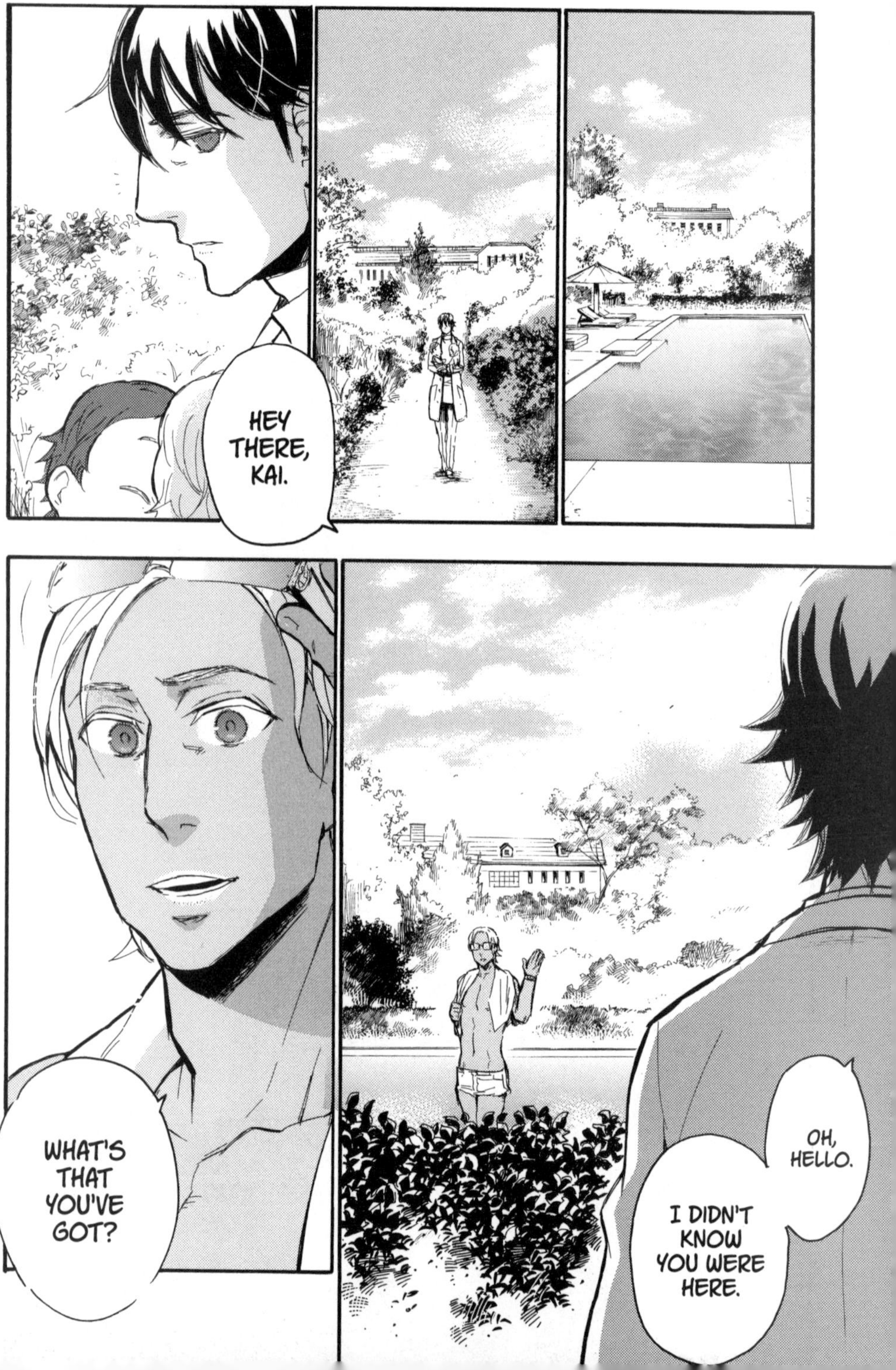
HEY THERE, KAI.
OH, HELLO.
I DIDN'T KNOW YOU WERE HERE.
WHAT'S THAT YOU'VE GOT?

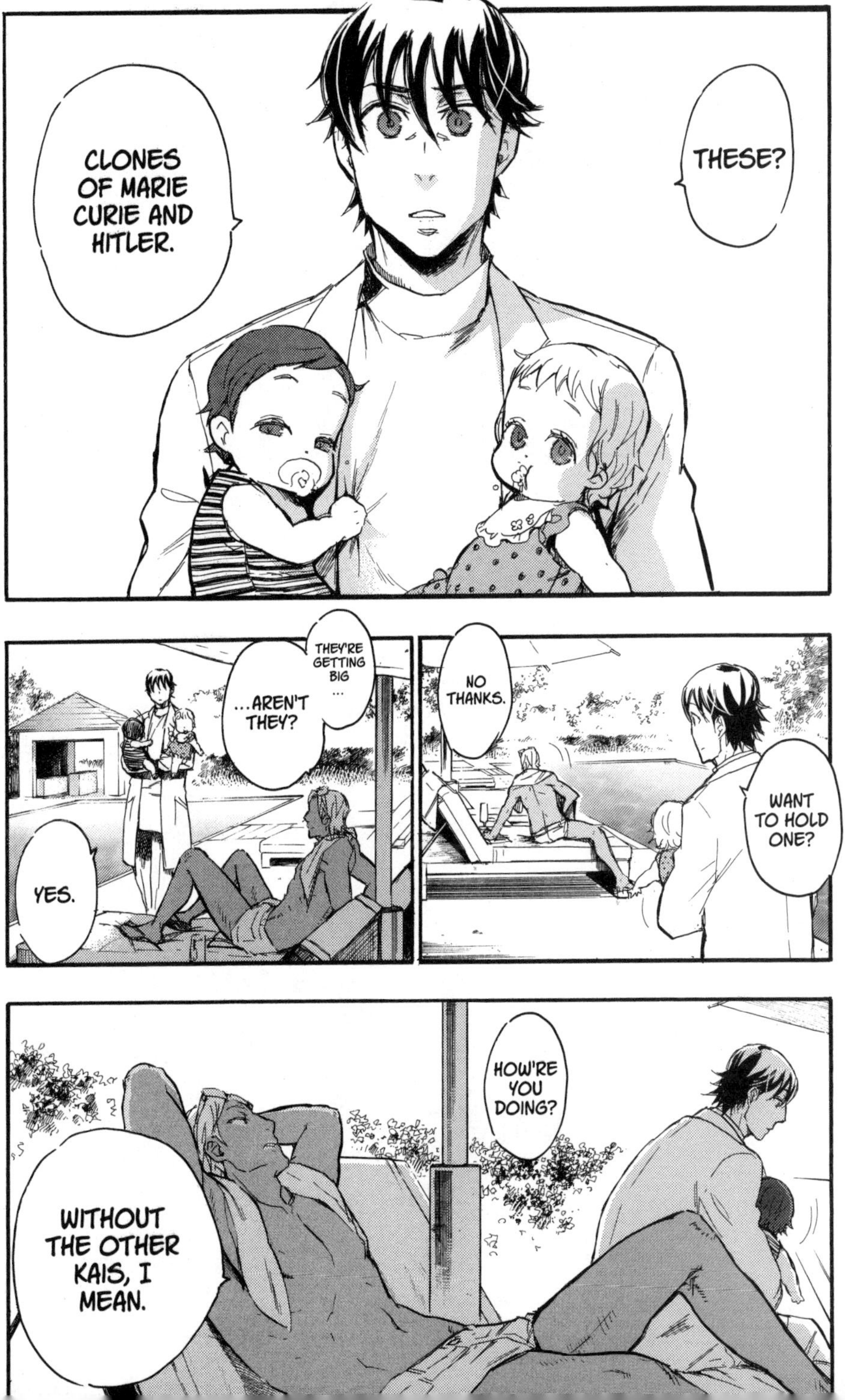
THESE?
CLONES OF MARIE CURIE AND HITLER.
WANT TO HOLD ONE?
NO THANKS.
THEY'RE GETTING BIG...
...AREN'T THEY?
YES.
HOW'RE YOU DOING?
WITHOUT THE OTHER KAIS, I MEAN.

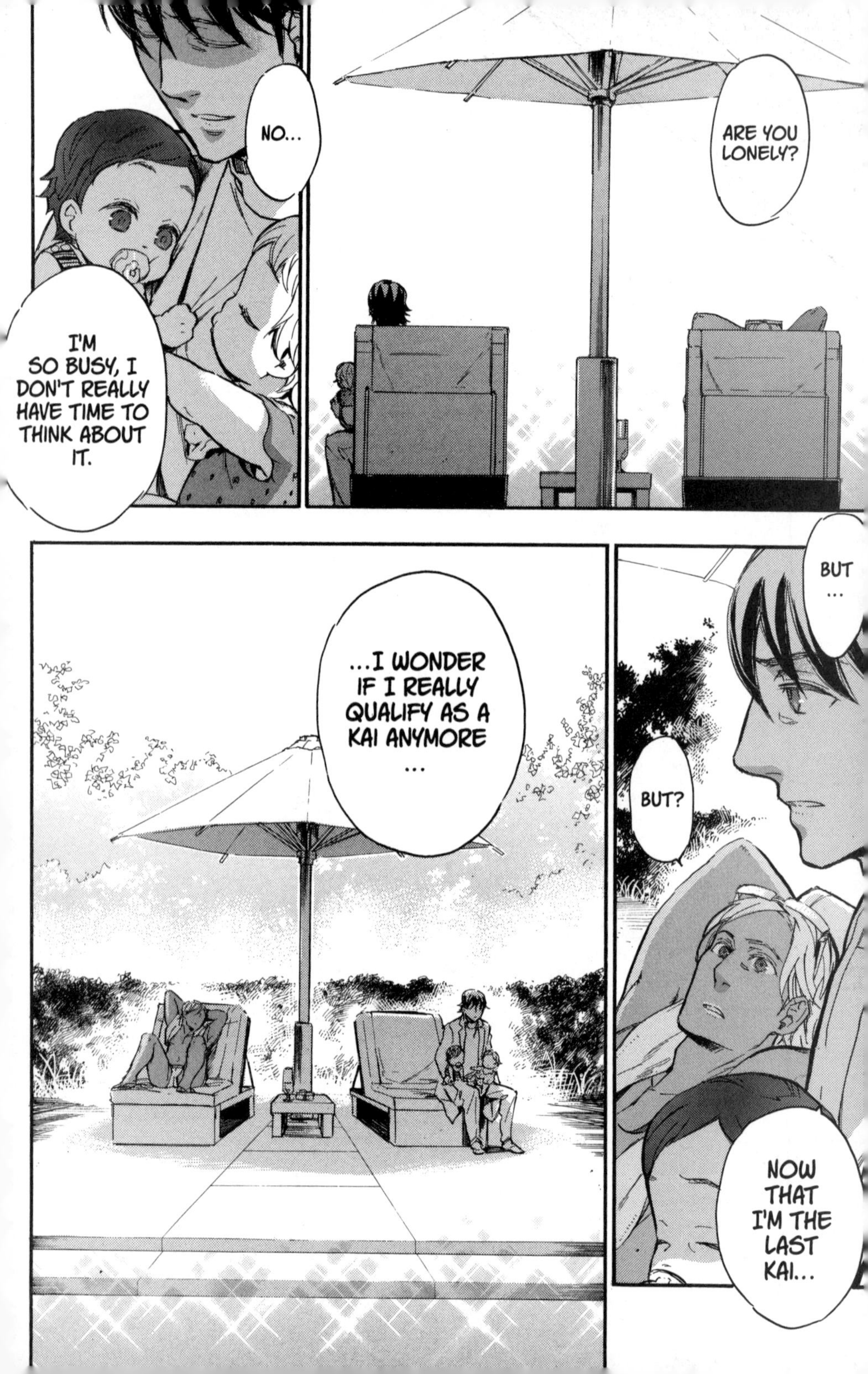
ARE YOU LONELY?
NO...
I'M SO BUSY, I DON'T REALLY HAVE TIME TO THINK ABOUT IT.
BUT...
BUT?
NOW THAT I'M THE LAST KAI...
...I WONDER IF I REALLY QUALIFY AS A KAI ANYMORE...

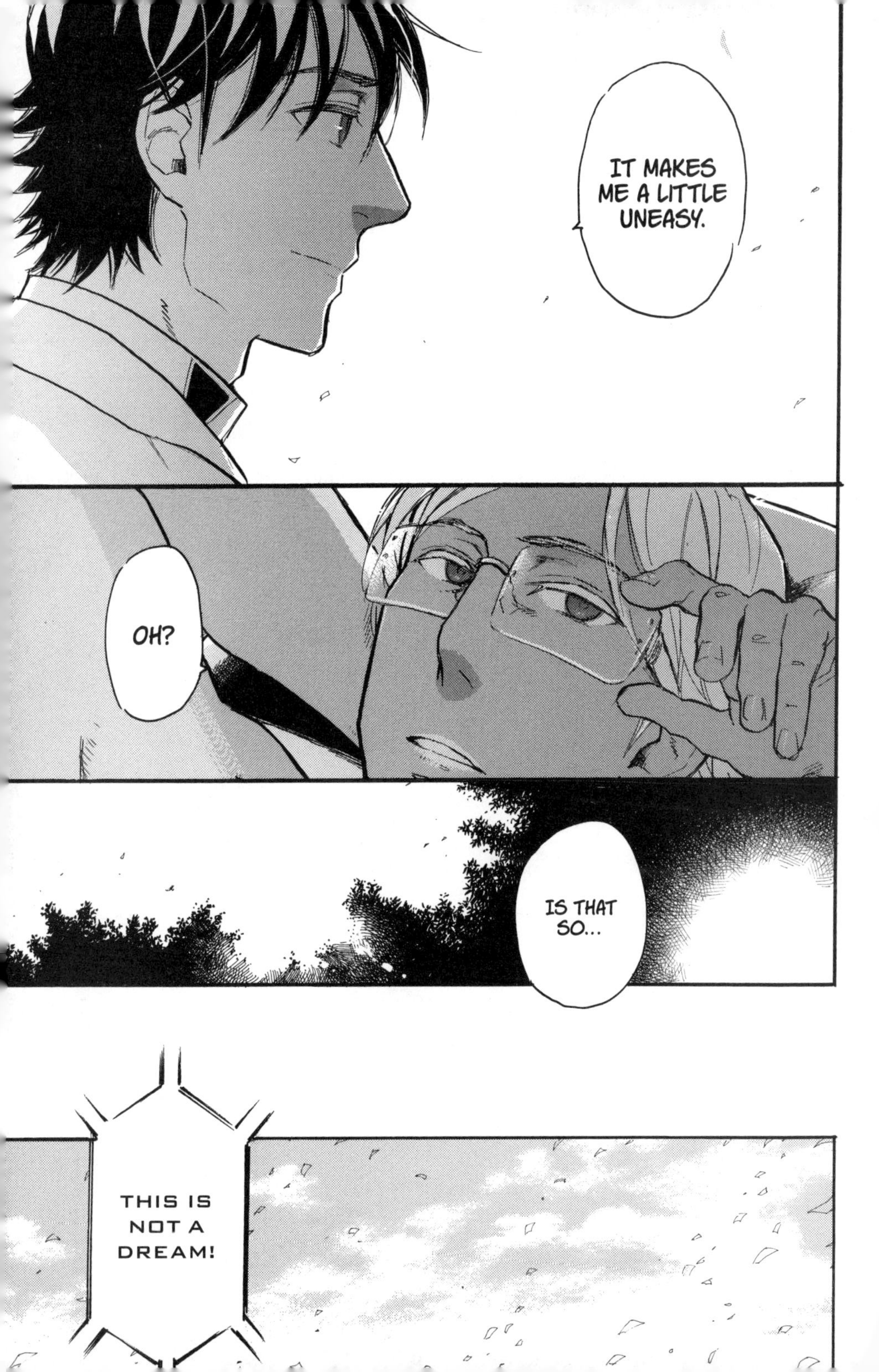
IT MAKES ME A LITTLE UNEASY.
OH?
IS THAT SO...
THIS IS NOT A DREAM!

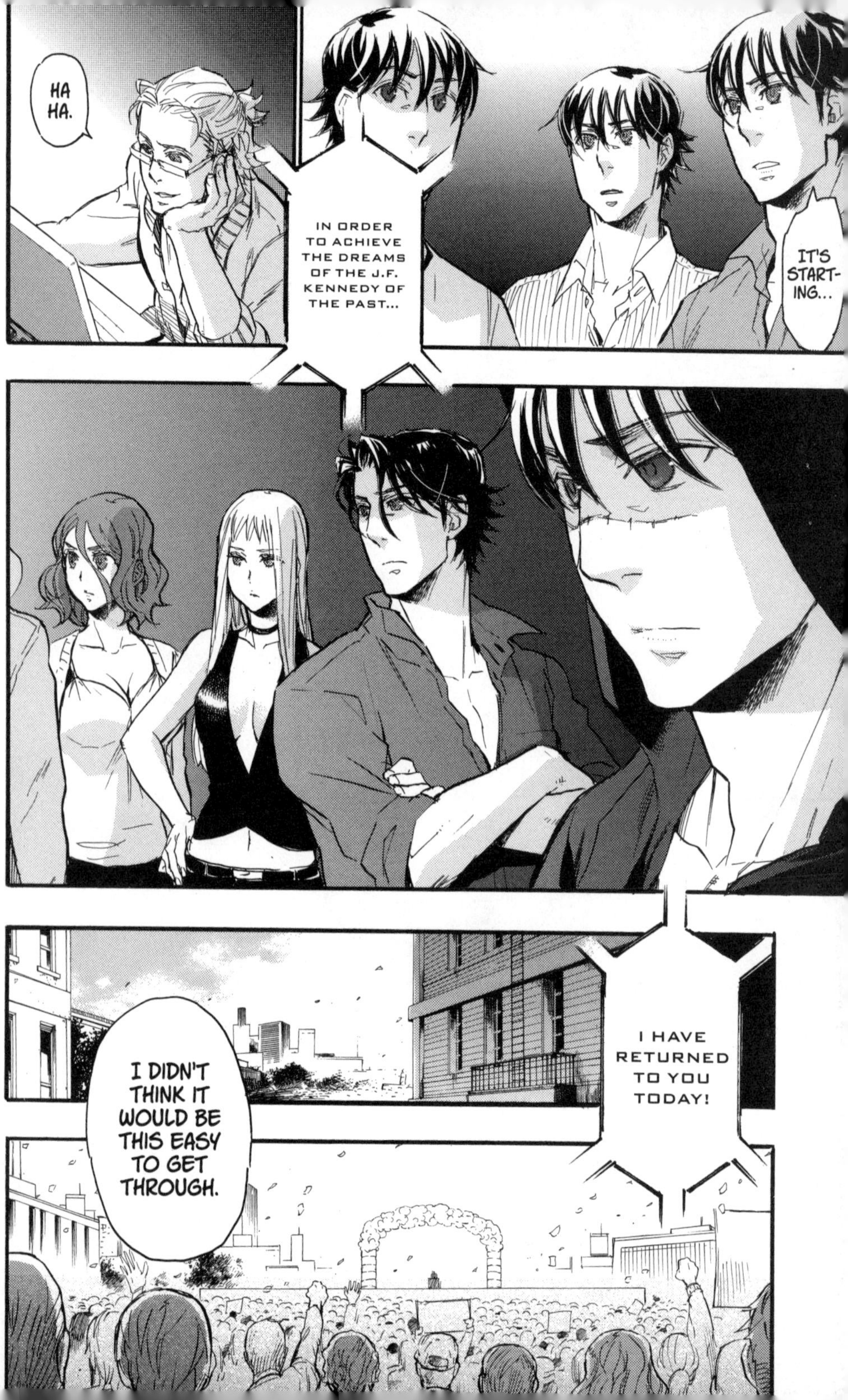
IT'S START-ING...
IN ORDER TO ACHIEVE THE DREAMS OF THE J.F. KENNEDY OF THE PAST...
HA HA.
I HAVE RETURNED TO YOU TODAY!
I DIDN'T THINK IT WOULD BE THIS EASY TO GET THROUGH.

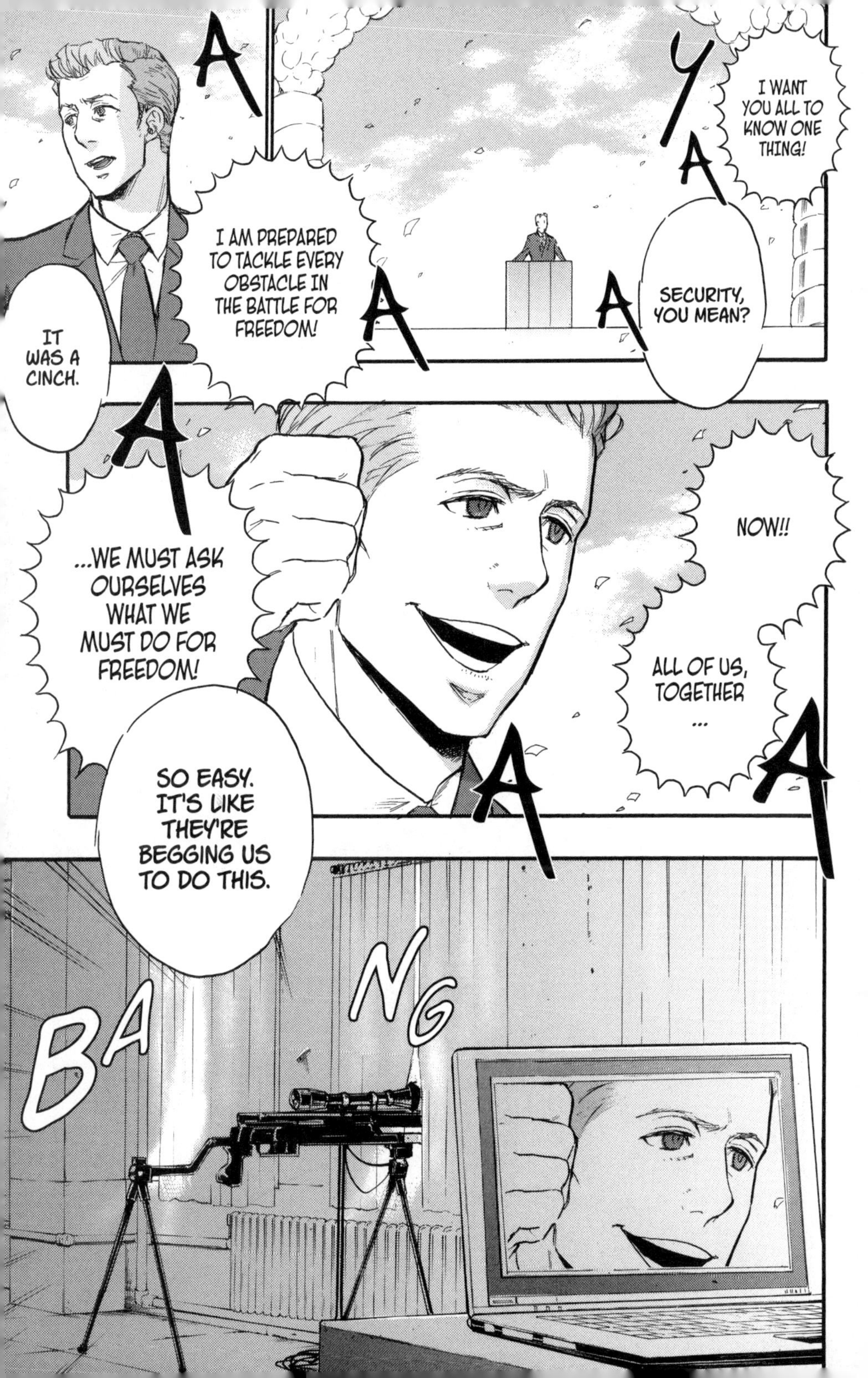
I WANT YOU ALL TO KNOW ONE THING!
SECURITY, YOU MEAN?
I AM PREPARED TO TACKLE EVERY OBSTACLE IN THE BATTLE FOR FREEDOM!
IT WAS A CINCH.
NOW!!
ALL OF US, TOGETHER ...
...WE MUST ASK OURSELVES WHAT WE MUST DO FOR FREEDOM!
SO EASY. IT'S LIKE THEY'RE BEGGING US TO DO THIS.
BANG

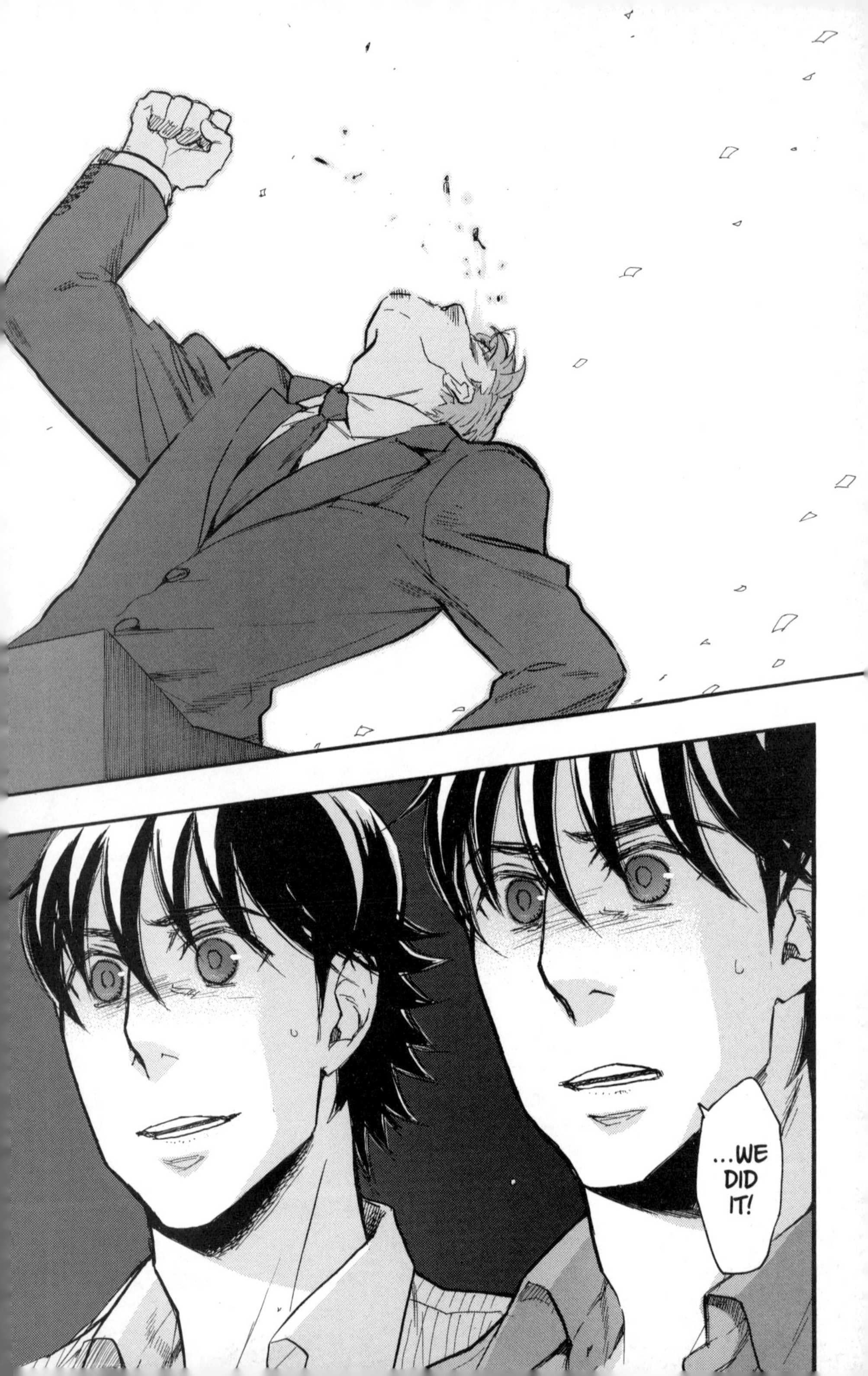
...WE DID IT!

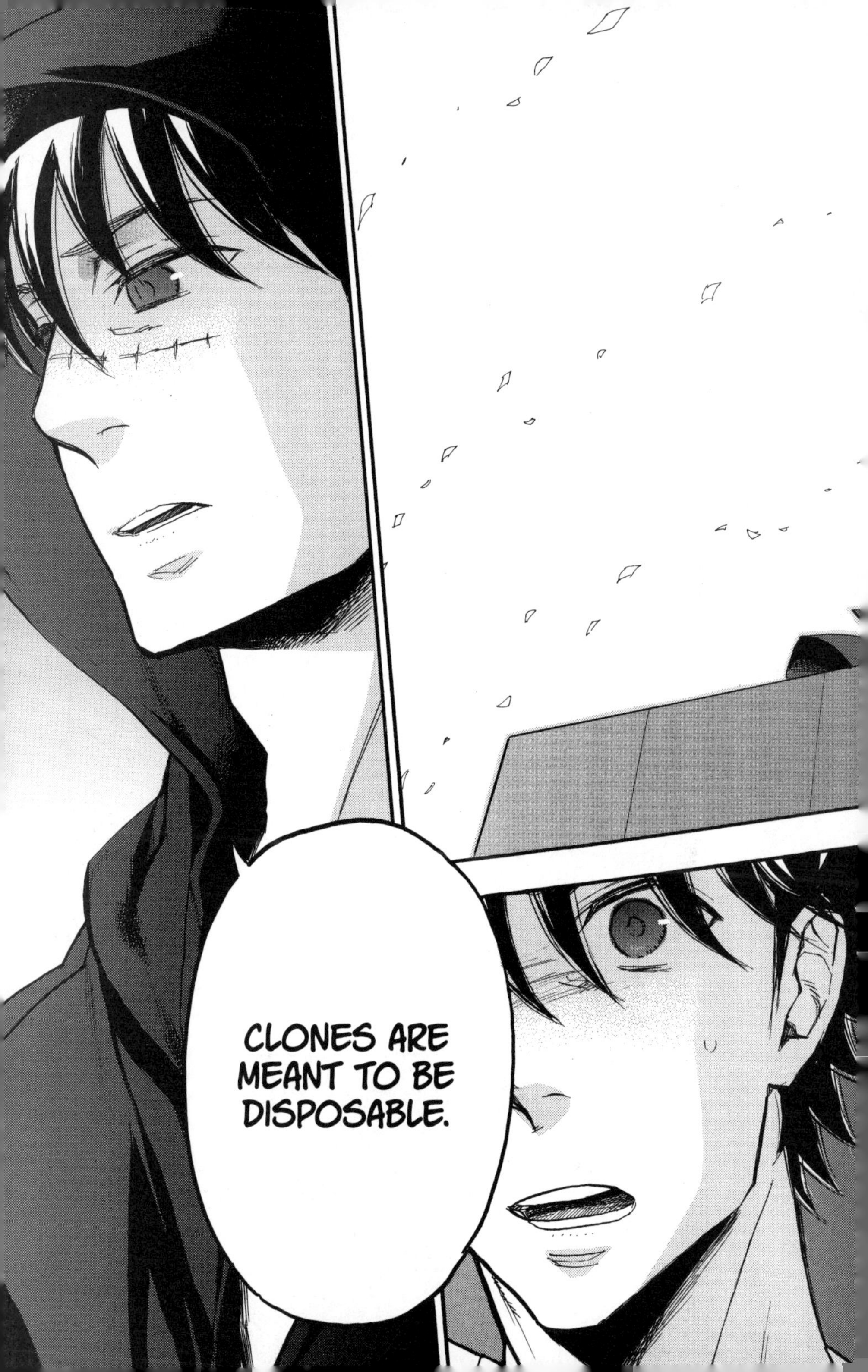
CLONES ARE MEANT TO BE DISPOSABLE.

FO OM

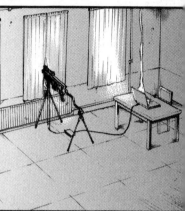

NOW
...

...
LET US
BEGIN.

NEXT
UP IS ST.
KLEIO...

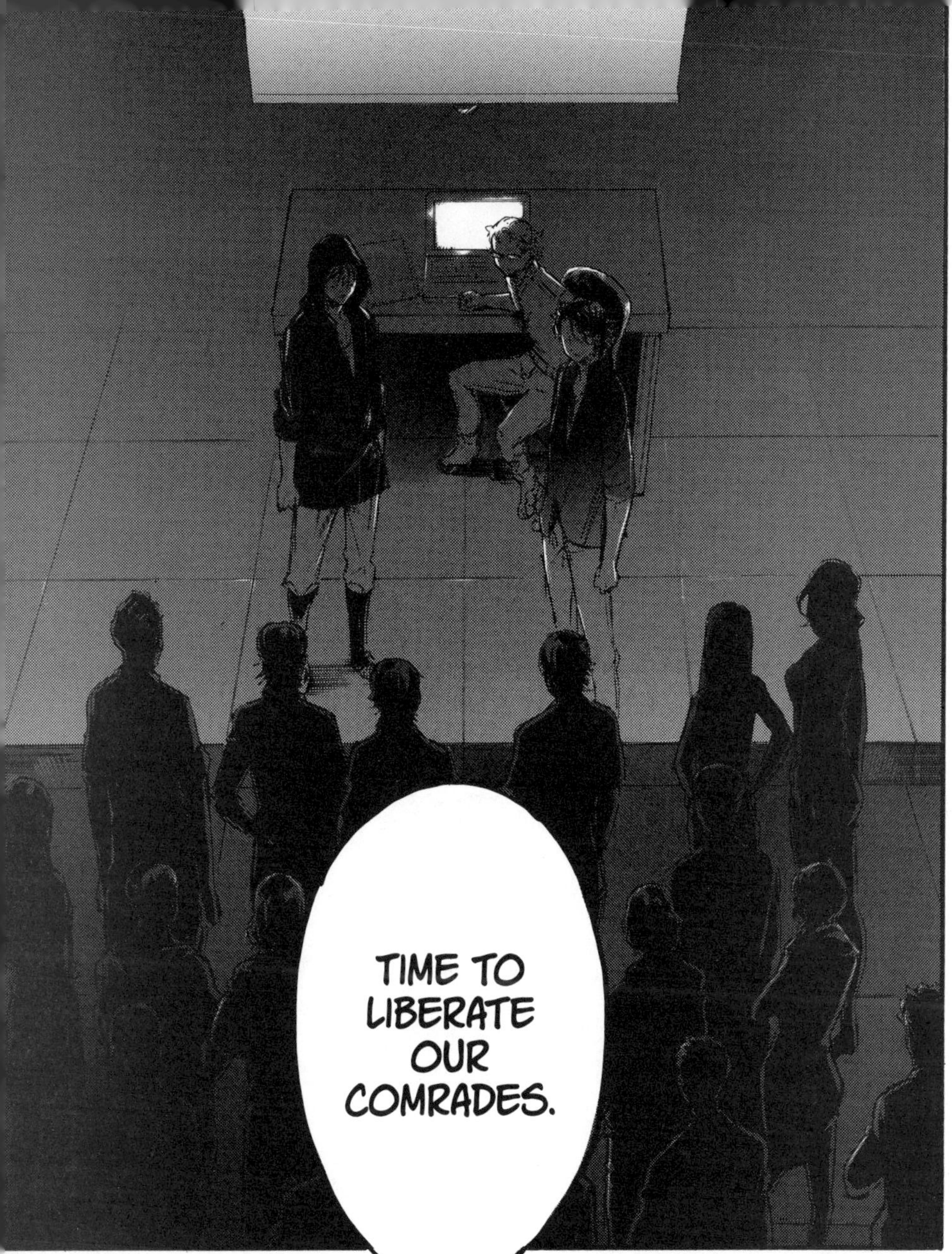
TIME TO LIBERATE OUR COMRADES.

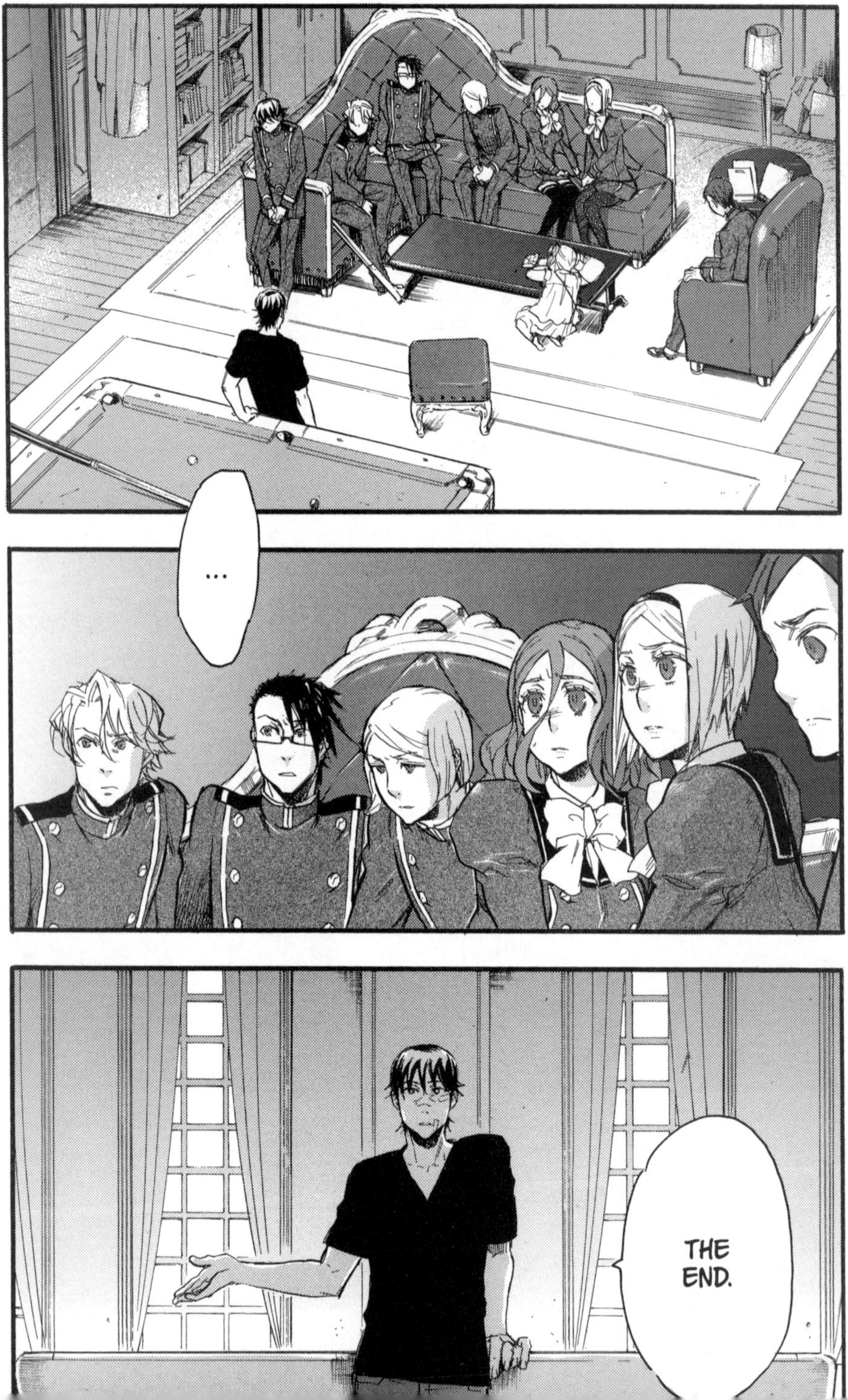
...
THE END.

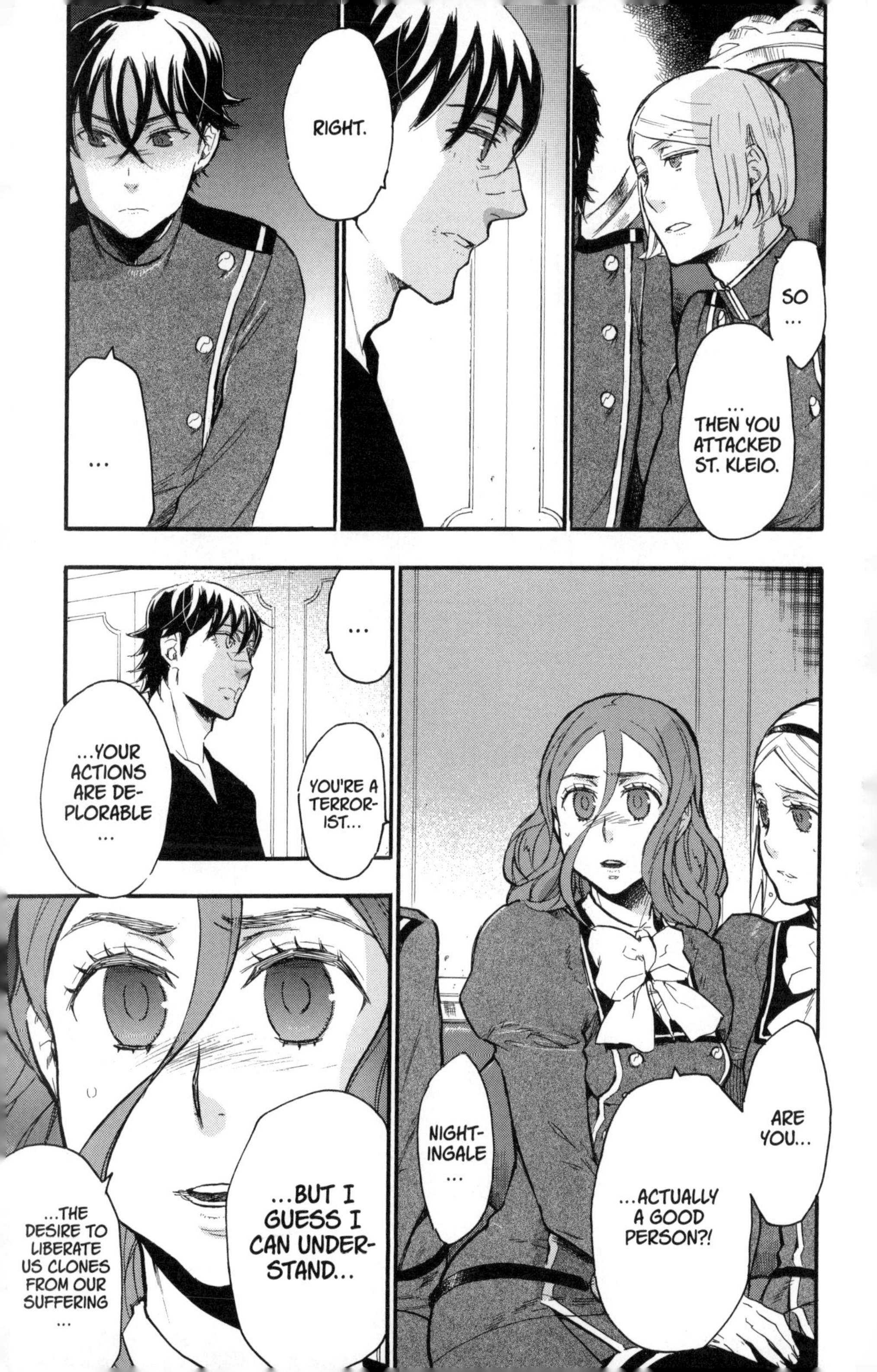
SO...
...THEN YOU ATTACKED ST. KLEIO.
RIGHT.
...
ARE YOU...
...ACTUALLY A GOOD PERSON?!
NIGHT-INGALE...
...
YOU'RE A TERROR-IST...
...YOUR ACTIONS ARE DE-PLORABLE...
...BUT I GUESS I CAN UNDER-STAND...
...THE DESIRE TO LIBERATE US CLONES FROM OUR SUFFERING...

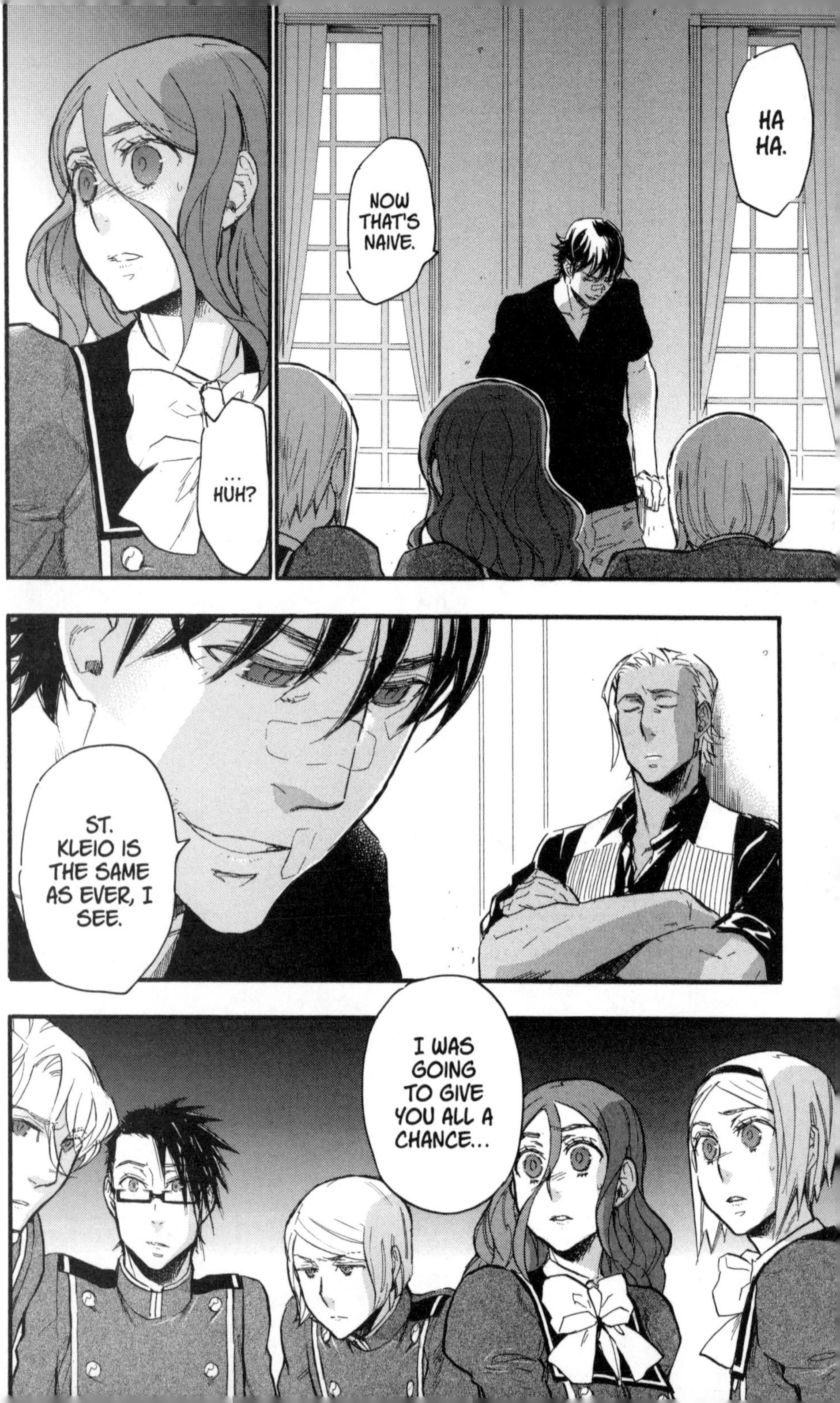
HA HA.
NOW THAT'S NAIVE.
... HUH?
ST. KLEIO IS THE SAME AS EVER, I SEE.
I WAS GOING TO GIVE YOU ALL A CHANCE...

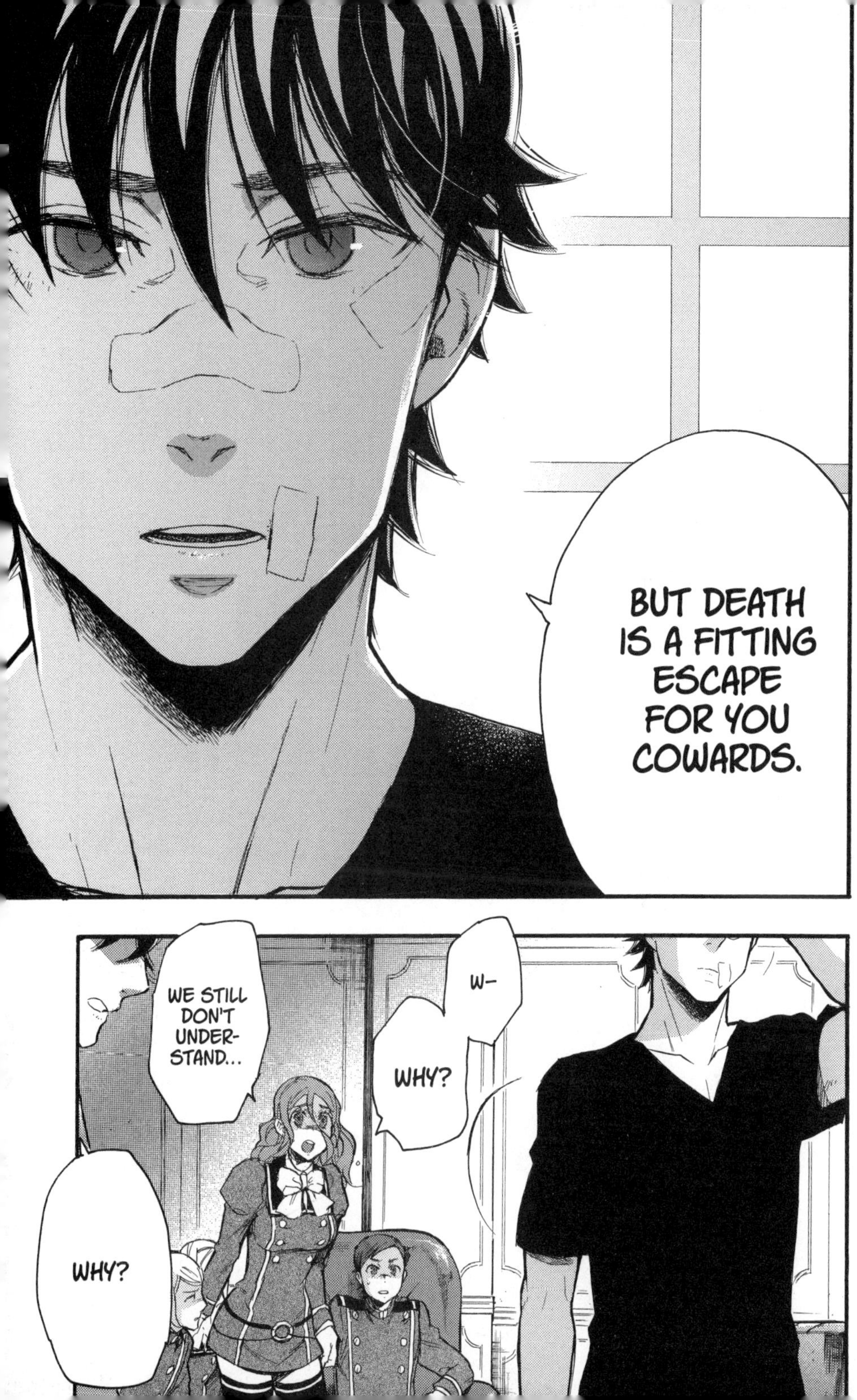
BUT DEATH IS A FITTING ESCAPE FOR YOU COWARDS.
W-
WHY?
WE STILL DON'T UNDER-STAND...
WHY?

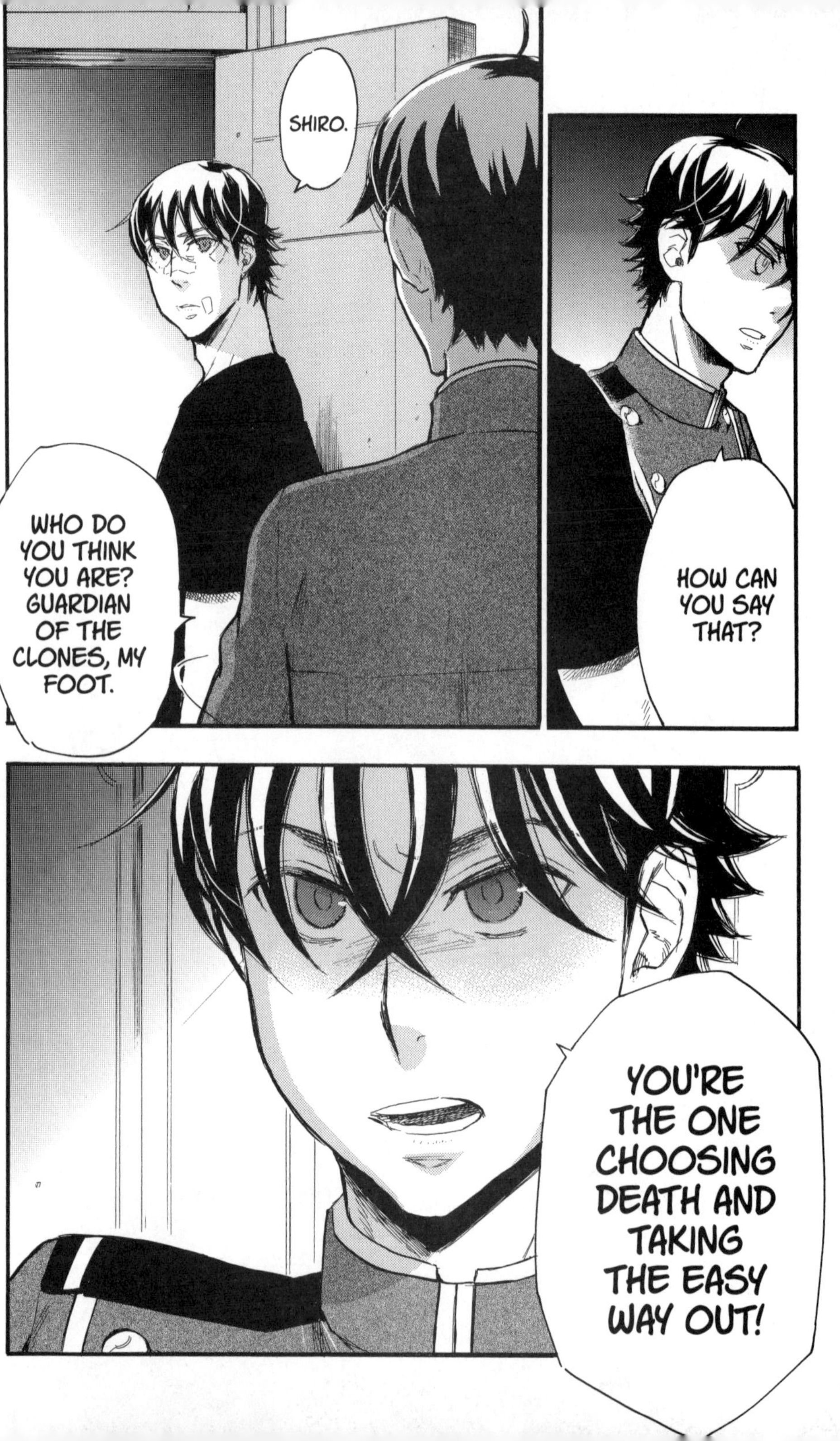
HOW CAN YOU SAY THAT?
SHIRO.
WHO DO YOU THINK YOU ARE? GUARDIAN OF THE CLONES, MY FOOT.
YOU'RE THE ONE CHOOSING DEATH AND TAKING THE EASY WAY OUT!

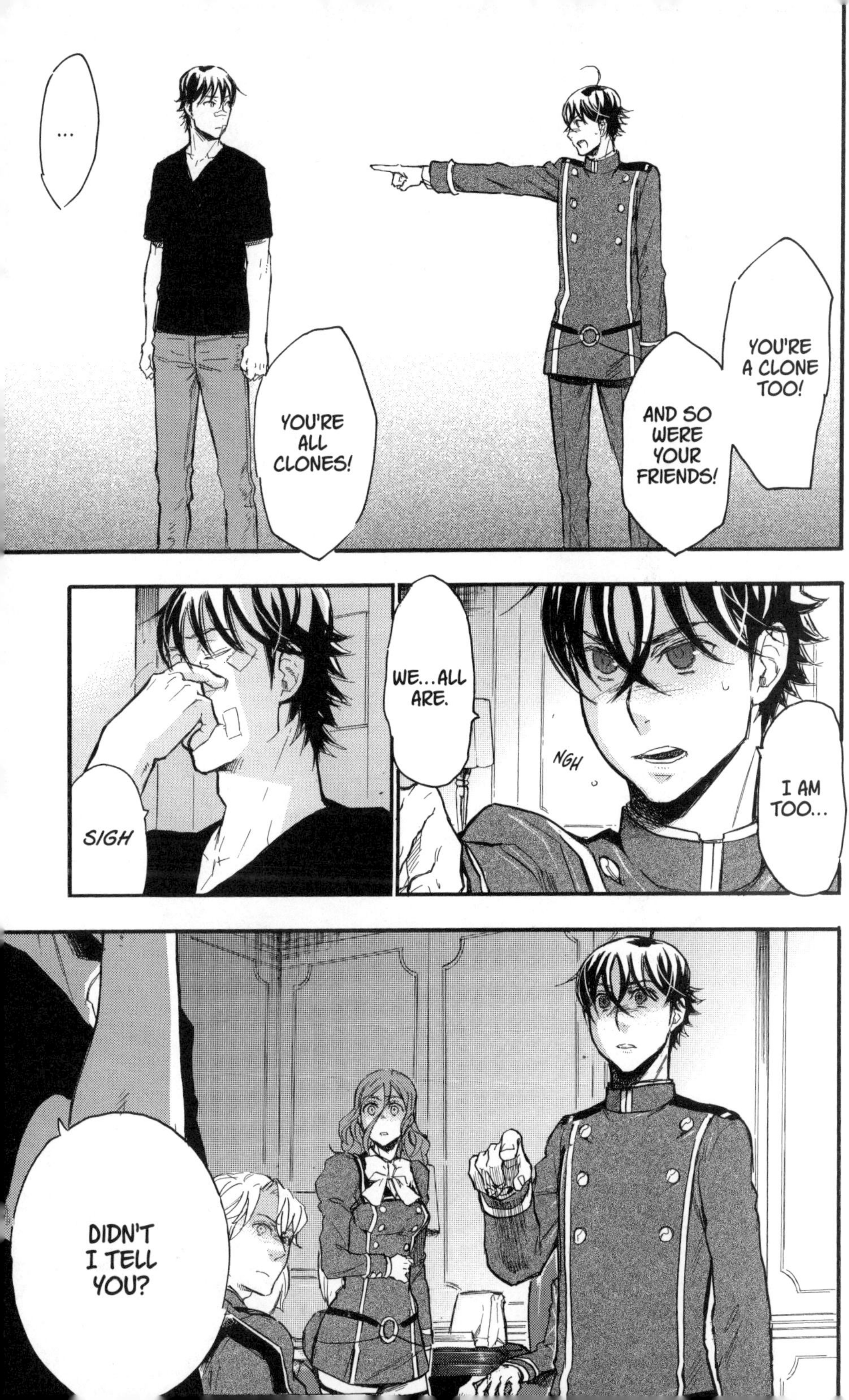
YOU'RE A CLONE TOO!
AND SO WERE YOUR FRIENDS!
YOU'RE ALL CLONES!
...
I AM TOO...
WE...ALL ARE.
NGH
SIGH
DIDN'T I TELL YOU?

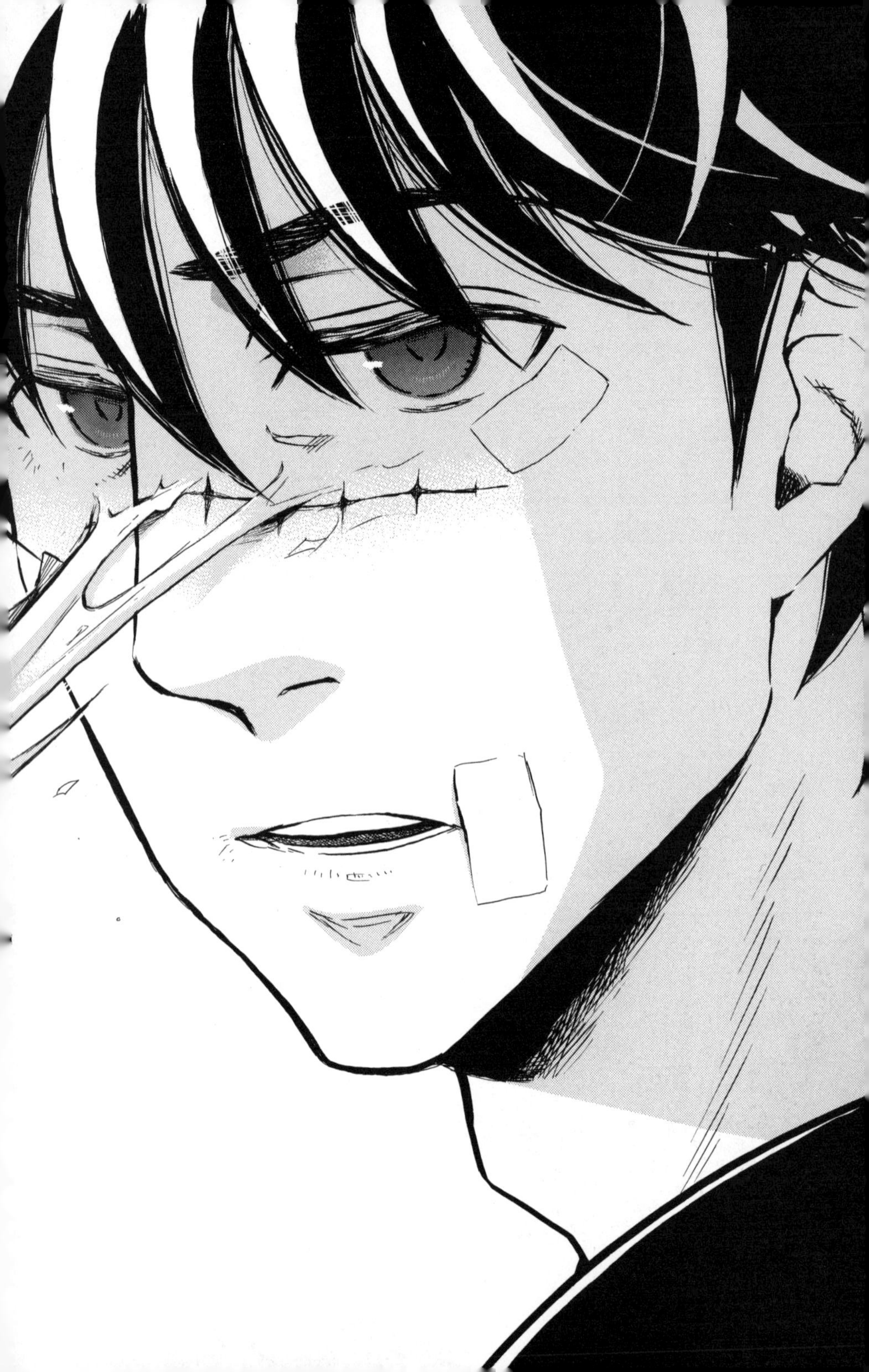

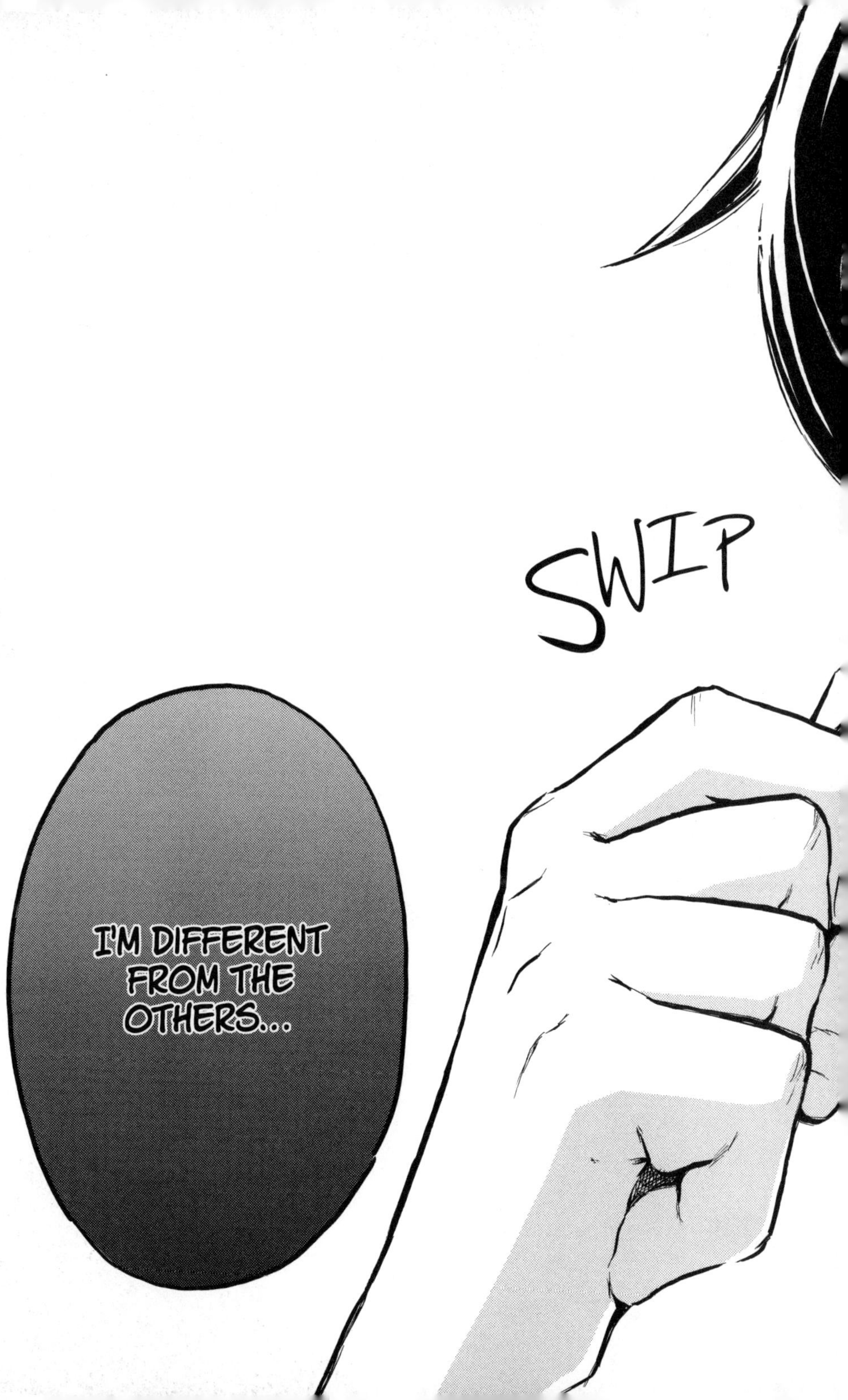
SWIP
I'M DIFFERENT FROM THE OTHERS...

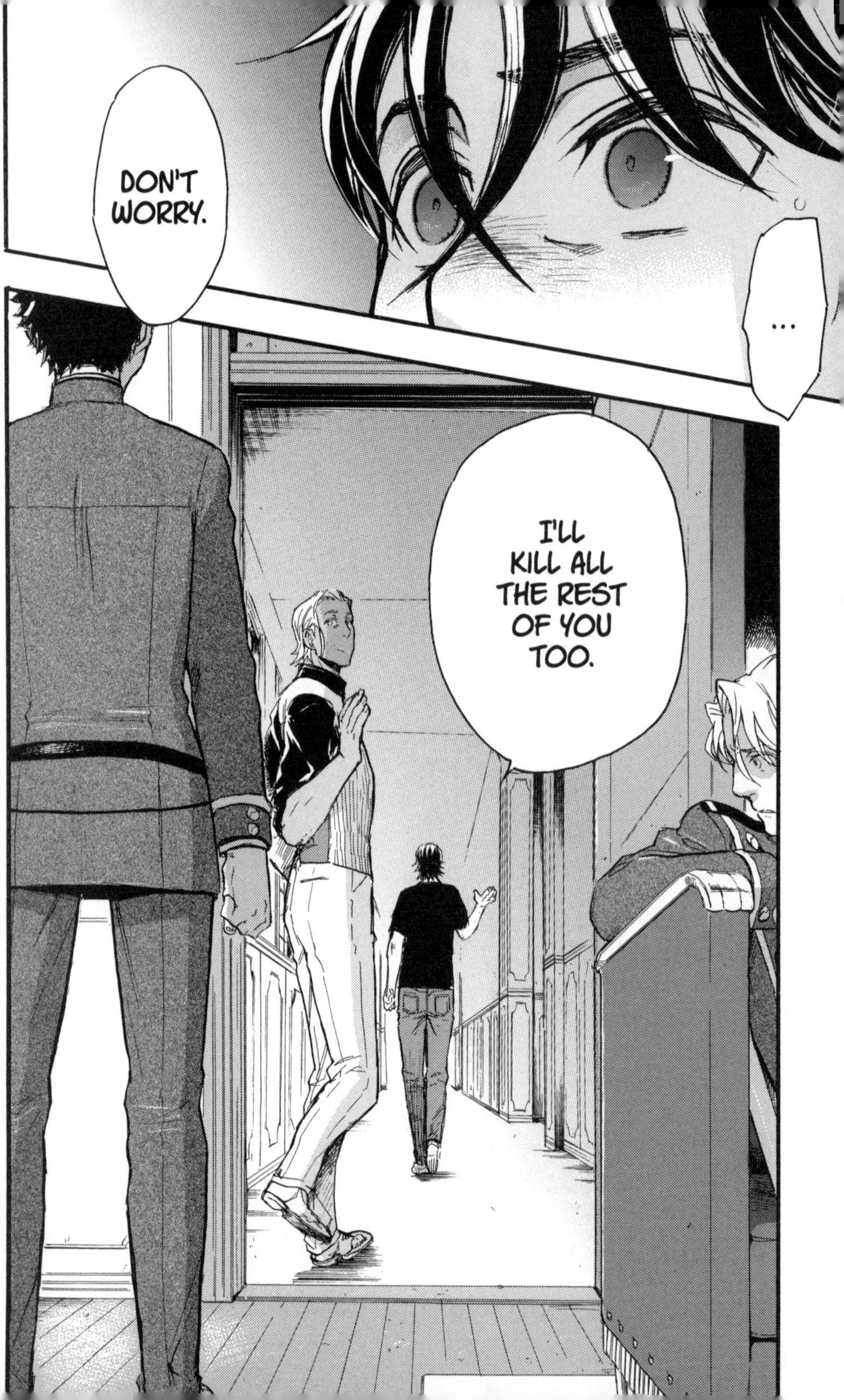
...
DON'T WORRY.
I'LL KILL ALL THE REST OF YOU TOO.

CHAPTER thirty-five

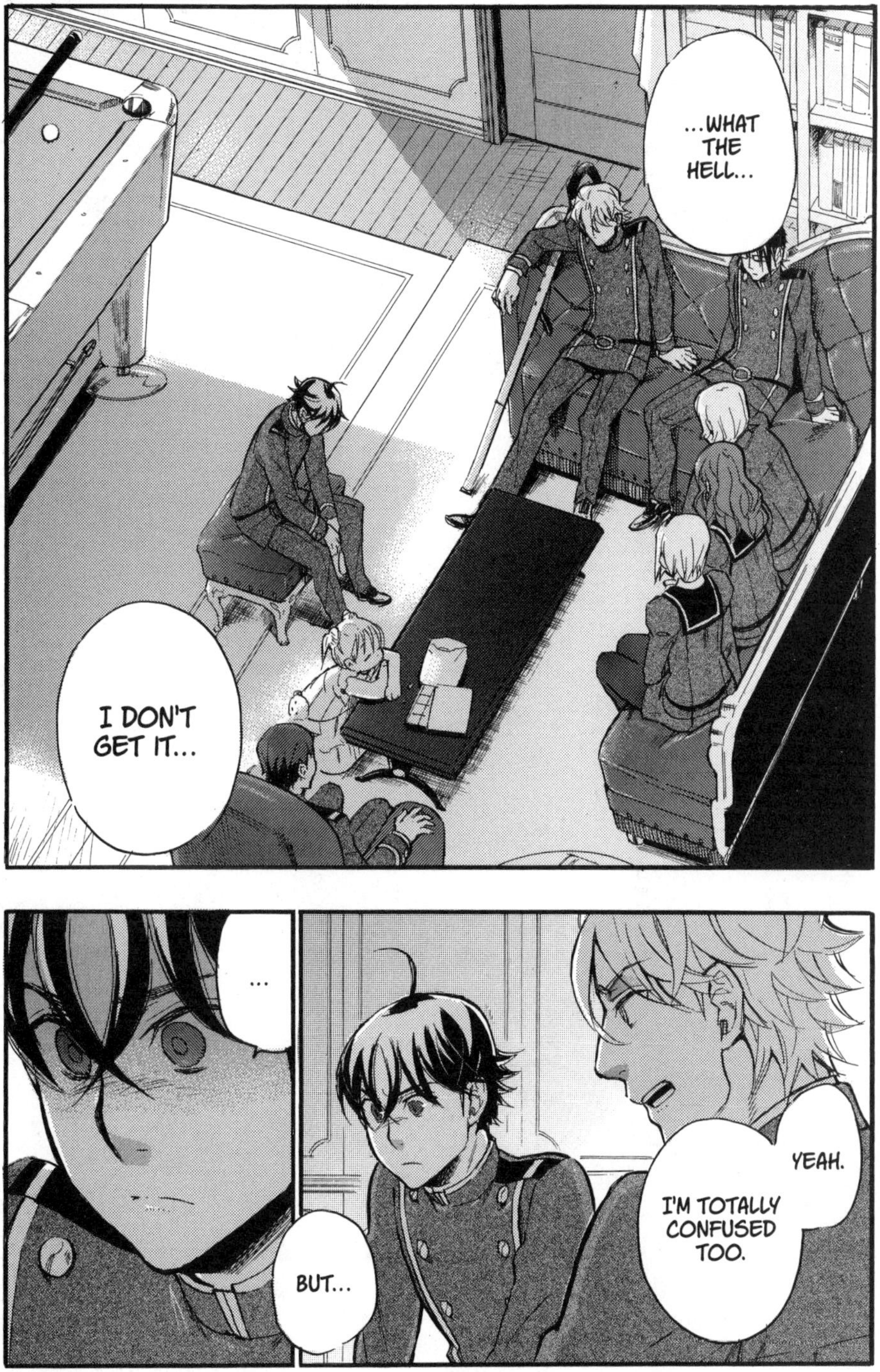
...WHAT THE HELL...
I DON'T GET IT...
YEAH.
I'M TOTALLY CONFUSED TOO.
BUT...
...

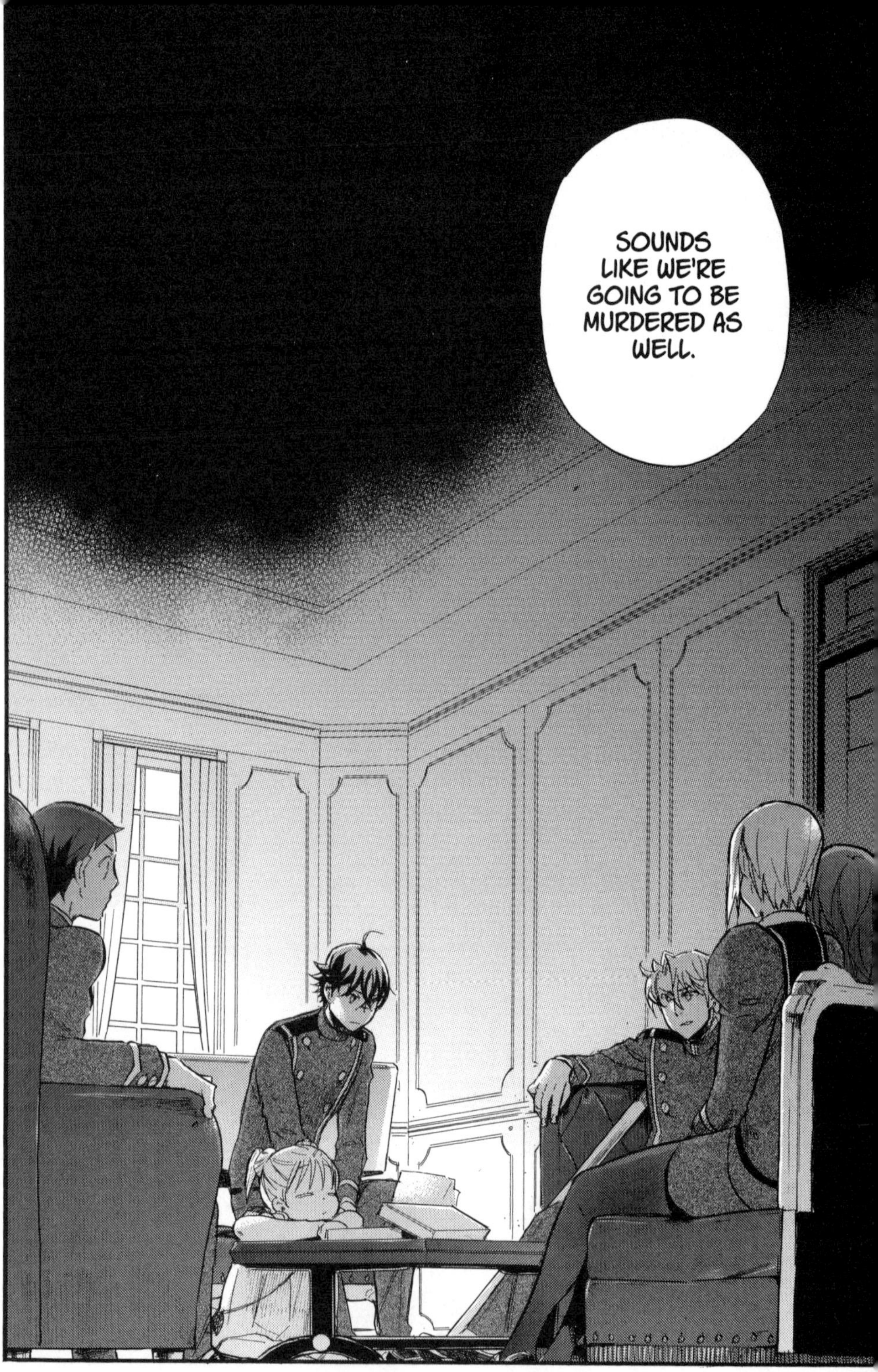
SOUNDS LIKE WE'RE GOING TO BE MURDERED AS WELL.

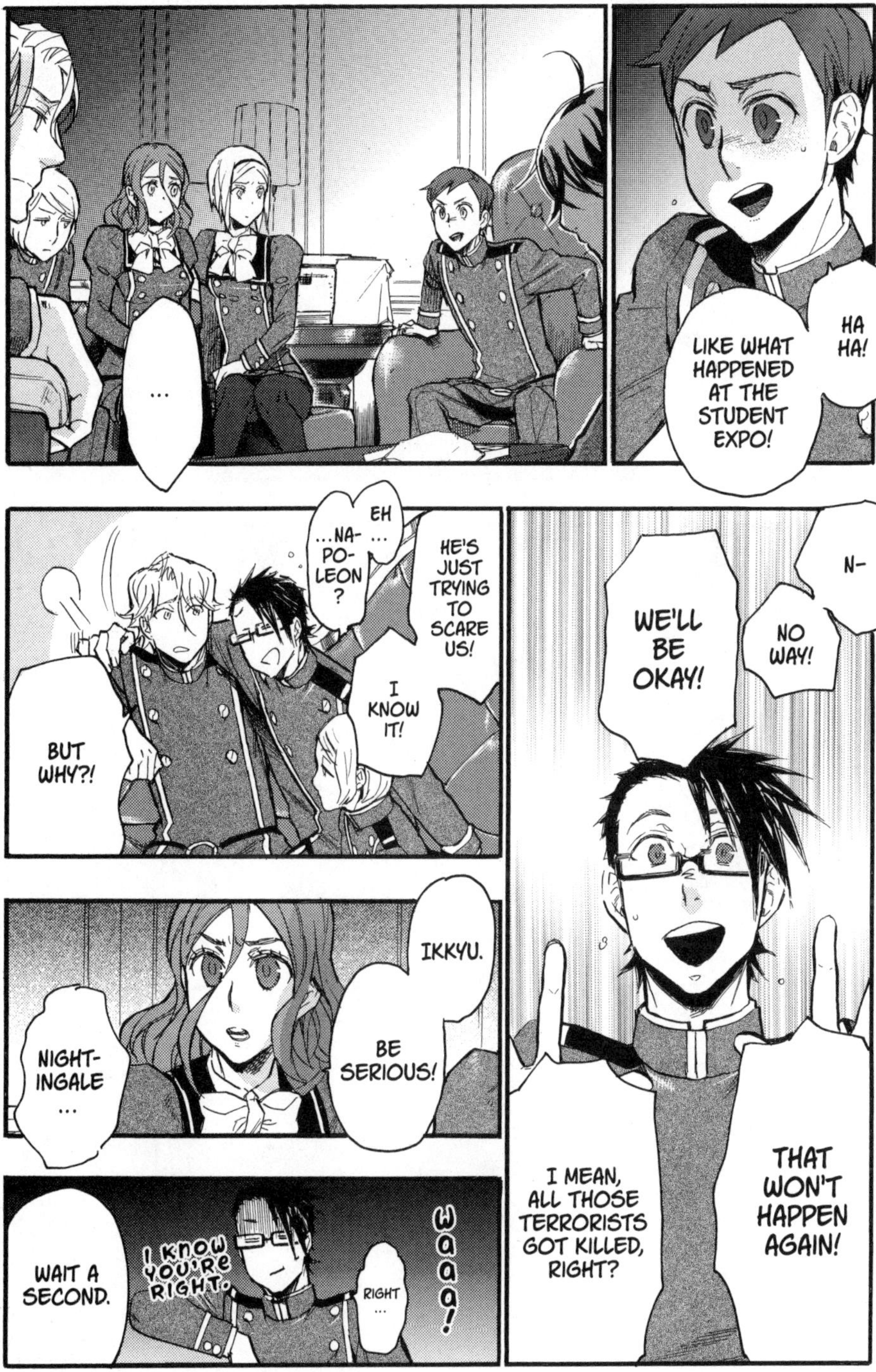
HA HA!
LIKE WHAT HAPPENED AT THE STUDENT EXPO!
...
N-
NO WAY!
WE'LL BE OKAY!
THAT WON'T HAPPEN AGAIN!
I MEAN, ALL THOSE TERRORISTS GOT KILLED, RIGHT?
HE'S JUST TRYING TO SCARE US!
EH...
...NA-PO-LEON?
I KNOW IT!
BUT WHY?!
IKKYU.
BE SERIOUS!
NIGHT-INGALE...
Waaa!
RIGHT...
I know you're right.
WAIT A SECOND.

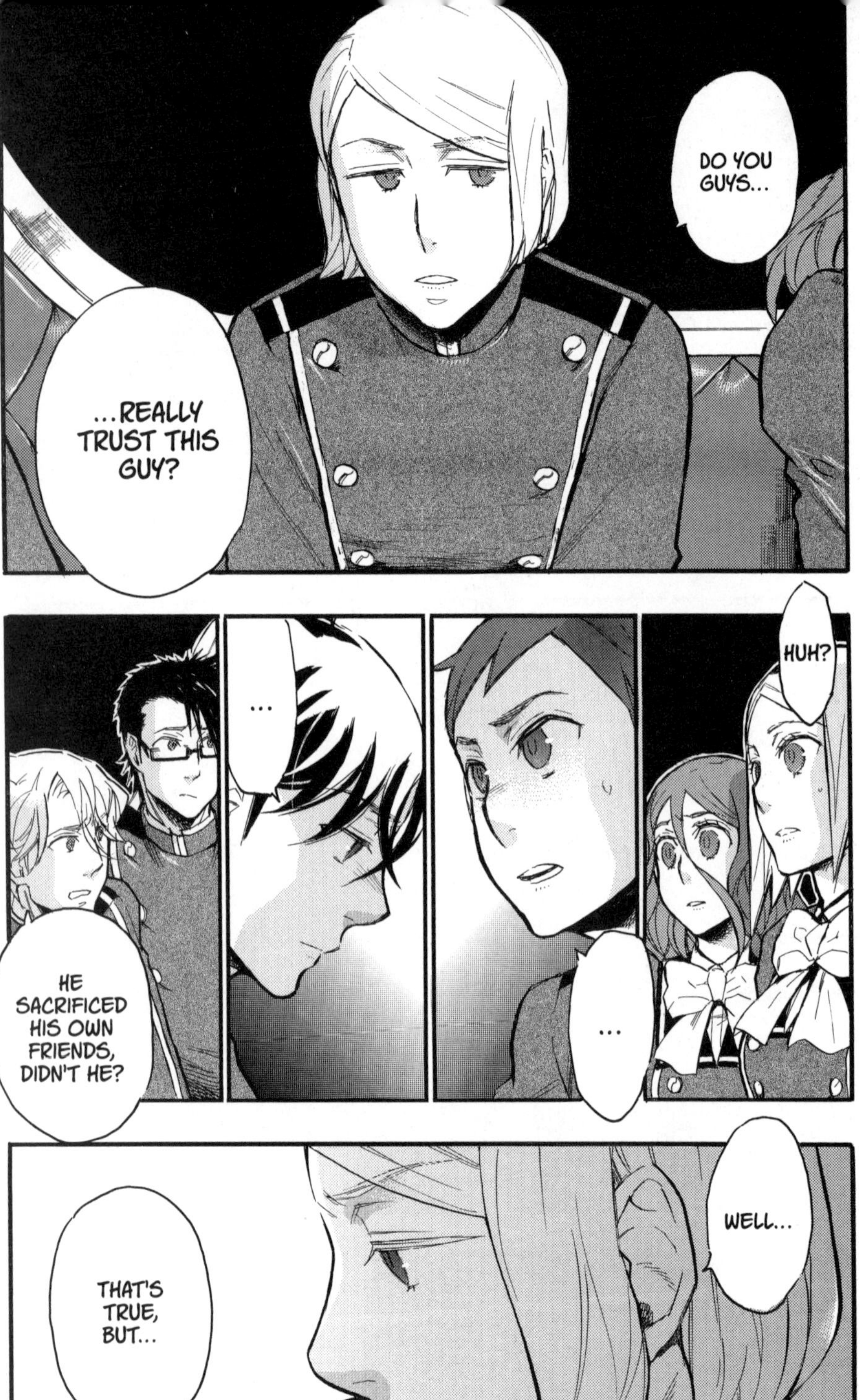
DO YOU GUYS...
...REALLY TRUST THIS GUY?
HUH?
...
...
HE SACRIFICED HIS OWN FRIENDS, DIDN'T HE?
WELL...
THAT'S TRUE, BUT...

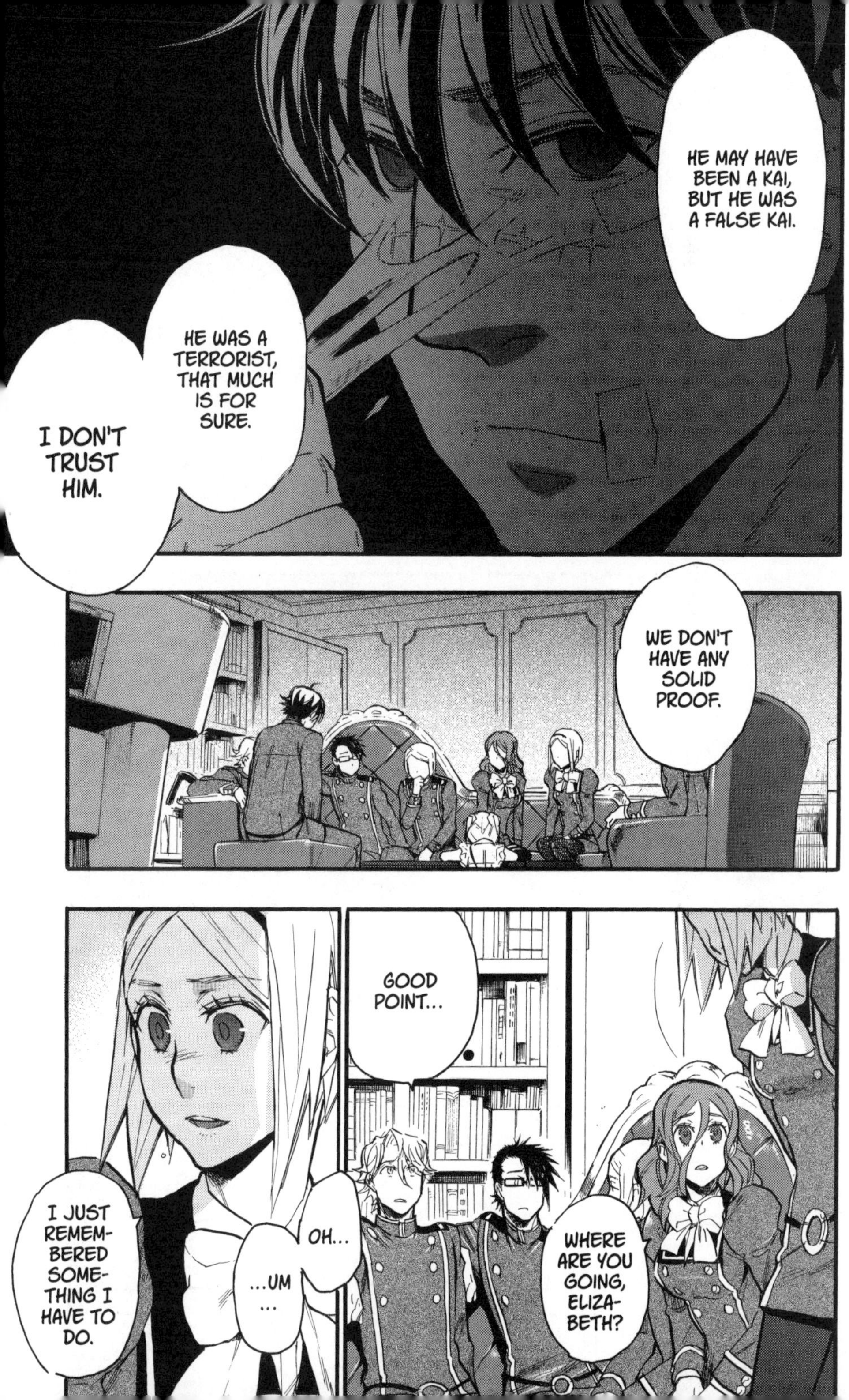
HE MAY HAVE BEEN A KAI, BUT HE WAS A FALSE KAI.
HE WAS A TERRORIST, THAT MUCH IS FOR SURE.
I DON'T TRUST HIM.
WE DON'T HAVE ANY SOLID PROOF.
GOOD POINT...
WHERE ARE YOU GOING, ELIZA-BETH?
OH...
...UM ...
I JUST REMEM-BERED SOME-THING I HAVE TO DO.

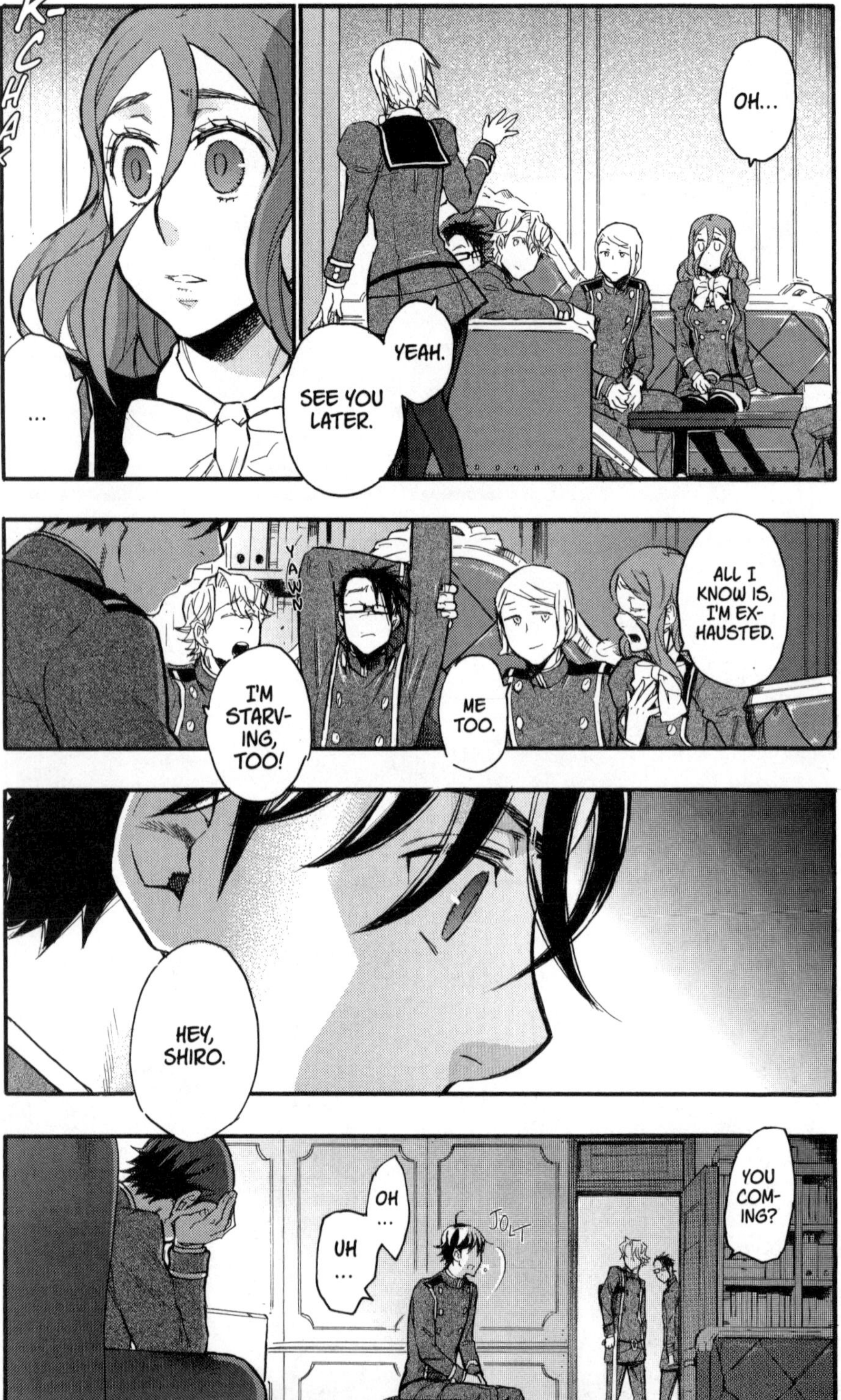
OH...
YEAH.
SEE YOU LATER.
K-CHAK
...
ALL I KNOW IS, I'M EX-HAUSTED.
ME TOO.
YAWN
I'M STARV-ING, TOO!
HEY, SHIRO.
YOU COM-ING?
JOLT
OH ...
UH ...

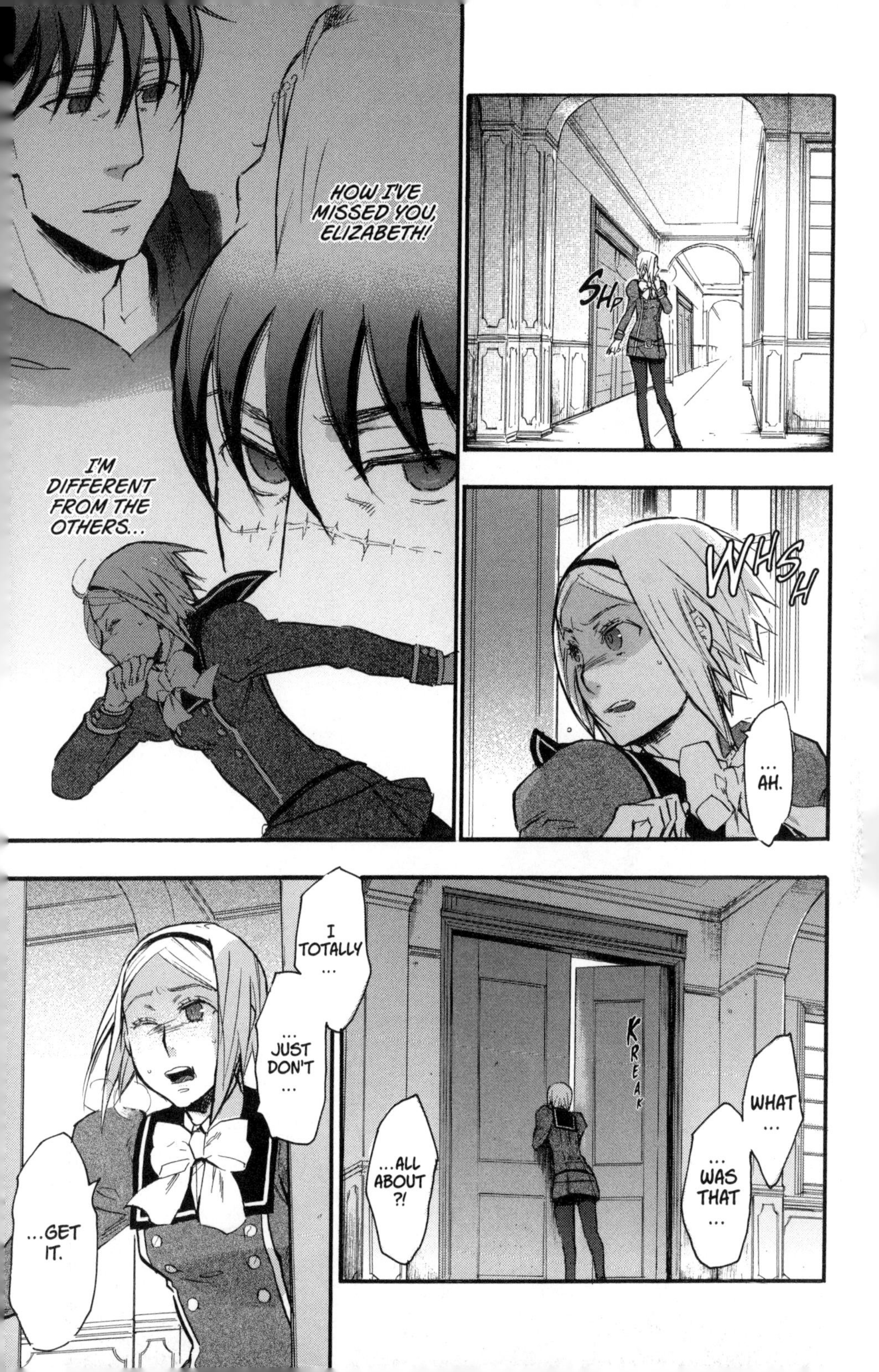
SHP
WHSH
...AH.
HOW I'VE MISSED YOU, ELIZABETH!
I'M DIFFERENT FROM THE OTHERS...
WHAT...
...WAS THAT...
...ALL ABOUT?!
KREAK
I TOTALLY...
...JUST DON'T...
...GET IT.

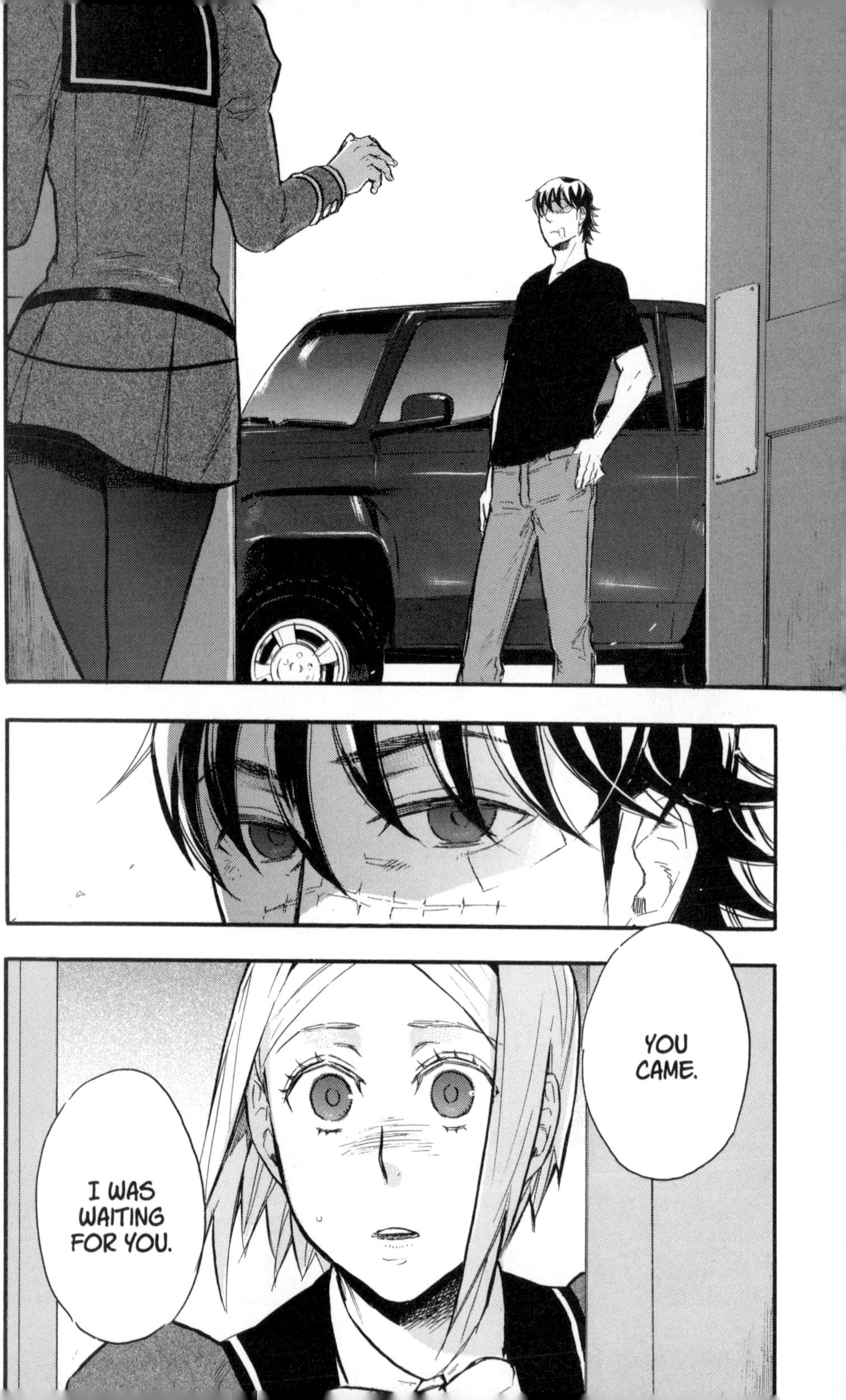
YOU CAME.
I WAS WAITING FOR YOU.

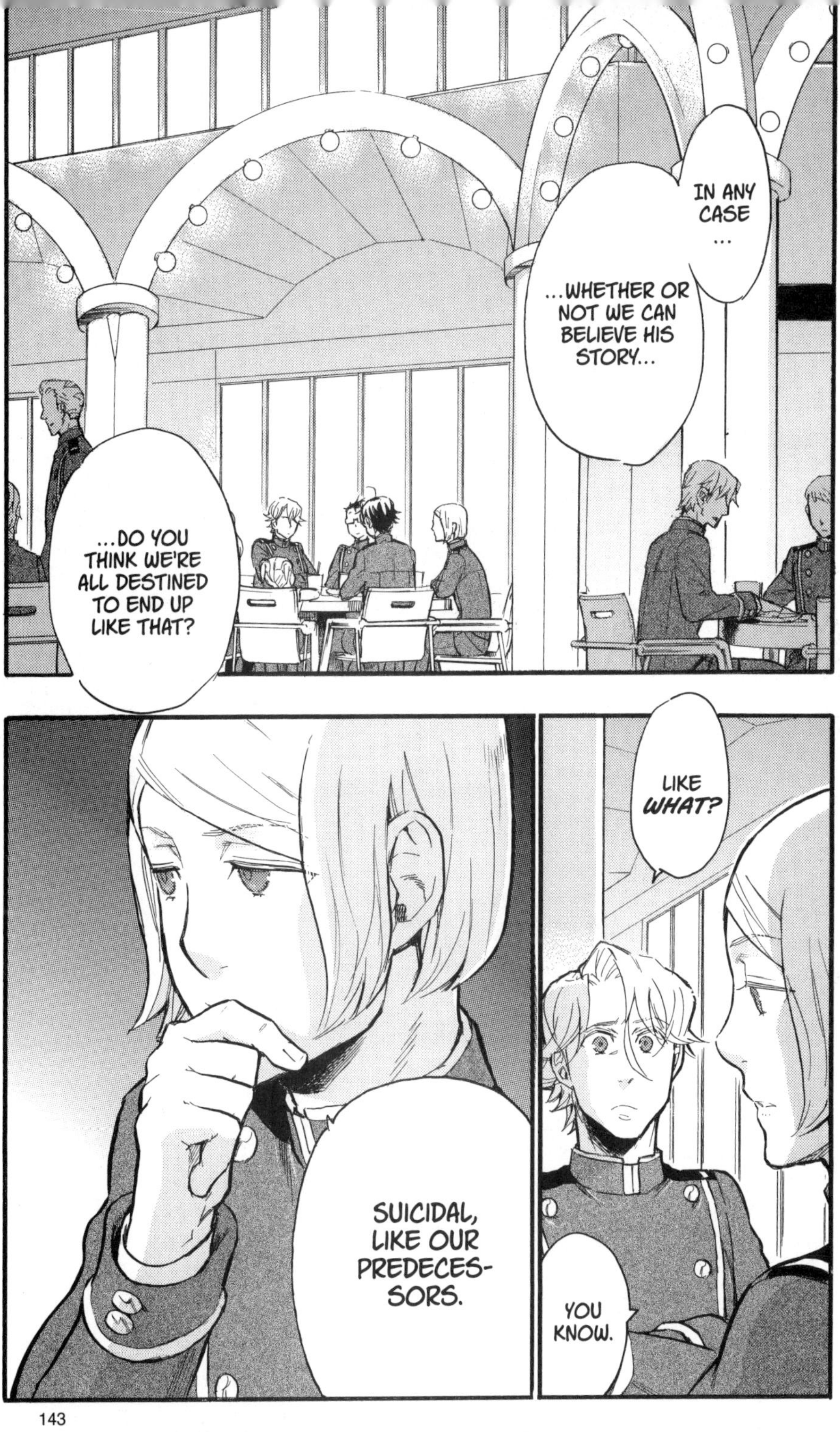
IN ANY CASE ...
...WHETHER OR NOT WE CAN BELIEVE HIS STORY...
...DO YOU THINK WE'RE ALL DESTINED TO END UP LIKE THAT?
LIKE *WHAT?*
YOU KNOW.
SUICIDAL, LIKE OUR PREDECES-SORS.

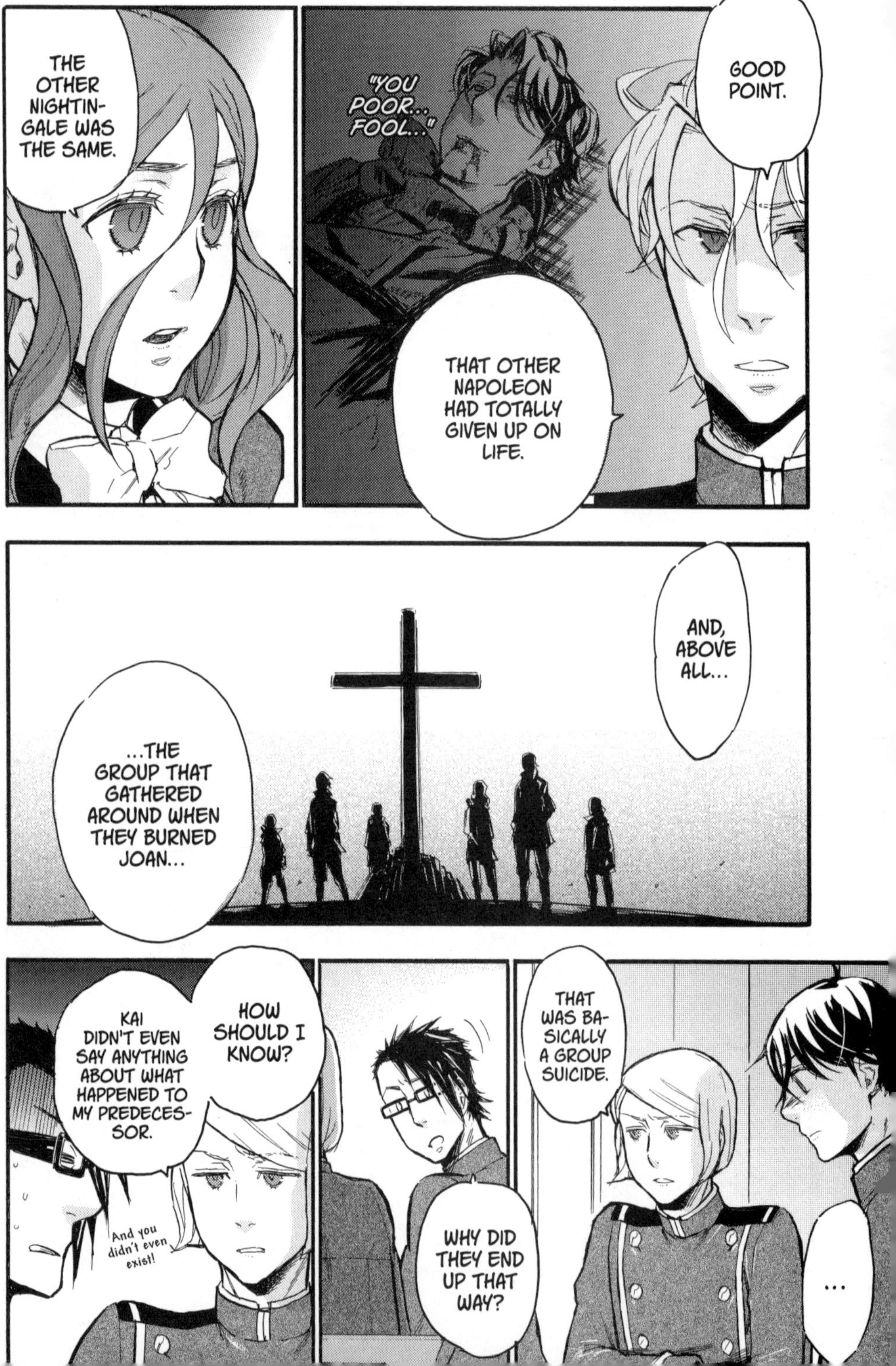
GOOD POINT.
"YOU POOR... FOOL..."
THAT OTHER NAPOLEON HAD TOTALLY GIVEN UP ON LIFE.
THE OTHER NIGHTIN-GALE WAS THE SAME.
AND, ABOVE ALL...
...THE GROUP THAT GATHERED AROUND WHEN THEY BURNED JOAN...
THAT WAS BA-SICALLY A GROUP SUICIDE.
...
WHY DID THEY END UP THAT WAY?
HOW SHOULD I KNOW?
KAI DIDN'T EVEN SAY ANYTHING ABOUT WHAT HAPPENED TO MY PREDECES-SOR.
And you didn't even exist!

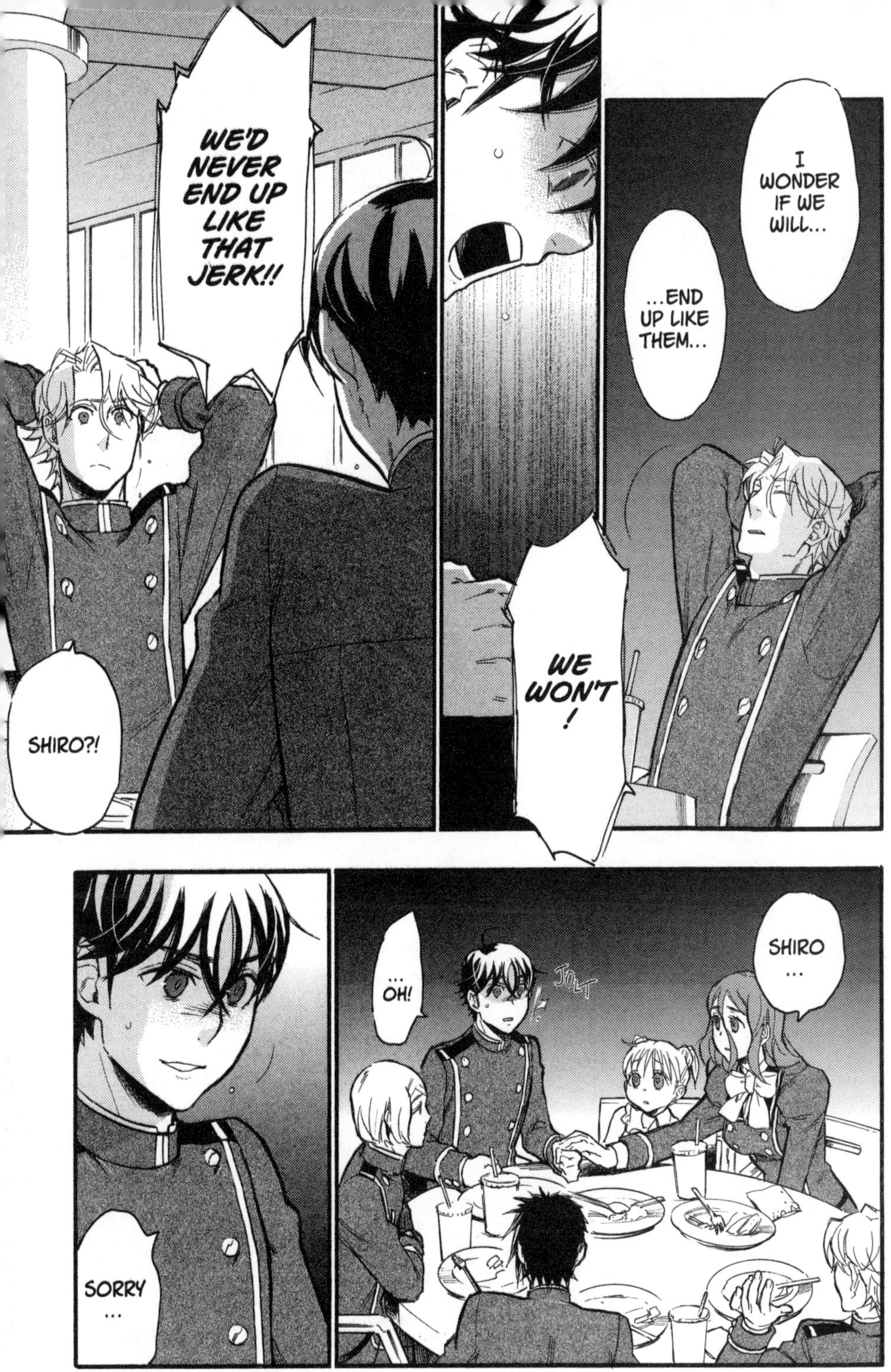
I WONDER IF WE WILL...
...END UP LIKE THEM...
WE WON'T!
WE'D NEVER END UP LIKE THAT JERK!!
SHIRO?!
SHIRO...
JOLT
...OH!
SORRY...

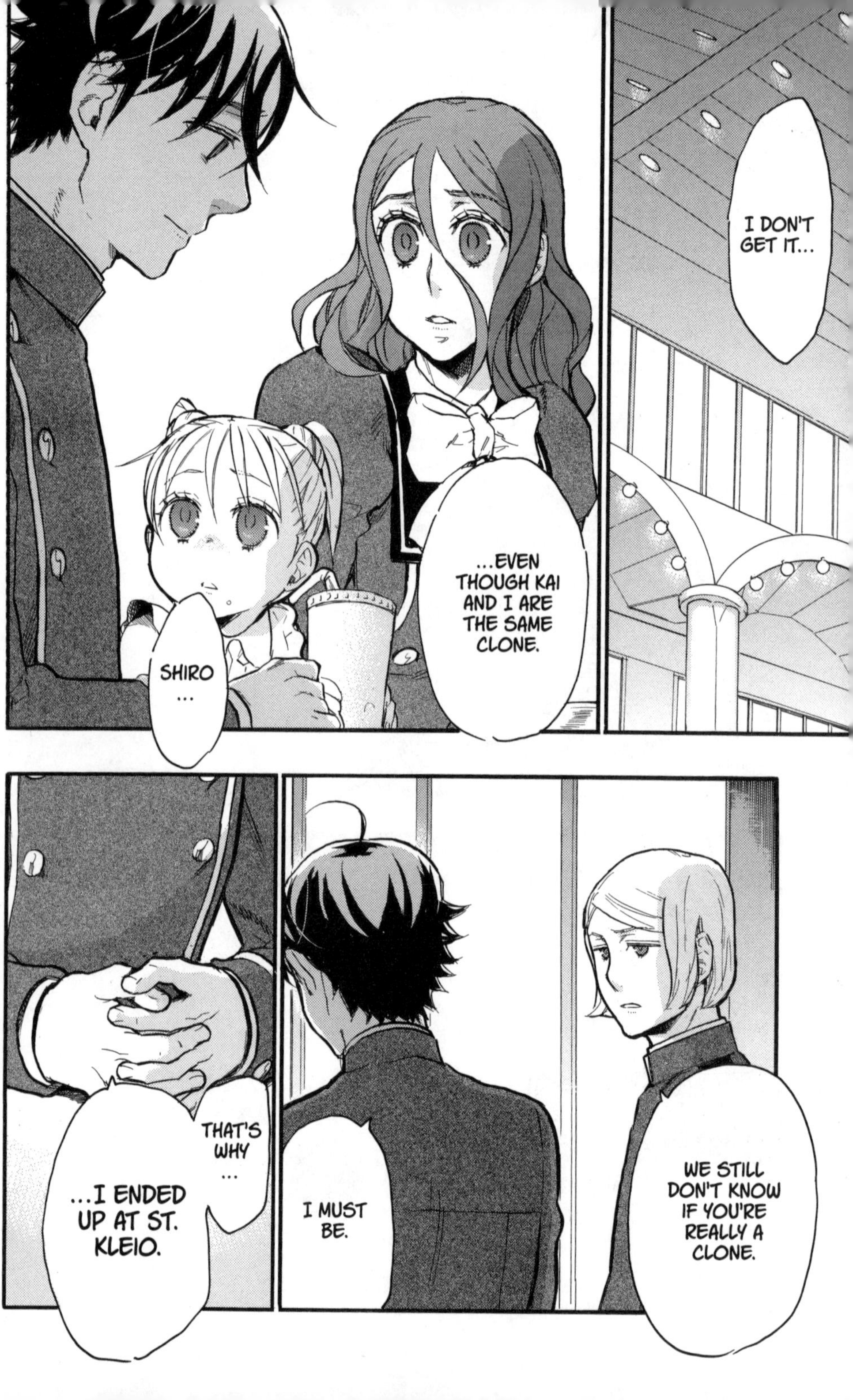
I DON'T GET IT...
...EVEN THOUGH KAI AND I ARE THE SAME CLONE.
SHIRO ...
WE STILL DON'T KNOW IF YOU'RE REALLY A CLONE.
I MUST BE.
THAT'S WHY ...
...I ENDED UP AT ST. KLEIO.

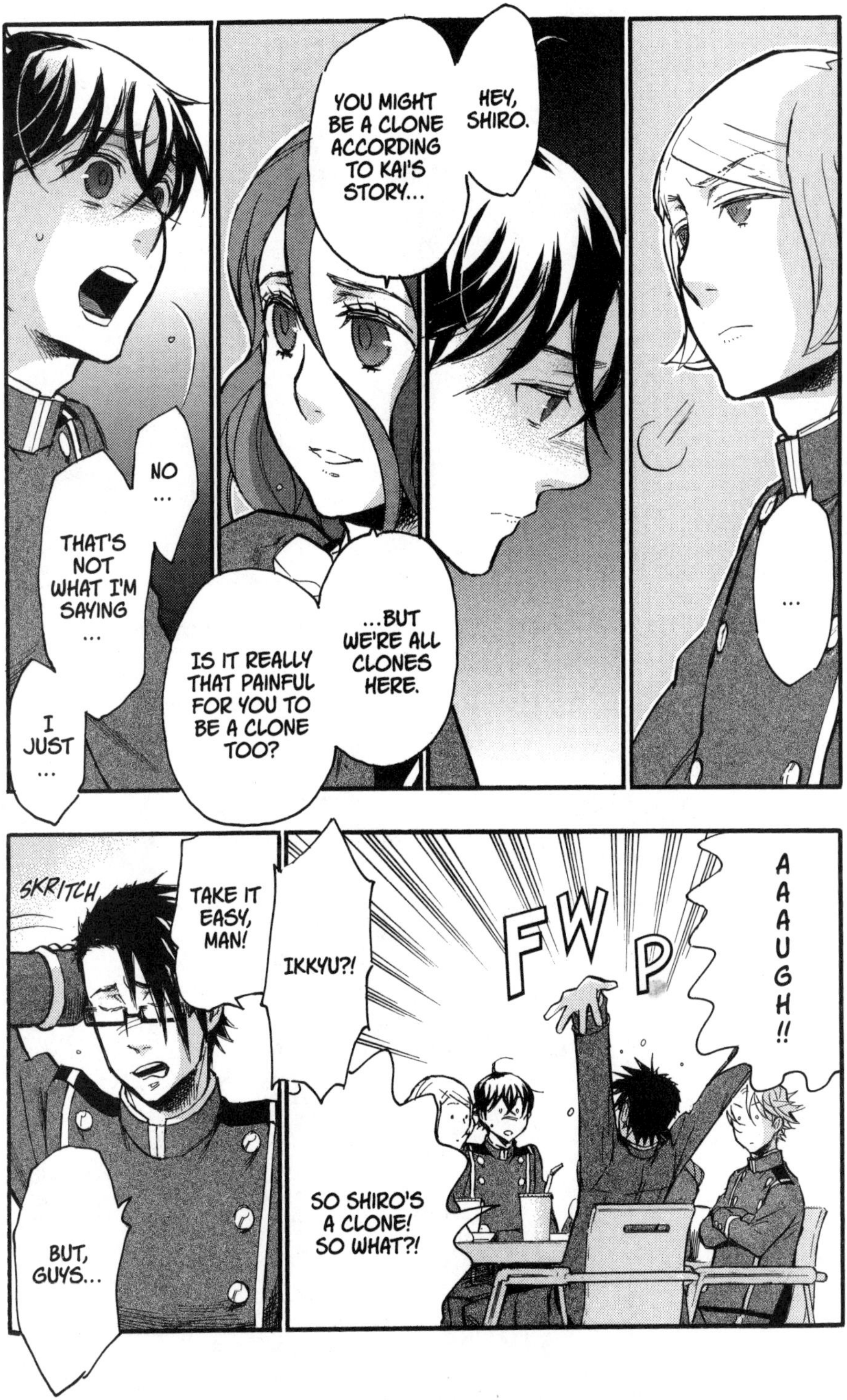
...
HEY, SHIRO.
YOU MIGHT BE A CLONE ACCORDING TO KAI'S STORY...
...BUT WE'RE ALL CLONES HERE.
IS IT REALLY THAT PAINFUL FOR YOU TO BE A CLONE TOO?
NO...
THAT'S NOT WHAT I'M SAYING...
I JUST...
AAAAUGH!!
FWP
IKKYU?!
SO SHIRO'S A CLONE! SO WHAT?!
SKRITCH
TAKE IT EASY, MAN!
BUT, GUYS...

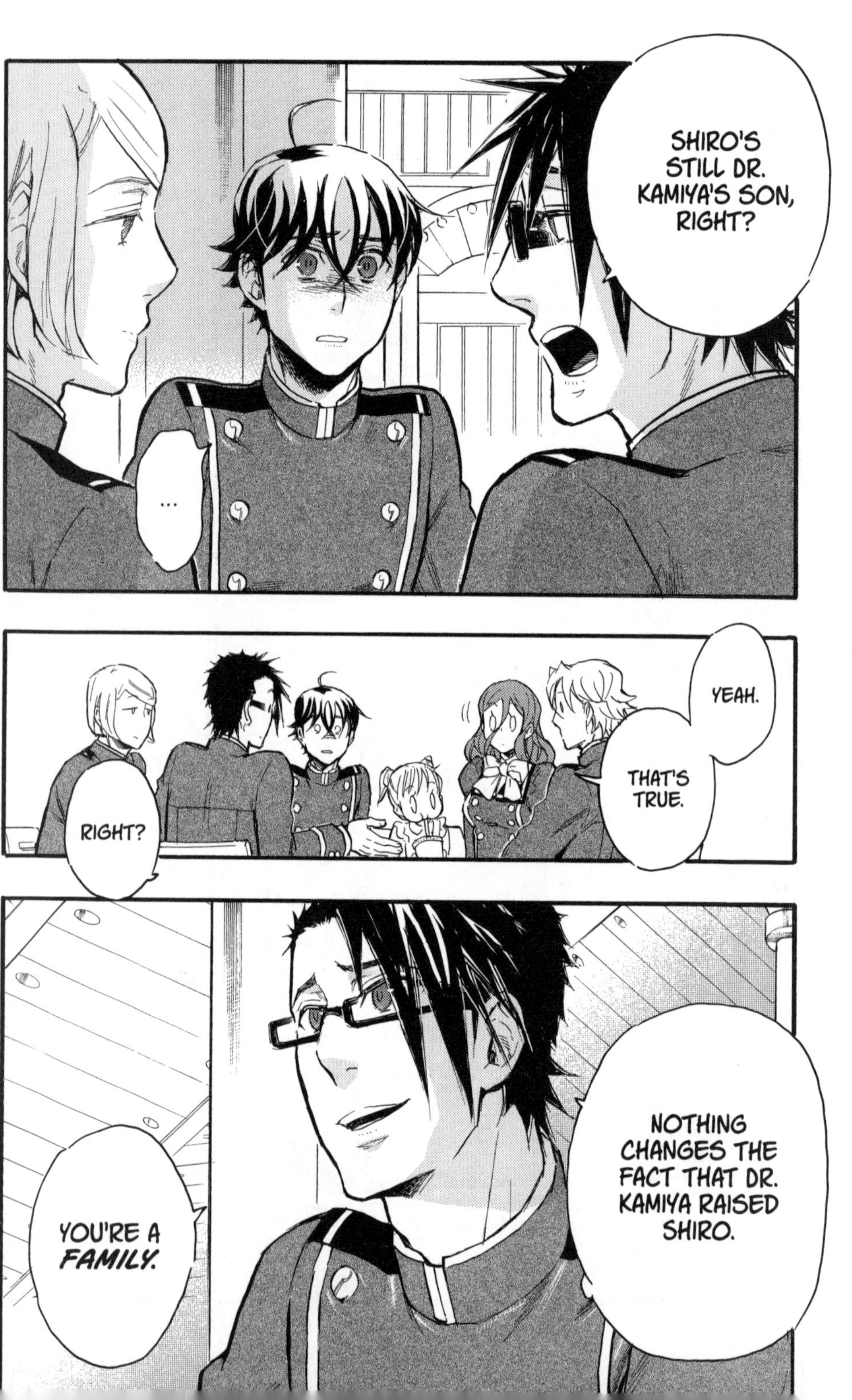
SHIRO'S STILL DR. KAMIYA'S SON, RIGHT?
...
YEAH.
THAT'S TRUE.
RIGHT?
NOTHING CHANGES THE FACT THAT DR. KAMIYA RAISED SHIRO.
YOU'RE A *FAMILY.*

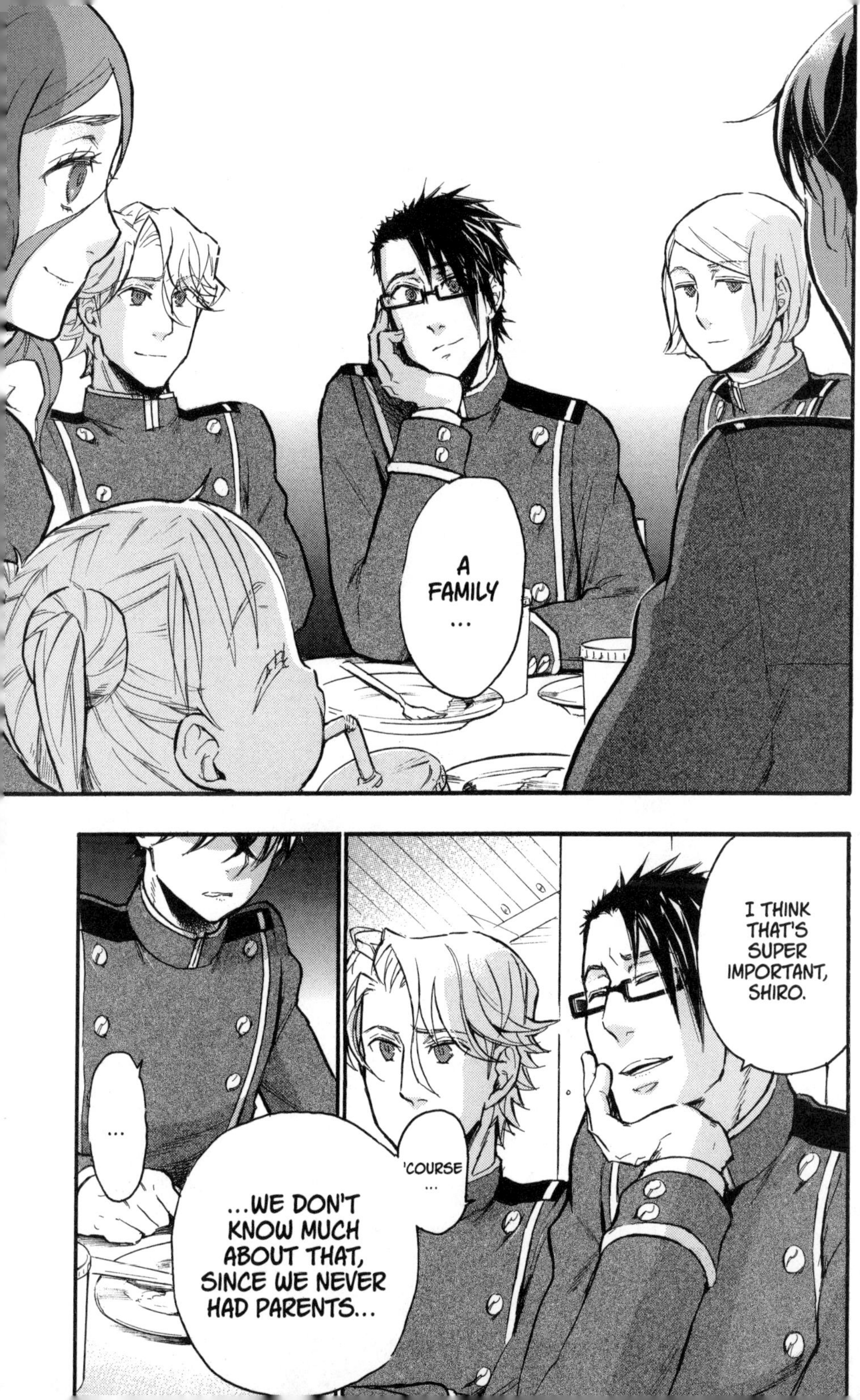
A FAMILY ...
I THINK THAT'S SUPER IMPORTANT, SHIRO.
'COURSE ...
...WE DON'T KNOW MUCH ABOUT THAT, SINCE WE NEVER HAD PARENTS...
...

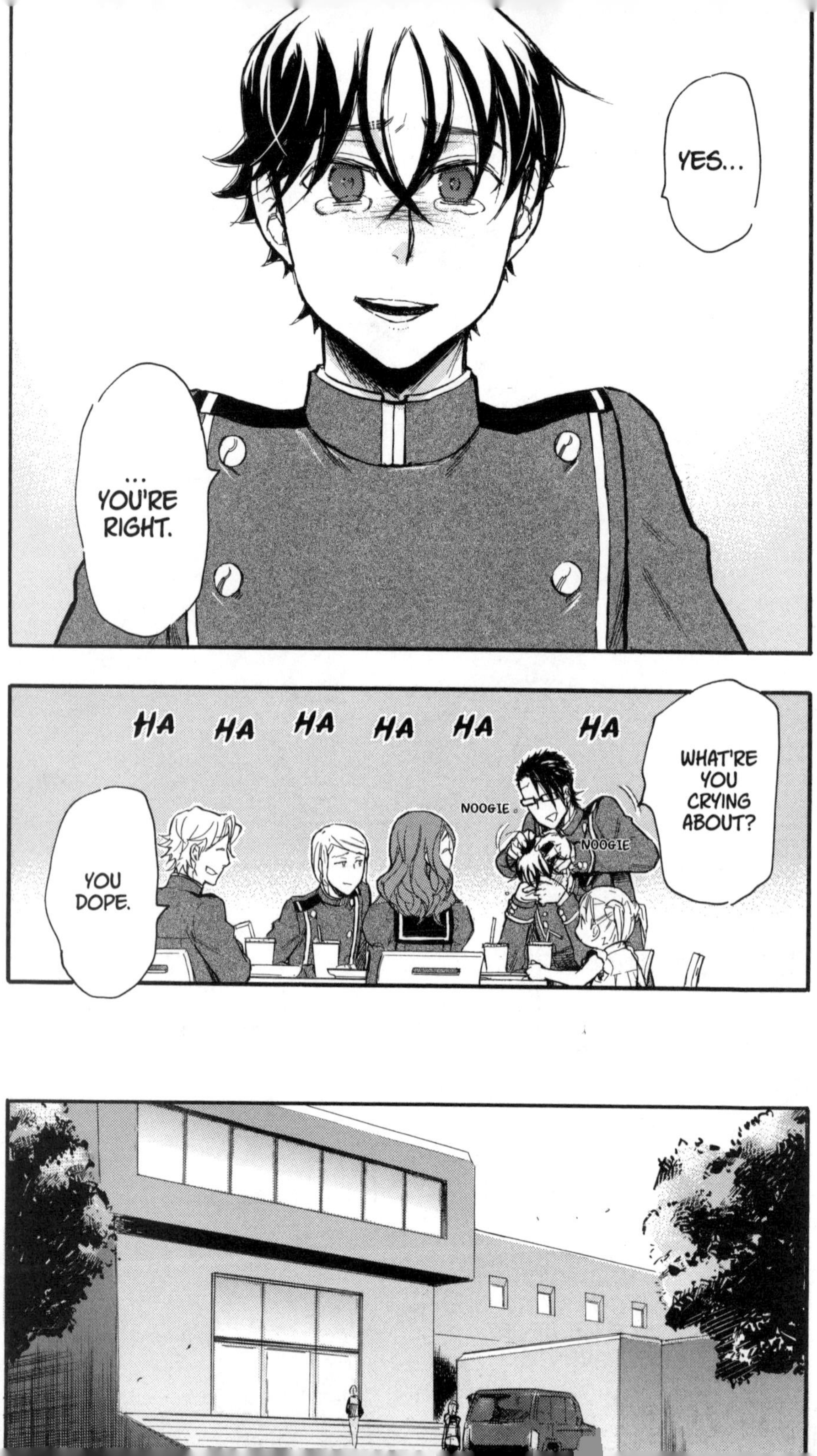
YES...
...YOU'RE RIGHT.
HA HA HA HA HA HA
WHAT'RE YOU CRYING ABOUT?
NOOGIE
NOOGIE
YOU DOPE.

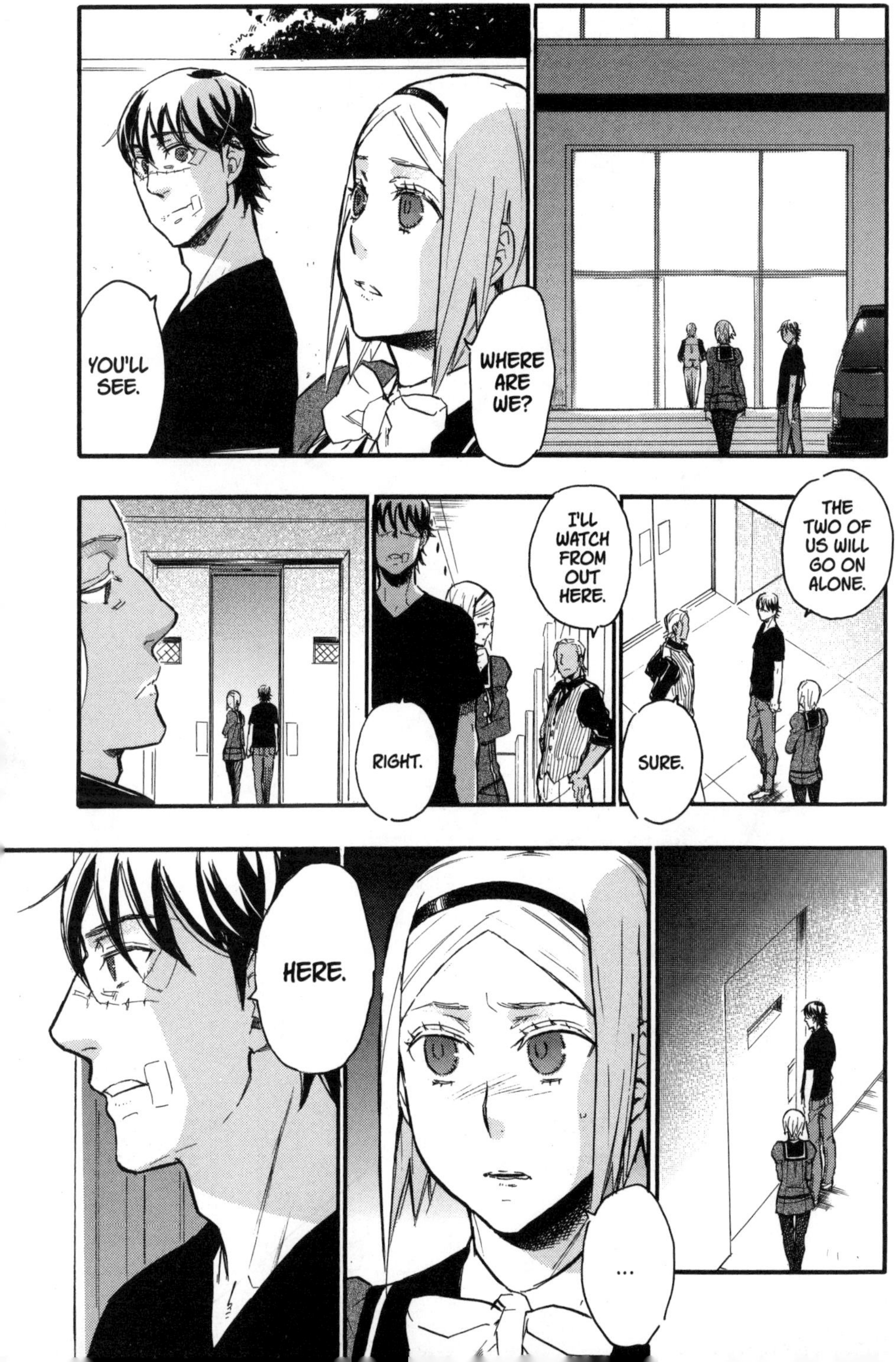
WHERE ARE WE?
YOU'LL SEE.
THE TWO OF US WILL GO ON ALONE.
SURE.
I'LL WATCH FROM OUT HERE.
RIGHT.
HERE.
...

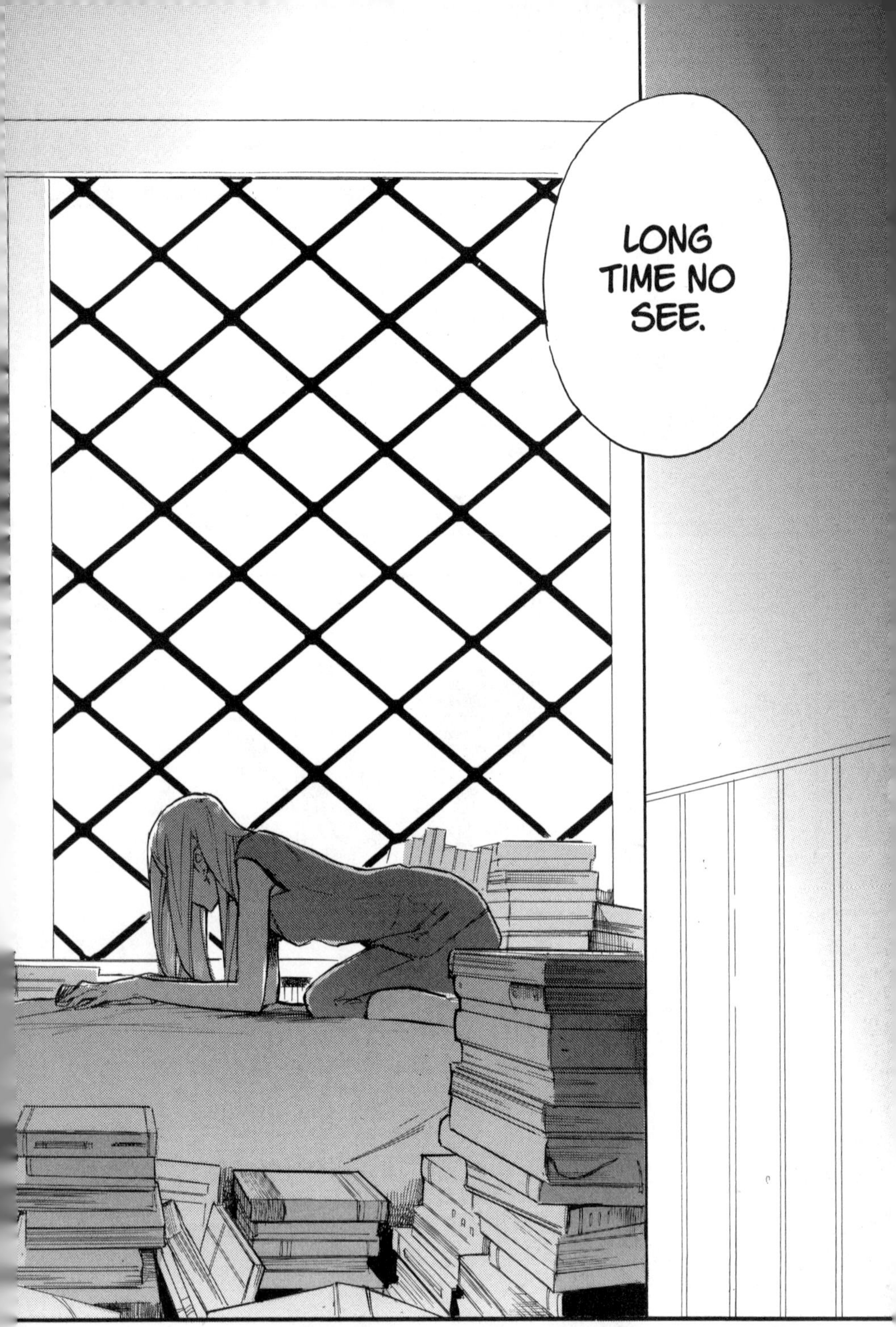
LONG TIME NO SEE.

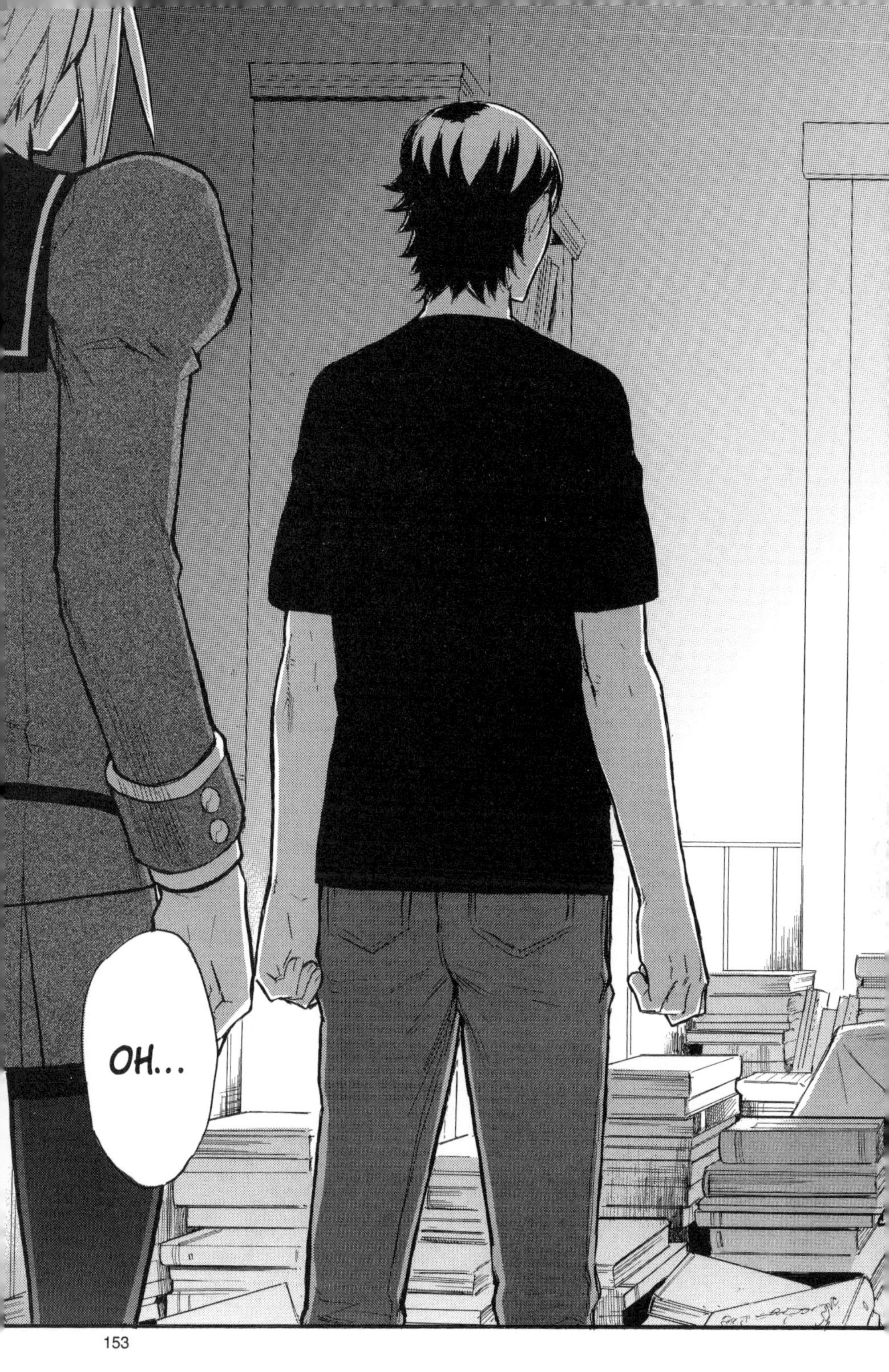
OH...

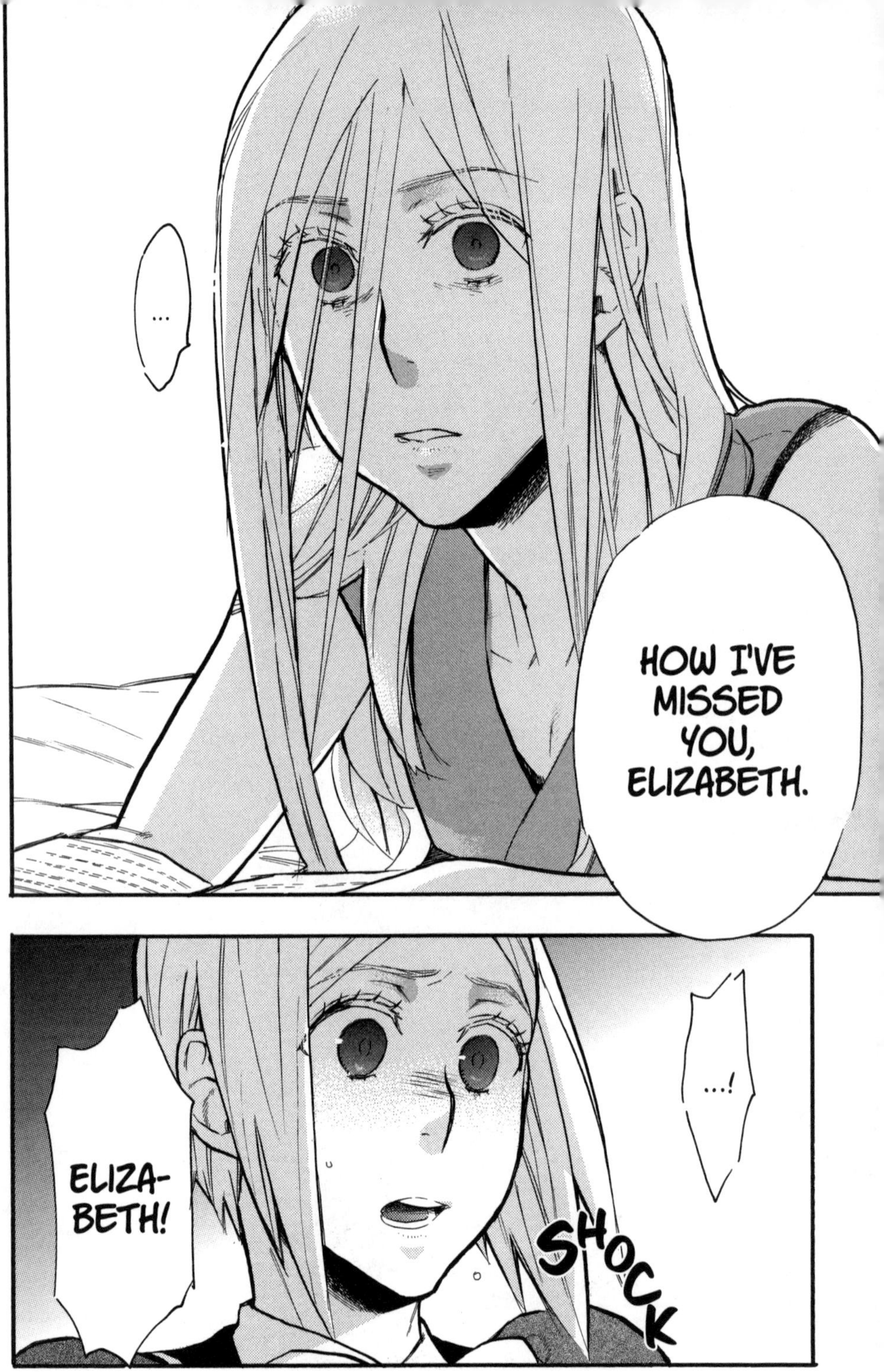
HOW I'VE MISSED YOU, ELIZABETH.
...
...!
SHOCK
ELIZA-BETH!

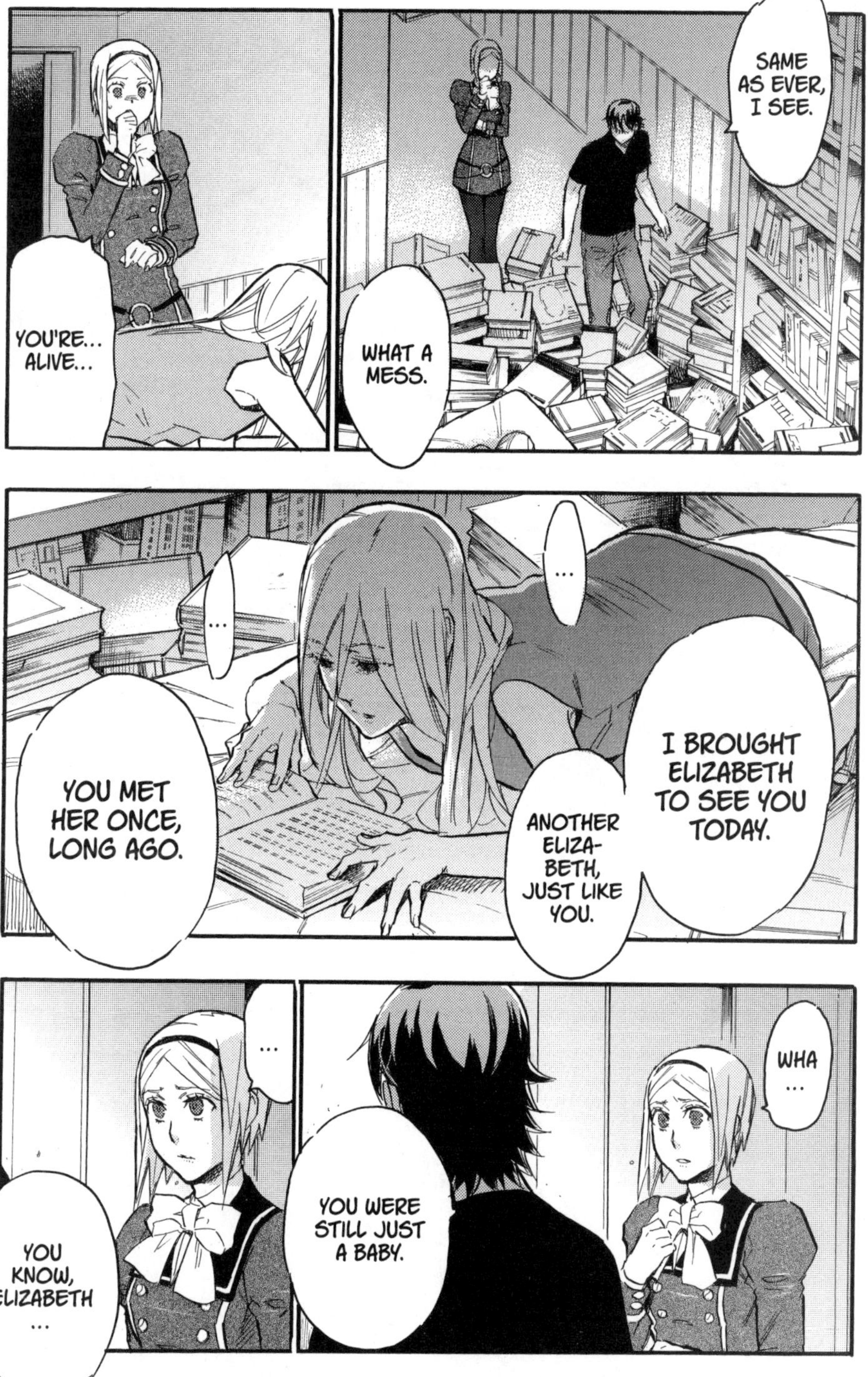
SAME AS EVER, I SEE.
WHAT A MESS.
YOU'RE... ALIVE...
...
...
I BROUGHT ELIZABETH TO SEE YOU TODAY.
ANOTHER ELIZA-BETH, JUST LIKE YOU.
YOU MET HER ONCE, LONG AGO.
WHA ...
...
YOU WERE STILL JUST A BABY.
YOU KNOW, ELIZABETH ...

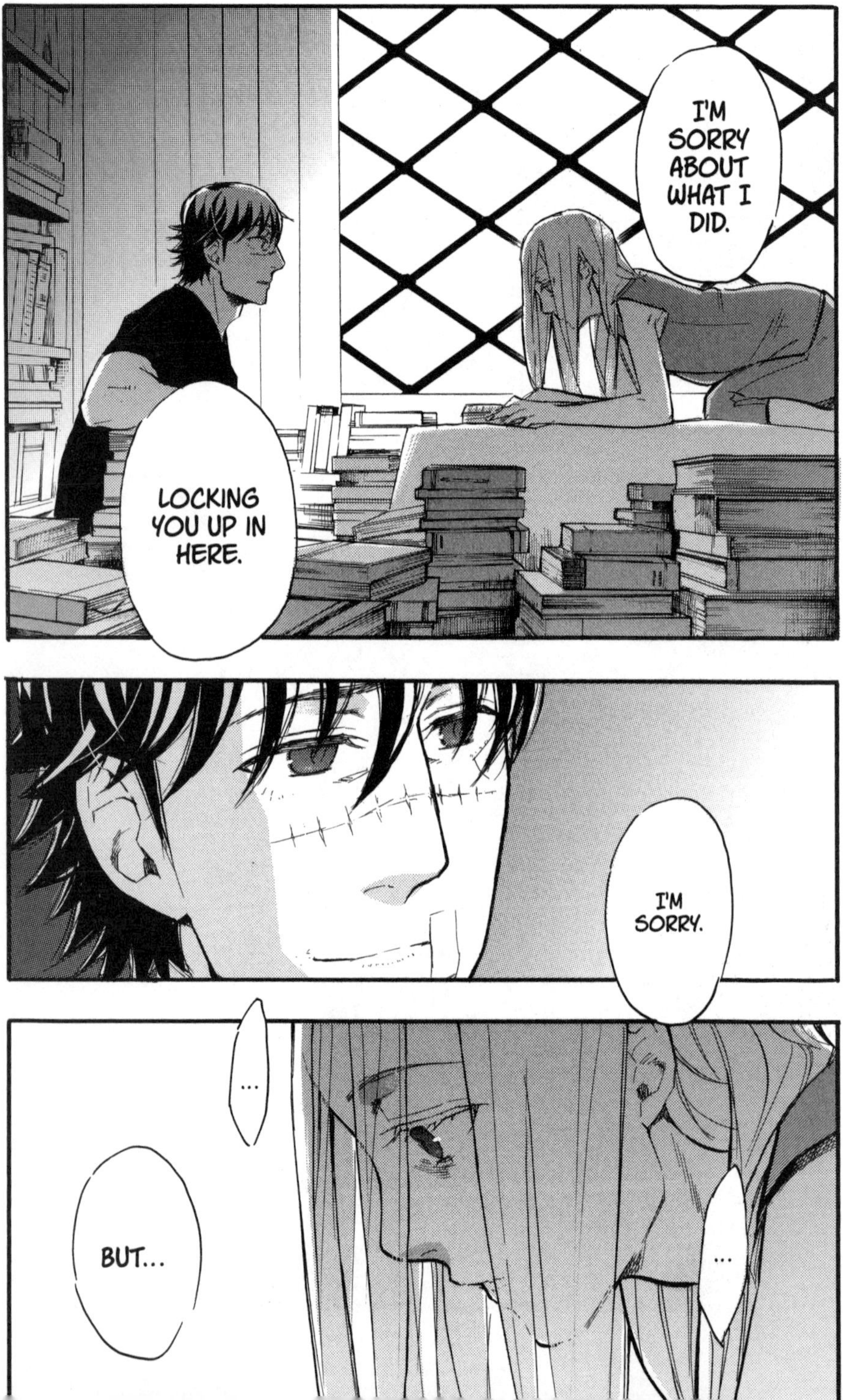
I'M SORRY ABOUT WHAT I DID.
LOCKING YOU UP IN HERE.
I'M SORRY.
...
...
BUT...

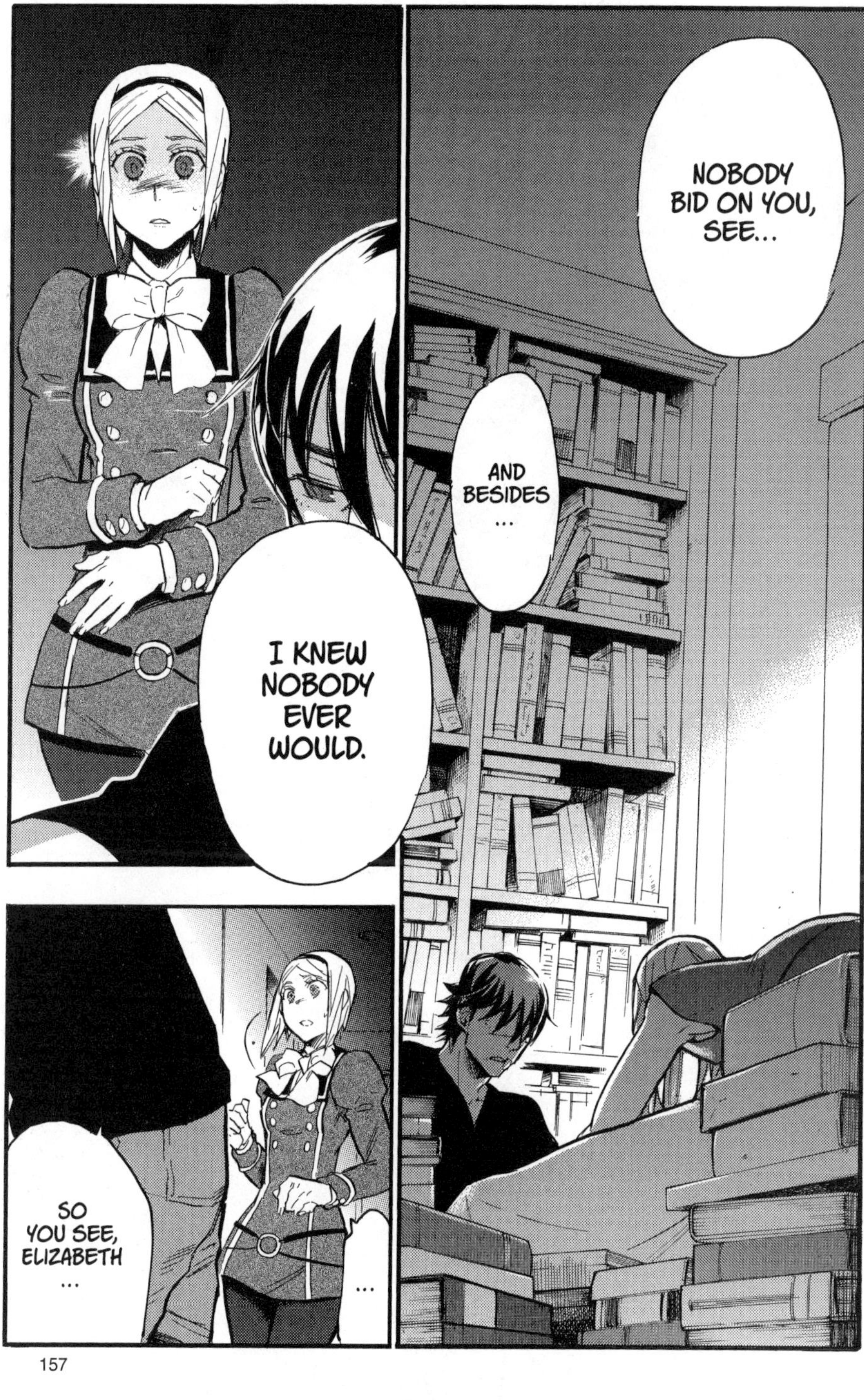
NOBODY BID ON YOU, SEE...
AND BESIDES ...
I KNEW NOBODY EVER WOULD.
SO YOU SEE, ELIZABETH ...
...

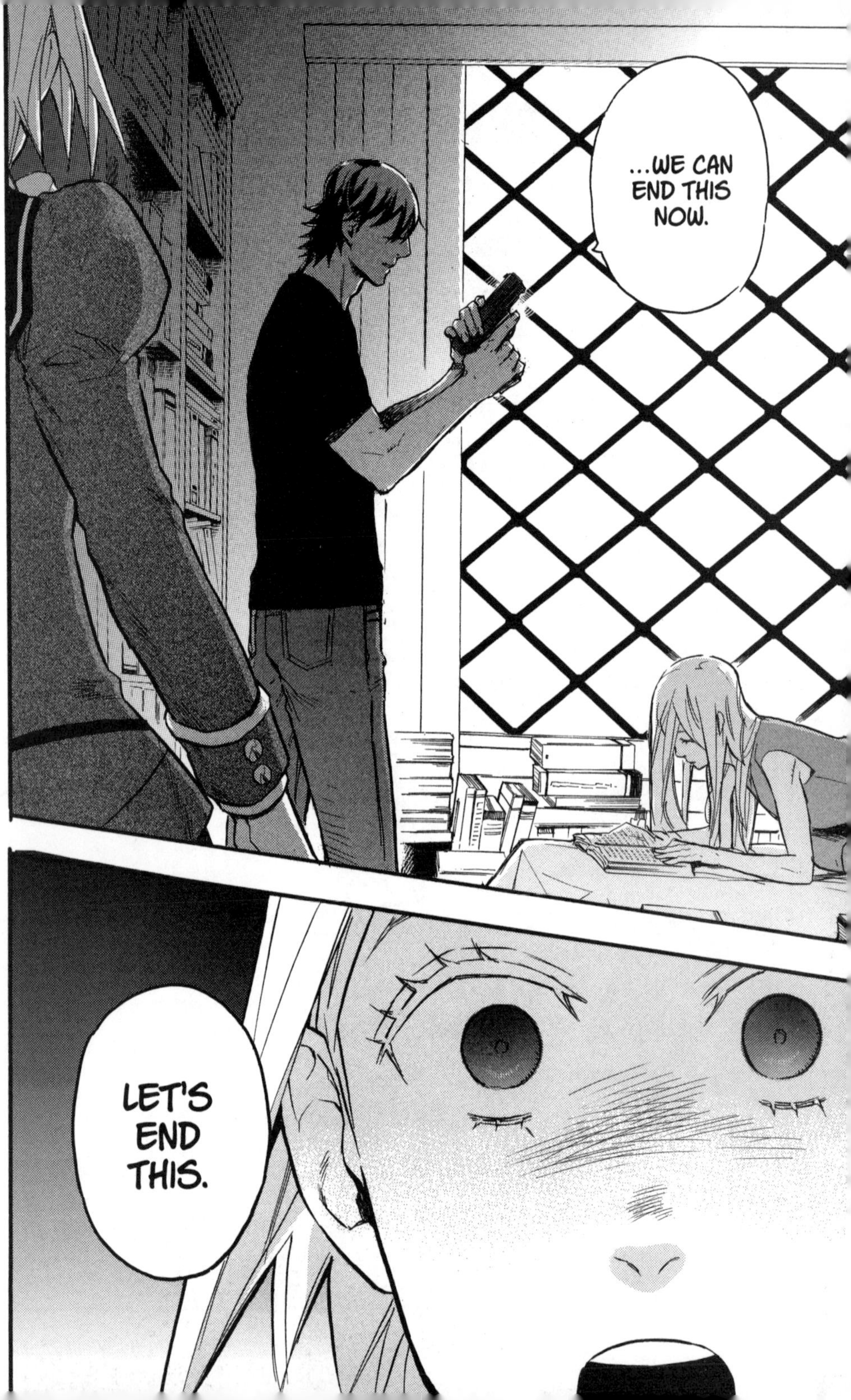
...WE CAN END THIS NOW.
LET'S END THIS.

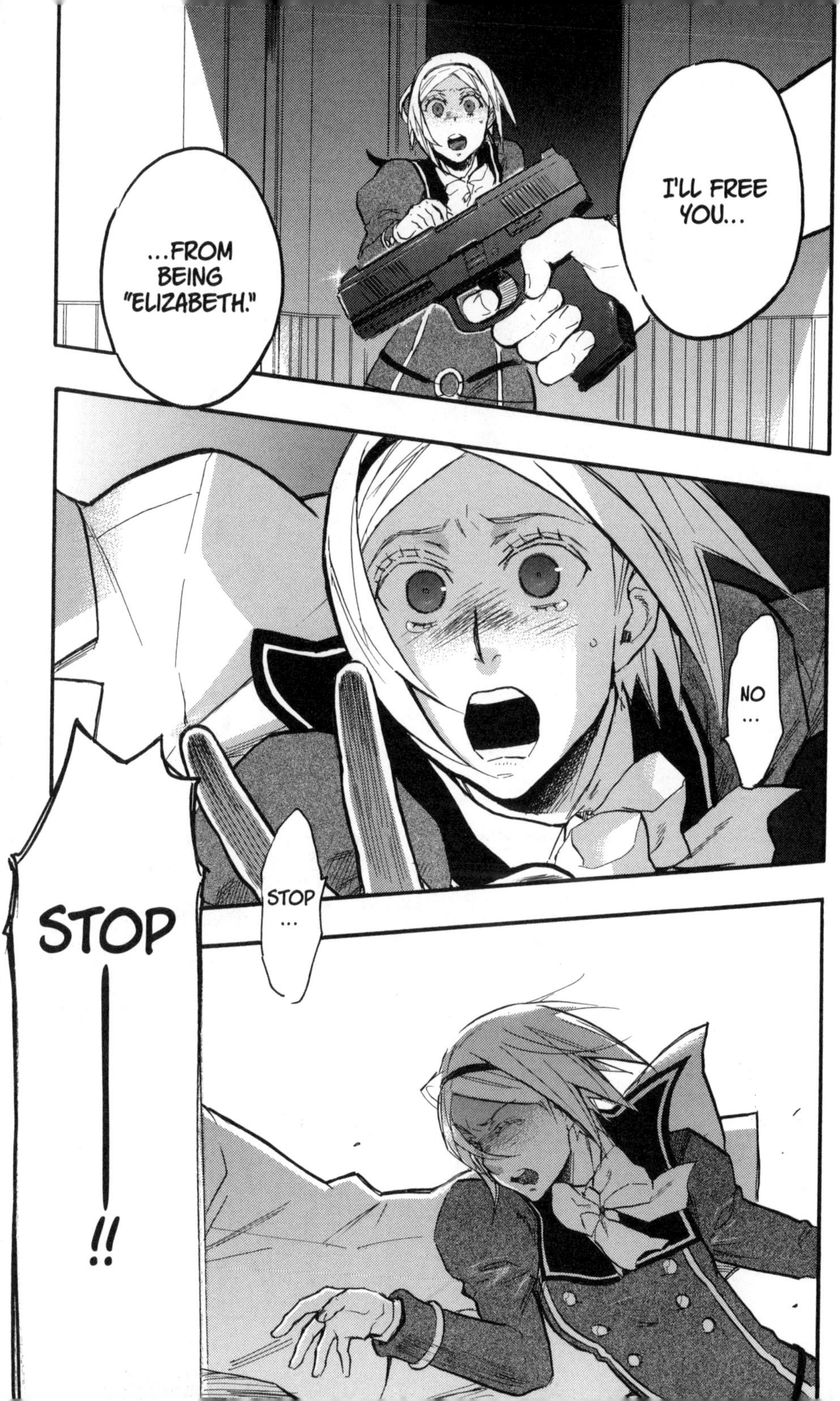
I'LL FREE YOU...
...FROM BEING "ELIZABETH."
NO...
STOP...
STOP——!!

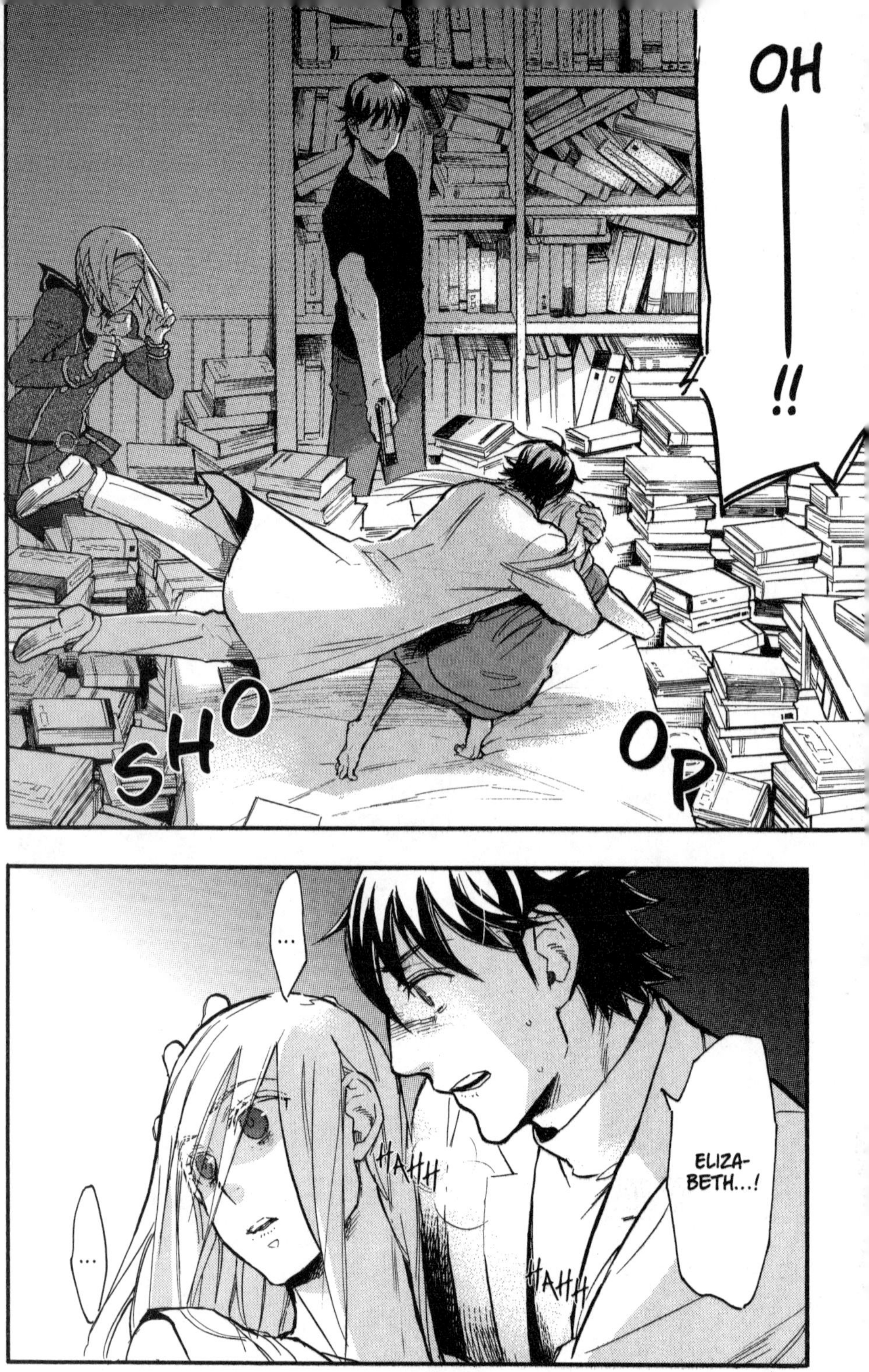
OH——!!
SHOOP
...
ELIZA-
BETH...!
HAHH
HAHH
...

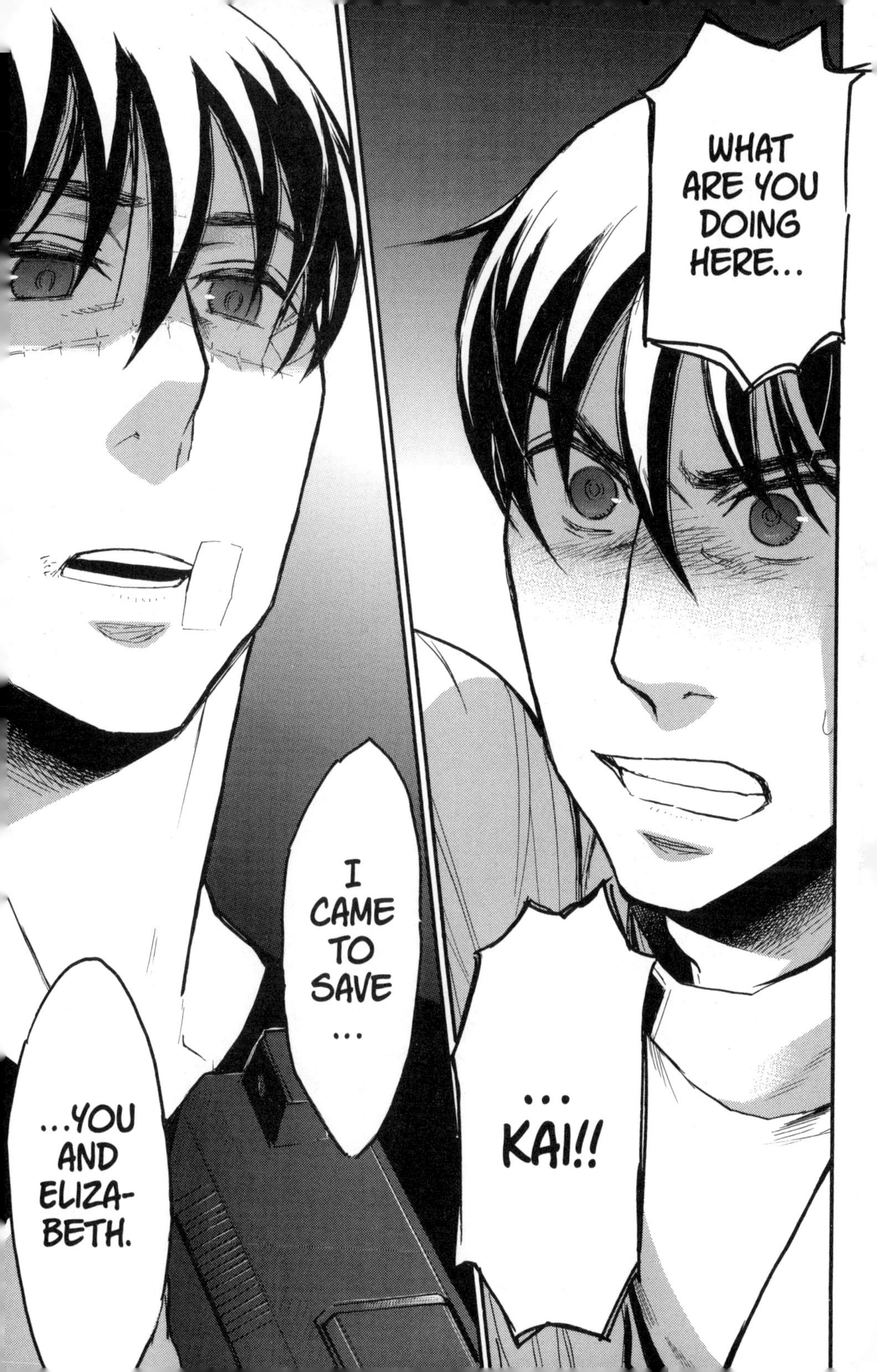
WHAT ARE YOU DOING HERE...
...KAI!!
I CAME TO SAVE ...
...YOU AND ELIZA-BETH.

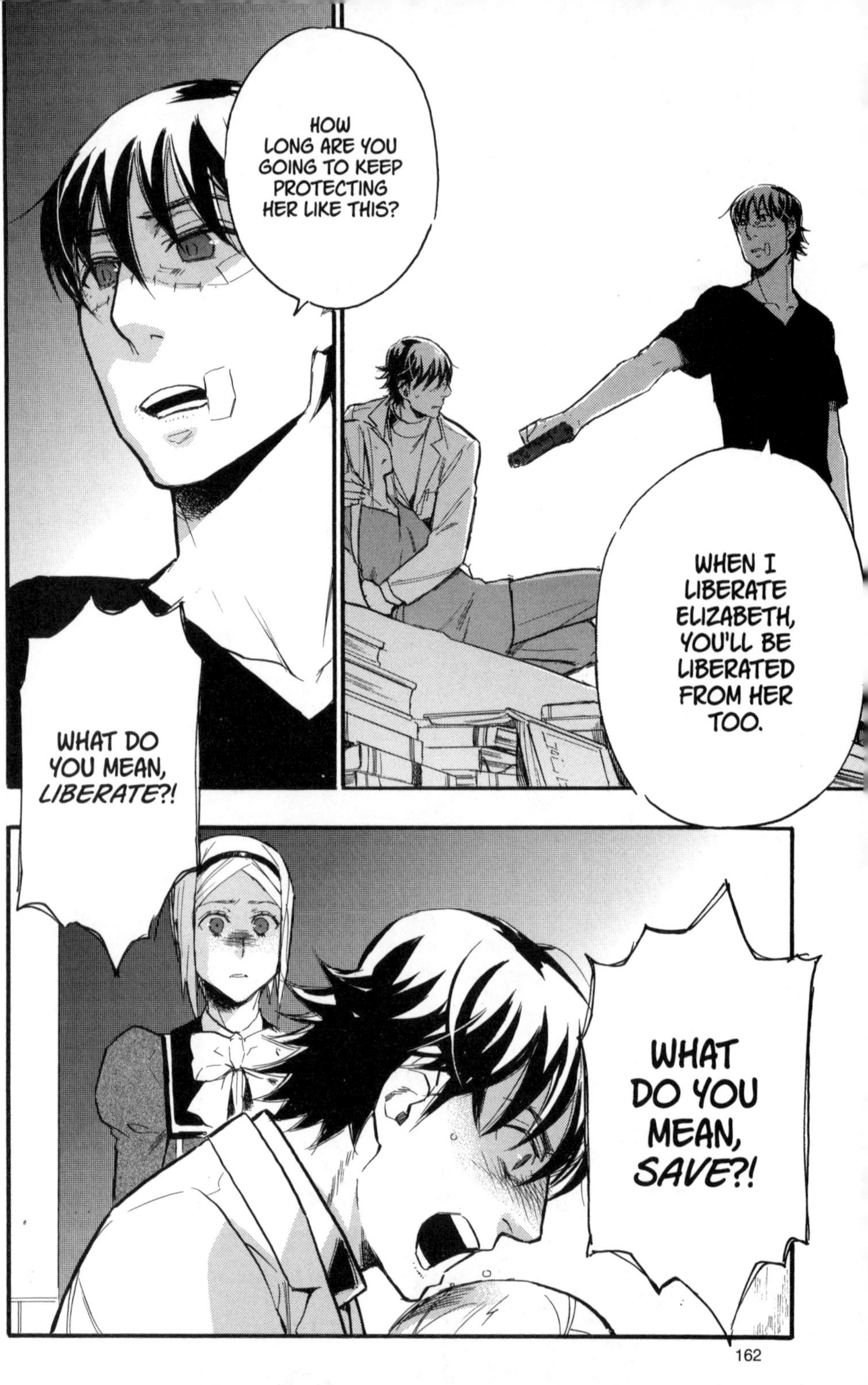
WHEN I LIBERATE ELIZABETH, YOU'LL BE LIBERATED FROM HER TOO.
HOW LONG ARE YOU GOING TO KEEP PROTECTING HER LIKE THIS?
WHAT DO YOU MEAN, *SAVE*?!
WHAT DO YOU MEAN, *LIBERATE*?!

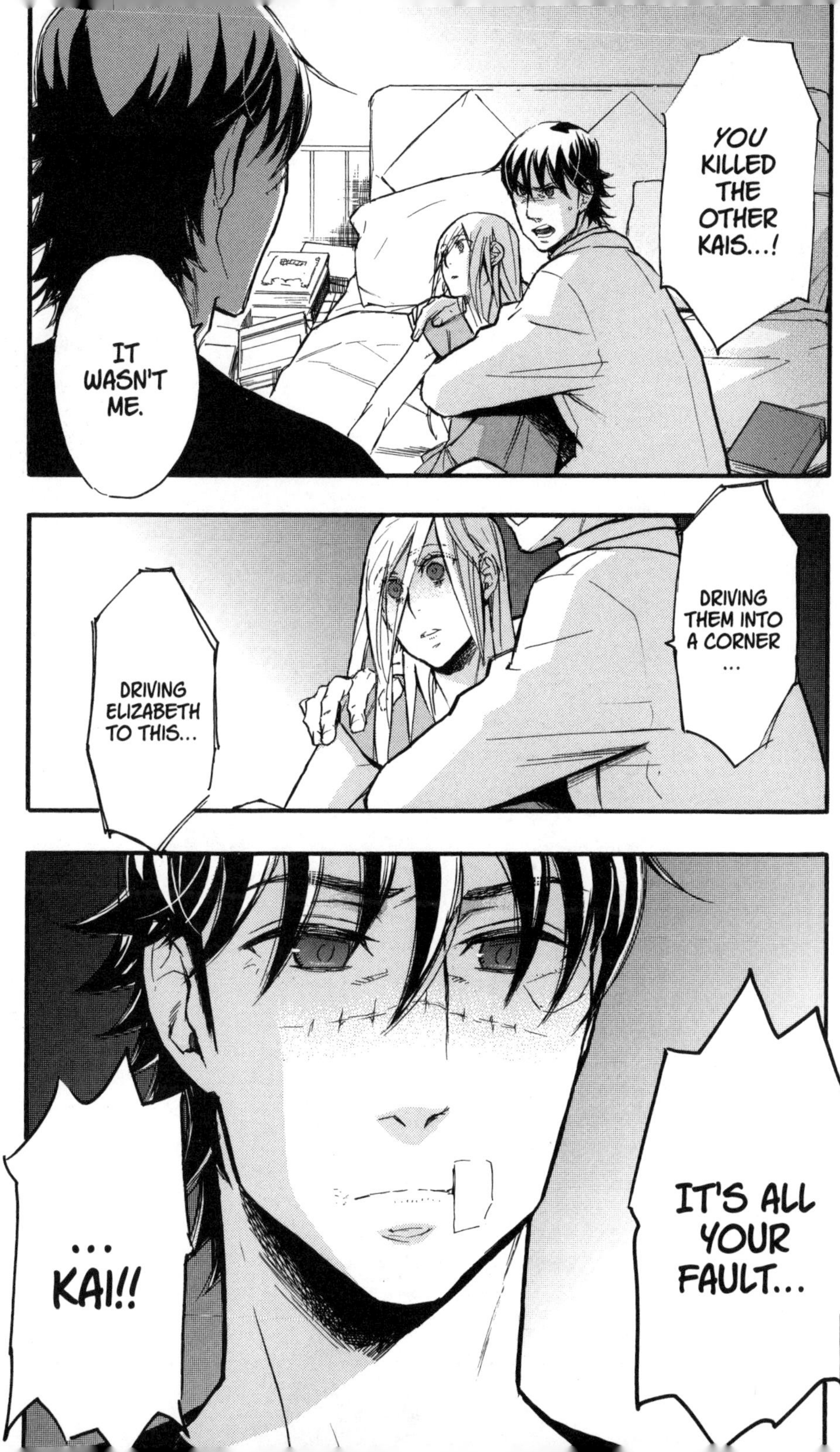
YOU KILLED THE OTHER KAIS...!
IT WASN'T ME.
DRIVING THEM INTO A CORNER ...
DRIVING ELIZABETH TO THIS...
IT'S ALL YOUR FAULT...
... KAI!!

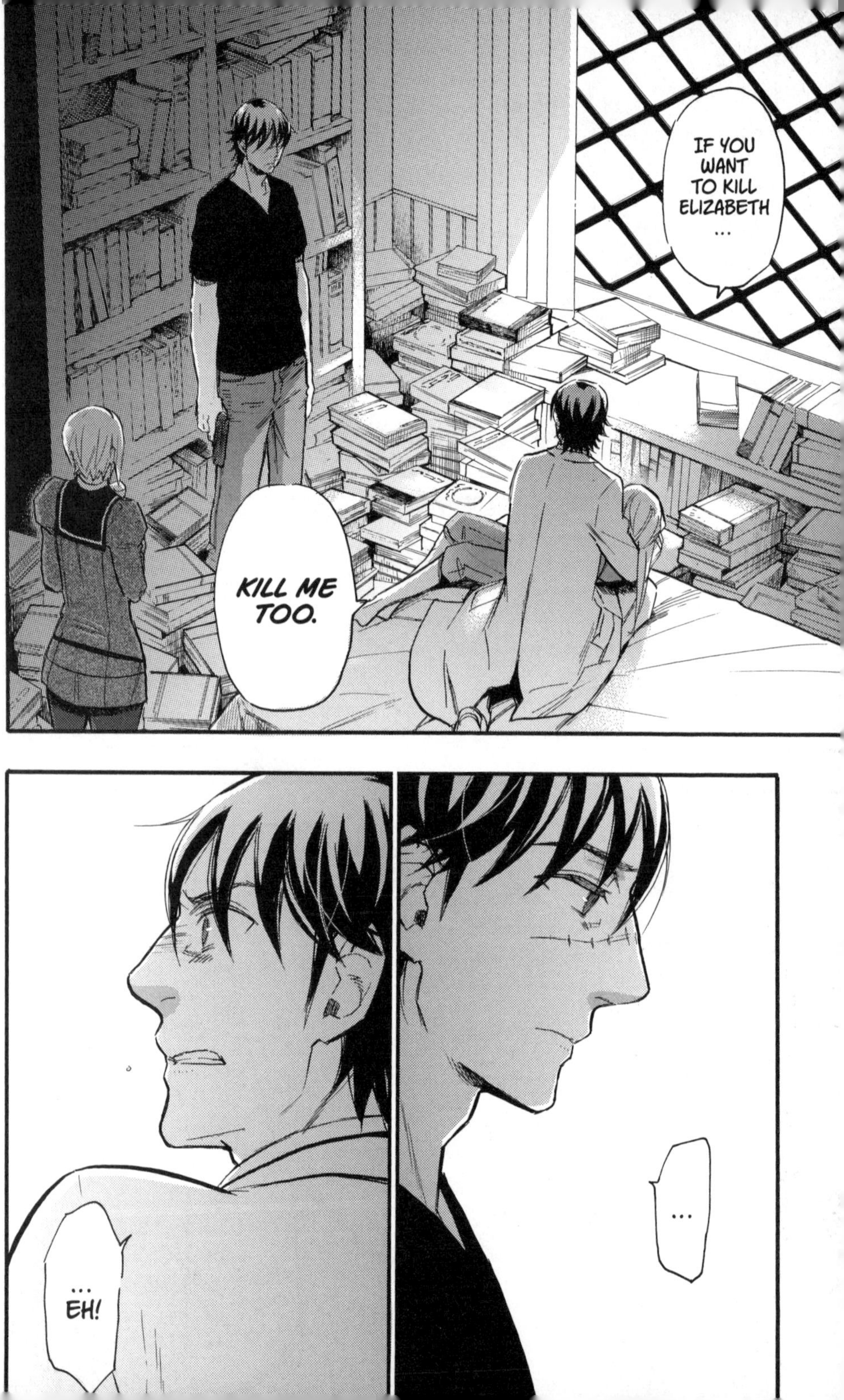
IF YOU WANT TO KILL ELIZABETH ...
KILL ME TOO.
...
... EH!

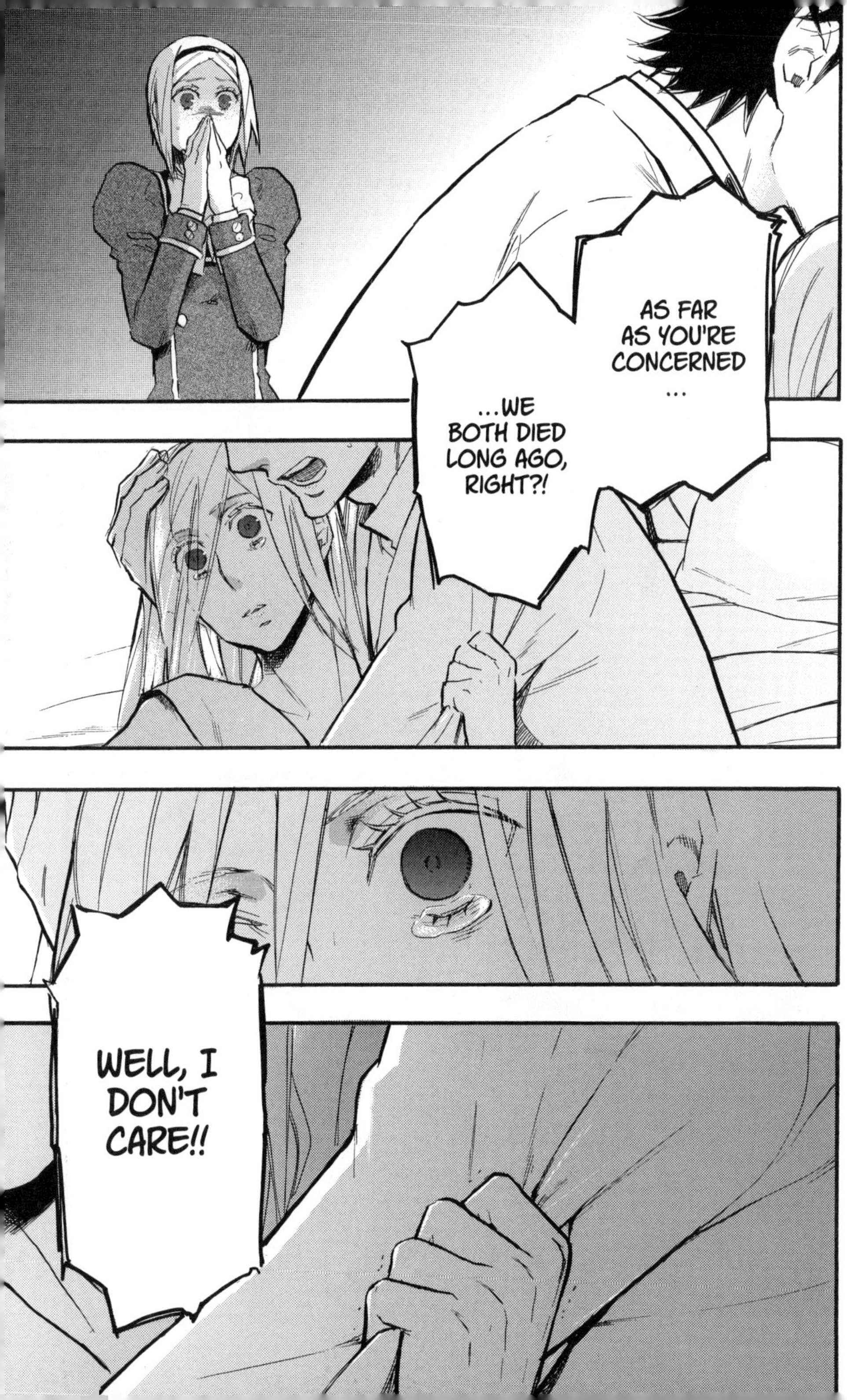
AS FAR AS YOU'RE CONCERNED ...
...WE BOTH DIED LONG AGO, RIGHT?!
WELL, I DON'T CARE!!

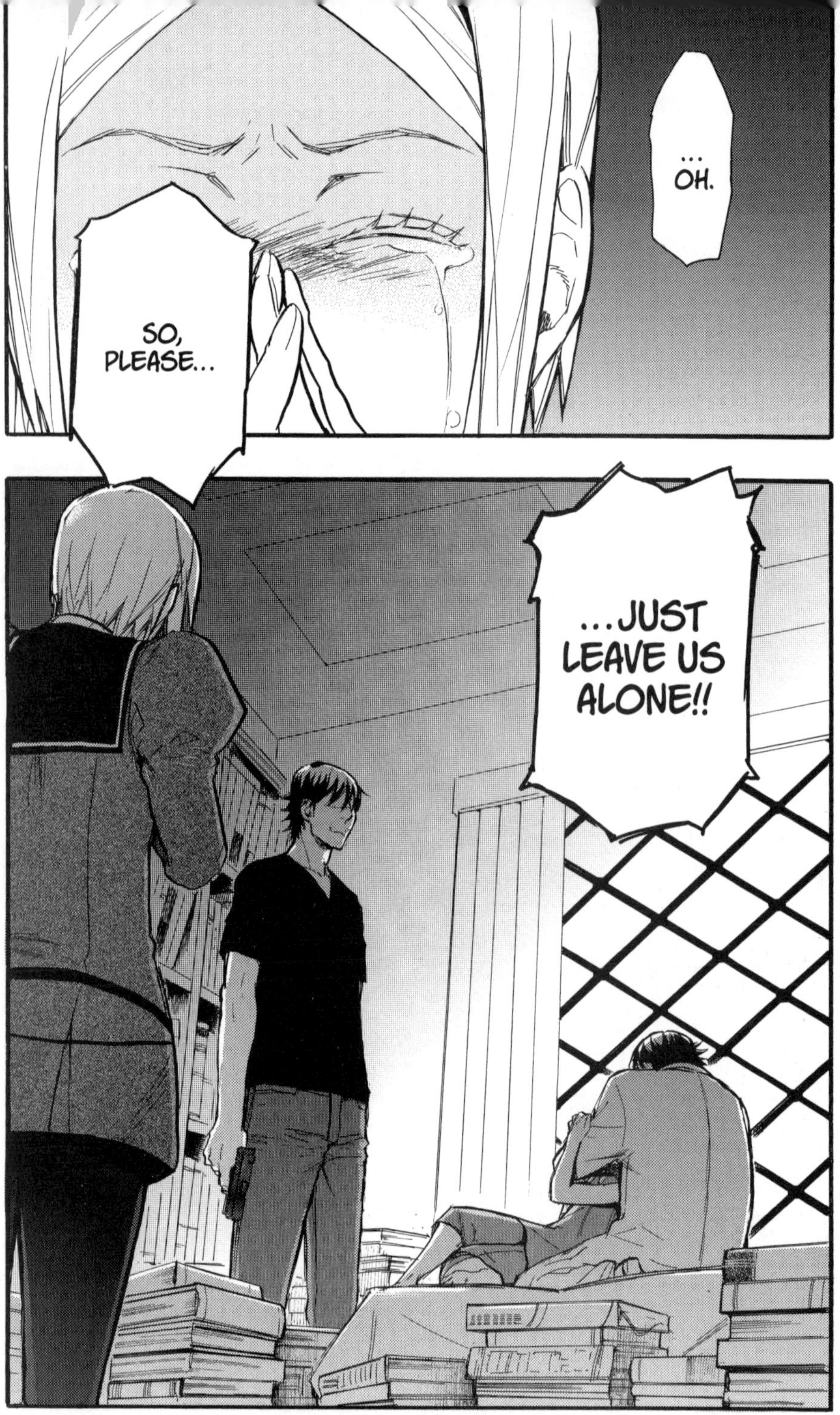

...OH.
SO, PLEASE...
...JUST LEAVE US ALONE!!

CHAPTER thirty-six

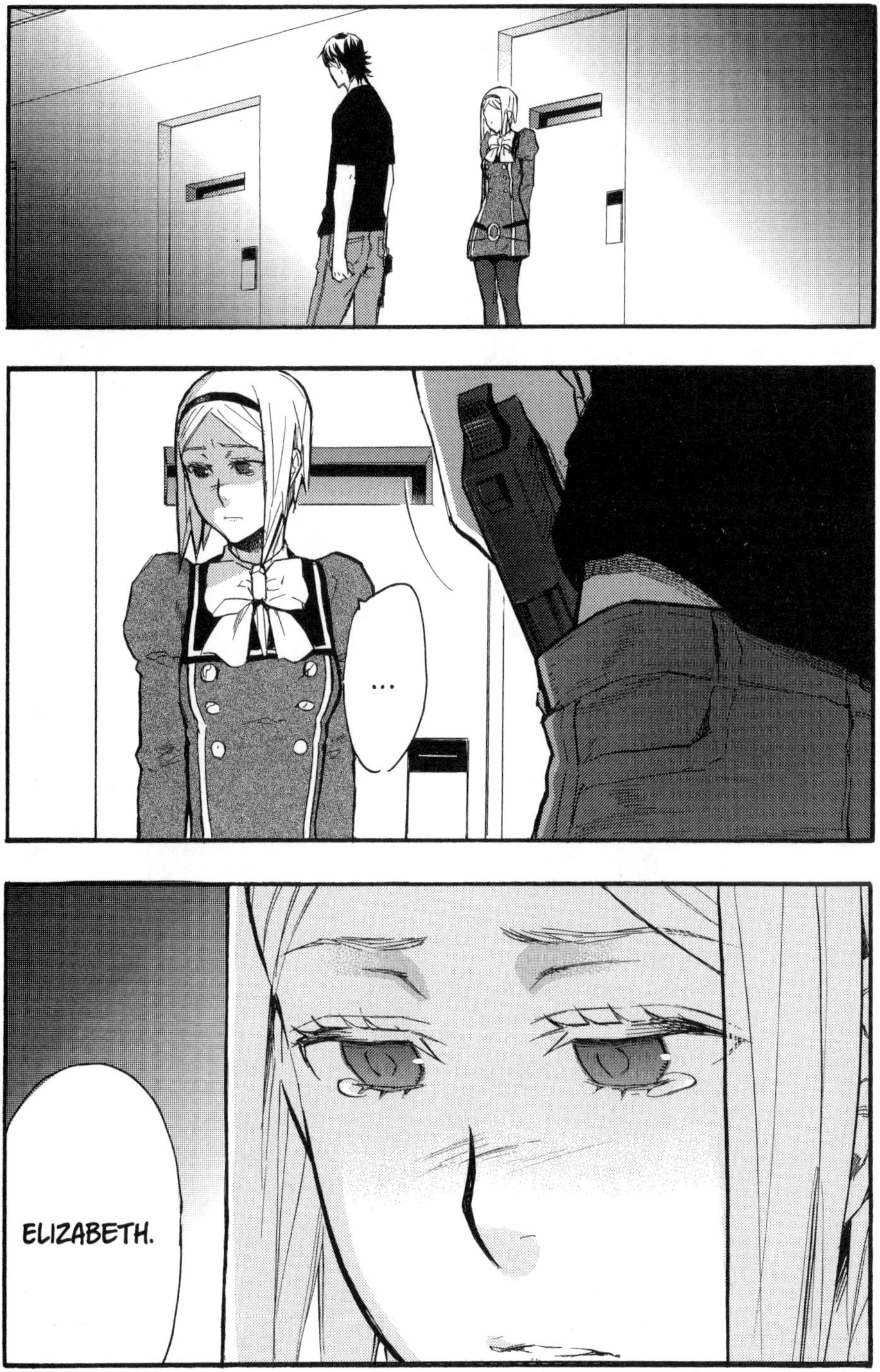
...
ELIZABETH.

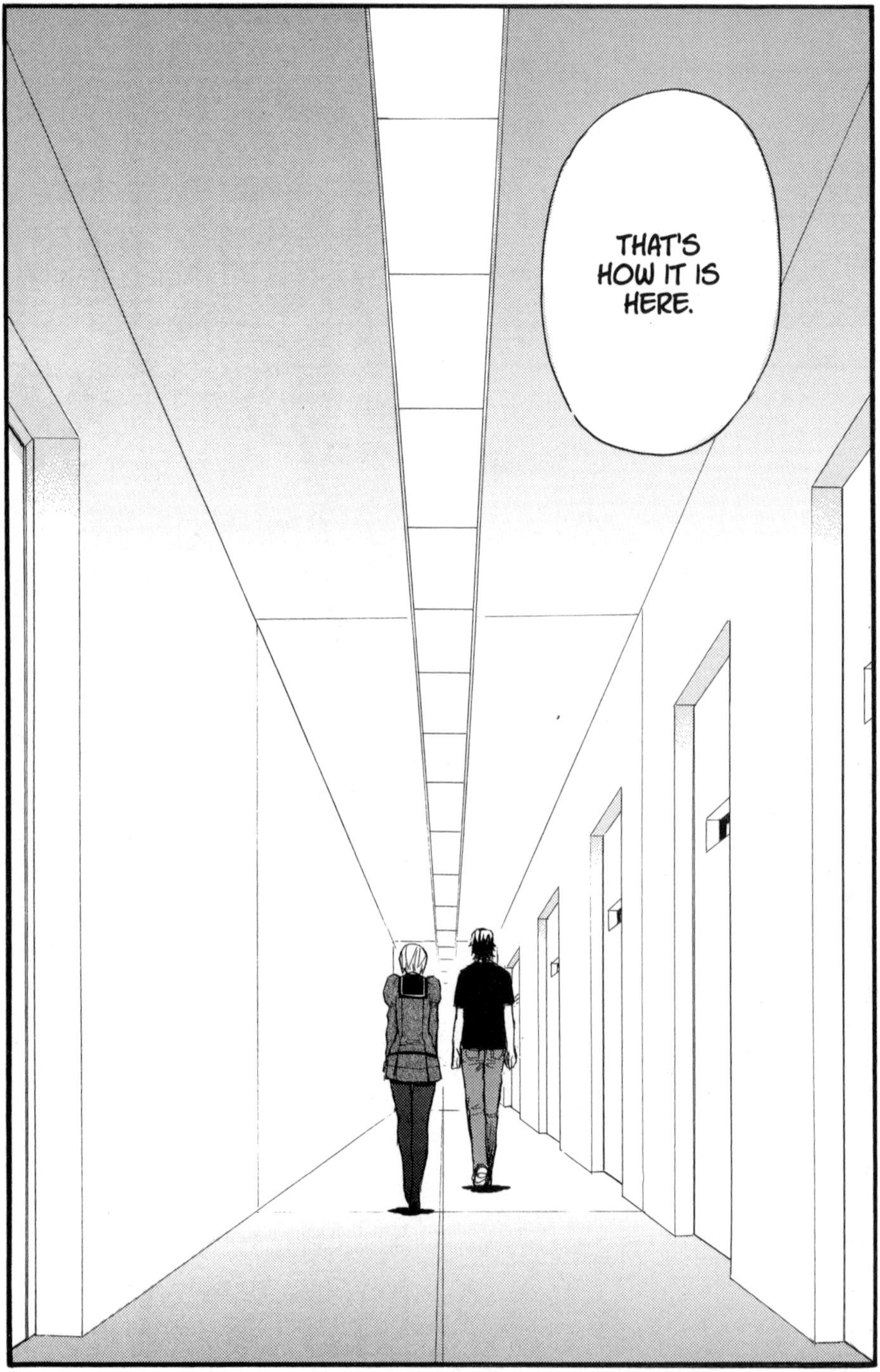
THAT'S HOW IT IS HERE.

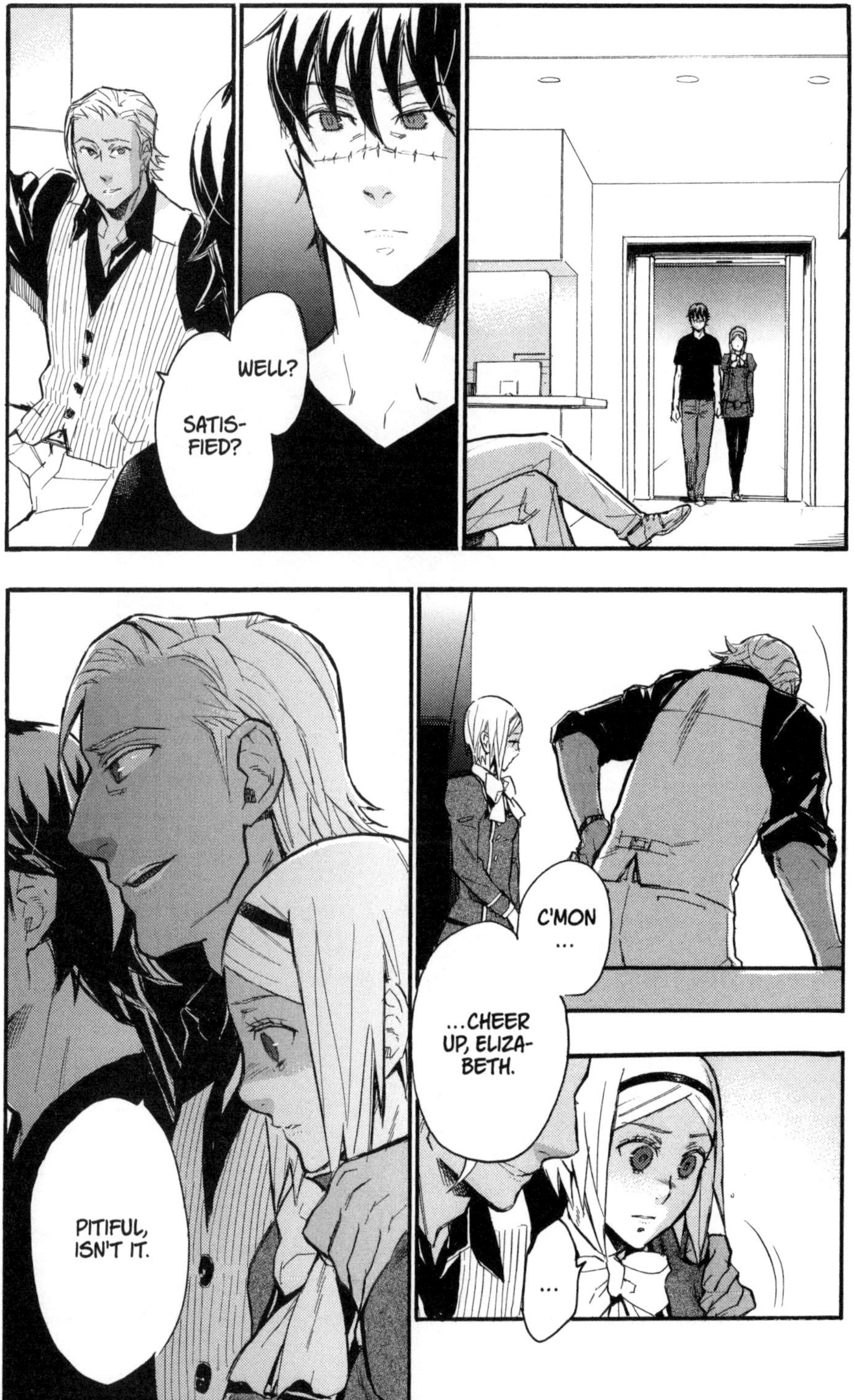
WELL?
SATISFIED?
C'MON ...
...CHEER UP, ELIZA-BETH.
...
PITIFUL, ISN'T IT.

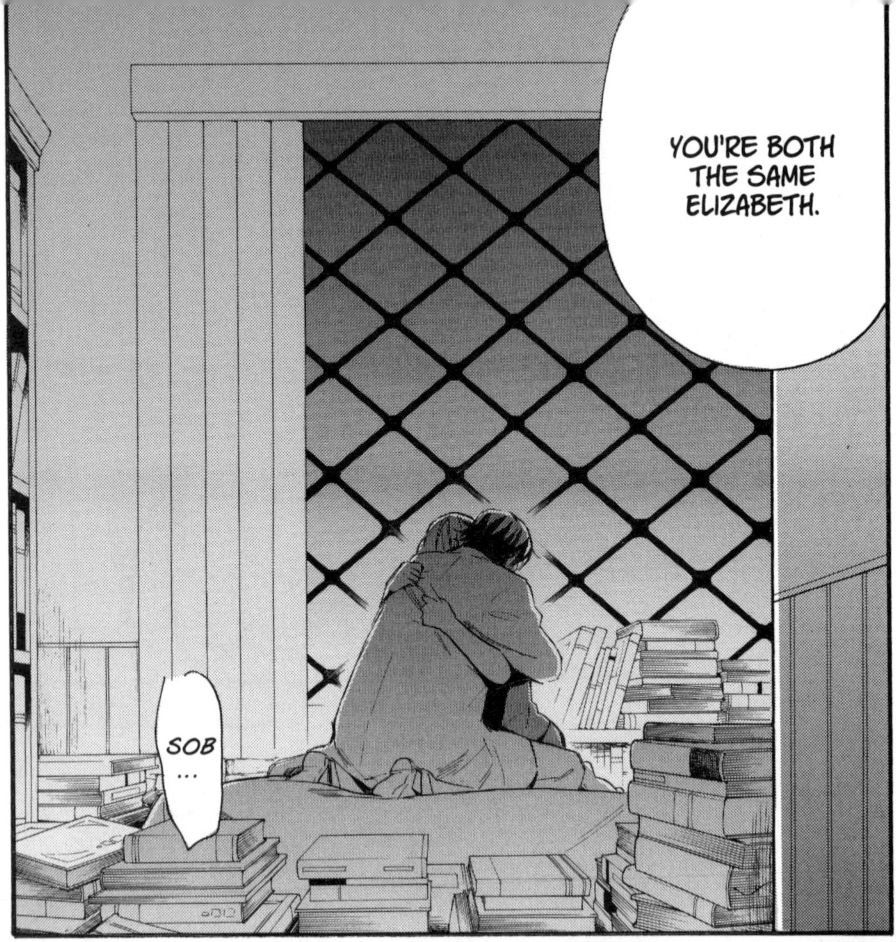
YOU'RE BOTH THE SAME ELIZABETH.
SOB ...

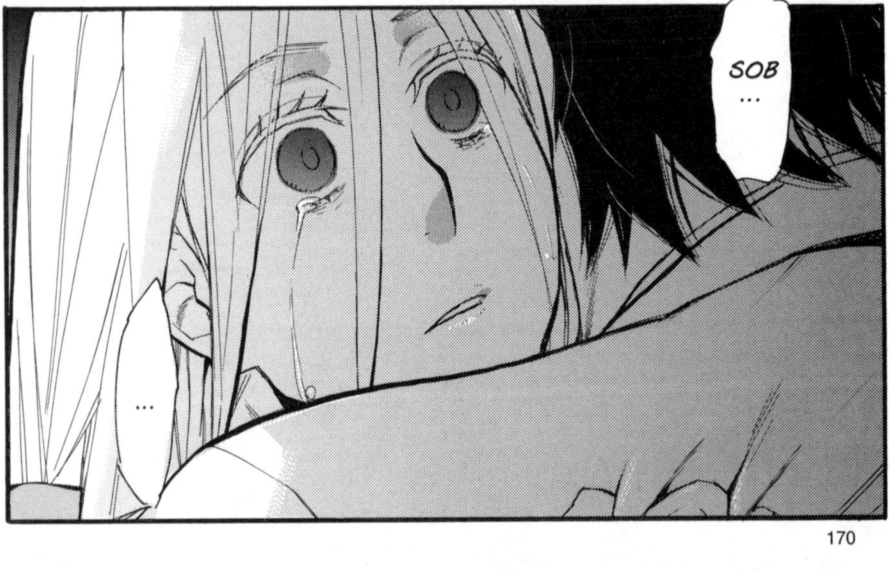
SOB ...
...

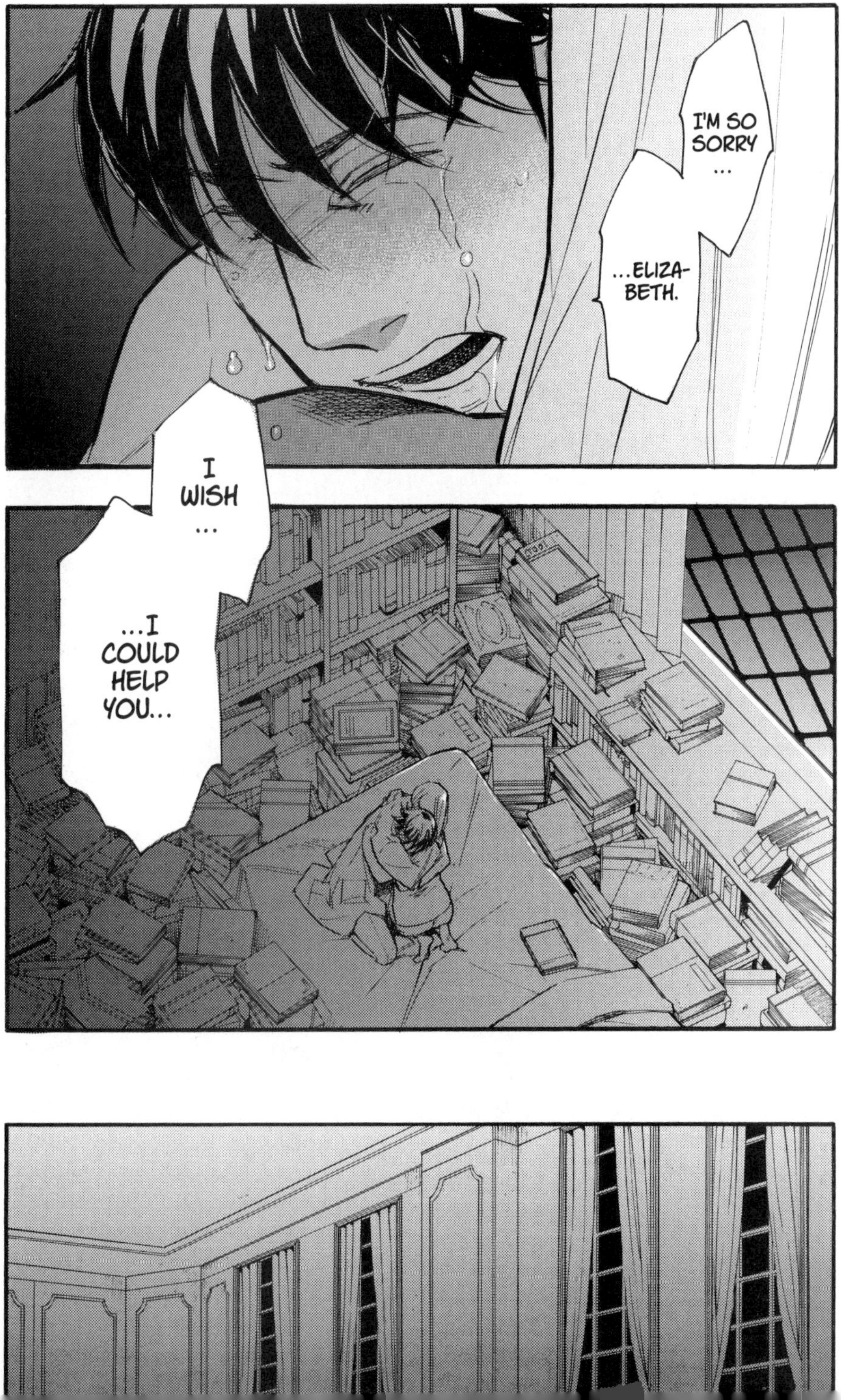
I'M SO SORRY ...
...ELIZA-BETH.
I WISH ...
...I COULD HELP YOU...

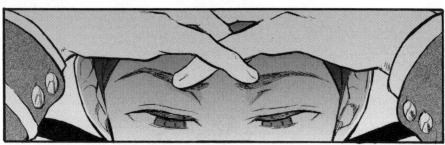

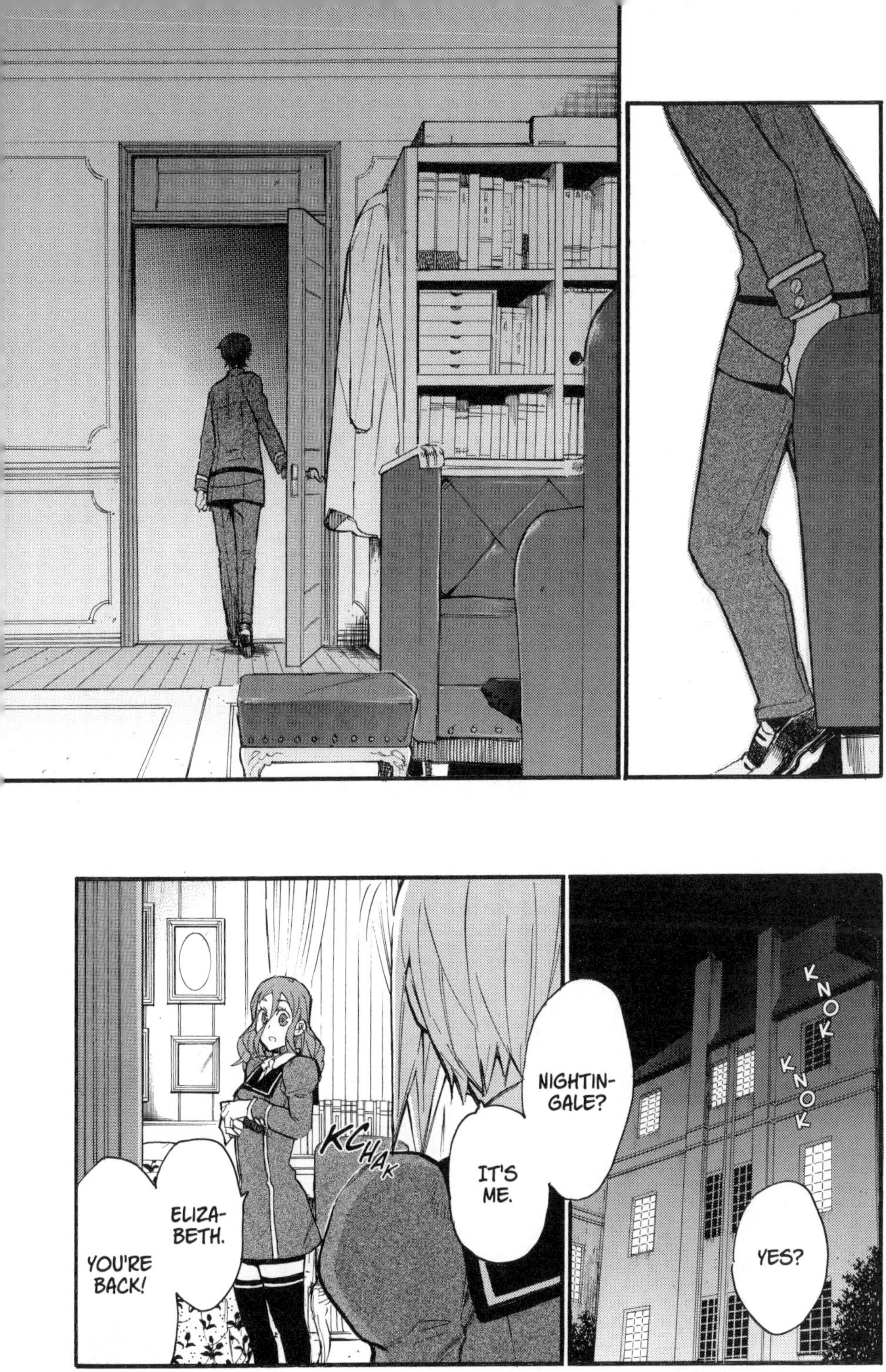
KNOK
KNOK
YES?
NIGHTIN-GALE?
IT'S ME.
KCHAK
ELIZA-BETH.
YOU'RE BACK!

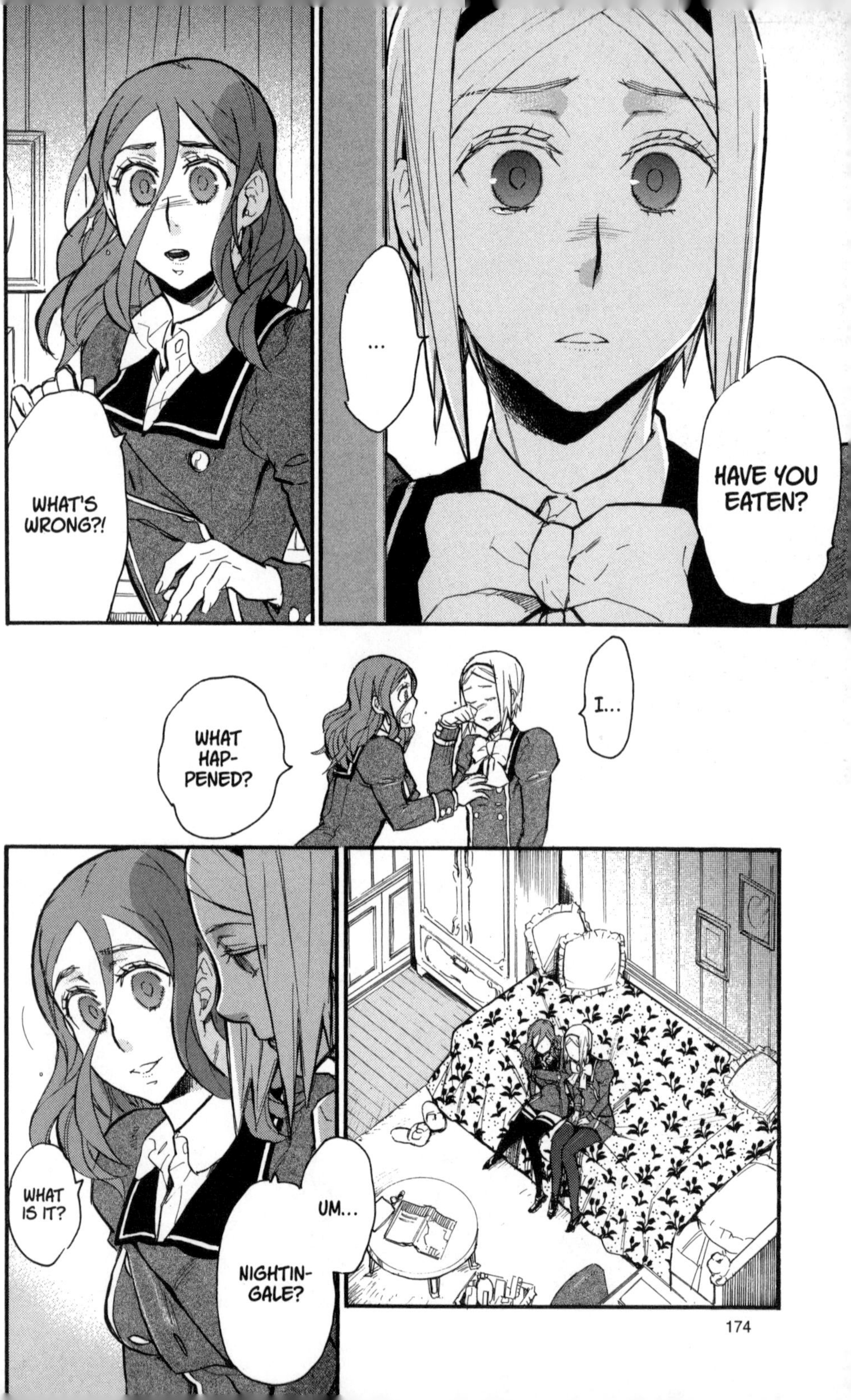
HAVE YOU EATEN?
...
WHAT'S WRONG?!
I...
WHAT HAPPENED?
UM...
NIGHTINGALE?
WHAT IS IT?

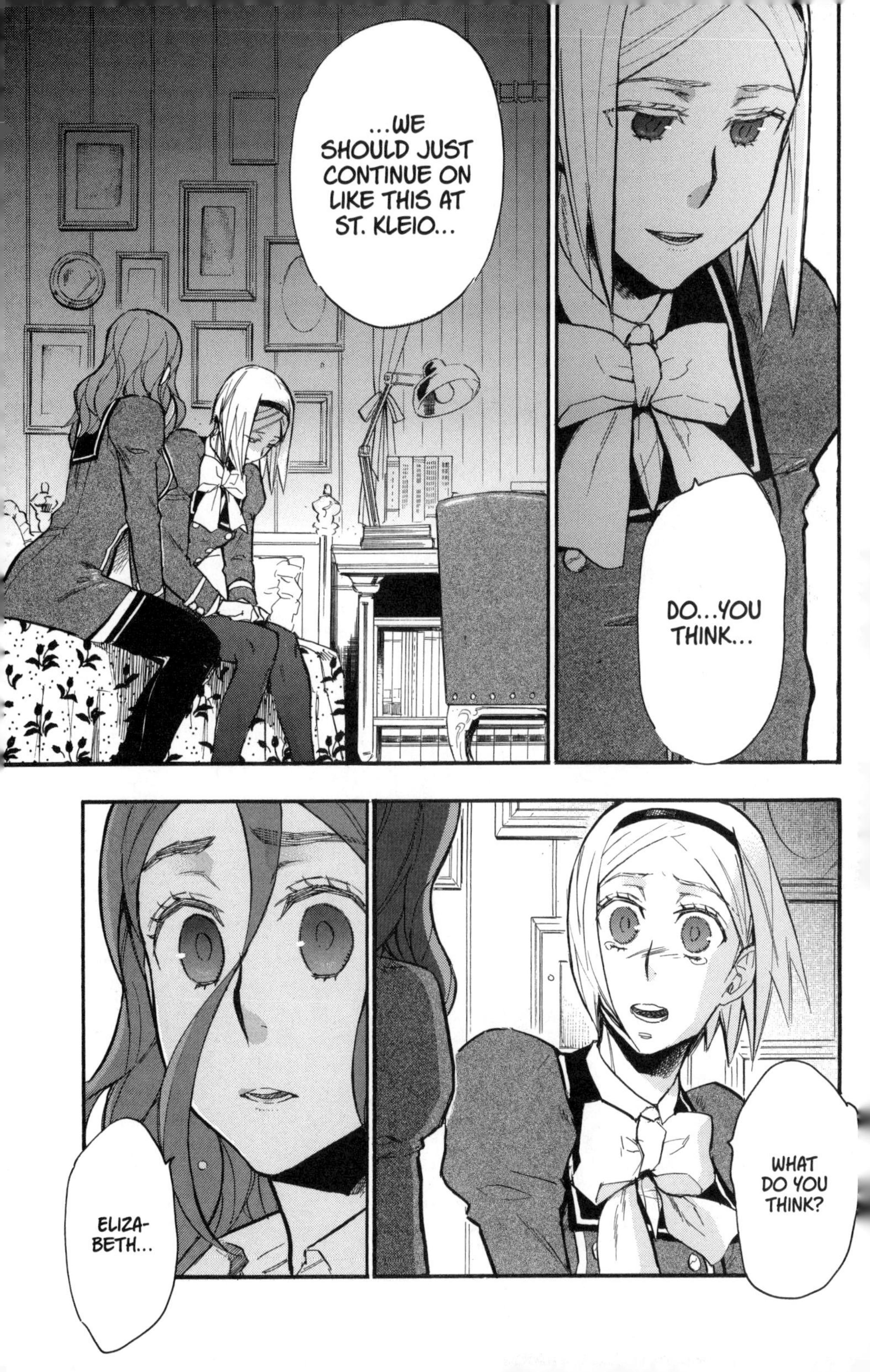
DO...YOU THINK...
...WE SHOULD JUST CONTINUE ON LIKE THIS AT ST. KLEIO...
WHAT DO YOU THINK?
ELIZA-BETH...

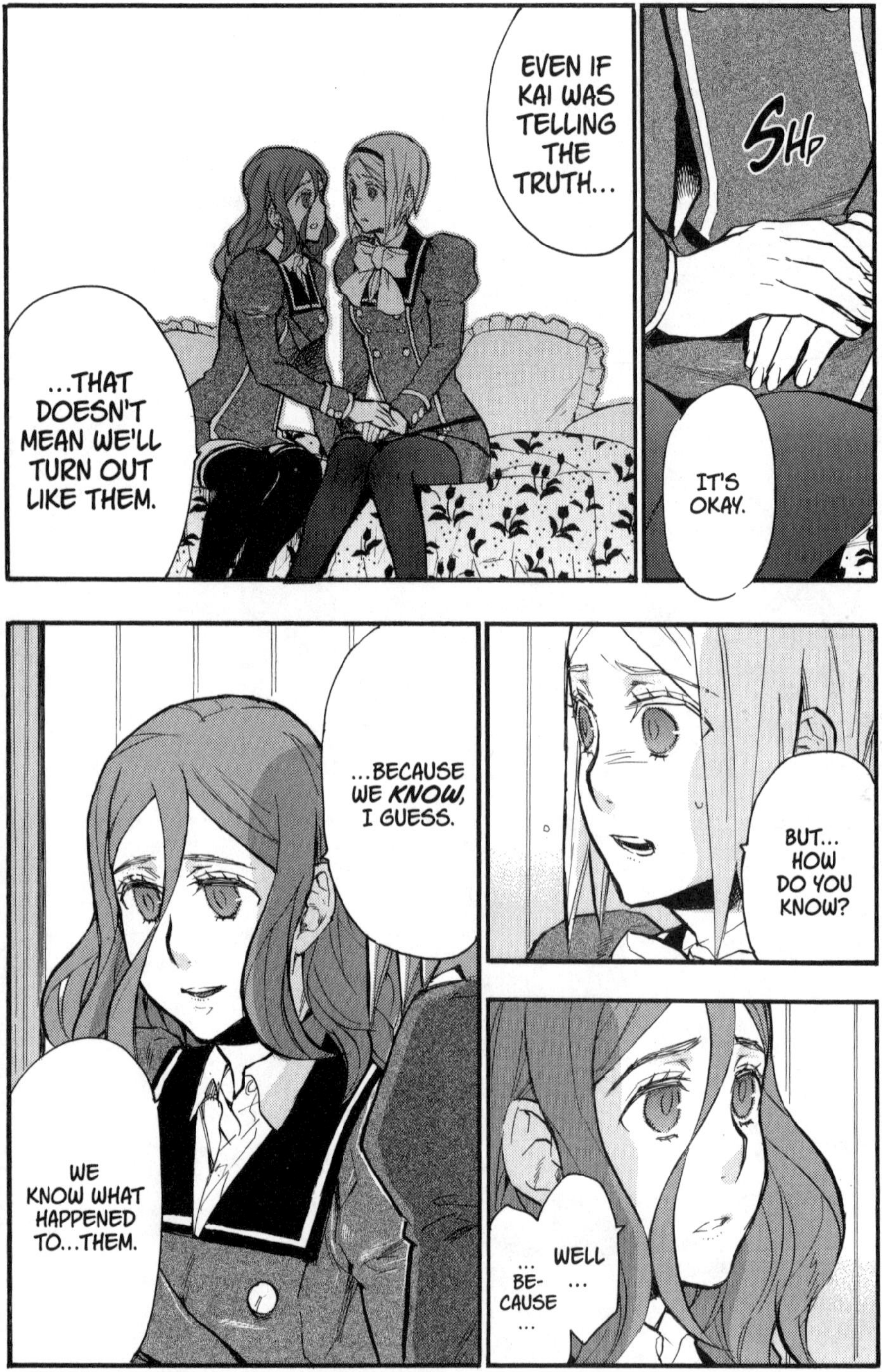
SHP
IT'S OKAY.
EVEN IF KAI WAS TELLING THE TRUTH...
...THAT DOESN'T MEAN WE'LL TURN OUT LIKE THEM.
BUT... HOW DO YOU KNOW?
WELL ... ... BE-CAUSE ...
...BECAUSE WE ***KNOW,*** I GUESS.
WE KNOW WHAT HAPPENED TO...THEM.

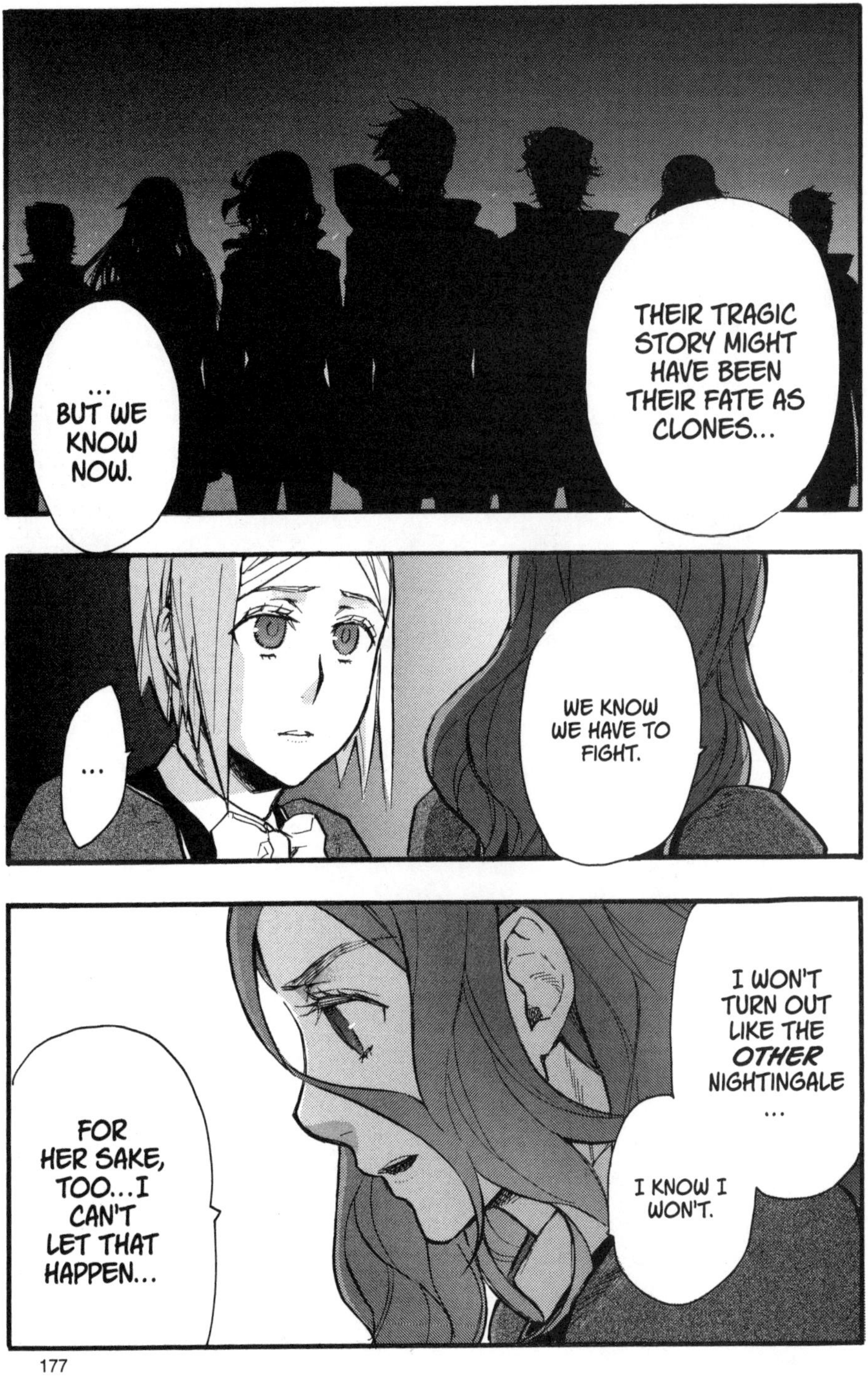
THEIR TRAGIC STORY MIGHT HAVE BEEN THEIR FATE AS CLONES...
... BUT WE KNOW NOW.
WE KNOW WE HAVE TO FIGHT.
...
I WON'T TURN OUT LIKE THE *OTHER* NIGHTINGALE ...
I KNOW I WON'T.
FOR HER SAKE, TOO...I CAN'T LET THAT HAPPEN...

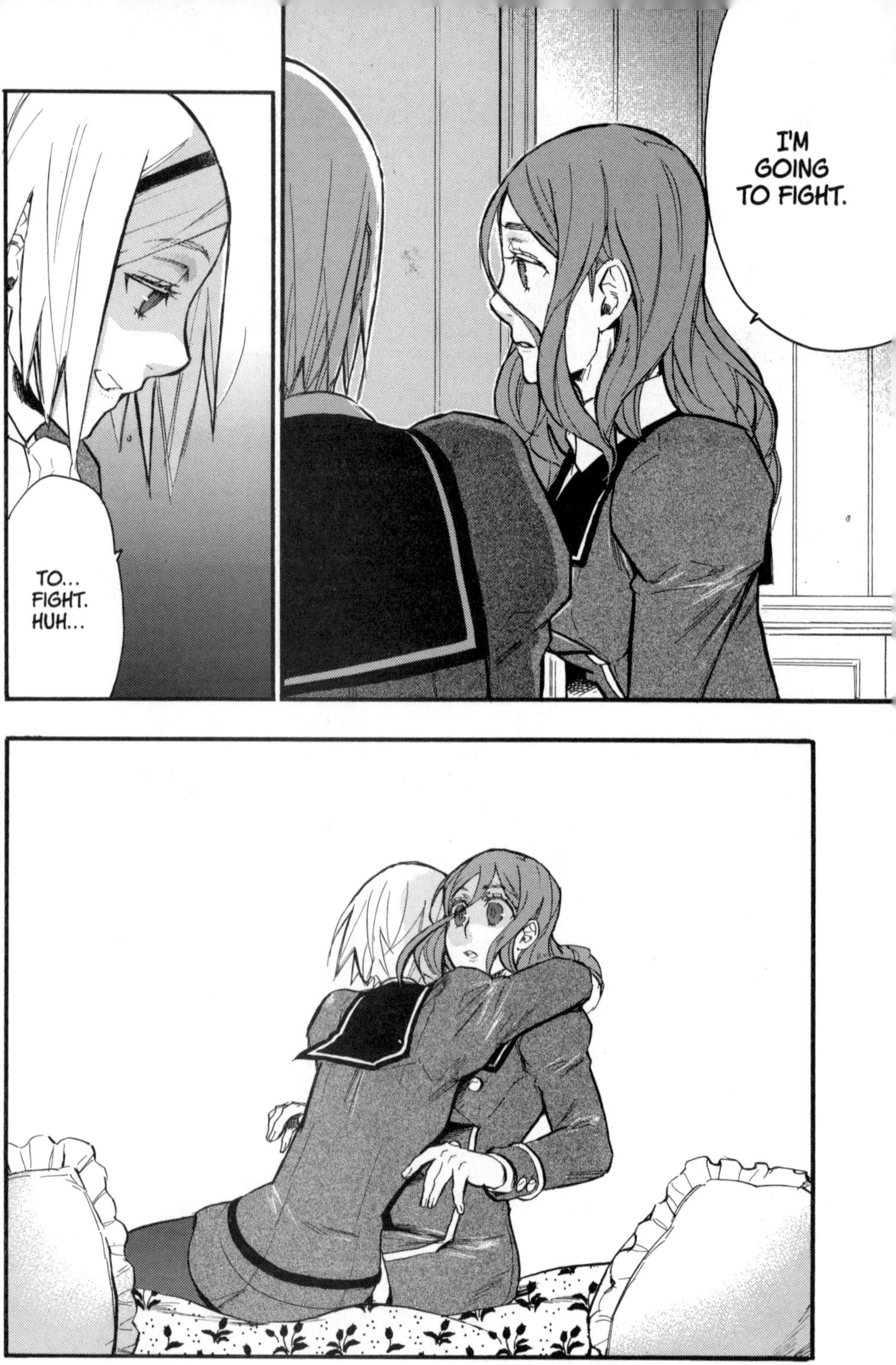
I'M GOING TO FIGHT.
TO... FIGHT. HUH...

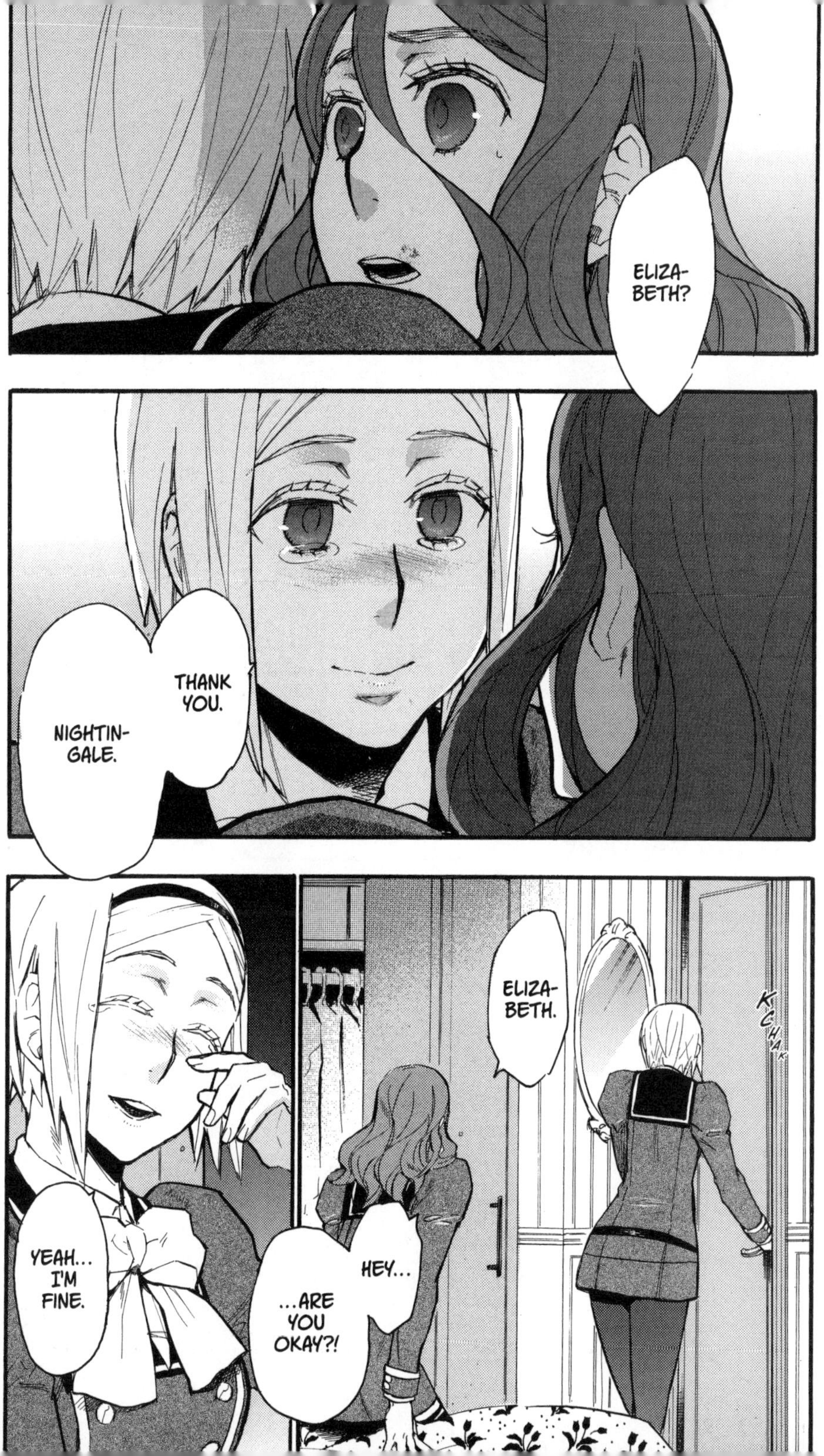
ELIZA-BETH?
THANK YOU.
NIGHTIN-GALE.
KCHAK
ELIZA-BETH.
HEY...
...ARE YOU OKAY?!
YEAH... I'M FINE.

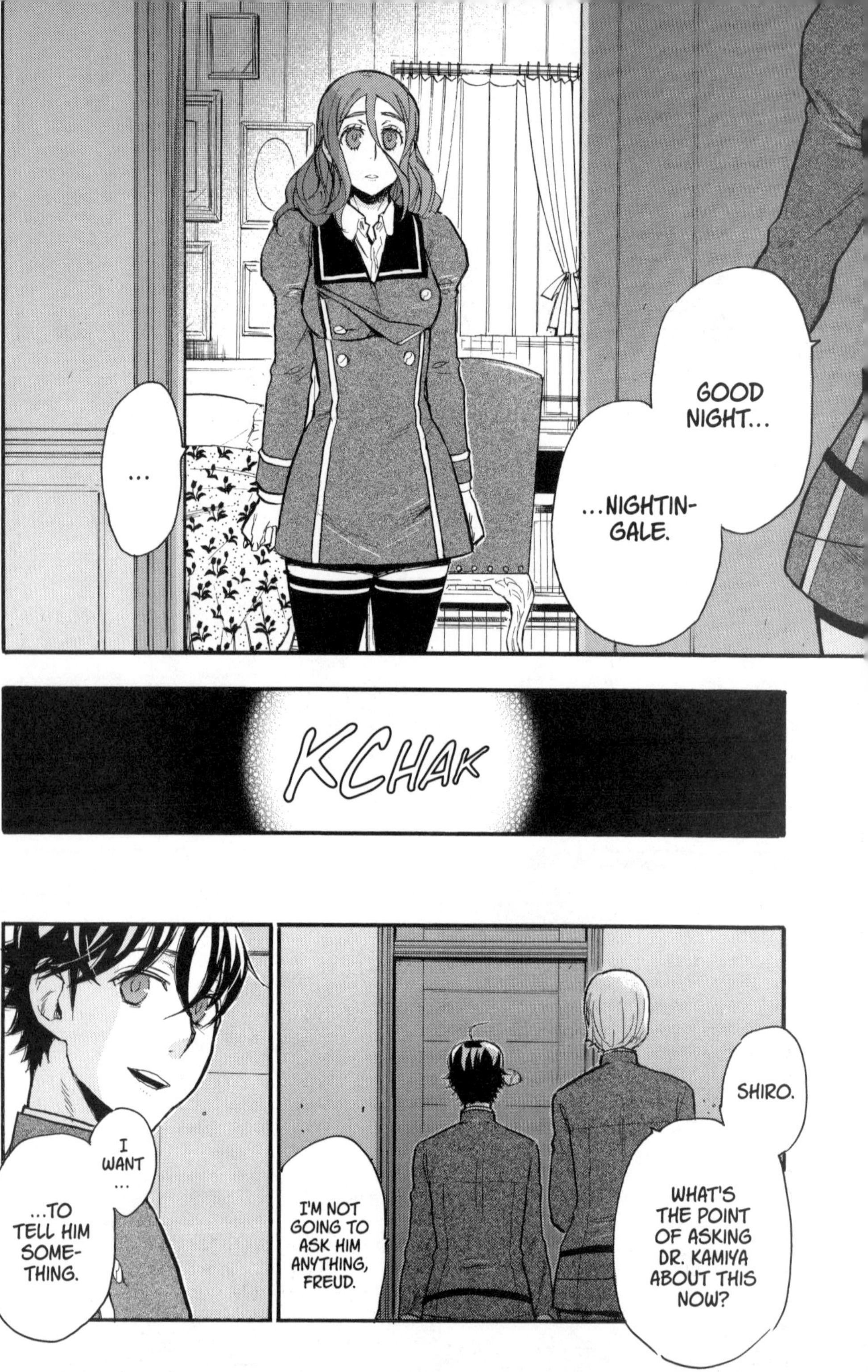
GOOD NIGHT...
...NIGHTIN-GALE.
...
KCHAK
SHIRO.
WHAT'S THE POINT OF ASKING DR. KAMIYA ABOUT THIS NOW?
I'M NOT GOING TO ASK HIM ANYTHING, FREUD.
I WANT...
...TO TELL HIM SOMETHING.

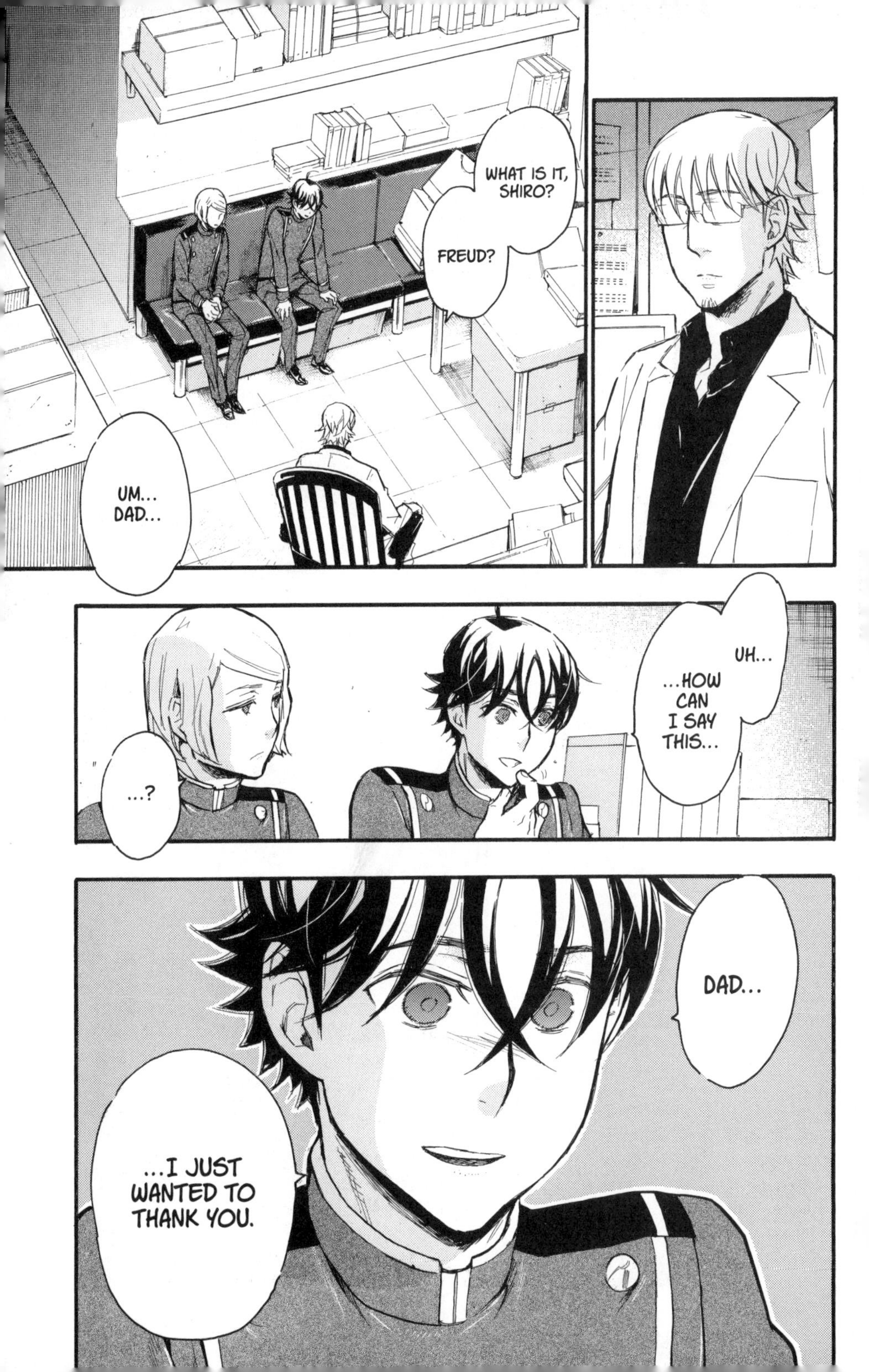
WHAT IS IT, SHIRO?
FREUD?
UM... DAD...
UH...
...HOW CAN I SAY THIS...
...?
DAD...
...I JUST WANTED TO THANK YOU.

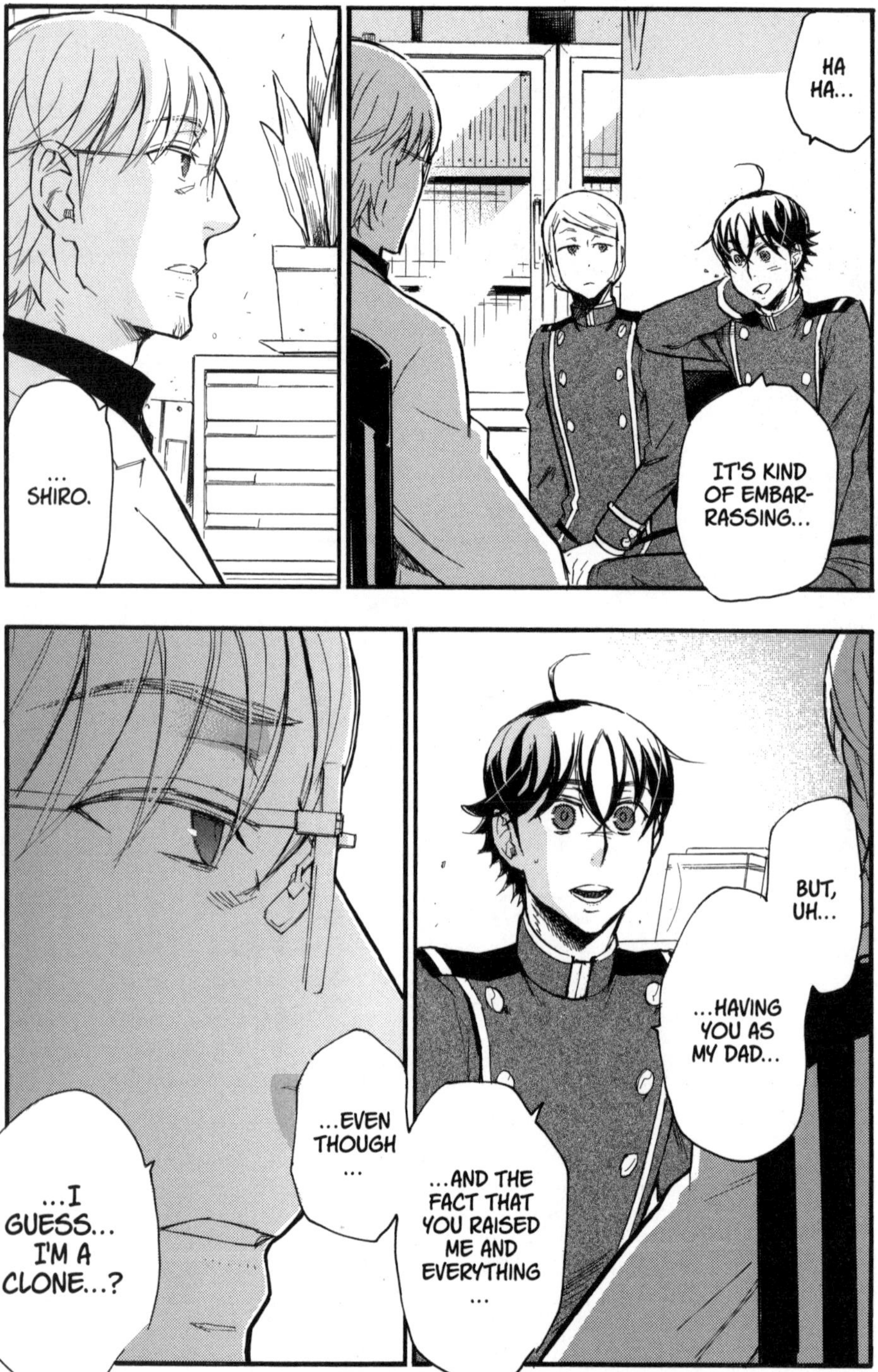
HA HA...
IT'S KIND OF EMBARRASSING...
... SHIRO.
BUT, UH...
...HAVING YOU AS MY DAD...
...AND THE FACT THAT YOU RAISED ME AND EVERYTHING ...
...EVEN THOUGH ...
...I GUESS... I'M A CLONE...?

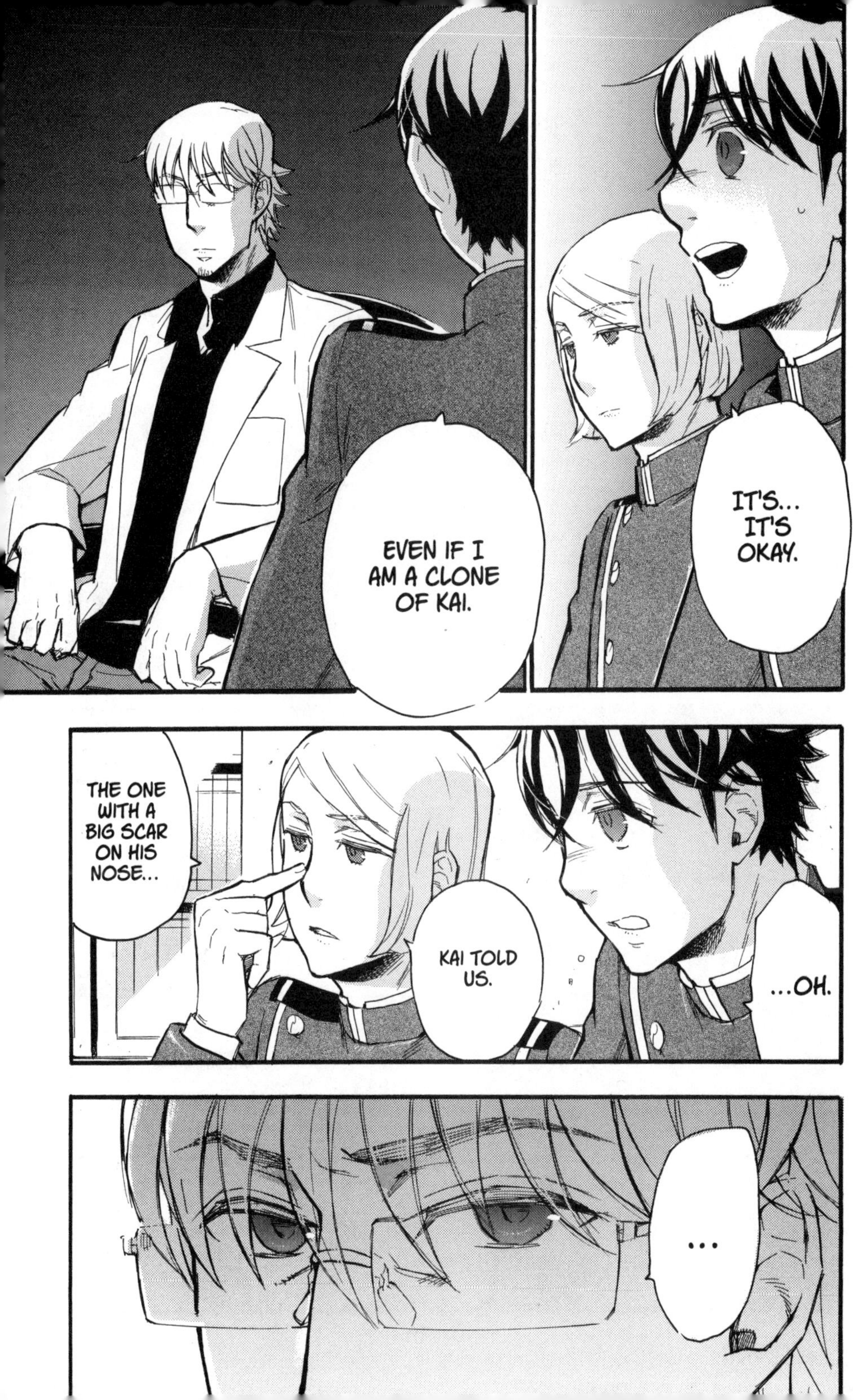
IT'S... IT'S OKAY.
EVEN IF I AM A CLONE OF KAI.
...OH.
KAI TOLD US.
THE ONE WITH A BIG SCAR ON HIS NOSE...
...

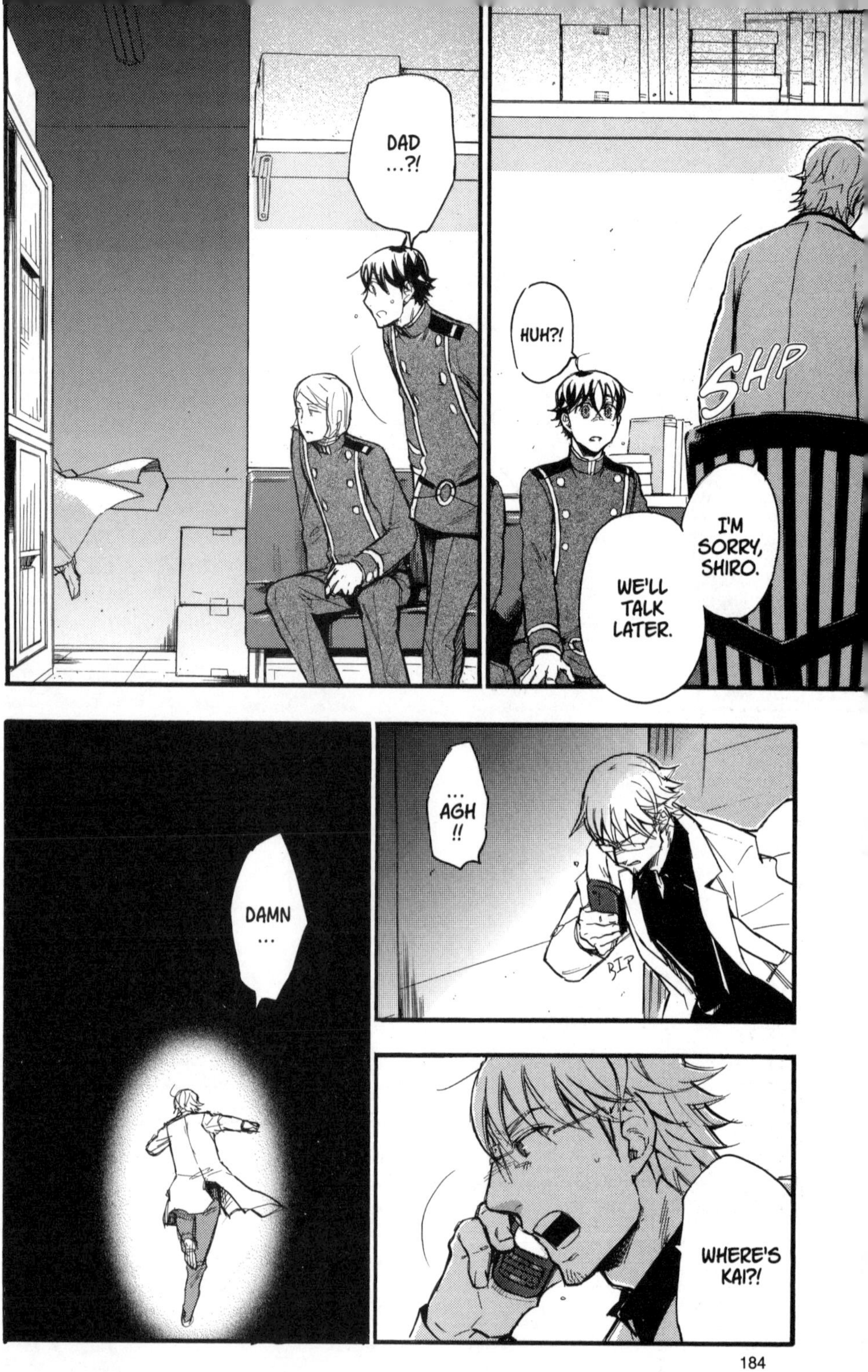
HUH?!
SHP
I'M SORRY, SHIRO.
WE'LL TALK LATER.
DAD ...?!
... AGH !!
BIP
WHERE'S KAI?!
DAMN ...

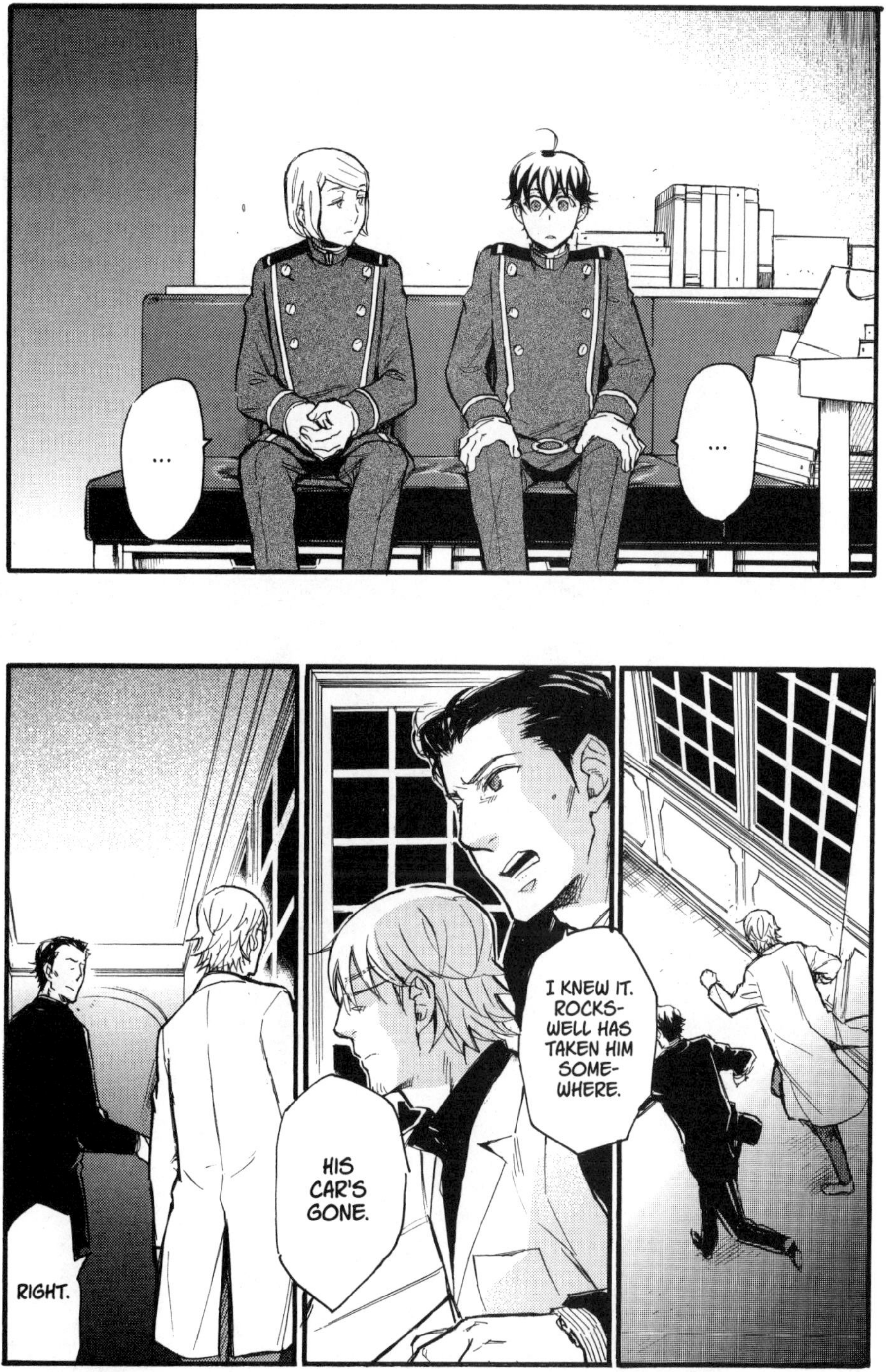
...
...
I KNEW IT. ROCKS-WELL HAS TAKEN HIM SOME-WHERE.
HIS CAR'S GONE.
RIGHT.

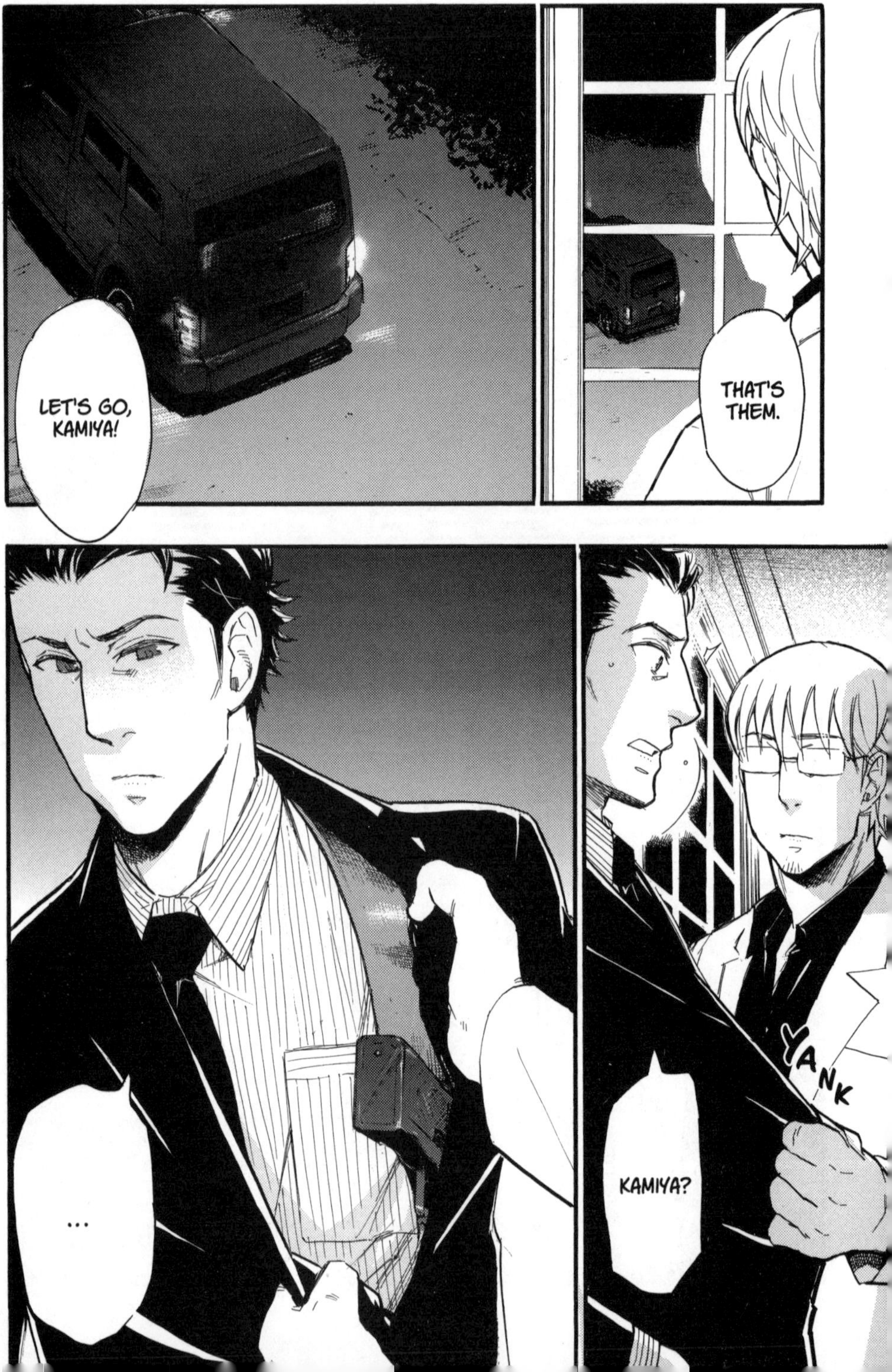
THAT'S THEM.
LET'S GO, KAMIYA!
YANK
KAMIYA?
...

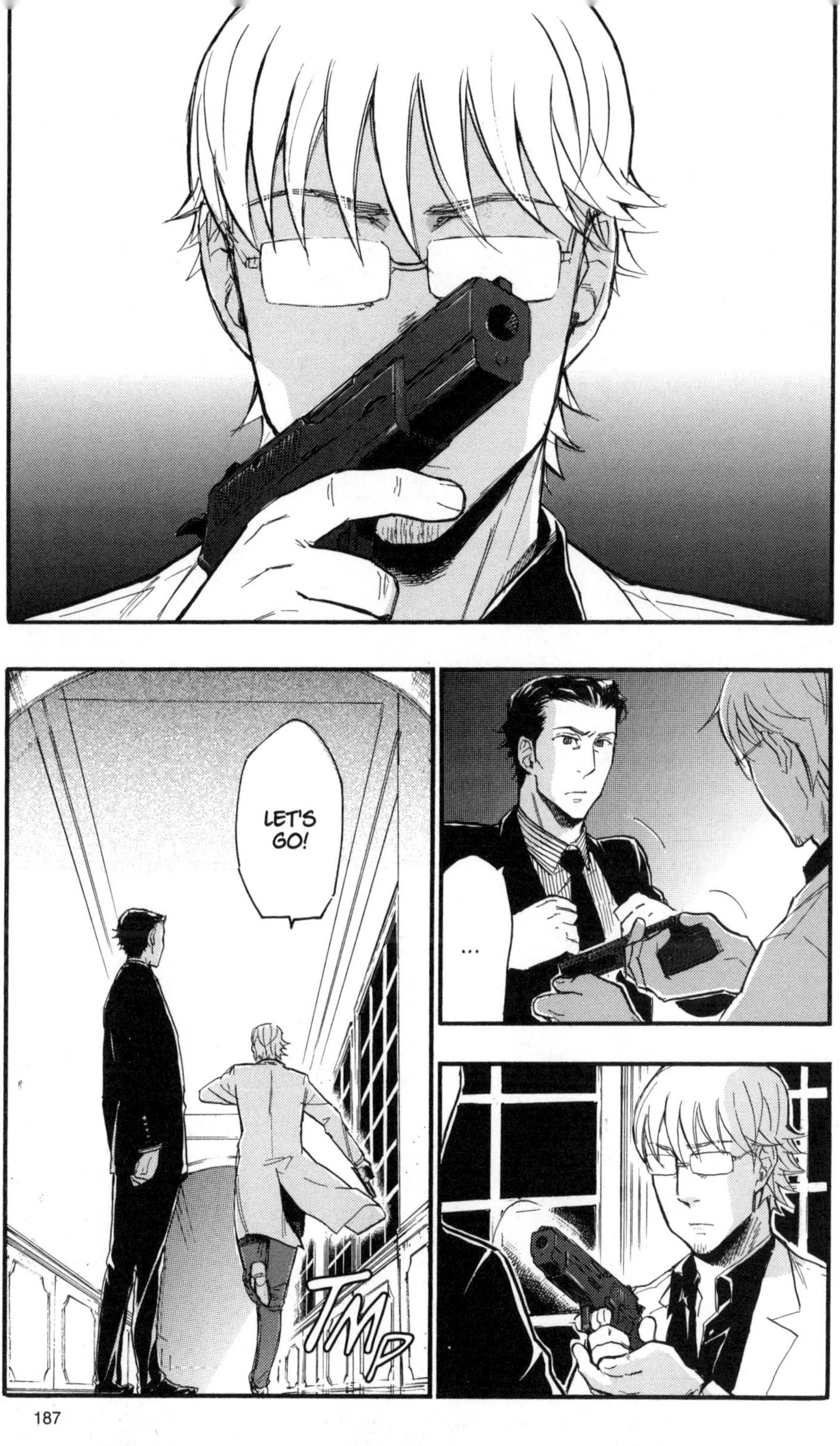
...
LET'S GO!
TMP

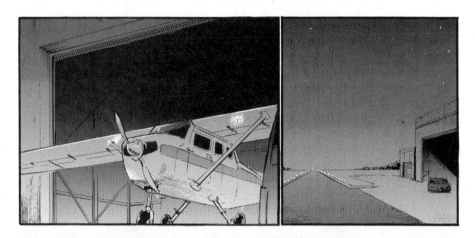

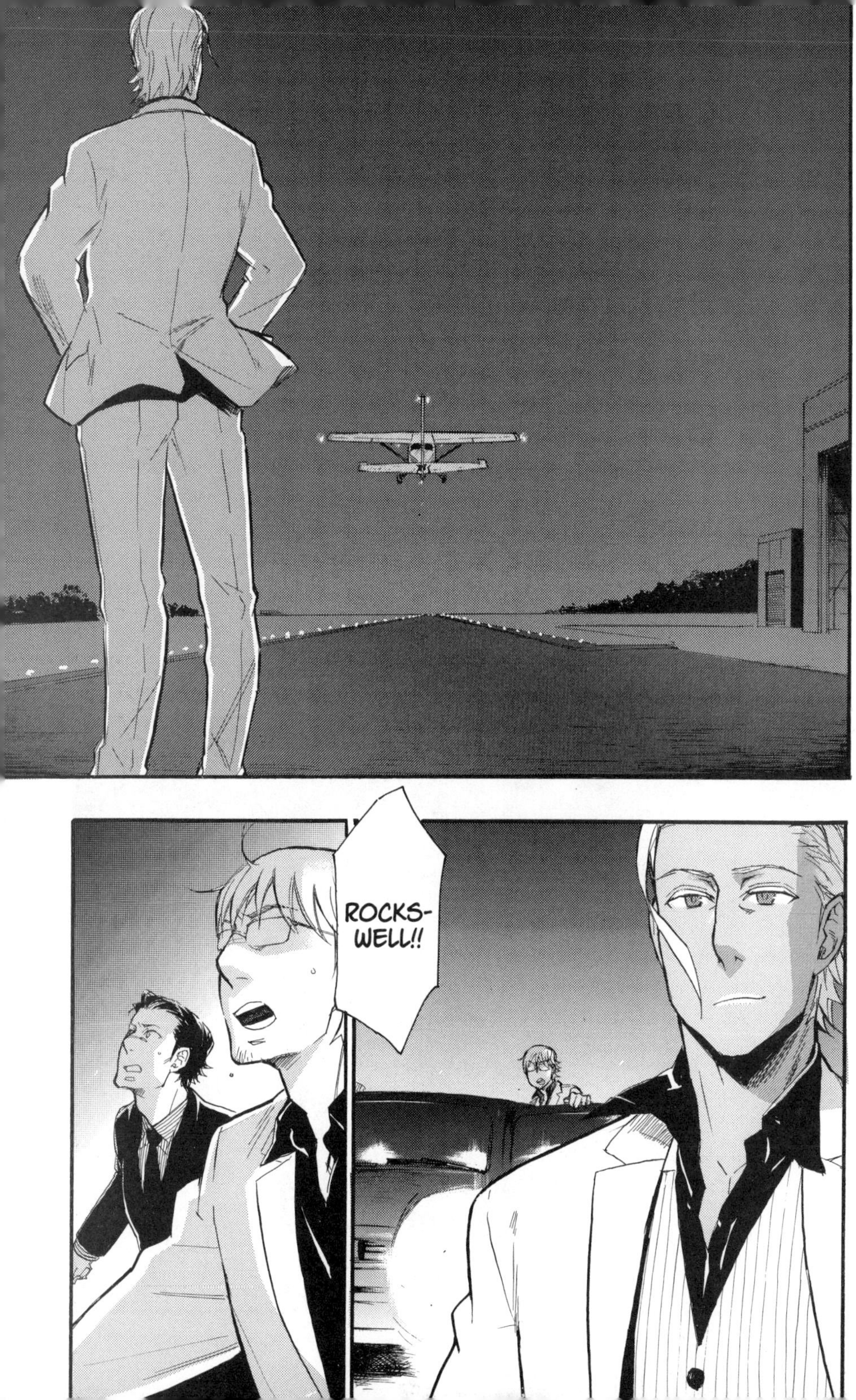
ROCKS-
WELL!!

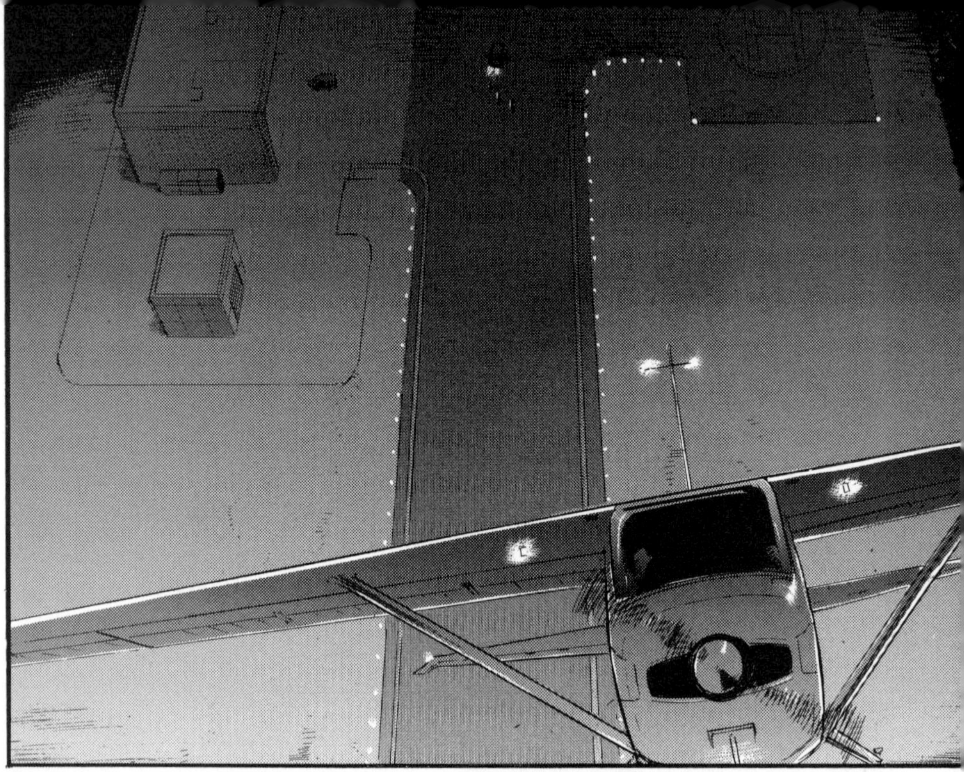

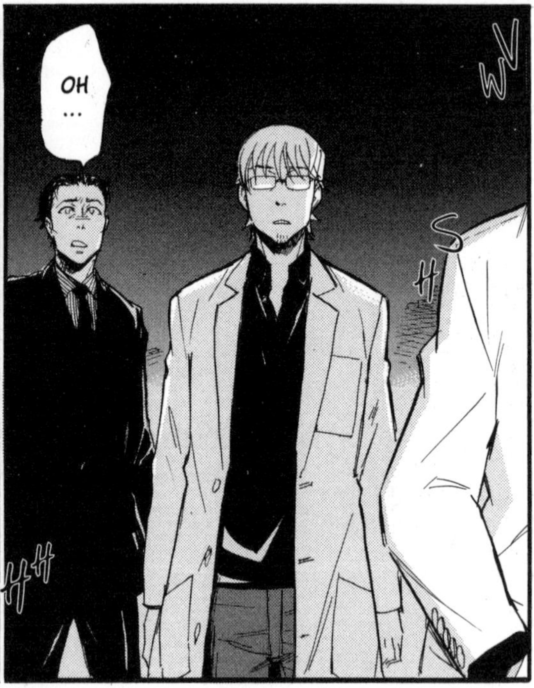
OH ...

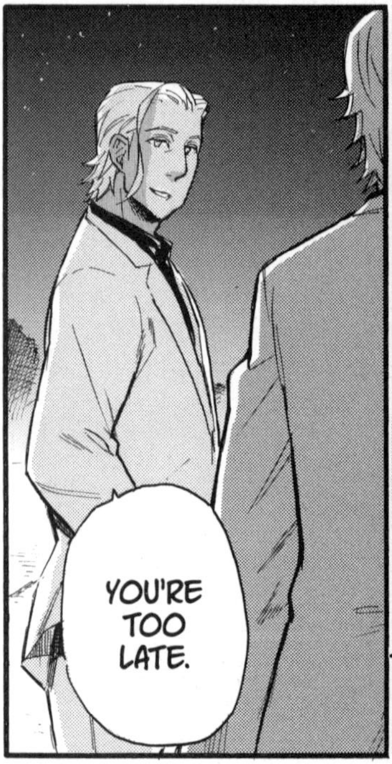
YOU'RE TOO LATE.

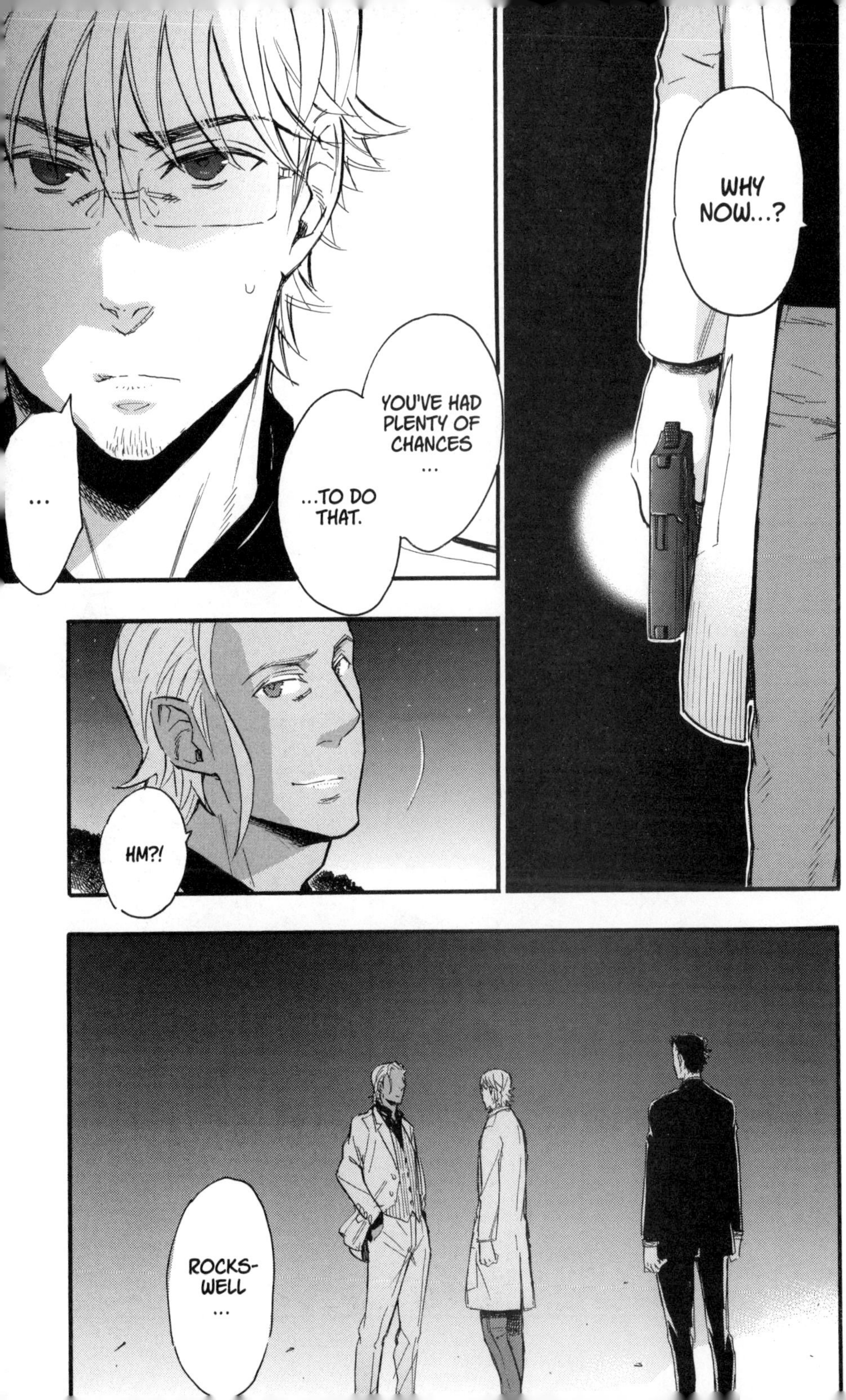
WHY NOW...?
YOU'VE HAD PLENTY OF CHANCES ...
...TO DO THAT.
...
HM?!
ROCKS-WELL ...

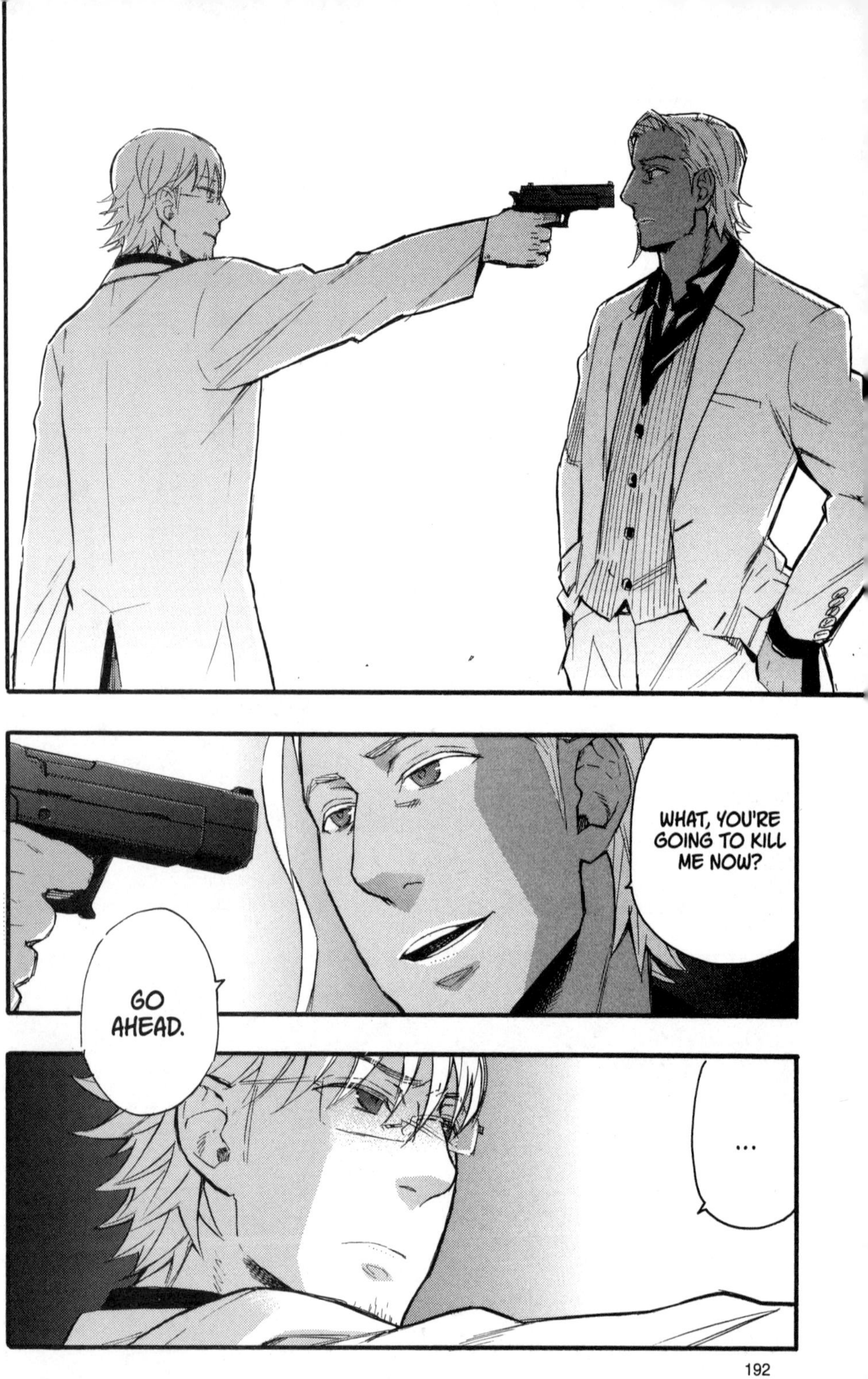
WHAT, YOU'RE GOING TO KILL ME NOW?
GO AHEAD.
...

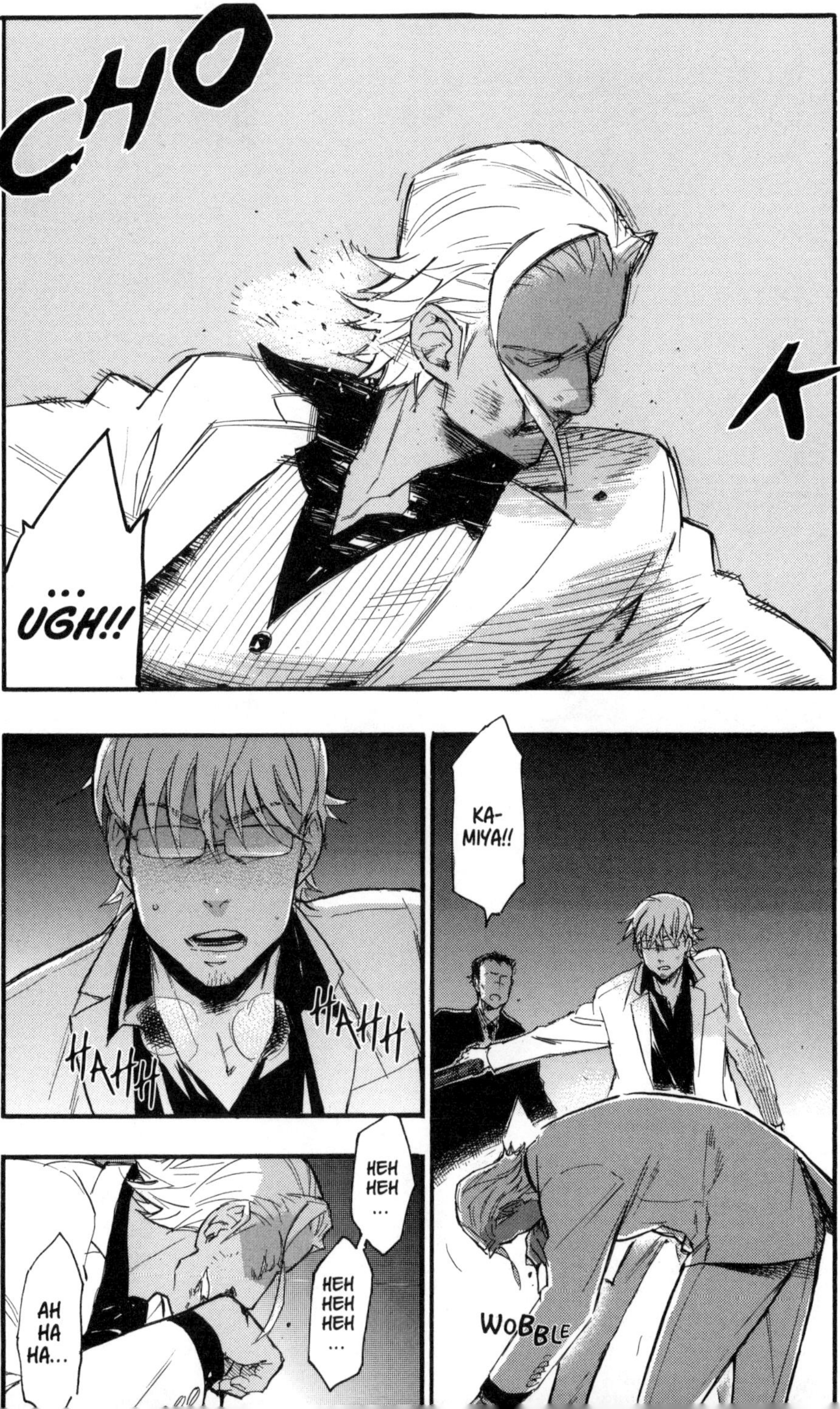
CHO
K
... UGH!!
KA-MIYA!!
WOBBLE
HAHH
HAHH
HEH HEH ...
HEH HEH HEH ...
AH HA HA...

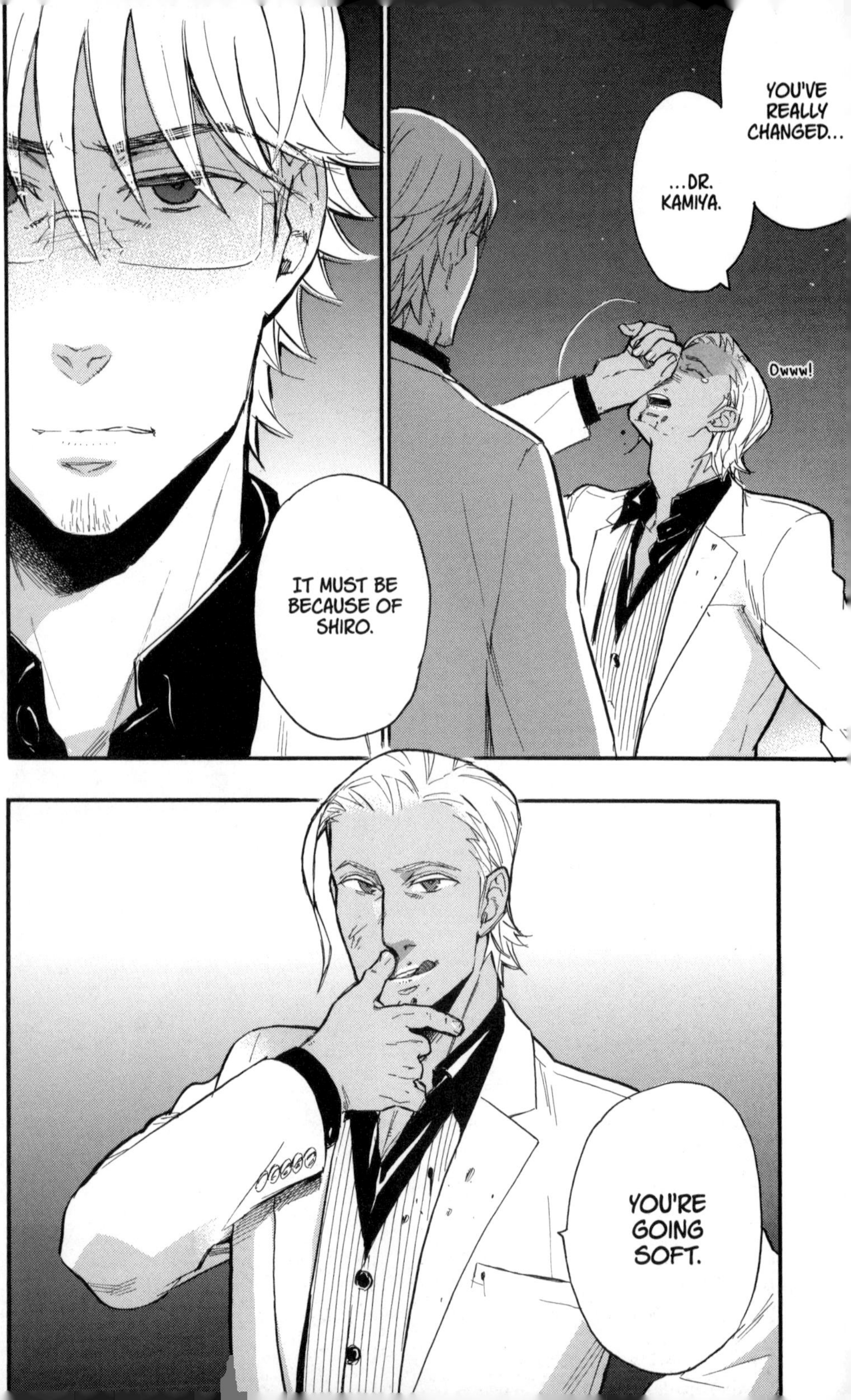
YOU'VE REALLY CHANGED...
...DR. KAMIYA.
Owww!
IT MUST BE BECAUSE OF SHIRO.
YOU'RE GOING SOFT.

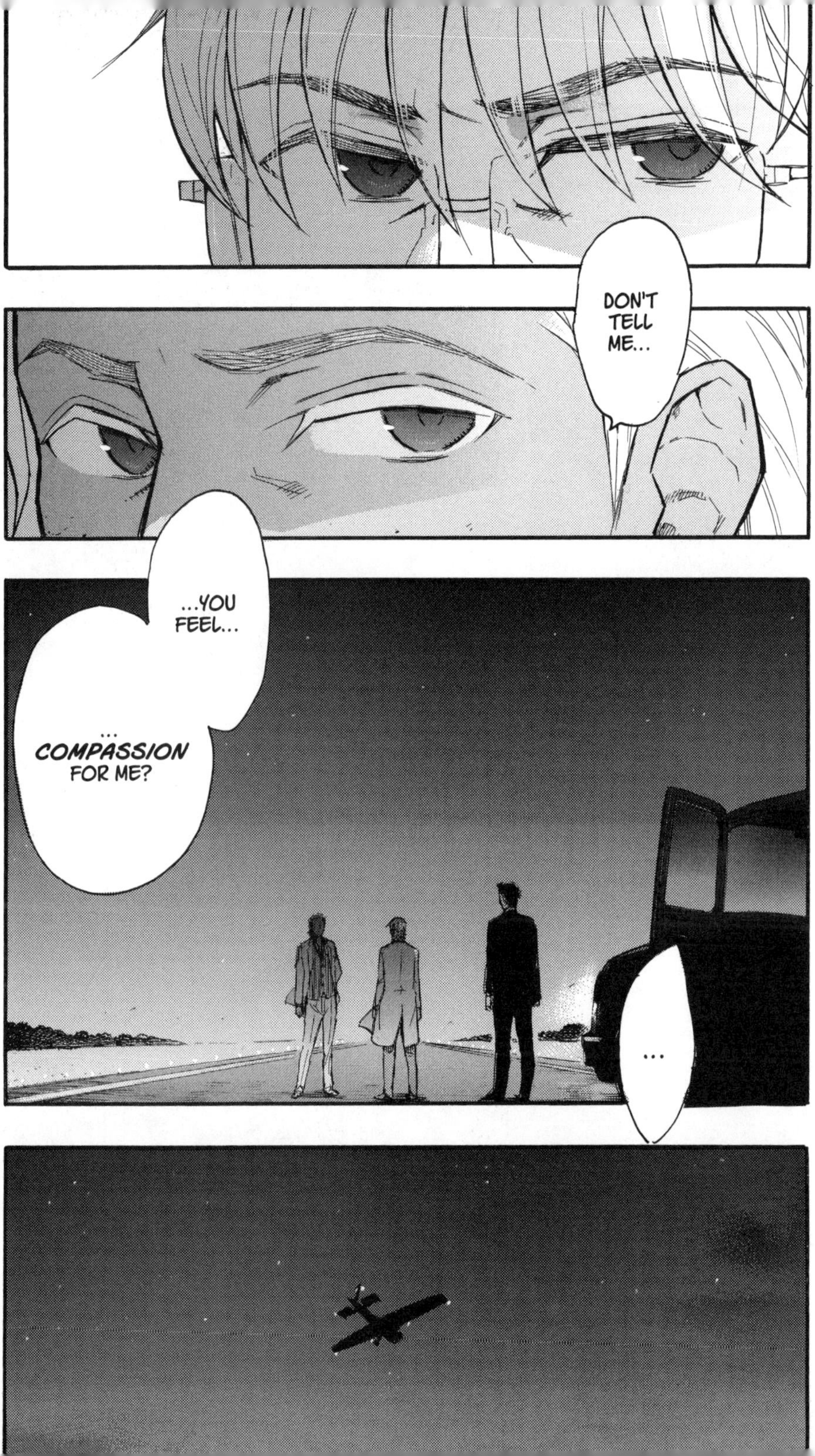
DON'T TELL ME...
...YOU FEEL...
... COMPASSION FOR ME?
...

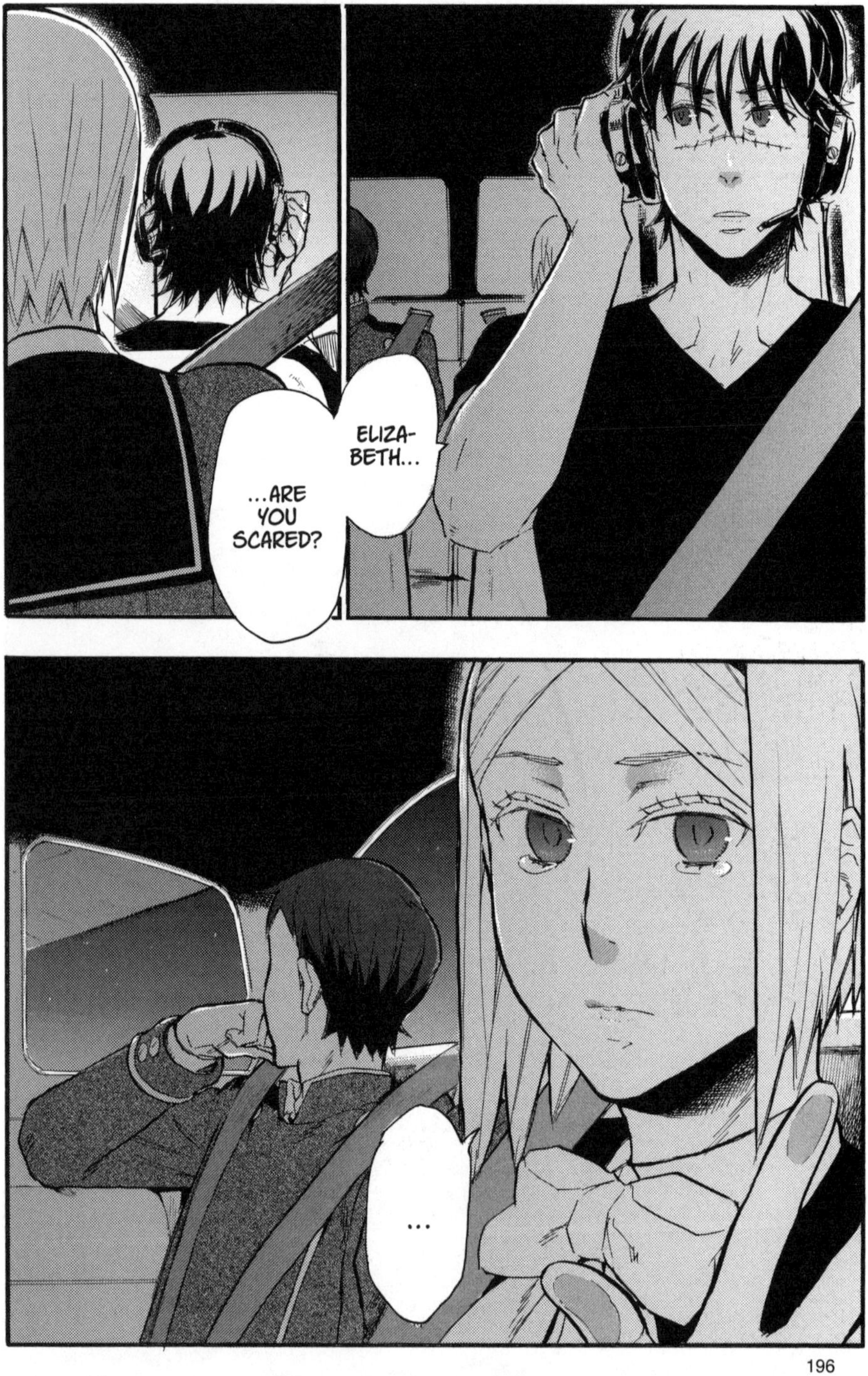
ELIZA-BETH...
...ARE YOU SCARED?
...

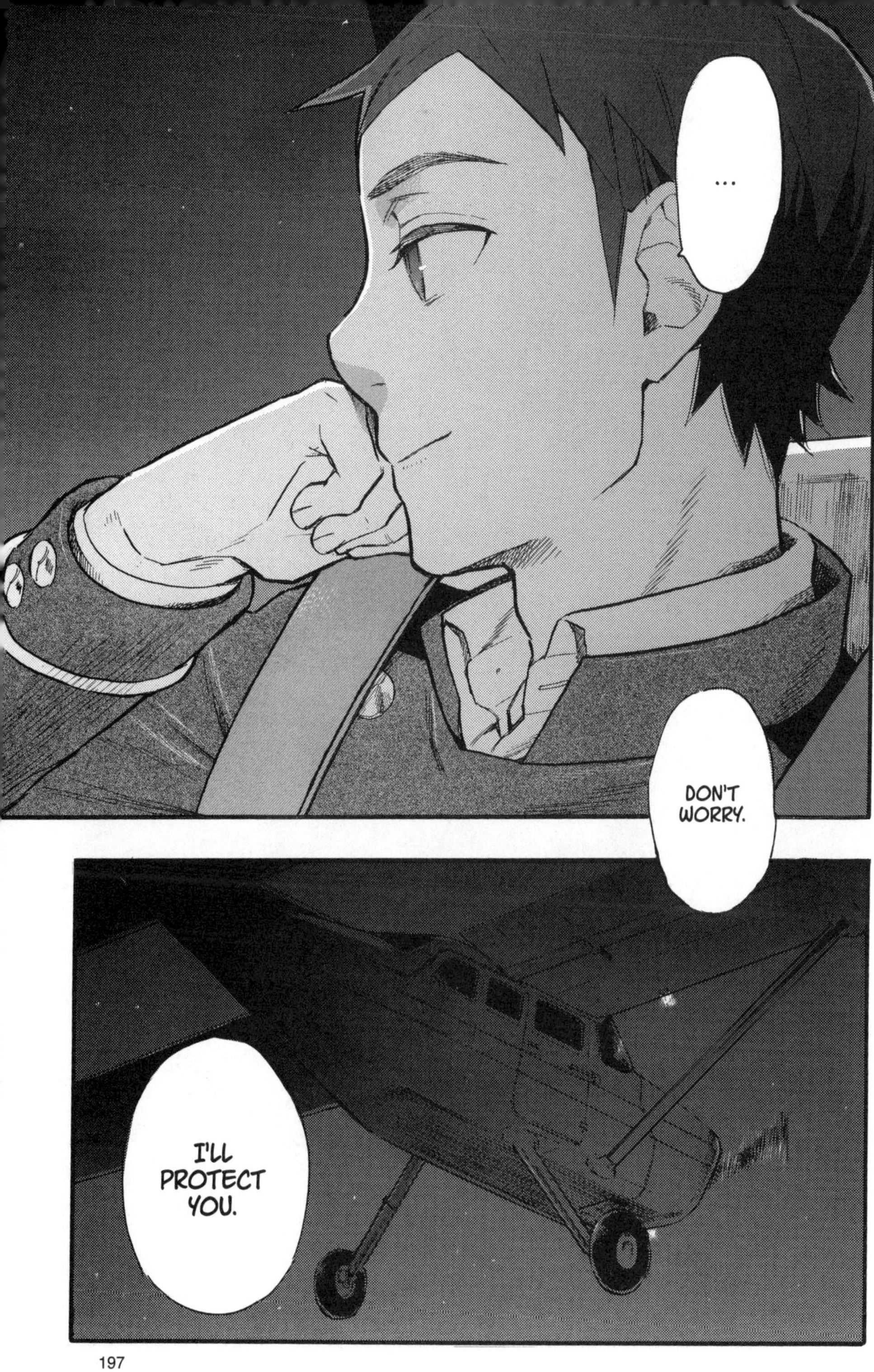
...
DON'T WORRY.
I'LL PROTECT YOU.

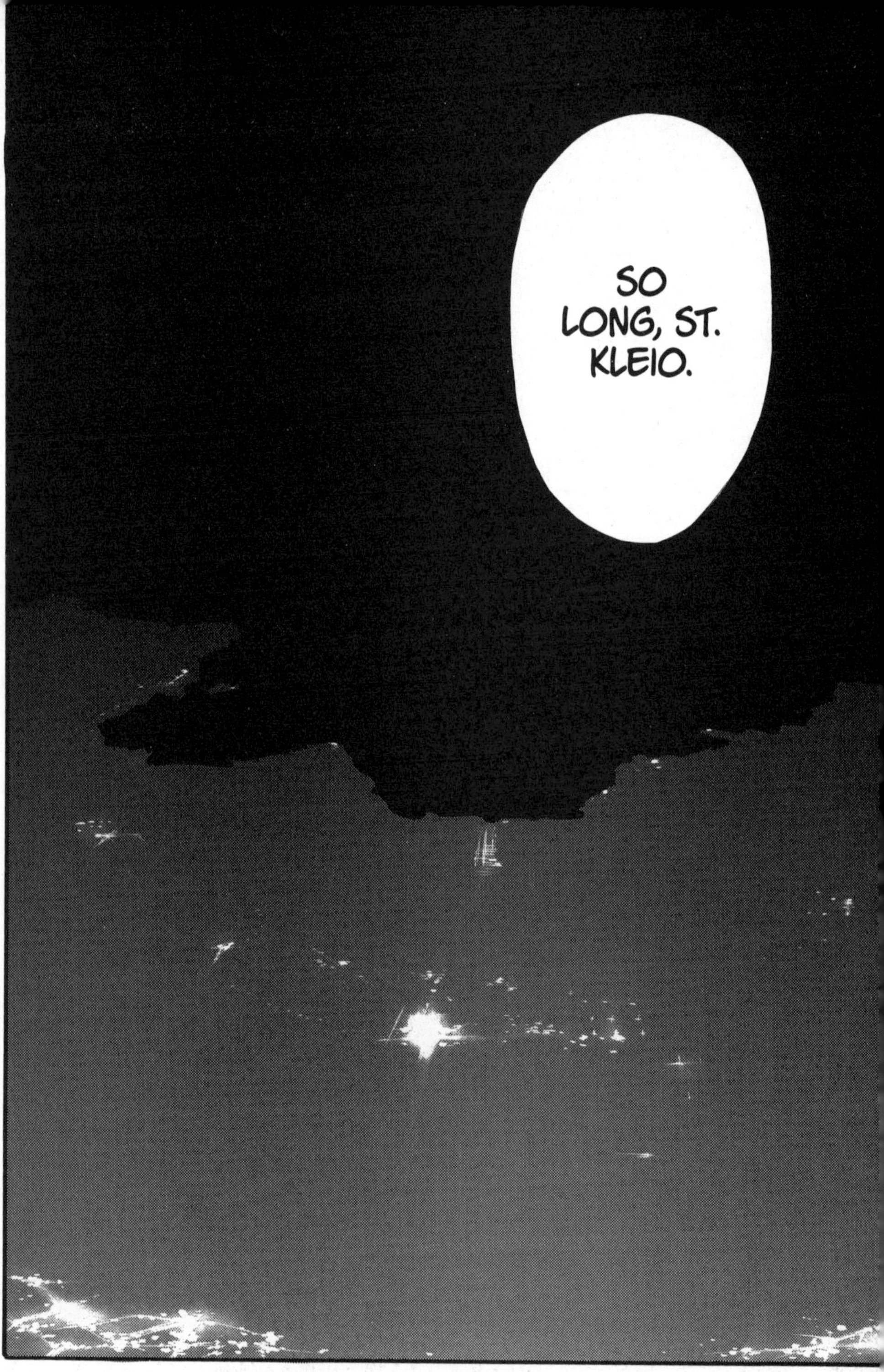
SO LONG, ST. KLEIO.

afterschool charisma

VOLUME SIX

end

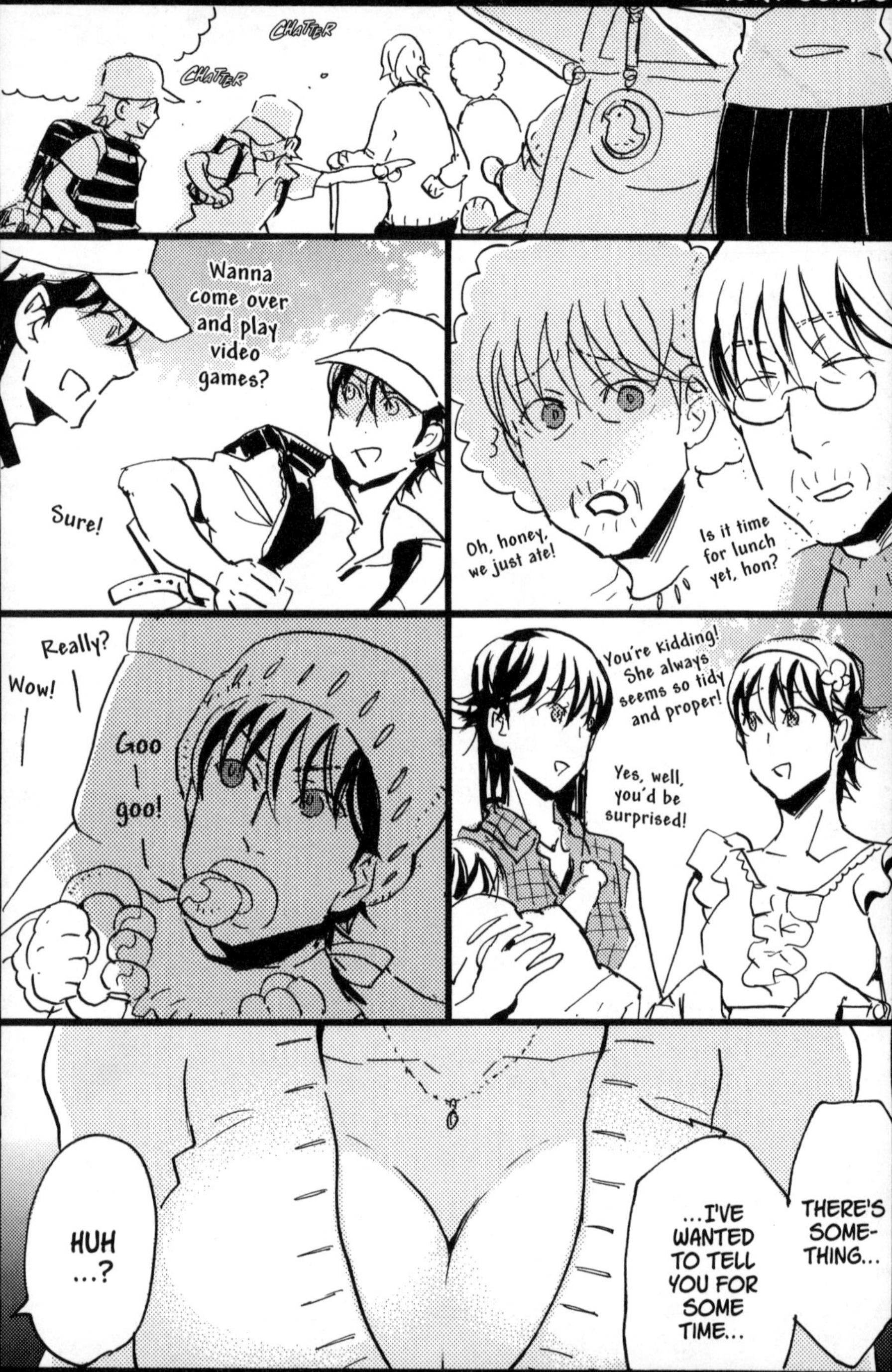
CHATTER
CHATTER
Is it time for lunch yet, hon?
Oh, honey, we just ate!
Wanna come over and play video games?
Sure!
You're kidding! She always seems so tidy and proper!
Yes, well, you'd be surprised!
Really?
Wow!
Goo goo!
THERE'S SOME-THING...
...I'VE WANTED TO TELL YOU FOR SOME TIME...
HUH ...?

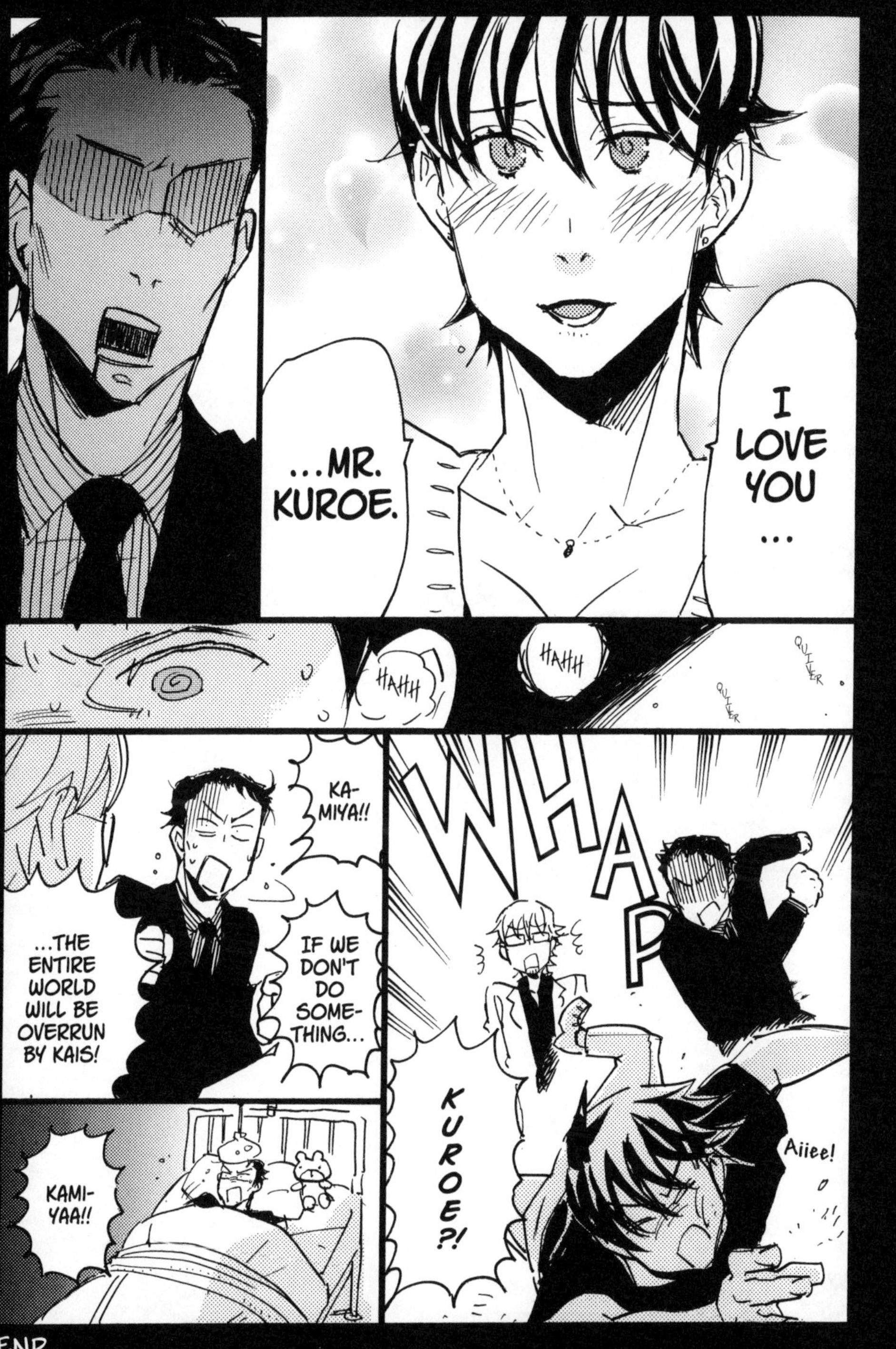
I LOVE YOU...
...MR. KUROE.
QUIVER
QUIVER
HAHH
HAHH
WHAP
Aiiee!
KUROE?!
KA-MIYA!!
IF WE DON'T DO SOME-THING...
...THE ENTIRE WORLD WILL BE OVERRUN BY KAIS!
KAMI-YAA!!

END

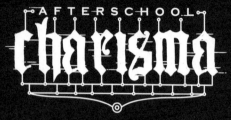

AFTERSCHOOL CHARISMA

AFTERSCHOOL CHARISMA
VOLUME 6
VIZ SIGNATURE EDITION

STORY & ART BY KUMIKO SUEKANE

Original Japanese edition "HOUKAGO NO CARISMA"
published by SHOGAKUKAN Inc.

Original Japanese cover design by Mitsuru KOBAYASHI (GENI A LÒIDE)

TRANSLATION -o- CAMELLIA NIEH
TOUCH UP ART & LETTERING -o- ERIKA TERRIQUEZ
DESIGN -o- FAWN LAU
EDITOR -o- MEGAN BATES

Printed in the U.S.A

Published by VIZ Media, LLC
P.O. Box 77010
San Francisco, CA 94107

10 9 8 7 6 5 4 3 2 1
First printing, July 2012

www.viz.com

RATED T+ FOR OLDER TEEN
PARENTAL ADVISORY
AFTERSCHOOL CHARISMA is rated T+ for Older Teen and is recommended for ages 16 and up.
ratings.viz.com

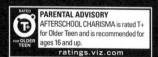

VIZ SIGNATURE
WWW.SIGIKKI.COM

I'll tell you a story
about the sea.
It's a story that
no one knows yet.
The story of the sea
that only I can tell...
Children of the Sea
BY DAISUKE IGARASHI
Children of the Sea
DAISUKE IGARASHI
1
Uncover the mysterious tale
with Children of the Sea—
BUY THE MANGA TODAY!
Read a FREE preview
at www.sigikki.com
On sale at store.viz.com
Also available at your local bookstore and comic sto
SIG IKKI
VIZ SIGNATURE
KAIJU NO KODOMO © 2007 Daisuke IRAGASHI/Shogakukan
RATED T+ FOR OLDER TEEN
ratings.viz.com
VIZ media
www.viz.com

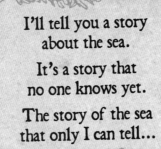

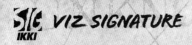

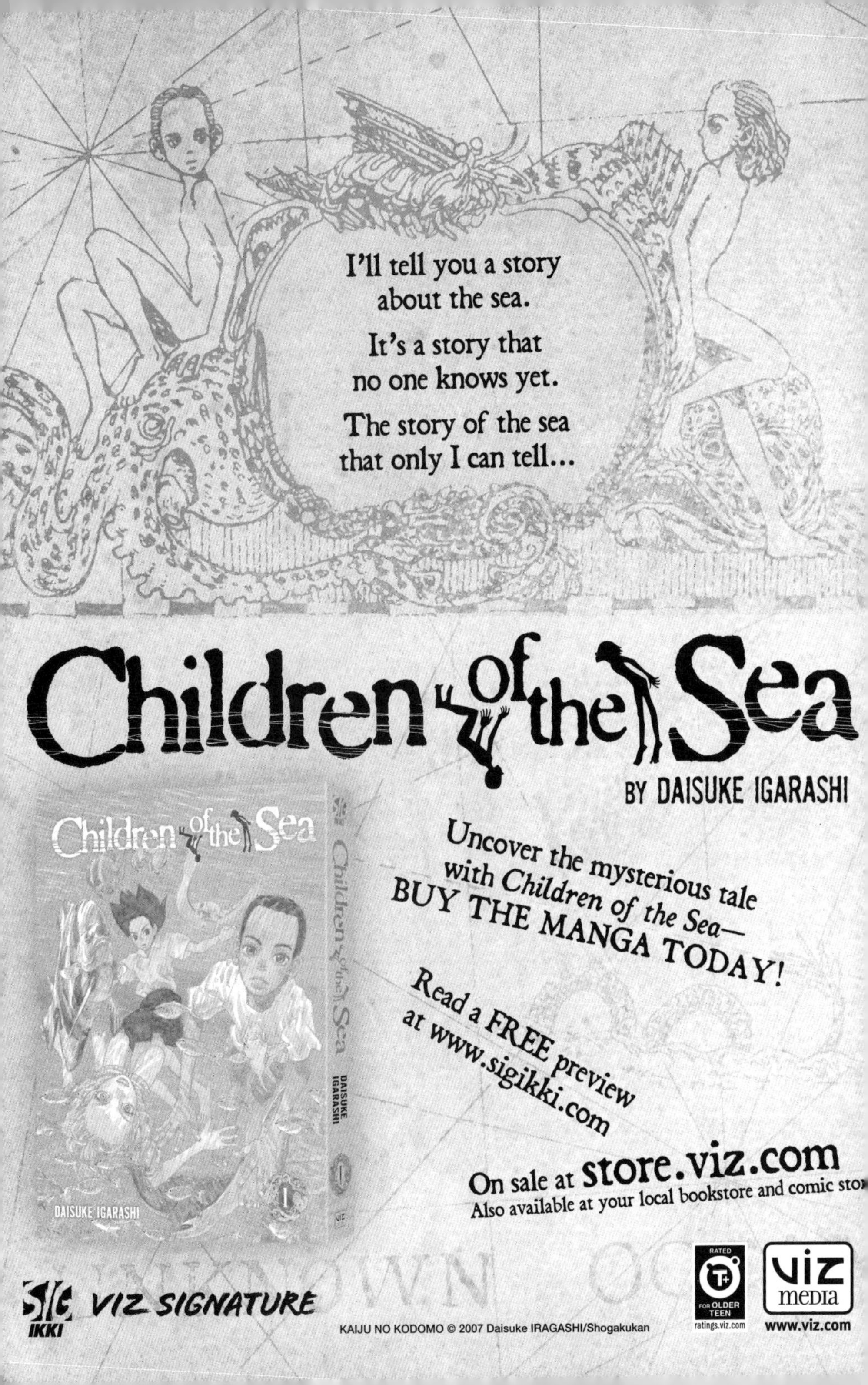

All My Darling Daughters

Story & Art by **Fumi Yoshinaga**

Eisner-nominated author and creator of *Antique Bakery* and *Ōoku*

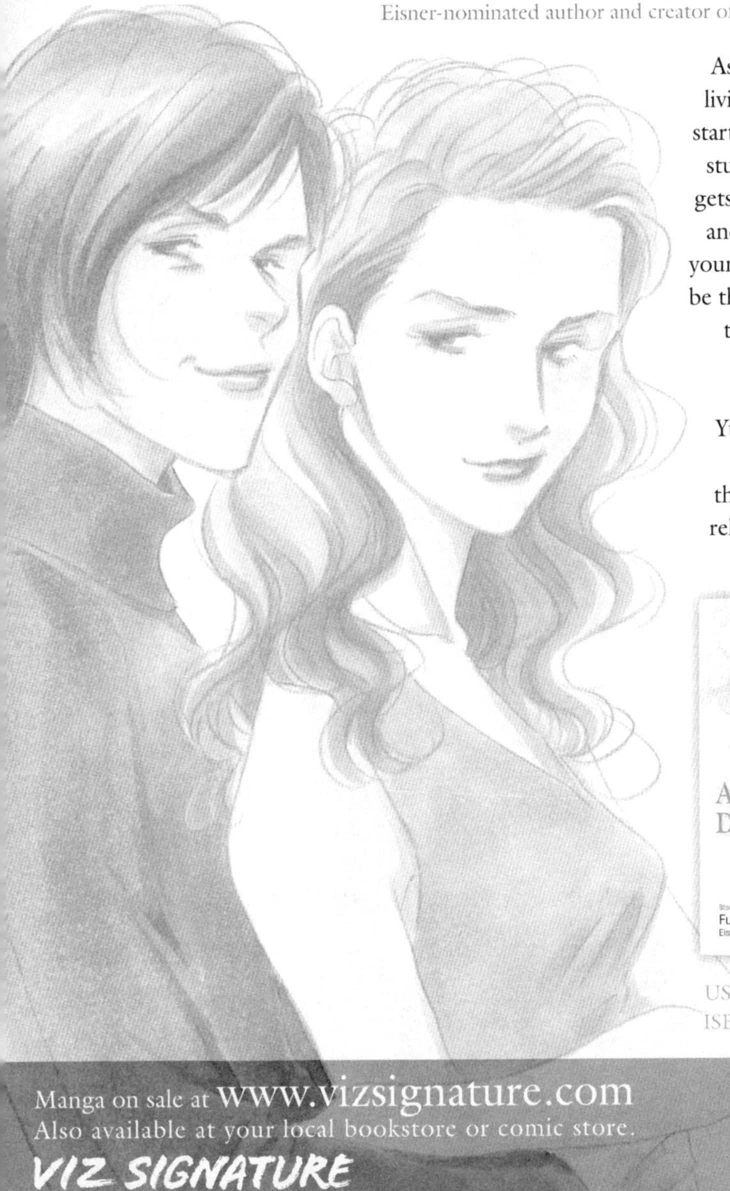

As an adult woman still living at home, Yukiko is starting to feel a little bit… stuck. When her mother gets engaged to an ex-host and aspiring actor who's younger than Yukiko, will it be the motivation she needs to move on and out?

Follow the lives of Yukiko and her friends in five short stories that explore their lives, relationships, and loves.

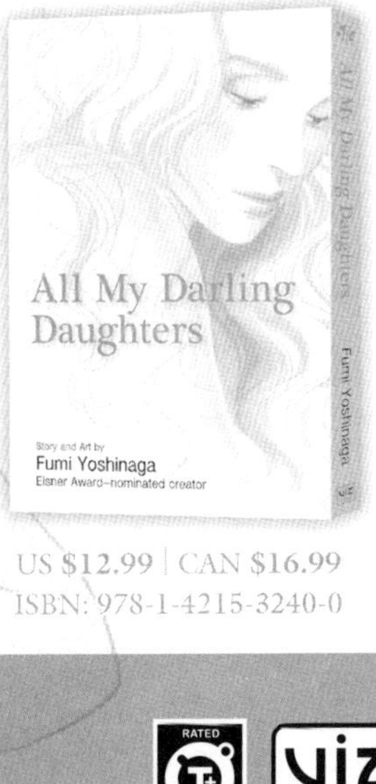
All My Darling Daughters
Fumi Yoshinaga
All My Darling Daughters
Story and Art by
Fumi Yoshinaga
Eisner Award–nominated creator

US $12.99 | CAN $16.99

ISBN: 978-1-4215-3240-0

Manga on sale at **www.vizsignature.com**
Also available at your local bookstore or comic store.

VIZ SIGNATURE

RATED T+ FOR OLDER TEEN ratings.viz.com

VIZ MEDIA www.viz.com

A story about *love* lost...and *found* again

ristorante Paradiso

Story and Art by NATSUME ONO
Creator of *Gente*, *House of Five Leaves* and *not simple*

Upon finding the mother who abandoned her, Nicoletta is offered a place to live but introduced as a "daughter of an old friend." When Nicoletta starts to fall for an older man, she turns to her mother for advice and begins an unexpected friendship! Can Nicoletta learn everything she needs about love from the woman who never gave it to her?

$12.99 USA $16.99 CAN * | ISBN: 978-1-4215-3250-9

Manga on sale at
store.viz.com/signature
Also available at your local bookstore or comic store.

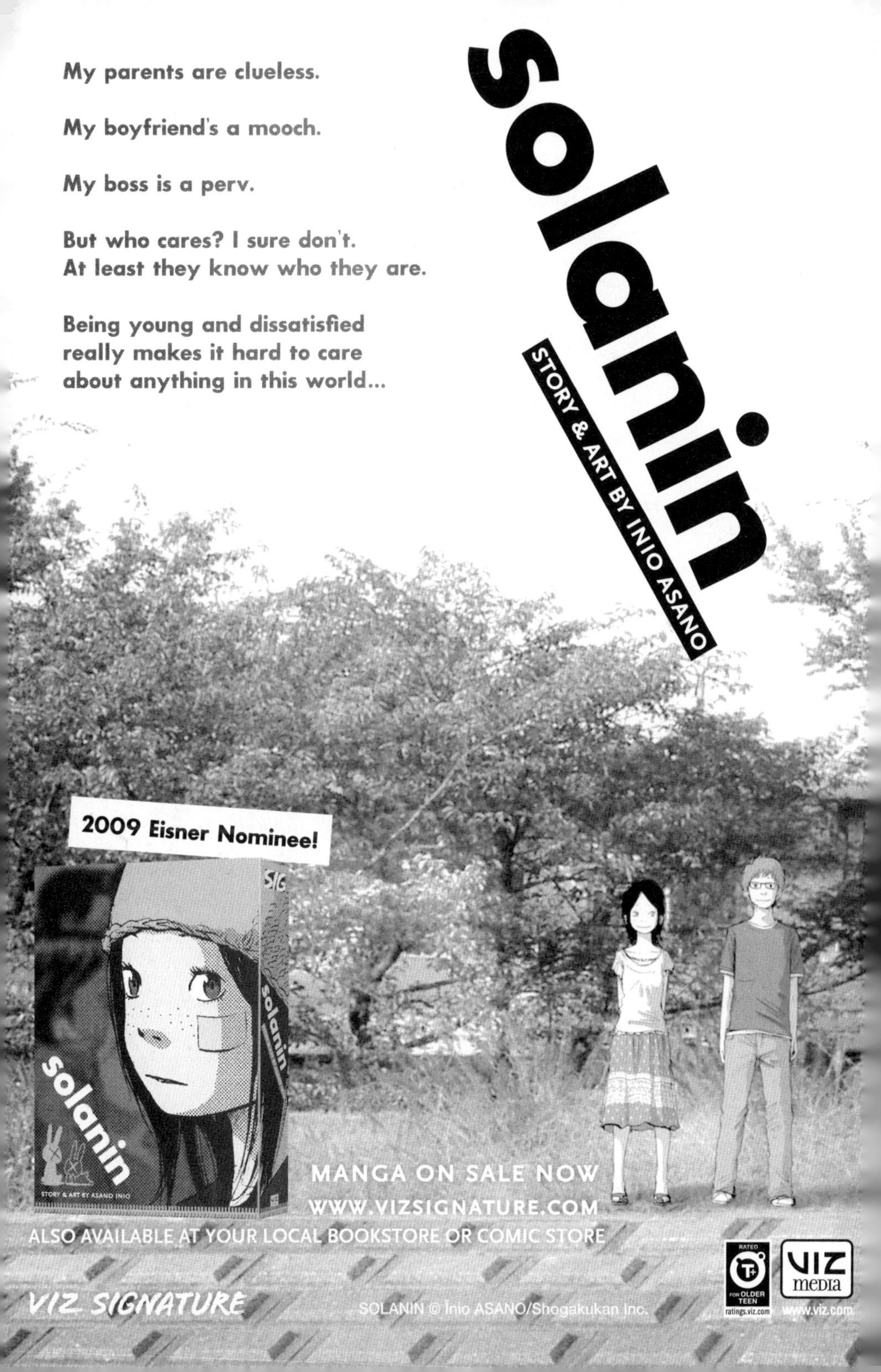
My parents are clueless.
My boyfriend's a mooch.
My boss is a perv.
But who cares? I sure don't.
At least they know who they are.
Being young and dissatisfied
really makes it hard to care
about anything in this world...
solanin
STORY & ART BY INIO ASANO
2009 Eisner Nominee!
solanin
STORY & ART BY ASANO INIO
MANGA ON SALE NOW
WWW.VIZSIGNATURE.COM
ALSO AVAILABLE AT YOUR LOCAL BOOKSTORE OR COMIC STORE
VIZ SIGNATURE
SOLANIN © Inio ASANO/Shogakukan Inc.
RATED T+ FOR OLDER TEEN
ratings.viz.com
VIZ media
www.viz.com

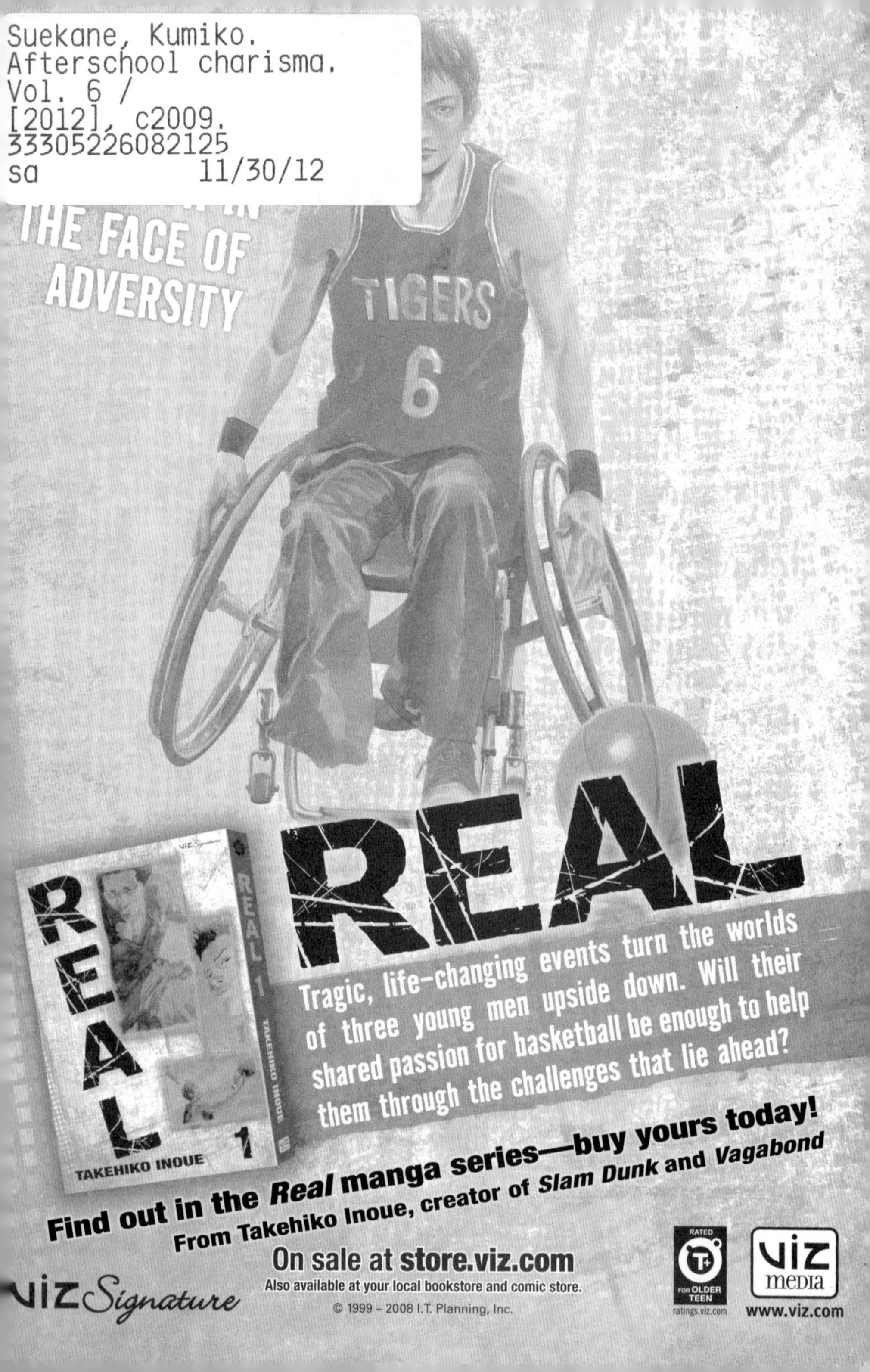
THE FACE OF ADVERSITY
TIGERS
6
REAL
REAL 1 TAKEHIKO INOUE
Tragic, life-changing events turn the worlds of three young men upside down. Will their shared passion for basketball be enough to help them through the challenges that lie ahead?
Find out in the Real manga series—buy yours today!
From Takehiko Inoue, creator of Slam Dunk and Vagabond
On sale at store.viz.com
Also available at your local bookstore and comic store.
© 1999 – 2008 I.T. Planning, Inc.
VIZ Signature
RATED T+ FOR OLDER TEEN
ratings.viz.com
VIZ media
www.viz.com